Solutions Architect's Handbook

Second Edition

Kick-start your career as a solutions architect by learning architecture design principles and strategies

Saurabh Shrivastava

Neelanjali Srivastav

BIRMINGHAM—MUMBAI

Solutions Architect's Handbook

Second Edition

Copyright © 2022 Packt Publishing

Producer: Suman Sen
Acquisition Editor – Peer Reviews: Saby Dsilva
Project Editor: Amisha Vathare
Content Development Editor: Edward Doxey
Copy Editor: Safis Editing
Technical Editor: Karan Sonawane
Proofreader: Safis Editing
Indexer: Hemangini Bari
Presentation Designer: Ganesh Bhadwalkar

First published: March 2020
Second edition: January 2022

Production reference: 5210422

Published by Packt Publishing Ltd.
Livery Place
35 Livery Street
Birmingham
B3 2PB, UK.

ISBN 978-1-80181-661-8

`www.packt.com`

To our loving daughter, Sanvi, who fills our lives with happiness and joy.

– Saurabh and Neelanjali

Contributors

About the authors

Saurabh Shrivastava is a technology leader, author, inventor, and public speaker with over 18 years of experience in the IT industry. He currently works at **Amazon Web Services (AWS)** as a Global Solutions Architect Leader and enables global consulting partners and enterprise customers on their journey to the cloud. Saurabh led the AWS global technical partnerships, set his team's vision and execution model, and nurtured multiple new strategic initiatives.

Saurabh has authored various blogs and whitepapers across a diverse range of technologies, such as big data, IoT, machine learning, and cloud computing. He is passionate about the latest innovations and their impact on our society and daily life. He holds a patent in the area of cloud platform automation. Before AWS, Saurabh worked as an enterprise solution architect, software architect, and software engineering manager in Fortune 50 enterprises, start-ups, and global product and consulting organizations.

Neelanjali Srivastav is a technology leader, product manager, agile coach, and cloud practitioner with over 16 years of experience in the software industry. She currently works at **Amazon Web Services (AWS)** as a Senior Product Manager and enables global customers on their data journey to the cloud. Neelanjali evangelizes and enables AWS customer and partners in AWS database, analytics, and machine learning services. She sets the product vision and cultivates new products in incubation.

Before AWS, Neelanjali led teams of software engineers, solutions architects, and systems analysts to modernize IT systems and develop innovative software solutions for large enterprises. Neelanjali has held multiple roles in the IT services industry and R&D, focusing on enterprise application management, cloud service management, and orchestration.

About the reviewer

Kamesh Ganesan is a cloud evangelist, a seasoned technology professional, and an author and leader with over 24 years of IT experience in all major cloud technologies, including AWS, Azure, GCP, Oracle and Alibaba Cloud. He has over 50 IT certifications, including many cloud certifications. He has architected and delivered mission-critical and innovative technology solutions that have helped his enterprise, commercial, and government clients to be very successful. He has authored AWS and Azure books and reviewed many IT/cloud technology books and courses.

I am extremely thankful for all God's blessings in my life. A special thanks to my wife, Hemalatha, for her motivation and continuous support in all my pursuits and many thanks to my kids, Sachin and Arjun, for their unconditional love. I am very grateful to my father, Ganesan, and mother, Kasthuri, for their unwavering encouragement throughout my life.

Forewords

A Solutions Architect requires a unique skill set with breadth and depth of technology and the ability to tie that skill set back to business and derive a return on investment. As cloud adoption accelerates, enterprises are looking for solutions architects to help their digital journey, keeping the cloud at the core of their strategy. The cloud has a very different value proposition to on-premises systems, and comes with several tools and services, replacing the costly third-party licensed software. You can achieve desired reliability and scalability in the cloud in minutes to capture high growth and seasonality. You can use cloud native services to build high-performance applications while keeping your costs low. As per my 25+ years tenure in the IT industry building complex and highly scalable applications, I strongly believe that the right architectural choice enables customers to get the most from their cloud strategy.

The *Solutions Architect's Handbook* fills the skill gap by providing architecture best practices through the lens of cloud architecture. The book starts by clarifying the roles and responsibilities of solutions architects, and then helps build a strong foundation by walking through the design principle of the architecture. Keeping cloud strategy at the core, the book covers a broad range of topics, from migration to the cloud, to designing cloud native solution architecture. The book has done a good job of addressing 30+ core application development architecture design patterns with reference architectures to visualize them. Solutions architects need to look at all aspects of application design and this book dives deep into each of these topics to optimize your architecture for security, reliability, performance, cost, and operational excellence.

My favorite part of the 2nd edition of the book is the addition of new architectural patterns and the latest technology trends. It discusses big data design patterns such as data lake, lake house, and data mesh in detail, covering the reference architecture and best practices. The book goes into details about various streaming technologies, an upcoming industry trend to get faster business insight. Further, the book provides details on machine learning architecture, MLOps to put ML models in production, Quantum computing, and industrial IoT.

I often see people looking to upgrade their skills or change their career paths to become solutions architects. Saurabh has put his years of experience into this book, making it very easy for anyone looking to upskill in their current role or exploring future technologies. Starting with an introduction to the function and the role, he goes into design patterns and migration strategies before covering technology and trends. For a new or existing solutions architect who is looking to keep their skills sharp in the cloud era, this book hits all the key areas.

Rajesh Sheth

General Manager, AWS Messaging and Streaming

During the last two years, the COVID-19 pandemic has led to an acceleration of digital transformations and the adoption of cloud technologies. Solutions Architects have had to adapt to these compressed timeframes to not just move to the cloud but also to build microservice-based cloud native architectures. They have been presented with unique challenges related to scaling, operational resiliency, disaster recovery, and business continuity, building insights and automations to meet these changes. We are seeing a shift in the mindset of building distributed applications and the rapid adoption of cloud native technologies. The second edition covers these new design patterns and covers some of the anti-patterns observed.

The broader technology areas covered in this book really amazes me. Architecture and design patterns, from cloud migration and modernization to the Internet of Things/Edge, to machine learning make this book a real page turner. The breadth of topics, from legacy modernization including mainframe to emerging technologies such as quantum computing, provides a great insight into trends and best practices for everyone looking to apply them in their roles as Solutions Architects.

Solutions Architect's Handbook is the go-to guide for understanding various functions in the age of cloud computing, covering functional architectures to integrations to extensibility, reusability, usability, accessibility, costs, security, and more. I have never seen a more holistic approach to sharing best practices and patterns. Saurabh and Neel, through their experiences, have authored this book, which should be referenced by aspiring as well as experienced architects.

Rohan Karmarkar

Director, Solutions Architecture, AWS

The technology realm has always been fast-moving and in order to keep growing in their careers, IT professionals need to incrementally acquire new skills over time. However, in the last decade this trend has become dominant, with cloud computing becoming the 'new normal.' Now, almost every day, there are new announcements, features, and service updates by cloud providers, which has necessitated the focus on a continuous learning culture for everyone. Along with this, now, the typical boundaries between the usual roles of developer, database administrator, security professional, build/release engineer, and so on have started to blur, resulting in new roles being created to focus on big-picture and end-to-end ownership. One such role is that of a 'Solutions Architect,' which started to evolve from existing roles in the industry like 'Application Architect' and 'IT Architect' and has now become mainstream. There are also variations of this role, however, the most common avatar is that of 'Cloud Solutions Architect,' which is a pretty dynamic role in itself.

Often, IT professionals want to switch roles, however they lack direction on how to be successful on that path. This book focusses on this very aspect; an effective transition from an existing IT role to that of a Solutions Architect. It explains in a very logical manner the steps to embark on that journey. It starts off with a simple, very relatable explanation of what this role entails and how it differs from a few of the other similar type of profiles. Next, it goes into the technical skills and knowledge needed to be a successful Solutions Architect. This begins with basic design pillars and architectural principles (like high availability, reliability, performance, security, and cost optimizations), followed by a dive deep into each one of those. The book also covers some key concepts around cloud native architectures, DevOps, data engineering, and machine learning domains, which are the cornerstone of any modern-day architecture. In the latest revision of the book, Saurabh and Neelanjali have also included very insightful details on machine learning/MLOps, **Internet of Things (IoT)** architectures, data architecture best practices, and quantum computing. All these areas are slowly becoming pivotal to the enterprise IT landscape, and hence it's essential for Solutions Architects to be aware to stay ahead of the learning curve.

I have personally been through this journey of being a Solutions Architect, from a development team leader, and so has Saurabh, and we always wished there was a hand book available that could help us then. So, to fill that major gap in the industry, Saurabh has created this very detailed book, which is based on personal experiences and learnings that makes it a very relatable read for anyone from varying backgrounds. I highly recommend you read this book and keep it as a handy reference always, as in it you will find very important nuggets of knowledge that will help you be a successful Solutions Architect, and open up a new world of infinite possibilities!

Kamal Arora

Sr. Manager, Solutions Architecture, AWS
https://www.amazon.com/Kamal-Arora/e/B07HLTSNRJ/

Join our book's Discord space

Join the book's Discord workspace for a monthly *Ask me Anything* session with the authors: https://packt.link/SAHandbook

Table of Contents

Table of Contents

Preface

The *Solutions Architect's Handbook* guides readers to create robust, scalable, highly available, and fault-tolerant solutions by learning different aspects of solution architecture and next-generation architecture design in the cloud environment. This book will start by detailing solution architecture and how it fits in an agile enterprise environment. It will further take the reader through the journey of solution architecture design by providing detailed knowledge of design pillars, advanced design patterns, anti-patterns, and cloud-native aspects of modern software design. The reader will further dive deep into solution design performance optimization, security, compliance, reliability, cost optimization, and operational excellence. This book provides an in-depth understanding of the automation of security, infrastructure, DevOps, disaster recovery, and documentation of solution architecture. This book also provides a good understanding of future-proof architecture design with data engineering, machine learning, IoT, and quantum computing. As a bonus, this book also offers a soft-skill aspect of solution architect and continuous learning techniques.

Who this book is for?

This book is for software developers, system engineers, DevOps engineers, architects, and team leaders working in the IT industry who aspire to become solution architects and to design secure, reliable, highly performant, and cost-effective architectures.

What this book covers

Chapter 1, The Meaning of Solution Architecture, defines what solution architecture is and its importance. It explains various benefits of having a solution architecture in place and talks about architecting on the public cloud.

Chapter 2, Solution Architects in an Organization, discusses the different types of solution architect roles and how they fit in the organizational structure. It explores the various responsibilities of the solution architect in detail. It further explains the solution architect role fit in an agile organization along with agile processes.

Chapter 3, Attributes of the Solution Architecture, throws light on various attributes of solution architecture, such as scalability, resiliency, disaster recovery, accessibility, usability, security, and cost. It explains the co-existence and utilization of these architectural attributes to create an efficient solution design.

Chapter 4, Principles of Solution Architecture Design, talks about architecture principles to create scalable, resilient, and high-performance architecture. It explains efficient architecture design by applying security measures, overcoming constraints, and applying changes along with testing and automation approaches. It explores architecture principles to use service-oriented architecture and a data-driven approach.

Chapter 5, Cloud Migration and Hybrid Cloud Architecture Design, explains the benefits of the cloud and approaches to designing cloud-native architecture. It gives an understanding of different cloud migration strategies and migration steps. It talks about hybrid cloud design and explores popular public cloud providers.

Chapter 6, Solution Architecture Design Patterns, explores various architecture design patterns such as layered, microservice, event-driven, queue-based, serverless, cache-based, and service-oriented patterns, with examples. It demonstrates the applicability of solution architecture attributes and principles to design the best architecture as per business requirements.

Chapter 7, Performance Considerations, provides an understanding of essential attributes of application performance improvement such as latency, throughput, and concurrency. It explains various technology choices to improve performance at the multiple layers of architecture such as compute, storage, database, and networking, along with performance monitoring.

Chapter 8, Security Considerations, talks about various design principles applicable to securing your workload. Security needs to be applied at every layer and every component of architecture, and this chapter helps you to get an understanding of the right selection of technology to ensure your architecture is secure at every layer. It explores industry compliance applicable to architecture design as needed and explains security in the cloud with a shared responsibility model.

Chapter 9, Architectural Reliability Considerations, talks about design principles to make your architecture reliable. It explores various disaster recovery techniques to ensure high application availability and data replication methods for business process continuation. It explains best practices and the role of the cloud in applications to achieve reliability.

Chapter 10, Operational Excellence Considerations, talks about various processes and methods to achieve operational excellence for applications. It explains best practices and technology selections to apply throughout application design, implementation, and post-production to improve application operability. It also explores operational excellence for cloud workloads.

Chapter 11, Cost Considerations, talks about various techniques to optimize cost without risking business agility and outcomes. It explains multiple methods to monitor costs and apply governance for cost control. It helps you to understand cost optimization using the cloud.

Chapter 12, DevOps and Solution Architecture Framework, explains the importance of DevOps in application deployment, testing, and security. It explores DevSecOps and its role in the application's continuous deployment and delivery pipeline. It also talks about DevOps and best practices and different tools and techniques to implement them.

Chapter 13, Data Engineering for Solution Architecture, talks about how to design big data and analytics architecture. It explains steps to create a big data pipeline, including data ingestion, storage, processing, and visualization. It helps you to understand different big data architecture patterns, such as data lakes, data meshes, and lakehouses, with data architecture best practice.

Chapter 14, Machine Learning Architecture, explores details about machine learning and model evaluation techniques, and provides an overview of various machine learning algorithms. It talks about machine learning architecture patterns with reference architectures on a cloud platform. The chapter further explains the concept of MLOps with best practices and deep learning technologies.

Chapter 15, The Internet of Things Architecture, explains the IoT and various components of IoT architecture. It talks about industrial IoT and the digital twin concept along with giving insight into analytics for IoT data and IoT device management at scale.

Chapter 16, Quantum Computing, explains the working of quantum computers with real-life use cases. It provides details on building blocks of quantum computing and how quantum computers work in a very simplified manner. It talks about quantum gates, quantum circuits, and various types of quantum computing along with their availability on cloud platforms.

Chapter 17, Rearchitecting Legacy Systems, talks about various challenges and modernization drivers for legacy systems. It explains strategies and techniques for modernizing legacy systems as the public cloud is becoming a go-to strategy for many organizations. The chapter explores the cloud migration of legacy systems along with details on mainframe migration and modernization.

Chapter 18, Solution Architecture Document, talks about the solution architecture document with its structure and various details that need to be accommodated for in the documentation. It explores various IT procurement documentation such as RFP, RFI, and RFQ, where solution architects participate in providing feedback.

Chapter 19, Learning Soft Skills to Become a Better Solution Architect, talks about various soft skills required for a solution architect to be successful in the role. It helps you to understand methods to acquire strategic skills such as pre-sales and executive communication and develop design thinking and personal leadership skills such as thinking big and ownership. It also explores techniques to establish yourself as a leader and continue improving your skillset.

To get the most out of this book

Prior experience of software architecture design will be helpful to follow this book. It's good to have a basic understanding of any popular public cloud provider such as AWS. However, there are no specific prerequisites to understand this book. All the examples and relevant instructions are provided in the various chapters. This book takes you through the deep concept of solution architecture design and does not require knowledge of any particular programming language, framework, or tool.

Download the color images

We also provide a PDF file that has color images of the screenshots/diagrams used in this book. You can download it here: https://static.packt-cdn.com/downloads/9781801816618_ColorImages.pdf.

Conventions used

There are a number of text conventions used throughout this book.

CodeInText: Indicates code words in text, database table names, folder names, filenames, file extensions, pathnames, dummy URLs, user input, and Twitter handles. For example; "IoT platforms need to support SigV4, X.509 and custom authentication, while providing fine-grained access control with IoT policies down to the MQTT topic level."

A block of code is set as follows:

```
<message name="GetOrderInfo">
    <part name="body" element="xsd1:GetOrderRequest"/>
</message>
```

Bold: Indicates a new term, an important word, or words that you see on the screen, for example, in menus or dialog boxes. For example: "Cloud providers such as **AWS**, **Microsoft Azure**, and **GCP** provide many options out of the box that can help you to modernize your system."

 Warnings or important notes appear like this.

 Tips and tricks appear like this.

Get in touch

Feedback from our readers is always welcome.

General feedback: Email feedback@packtpub.com, and mention the book's title in the subject of your message. If you have questions about any aspect of this book, please email us at questions@packtpub.com.

Errata: Although we have taken every care to ensure the accuracy of our content, mistakes do happen. If you have found a mistake in this book we would be grateful if you would report this to us. Please visit http://www.packtpub.com/submit-errata, selecting your book, clicking on the Errata Submission Form link, and entering the details.

Piracy: If you come across any illegal copies of our works in any form on the Internet, we would be grateful if you would provide us with the location address or website name.

Please contact us at copyright@packtpub.com with a link to the material.

If you are interested in becoming an author: If there is a topic that you have expertise in and you are interested in either writing or contributing to a book, please visit http://authors.packtpub.com.

Share Your Thoughts

Once you've read *Solutions Architect's Handbook - Second Edition,* we'd love to hear your thoughts! Please click here to go straight to the Amazon review page for this book and share your feedback.

Your review is important to us and the tech community and will help us make sure we're delivering excellent quality content.

1

The Meaning of Solution Architecture

This book will be your first step in the solution architecture world, acting as a comprehensive guide to learn all about solution architecture, and allowing you to become a professional solution architect. In this chapter, we will explore the meaning of solution architecture, and how it is the foundation of solution development in an organization. A robust solution architecture design helps successful software application development in a complex organization, covering all aspects, from IT infrastructure, application security, and reliability, to operational aspects in production.

For successful application development, defining the solution architecture should be the first step, which then lays out the foundations and the robust building blocks of implementation. Solution architecture handles critical, non-functional requirements such as scalability, high availability, maintainability, performance, and security while keeping business requirements in mind.

A solution architect is a person who is responsible for designing solution architecture by collaborating with and across stakeholders. The solution architect analyzes the functional requirements and defines non-functional requirements in order to cover all aspects of the solution—and avoid any surprises. Each solution has multiple constraints, such as cost, budget, timeline, and regulatory constraints, so the solution architect must consider them while selecting technology during the application design process to solve a given business problem.

The solution architect develops a proof of concept and prototype in order to evaluate various technology platforms, and then chooses the best strategy for solution implementation.

They mentor the team throughout solution development and provide post-launch guidance to maintain and scale the final product.

In this chapter, you will learn about the following topics:

- What is solution architecture?
- The evolution of solution architecture
- Why is solution architecture important?
- The benefits of solution architecture
- Solution architecture in the public cloud

By the end of this chapter, you will have learned about the benefits of solution architecture to every aspect of an enterprise application. You will evaluate solution architecture in the public cloud and develop a cloud-native approach to architecture design.

What is solution architecture?

Asking this question to a variety of professionals may lead to ten different answers for the definition of solution architecture. In fact, they may all be correct, within the context of a given organization's structure. Each organization may see solution architecture from a different perspective, based on their business needs, organizational hierarchy, and solution complexity.

In a nutshell, solution architecture can be described as defining and foreseeing multiple aspects of a business solution, from both strategic and transactional perspectives. "Strategic" means that a solution architect defines a long-term vision for a software application to ensure it stays relevant, regardless of future changes, with possible extensions to address increasing user workload and additional feature demand. "Transactional" means an application should handle the current customer workload and address daily business challenges without any issues.

Solution architecture is not just about providing a software solution. It covers all aspects of a system, which includes, but is not limited to, system infrastructure, networking, security, compliance requirement, system operation, cost, and reliability. As can be seen in *Figure 1.1*, there are many aspects that a solution architect may need to address.

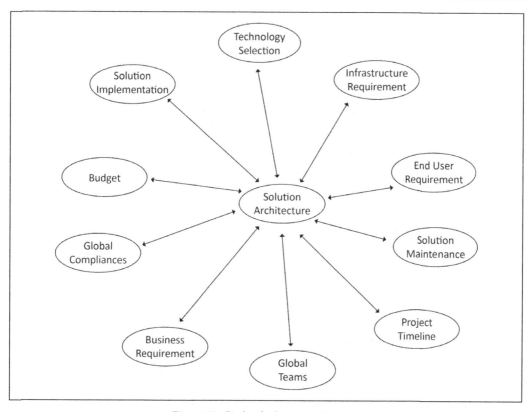

Figure 1.1: Circle of solution architecture

A good solution architect addresses the most common aspects of the software solution in an organization:

- **Globally distributed teams**: In this age of globalization, almost every product has users distributed across the globe, and stakeholder groups to take care of customer needs. Often, the software development team has an onshore-offshore model, where a team works across different time zones to increase productivity and optimize project costs. Solution design needs to consider a globally distributed team structure. This means solution development and operation should not be people-dependent but utilize tools to scale and collaborate regardless of team members' work locations and time zones.

- **Global compliance requirement**: When you are deploying your solution globally, each country and region has its laws and compliance regulations, which your solution must adhere to. Some examples are as follows:
    - The **Federal Risk and Authorization Management Program (FedRAMP)** and **Department of Defense Cloud Computing Security Requirements Guide (DoDSRG)** for the USA
    - The **General Data Protection Regulation (GDPR)** for Europe
    - The **Information Security Registered Assessors Program (IRAP)** for Australia
    - The **Center for Financial Industry Information Systems (FISC)** for Japan
    - The **Multi-Tier Cloud Security (MTCS)** standard for Singapore
    - The **G-Cloud** for the UK
    - The **IT-Grundschutz** for Germany
    - The **Multi-Level Protection Scheme (MLPS)** Level 3 for China
- Compliance requirements are different between industries; for example, the **International Organization for Standardization (ISO) 9001** (which is primarily for healthcare, life sciences, medical devices, and the automotive and aerospace industries), the **Payment Card Industry Data Security Standard (PCI DSS)** for finance, and the **Health Insurance Portability and Accountability Act (HIPAA)** for healthcare. Solution architecture needs to consider any compliance adherence in the design phase. You will learn more about compliance in *Chapter 8, Security Considerations*.
- **Cost and budget**: Solution architecture gives a good estimation of the overall cost of the project, which helps to define a budget. This includes **capital expenditure (CapEx)**, which is the upfront cost, and **operational expenditure (OpEx)**, an ongoing cost. It helps management to create an overall budget for human resources, infrastructure resources, and other licensing-related costs.
- **Solution implementation component**: Solution architecture provides a high-level overview of different implementation components of the product beforehand, which helps to plan execution.
- **Business requirements**: Solution architecture considers all business requirements, both functional and non-functional. A functional requirement addresses the application features that an end user will directly interact with. Non-functional requirements are not directly related to customer-facing feature enhancement, but impact the overall application in terms of critical factors, including performance, scalability, and availability. It ensures that business requirements are compatible, allowing them to be converted into the technical implementation stage, and strikes a balance between stakeholders.

- **IT infrastructure requirements**: Solution architecture determines what kind of IT infrastructure is required to execute the project; this includes computing, storage, network, and considerations, and helps to plan the IT resources more effectively.

- **Technology selection**: During solution design, a solution architect creates a prototype, which considers the corporate requirements, and then recommends the right technology and tools for implementation. Solution architecture aims to build in-house rather than third-party tool sourcing while defining software standards across the organization.

- **End user requirements**: Solution architecture pays special attention to the requirements of the end user who will be the actual consumer of the product. It helps to discover the hidden requirements that a product owner may not be able to capture. During implementation and launch, the solution architect provides a standard document and standard language structure in order to make sure that all of the requirements have been met to satisfy the user's needs.

- **Solution maintenance**: Solution architecture is not just about solution design and implementation, but also takes care of post-launch activities, such as solution scalability, disaster recovery, and operational excellence.

- **Project timeline**: Solution architecture designs the layout details of each component with their complexity, which further helps to define the project milestones and timeline by providing resource estimation and associated risks.

An industry-standard and well-defined solution architecture addresses all business requirements within a technical solution and makes sure to deliver the desired result in order to satisfy the stakeholders, as per their expectations in terms of the quality, availability, maintainability, and scalability of the solution.

The initial design of a solution architecture may be conceived at a very early stage during the pre-sales cycle, such as the **request for proposal (RFP)** or the **request for information (RFI)**, and is followed by the creation of a prototype or proof of concept, in order to discover any solution risk. The solution architect also identifies whether to build a solution or to source it. It helps to identify the appropriate technology, while also keeping an organization's critical security and compliance requirements in mind.

There are two primary situations for creating a solution architecture:

- First, enhancing technology for an existing application, which may include hardware refresh or software re-architecting.

- Second, creating a new solution from the ground up, where you get more flexibility to choose the best fit of technology to address a business requirement.

However, while re-architecting an existing solution, you need to consider the minimal impact on the current environment. Solution architects may decide to completely rebuild if re-architecting the existing solution is not worth it, and a better solution can be provided through a full rebuild approach.

Put simply, solution architecture is about looking at all the aspects of the system in order to generate a technical vision, which provides steps to implement the business requirements. Solution architecture can define an implementation for a project, or a group of projects in a complex environment, by putting together all of the different pieces that are related to data, infrastructure, networking, and software applications. A good solution architecture not only satisfies the functional and non-functional requirements but also addresses system scalabilities and maintenance in the long run.

We have now briefly covered the role of solution architecture and its different aspects. In the next section, we will look at the evolution of solution architecture.

The evolution of solution architecture

Solution architecture has evolved with technological modernization. Today, solution architecture design has changed drastically compared to a couple of decades ago, due to the increasing use of the internet, the availability of high-bandwidth networks, the low cost of storage, and compute availability.

Back in the days before the era of the internet, most solution designs focused on providing a thick desktop client that was capable of operating with low bandwidth and working offline when a system could not connect to the internet.

This technology has evolved over the two decades. **Service-oriented architecture (SOA)** started taking shape for distributed design, and applications started moving from monolithic to *modern n-tier architecture*, where the frontend server, application server, and database were live in their own compute and the storage layer. These SOAs are mostly achieved by an XML-based messaging protocol, called **Simple Object Access Protocol (SOAP)**. A major component of this is its ability to follow a client-server model in order to create services.

In this age of digitization, you will see microservice-based solution design becoming increasingly popular, which is based on **JavaScript Object Notation (JSON)** messaging and the **Representational State Transfer (REST)** service. These are web APIs, which do not require XML-based web service protocols (SOAPs) to support their interfaces. They rely on web-based HTTP protocols such as POST, GET, UPDATE, DELETE, and so on. You will learn more about different architecture patterns in great detail in *Chapter 6, Solution Architecture Design Patterns*.

The microservice architecture addresses the need for changing requirements in an agile environment, where any solution changes need to be accommodated and deployed rapidly. Organizations have to be agile to stay ahead of the competition, which forces solution architecture to be flexible compared to the waterfall model, where you have a long cycle before project release.

The web-based microservice architecture is fueled by an almost unlimited resource capability, which is available from cloud providers, and can scale in minutes or seconds. It's becoming easier to innovate, experiment, and change as solution architects and developers can risk failing without impacting business functions.

Why is solution architecture important?

Solution architecture is a component of the foundation of an overall enterprise software solution that addresses specific problems and requirements. As the project size increases, the team becomes distributed globally. It is required to have solution architecture in place for long-term sustainability and a solid foundation.

Solution architecture addresses various solution needs, keeping the business context intact. It specifies and documents technology platforms, application components, data requirements, resource requirements, and many important non-functional requirements, such as scalability, reliability, performance, throughput, availability, security, and maintainability.

Solution architecture is vital for any industry to solve business problems using software applications. In the absence of solution architecture, there is a chance that software development could fail: projects can get delayed, go over budget, and not deliver enough in the form of functionalities. This scenario can be drastically improved by creating a solution architecture and applying experience and knowledge—all of which are provided by a solution architect. It helps to keep stakeholders from all areas, from non-technical business functions through to technical development, on the same page, which avoids confusion, keeps the project on track, within schedule and on time, and helps to derive maximum **return on investment (ROI)**.

Often, the solution architect requires customer collaboration in order to understand specifications. In a solution architect's role, the architect needs to call on multiple skillsets, from technical leaders and experts to business analysts and project management. We will learn more about the solution architect's role in *Chapter 2, Solution Architects in an Organization*.

A good solution architecture puts specifications in place with a well-defined solution, which helps us to deliver and accomplish the final product, along with smooth product operability after launch.

A single problem can have multiple solutions, and each solution has its constraints. Solution architecture considers all the solutions and finds the best one by creating a hands-on proof of concept that accommodates all of the business and technical limitations.

Let's learn about the various benefits of solution architecture in detail.

The benefits of solution architecture

Now that we have detailed the importance of solution architecture, we will now provide more details on the benefits of solution architecture in various aspects of an organization; *Figure 1.2* is a breakdown of the potential benefits bestowed upon an organization when employing the role of solution architect in the business.

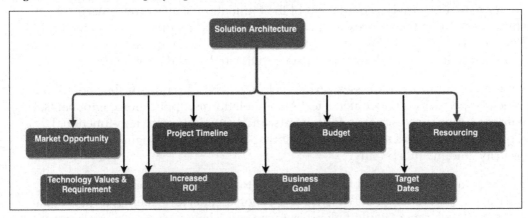

Figure 1.2: A solution architecture's beneficial attributes

The preceding diagram highlights the following attributes of a good solution architecture:

- **Technology values and requirements**: Solution architecture determines the ROI, which solution can be obtained by a particular technology selection, and the market trends. The solution architect evaluates which technology an organization or project should adopt in order to achieve long-term sustainability, maintainability, and team comfort.

- **Business goal**: The primary responsibility of a solution architecture design is to accommodate the needs of the stakeholders and adapt it to their requirements. Solution architecture converts business goals into a technical vision by analyzing market trends and implementing best practices. Solution architecture needs to be flexible enough to meet new, challenging, demanding, and rapidly changing business requirements.

- **Target dates**: A solution architect continuously works with all stakeholders, including the business team, customers, and the development team. A solution architect defines the process standard and provides guidelines for solution development. They make sure that the overall solution is in alignment with the business objective and launch timeline, to ensure minimal chances of target date slippage.

- **Increased ROI**: Solution architecture determines the ROI and helps to measure the success of the project. Solution architecture forces a business to think about how to reduce costs and remove process wastage by applying automation in order to improve the overall ROI.

- **Market opportunity**: Solution architecture involves the process of analyzing and continuously evaluating the latest trends in the market. It also helps with backing up and promoting new products.

- **Budget and resourcing**: For a better budget, it is always recommended to invest well in estimation. A well-defined solution architecture helps us to understand the amount of resources that are required for project completion. This helps in the formulation of better budget forecasting and resource planning.

- **Project timeline**: Defining an accurate project timeline is critical for solution implementation. A solution architect determines the resources and effort that will be required during the design phase, which should help define the schedule.

Now you have had a high-level overview of solution architecture and its benefits, Let's investigate more closely the everyday aspects of solution architecture.

Addressing the business needs and quality of delivery

In the life cycle of product development, the most challenging phase is to establish the nature of the requirements, especially when multiple elements are competing to be addressed as high priority and are evolving rapidly. This is even more challenging when there are different views of the same requirement from various stakeholders. For example, a business user analyzes the page design from a user point of view, while a developer is looking at it from the perspective of implementation feasibility and load latency. This can cause conflicts and misunderstandings of the requirements between functional and technical members. In such cases, solution architecture helps to bridge the gap and define a standard that all members can understand.

Functional requirements are product features to accommodate user requirements and address the primary need of a given business problem. When users interact with software applications, they interact with functional requirements directly. For example, in an e-commerce application, examples of functional requirements are that users see their order history, search for merchandise, add them into the cart, and make payment using their preferred payment method. While the primary responsibility for the collection of functional requirements resides with the product owner, a solution architect makes sure of their design and implementation in such a way that it can scale as per user demand and accommodate any future extension.

Solution architecture defines standard documentation that explains the technical aspects to non-technical stakeholders and updates them regularly. As a solution architecture's design spans across the organization and different teams, it can help to discover hidden requirements. The solution architect makes sure that the development team knows about the requirements, and also maintains the cycle of progress.

A good solution architecture defines not only the solution design but also the success criteria in the form of qualitative and quantitative output, in order to ensure the quality of delivery. The qualitative output can be collected from user feedback, such as through sentiment analysis, while quantitative output may include latency, performance, load time on the technical side, and sales numbers on the business side. Taking continuous feedback and adapting to it is the key to high-quality delivery, which should adhere to all the phases of solution design and development.

Selecting the best technology platform

In a rapid and competitive market, the biggest challenge is maintaining the use of the best technologies. Today, when you have multiple resources all around the world, a specific technology should be chosen very carefully. The solution is the architecture design process, which can effectively tackle this problem.

The selection of the technology stack plays a significant role in efficient solution implementation by the team. In solution architecture, we should use different strategies to adopt various platforms, technologies, and tools. A solution architect should validate all of the needs carefully, and then evaluate and investigate the result using multiple parameters in order to find the best-fit solution for the product development by creating a working model of the product in the form of a prototype.

Good solution architecture addresses the depth of different tools and technologies by investigating all possible architectural strategies, based on the mixed use case, techniques, tools, and code reuse, which come as part of years of experience. The best platform simplifies the implementation process; however, the right technology selection is critical. This can be achieved by building a prototype according to the business requirement assessment, and the agility, speed, and security of the application.

Addressing solution constraints and issues

Any solution can be limited by various constraints and may encounter issues due to further complexities or unforeseen risks. Solution architecture needs to balance multiple constraints, such as resources, technologies, cost, quality, time to market, and frequently changing requirements.

Each project has its own specific goal, requirement, budget, and timeline. Solution architecture evaluates all of the possible critical paths and shares best practices to achieve a project goal in a given timeframe and budget. This is a systematic approach, where all tasks are interdependent of prior tasks; in order to achieve success in the project, all tasks need to be executed in sequence. A delay in one task can impact the project timeline and can result in the organization missing the market window to launch the product.

If there is an issue in the project development process, the probability of a project getting delayed is high. Sometimes, you encounter problems that are limitations of the adopted technology, or even of the solution environment. If you have a well-thought-out solution architecture, the most common issues are related to the non-functional requirements: resources and budgeting can mitigate problems encountered in the product development life cycle.

A solution architect helps to drive the project by diving deep into each component of it. They think of an out-of-the-box idea to save the project from unforeseen issues, such as those covered in disaster recovery, and will prepare a backup plan in the event that things do not work out with the main one. They evaluate the best possible way to execute the project by choosing the best practice and balancing constraints.

Helping in resource and cost management

There are always risks and uncertainties involved during solution implementation; it can become very tedious should a developer need to spend time on fixing a bug, for example. A good solution architecture controls the cost and budget and reduces uncertainty by providing developers with the required guidance in terms of priority, different communication services, and the details of each component.

Solution architecture also creates documentation that will be used to keep the system up to date, along with a deployment diagram, software patches, and a software release version, and enforces the runbook to tackle frequent issues and business continuation processes. It also addresses the indirect impacts of the cost of building a solution by considering extensibility, scalability, and other external factors that matter to the development environment.

Managing solution delivery and project life cycle

Lots of planning is involved in the inception stage of solution architecture. Solution architecture starts with a strategic view and provides more technical implementation input as you move forward with the solution implementation.

Solution architecture ensures an end-to-end solution delivery and impacts the overall project life cycle. It defines a process standard for different phases of the project life cycle and makes sure that it is applied across the organization so that other dependencies can be addressed as the implementation moves forward.

Solution architecture considers a holistic view of the project. It keeps syncing other dependent groups, such as security, compliance, infrastructure, project management, and support, in order to keep them engaged in different phases of the project life cycle as required.

Addressing non-functional requirements

Often, a solution architect has to deal with the **non-functional requirements (NFRs)** in an application. For project success, it is essential to address them, as they have a broader impact on the overall project and solution. These NFRs can make or break your user base, and address critical aspects of a solution, such as security, availability, latency concerns, maintenance, logging, masking confidential information, performance concerns, reliability, maintainability, scalability, and usability. If these are not considered on time, it can impact your project delivery. *Figure 1.3* shows some of the most common NFRs.

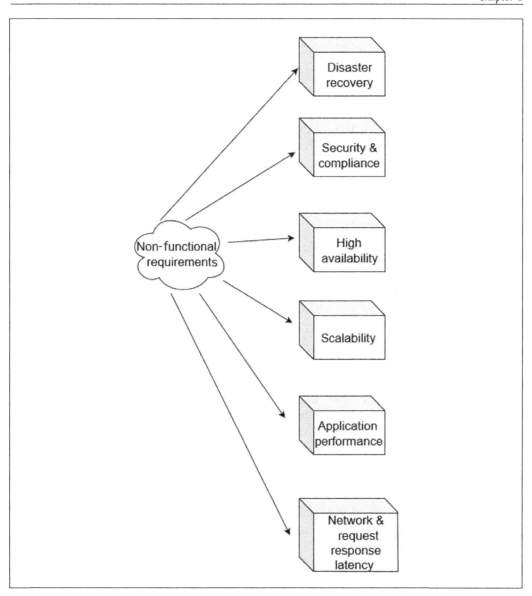

Figure 1.3: Non-functional attributes of solution architecture

As shown, NFRs include the following attributes of solution architecture. However, there can be more NFRs, depending on the type of project:

- **Disaster recovery**: To make sure the solution is up and running in case of any unforeseen events.

- **Security and compliance**: Put a safety net in place for a solution to save it from an external attack, such as a virus, malware, and so on. Also make sure that the solution complies with local and industry laws by meeting compliance requirements.

- **High availability**: To make sure the solution is always up and running.

- **Scalability**: To make sure the solution can handle the additional load in case of increasing demands.

- **Application performance**: To make sure the application is loading as per user expectation, and without much delay.

- **Network request and response latency**: Any activity performed on the application should be completed within an appropriate time, and should not be allowed to time out.

You will learn more details of the preceding attributes in *Chapter 3, Attributes of the Solution Architecture*. The solution architecture defines an initial framework for product development and the building blocks of the solution. While establishing a solution architecture, quality and customer satisfaction are always the main focus. Solution architecture needs to be built continuously by working on a proof of concept and exploring and testing until the desired quality is reached.

Solution architecture in the public cloud

Solution architecture in the cloud has become increasingly important these days and is becoming the "new normal" as more enterprises choose to migrate their workload to it. The public cloud has been a critical factor fueling start-up organizations' growth, as they do not need huge upfront investment. It provides flexibility to organizations to be run as an experiment, to be agile and innovative.

The great thing about cloud computing architecture is that you have an end-to-end view of all architecture components, including the frontend platforms, the application development platform, servers, storage, database, automation, delivery, and the networks that are required to manage the entire solution landscape.

Before jumping into solution architecture in the cloud, let's understand more about the public cloud and how it is becoming an essential and driving technology platform for businesses.

What is the public cloud?

The public cloud is based on the standard computing model in which a service provider makes resources, such as virtual machines, applications, and storage, available to their customers over the internet. Public cloud services offer a *pay-as-you-go* model.

In the cloud computing model, a public cloud vendor provides on-demand availability of IT resources, such as the server, database, network, and storage, which organizations can use with secure web-based interfaces, or through application programs over the internet. In most cases, the customer only pays for the services that they are using for the duration of utilization, which saves costs for them by optimizing IT resources to reduce idle time.

You can think of the public cloud in terms of an electric power supply model, where you switch on the light and pay only for the amount of electricity you use in units. As soon as you switch it off, you are not paying for it. It abstracts you from the complexity of power generation using turbines, resources to maintain the facility, a large infrastructure setup, and you use the entire service in a simplified way.

In addition to cost benefits, major public cloud providers, such as **Amazon Web Services (AWS)**, **Google Cloud Platform (GCP)**, and **Microsoft Azure** help to bring innovation by extending their technology platform through the cloud. These public cloud providers have mastered the scalability and future-looking architecture with comprehensive machine learning and analytics. With the public cloud, you get access to these cutting-edge technologies and the option of considering them to advance your architecture.

Public clouds, private clouds, and hybrid clouds

Here, you will get a high-level overview of the different types of cloud computing deployment models. You will learn more about the details in *Chapter 5, Cloud Migration and Hybrid Cloud Architecture Design*.

A **private cloud**, or **on-premises**, is registered to a single organization that owns and accesses it. Private clouds act as a replicate or extension of the company's existing data center. Often, a **public cloud** has a shared tenancy, which means virtual servers from multiple customers share the same physical server; however, they offer dedicated physical servers to customers if the customer wants it for a license or compliance need. A public cloud, such as AWS, Microsoft Azure, or GCP, utilizes massive IT infrastructure that can be accessed over the internet through a pay-as-you-go model.

A third model is the **hybrid cloud**, used by large enterprises who are moving their workload from on-premises to a cloud, where they still have a legacy application that cannot move to the cloud directly, or maybe they have a licensed application that needs to stay on-premises — or sometimes, due to compliance reasons, they need to secure data on-premises. In such a situation, the hybrid model helps when the enterprise has to maintain a partial environment on-premises and move other applications to the public cloud. Sometimes an organization moves to test and develop the environment to the public cloud and keep production environments on-premises. A hybrid model can vary depending upon the organization's cloud strategy.

As there are multiple public cloud providers in the market, you may start seeing the trends of **multi-cloud**. Enterprises choose to distribute their workload between different public cloud vendors to get the most out of each cloud technology or provide options to their team depending on their skill set.

The public cloud architecture

A typical definition of the public cloud is that it is a fully virtualized environment, which is accessible both over the internet or through a private network. However, in recent times, public cloud vendors have also started offering an on-premises physical infrastructure for better hybrid cloud adoption. The public cloud provides a multi-tenancy model, where IT infrastructure, such as storage and computational power, are shared between multiple customers; however, they are isolated at the software and logical network levels and do not interfere with each other's workload. In the public cloud, by creating network-level isolation, organizations can have their virtual private cloud, which is equivalent to the logical data center. Looking at organizations' regulatory needs, the public cloud also provides dedicated physical instances, however, those are also accessible over the web, but this is a less common option.

Public cloud storage achieves high durability and availability by creating a redundancy model using multiple data centers and robust data replication. This makes them achieve architecture resiliency and easy scalability. There are three major types of cloud computing models, as shown in *Figure 1.4*.

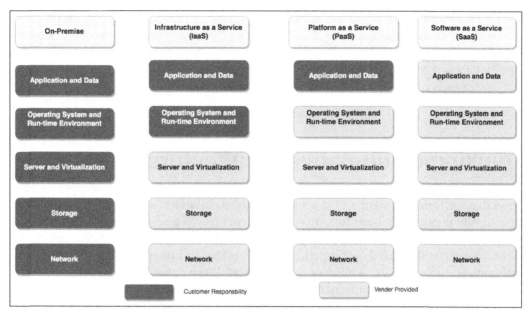

Figure 1.4: Types of cloud computing models

In *Figure 1.4* you can see a comparison between customer responsibilities in the on-premises environment with the cloud computing service model. In the on-premises environment, the customer has to manage everything, while in the cloud computing model, customers can offload responsibilities to the vendor and focus on their business needs. The following points are high-level details of services that are provided under different cloud computing models:

- **Infrastructure as a Service (IaaS)**: Here, a cloud vendor provides infrastructure resources, such as a compute server, networking components, and data storage space, as managed services. It helps customers to use IT resources without worrying about handling data center overheads, such as heating and cooling, racking and stacking, physical security, and so on.

- **Platform as a Service (PaaS)**: The PaaS model adds a layer of service where the cloud vendor takes care of the resources that are required for your development platform, such as the operating system, software maintenance, and patching, along with infrastructure resources. The PaaS model facilitates your team's focus on writing business logic and handling data by taking care of all of the burdens of platform maintenance for you.

- **Software as a Service (SaaS)**: The SaaS model adds one more layer of abstraction on top of the PaaS and IaaS models, wherein the cloud or software vendor provides ready-to-use software, and you pay for the service. For example, you use email services such as Gmail, Yahoo! Mail, AOL, and so on, where you get your own space for emails as a service, and you don't have to worry about underlying applications or infrastructures.

The fourth emerging model is the **Function as a Service (FaaS)** model, which is becoming popular in the building of serverless architecture through using services including AWS Lambda. You will learn more details about serverless architecture in *Chapter 6, Solution Architecture Design Patterns*.

As the public cloud functionality and the cost model are very different, let's learn how to develop a cloud-native approach to architecture design.

Thinking cloud-native architecture

With the increasing adoption of the cloud, cloud-native architecture is an upcoming trend that optimizes system architectures for cloud capabilities. Typical on-premises architecture is normally built for a fixed infrastructure, as adding new IT resources such as servers and computing power adds a considerable amount of time, cost, and effort. However, the cloud is charged based on usage, and provides ease through automation, such as in the scaling of servers up and down, on-demand, without worrying about a long procurement cycle. Cloud-native architecture primarily focuses on achieving on-demand scale, distributed design, and replacing failed components rather than fixing them.

The public cloud is not just about infrastructure, but most public cloud providers offer a broad range of managed services that allow the user to ignore underlying infrastructure and operation maintenance. For example, AWS provides Lambda, a serverless computing platform that can be used to run code without managing the server or runtime environment. Similarly, the Amazon DynamoDB database is highly scalable; tables can be created and data stored without managing a database server. Managed services make it easy to develop scalable applications rapidly.

In cloud-native architecture, you continually create automated operations for recovery, scalability, self-healing, and high availability using the cloud capabilities of continuous integration, deployment, and infrastructure automation. It encourages the continuous optimization of your application in terms of cost and performance, using new cloud capabilities that are released and improved upon every day.

You will learn more details about cloud-native architecture patterns in the next chapter.

Public cloud providers and cloud service offerings

There are several public cloud providers in the IT industry; among them, the key players are AWS, GCP, Microsoft Azure, and Alibaba Cloud. These providers offer an array of services, from computing, storage, networking, databases, and application development, to analytics and machine learning.

Figure 1.5 is a screenshot from the AWS console; you can see the array of services on offer in multiple areas. The highlighted EC2 service, known as Amazon Elastic Compute Cloud, allows you to spin up a virtual machine in minutes in the AWS cloud.

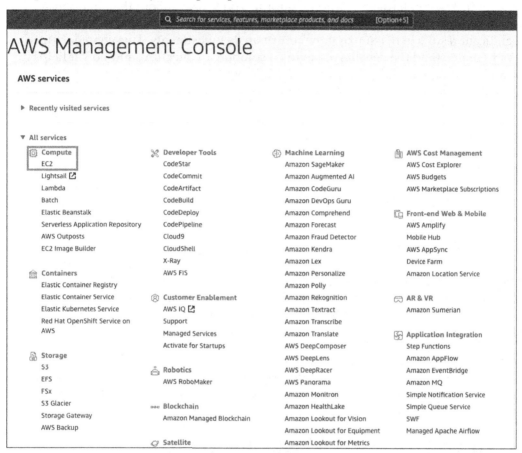

Figure 1.5: AWS console and service offerings

Public cloud vendors provide infrastructure and facilitate an array of services in various areas, such as analytics, machine learning, blockchain, robotics, application development, email, security, monitoring, and alerting. With the public cloud, different technical capabilities become more accessible to the development team, which helps drive innovation and reduce the time to market for the product launch.

Public cloud providers allow global infrastructure to spread across the world, which helps an application to be scaled globally near your user base. To encourage adoption, all cloud services provide a free-tier service, with lots of learning resources, so you can try your hand and develop your knowledge of them.

Summary

In this chapter, you have learned about the definition of solution architecture from industry standards in a simplified form. You learned about the importance of solution architecture, and how it can help an organization to achieve more significant results in maximizing the return on its investments. This chapter helped you to understand the benefits of having a solution architecture, and how it helps in different aspects of solution design and implementation.

In summary, solution architecture is a building block in a complex organization and is used to address all stakeholders' needs and establish a standard in order to fill the gap between business requirements and technical solutions. A good solution architect not only addresses functional requirements, but also puts long-term thought into, and takes care of, non-functional requirements, such as scalability, performance, resiliency, high availability, and disaster recovery. Solution architecture finds an optimal solution to accommodate the constraints of cost, resources, timelines, security, and compliance.

You have also explored the basics of cloud computing, solution architecture in the cloud environment, and the significant public cloud providers and their service offerings. This also aided in the gaining of a high-level overview of different cloud computing models, such as IaaS, PaaS, and SaaS, and the cloud computing deployment models in the public, private, and hybrid cloud. Finally, this chapter shed some light on the evolution of solution architecture design.

In the next chapter, you will learn all about the solution architect role itself—the different types of solution architect, the role's responsibilities with regards to solution architecture, and how these fit into an organizational structure and agile environment.

Join our book's Discord space

Join the book's Discord workspace for a monthly *Ask me Anything* session with the authors: https://packt.link/SAHandbook

2
Solution Architects in an Organization

A solution architect understands the needs and goals of an organization as part of a team—all stakeholders, processes, teams, and the organization's management affect solution architect roles and their work. In this chapter, you will learn and understand the role of the solution architect and how they fit into the organization. Following that, you will learn about the various types of solution architects, and how they coexist within an organization. An organization may need a generalist solution architect, along with other specialist solution architects that are required based on a project's complexity.

This chapter will provide details on the solution architect's responsibility and how it can impact an organization's success. A solution architect wears multiple hats, and business executives heavily depend on their experience and decision making to understand the technical vision.

The solution-and-software development methodology has evolved over the last few decades, from waterfall to agile, and is needed by a solution architect. This chapter will provide details about the agile methodology and the iterative approach that a solution architect should take for the continuous improvement of solution delivery. Agile thinking is extremely important for a solution architect.

In addition to solution design, solution architects need to handle various constraints to evaluate risk and plan mitigation strategies. Quality management also plays a significant role, and should not be overlooked. The solution architect plays an essential role throughout the solution's life cycle: from requirement collection, solution design, and solution implementation, to testing, and then on to the launch.

A solution architect needs to engage regularly post-launch to ensure the scalability, ready availability, and maintainability of the solution. For broader consumer products, the solution architect also needs to work with the sales team as a technology evangelist of the product through content publishing and public speaking in various forums.

In this chapter, you will learn about the following topics:

- Types of roles for a solution architect
- Understanding a solution architect's responsibilities
- Solution architects in an agile organization

Types of roles for a solution architect

In the previous chapter, you learned about solution architecture and how various stakeholders impact solution strategies—now, you will understand the solution architect's role. The software solution can develop without a solution architect, depending on the project's size, but for a large project it is a requirement to have a dedicated solution architect. The success or failure of the plan depends on the solution architect.

There is always a need for someone who can make architectural decisions for the team and drive team collaboration with stakeholders. Sometimes, it is required to have multiple solution architects in the team, depending on the size of the project. The different types of solution architect are depicted in *Figure 2.1*, showing how they have different responsibilities in the organization.

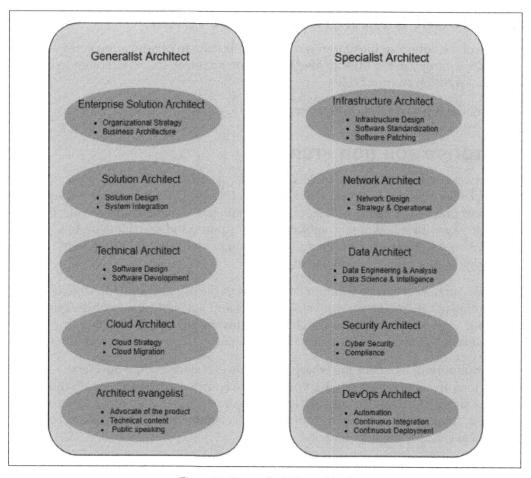

Figure 2.1: Types of solution architect

An organization can have multiple types of solution architect. Solution architects can be categorized as either **generalists** or **specialists**. Generalist solution architects have the breadth that comes from multiple technical domains, whereas specialist solution architects have very in-depth knowledge in their area of expertise, such as big data, security, or networking. A generalist solution architect needs to collaborate with a specialist solution architect to align with the project's requirements and complexity.

Generalist solution architect roles

The role of a solution architect varies from organization to organization and you may encounter a variety of job titles related to solution architect, the most common being generalist solution architect roles.

Details of the types of solution architect can be found in the following sections.

Enterprise solution architect

Do you ever think about how products launch in the information technology industry? This is where an enterprise solution role comes into the picture—they define best practices, culture, and suitable technologies. An enterprise architect works closely with stakeholders, subject matter experts, and management to identify organizational strategies for information technology and make sure that their knowledge aligns with company business rules.

Enterprise architects handle solution design across the organization; they create long-term plans and solutions with stakeholders and leadership. One of the most important aspects is to finalize which technologies should be used by the company, and ensure the company is using these technologies with consistency and integrity.

Another important aspect of the enterprise architect is defining the business architecture. In some organizations, you may see *business architect* as the job title. Business architecture fills the gap between organizational strategy and its successful execution. It helps convert a map strategy into executable action items and takes this to a tactical level for implementation.

Overall, enterprise architects are more aligned with company visions and responsibilities when it comes to defining organization-wide standards for the successful implementation of the business' vision.

Solution architect

In general, this book explores the role of a solution architect in a more generic way. Still, you often see solution architects with different titles, as per the organization's structure; for example, enterprise solution, software, or technical architects. In this section, you will find some distinct attributes related to the various titles. However, the responsibilities of the solution architect may overlap, depending on an organization's structure.

If you wish to know how a solution should be organized and delivered, then a solution architect plays an essential role in this context.

A solution architect designs the overall system, and how different systems integrate across different groups. A solution architect defines the expected outcome by working with business stakeholders and providing a clear understanding of the delivery objective on the part of the technical team.

The solution architect connects the dots across the organization and ensures consistency within different teams to avoid any issues that may appear late in the development process; they engage throughout the project life cycle and define monitoring and alerting mechanisms to ensure smooth operations after a product's launch. The solution architect also plays an essential role in project management by providing advice regarding resource, cost, and timeline estimation.

Overall, the solution architect gets to engage on a more tactical level compared to the enterprise architect. Sometimes, the solution architect takes on the role of an enterprise architect if more strategic involvement is required.

Technical architect

A technical architect may also be known as an application or software architect. A technical architect is responsible for software design and development. The technical architect works with the organization in terms of software engineering, and is more focused on defining technical details for software development by a team. They also work across the organization to understand how integration will work alongside other parts of the software module, which may be managed by other groups.

A technical architect can manage the details of API design and define API performance and scaling aspects. They make sure that the software is being developed consistently with the organization's standards and that they can easily integrate with components of other software applications.

The technical architect is a point of contact for any technical question related to the engineering team, and will have the ability to troubleshoot the system as required. For a small software development project, you may not see a technical architect role, as a senior engineer may take it up and work on software architecture design.

The technical architect mentors and supports the software engineering team by working closely with them and resolving any impediments that arise from cross-team integration or business requirements.

Cloud architect

The cloud architect role has only come into existence in the last decade, but as cloud adoption is increasing among enterprises, this is one role that is in great demand.

The cloud architect plans and designs the cloud environment and is responsible for deploying and managing the company's cloud computing strategies. Cloud architects provide breadth and depth for cloud services and can define the cloud-native design.

As you learned in the *Solution architecture in the public cloud* section in *Chapter 1, The Meaning of Solution Architecture,* use of the cloud is now very popular, and it has become the norm for organizations to move onto a public cloud. Major cloud providers, such as Amazon Web Services, Microsoft Azure, and Google Cloud Platform, are helping customers to adopt cloud platforms at exponential speed with SaaS, PaaS, and IaaS offerings. You will learn more about cloud architectures in *Chapter 5, Cloud Migration and Hybrid Cloud Architecture Design*.

There are a large number of enterprises that have an existing workload that they want to migrate into the cloud to utilize scalability, ease of business, and price benefits. A cloud architect can prepare a cloud migration strategy and develop a hybrid cloud architecture. A cloud architect can advise how on-premises applications will connect to the cloud and how different traditional offerings fit into a cloud environment.

For start-up businesses and enterprises starting in the cloud, a cloud architect can help to design a cloud-native architecture, which is more optimized for the cloud and uses the full capabilities it provides. The cloud-native architecture tends to be built on *pay-as-you-go* models to optimize cost and leverage the automation available in the cloud.

The cloud is now an essential part of enterprise strategy, and a cloud architect is a must-have if companies want to succeed in the modern era and keep up with the pace of innovation and automation.

Architect evangelist

An architect evangelist (also known as a technology evangelist) is a comparatively new role that offers a new paradigm in marketing, especially when it comes to the increasing adoption of complex solution platforms. People will always want to hear from an expert who has in-depth knowledge and the ability to answer their queries so that they can make an informed decision. Here, architect evangelists come into the picture with their expertise on a particular subject in a competitive environment.

An architect evangelist can design the architecture based on customer requirements, which resolves the customer's pain points and results in customer wins. The evangelist can be a trusted advisor for customers and partners, with a deep understanding of architectural issues, concepts, and market trends to help secure platform adoption and show revenue growth through market capture.

To increase platform adoption for the overall target audience, the architect evangelist writes public content, such as blogs, whitepapers, and articles. They speak on public platforms, whether it be an industry summit, technical talks, or conferences. They conduct technical workshops and publish tutorials to spread the word about their given product. This makes it very important for a solution architect to have excellent written and verbal communication skills; you will often see solution architects taking on technology evangelism as an additional responsibility.

Specialist solution architect roles

There may be other types of specialist solution architect, such as migration architect, storage architect, and machine learning architect. This, again, depends on the organization's structure. As per the project and organizational complexity, a solution architect can take on multiple roles, or different solution architects can have overlapping responsibilities.

Infrastructure architect

An infrastructure architect is a specialist architect role heavily focused on enterprise IT infrastructure design, security, and data center operation. They work closely with solution architects to make sure that the organization's infrastructure strategy is aligned with its overall business requirements, and they allocate appropriate resource capacity to fulfill this need by analyzing both the system requirements and the existing environment. They help reduce capital expenditure that could be utilized for operational spending to increase organizational efficiency and ROI.

The infrastructure architect is the backbone of the organization, since they define and plan overall IT resources, from storage servers to individual workspaces. The infrastructure architect creates detailed plans for procuring and setting up IT infrastructures. They define software standards, patching, and plan system updates across an organization. The infrastructure architect handles infrastructure security and makes sure all environments are protected from unwanted virus attacks. They also plan for disaster recovery and system backups to make sure business operations are always running.

In most e-commerce businesses, infrastructure architect roles become challenging, as they need to plan for periods when demands will peak, such as Thanksgiving in the USA, Boxing Day in Canada and the UK, or Diwali in India, when most consumers start shopping. They need to prepare enough server and storage capacity to accommodate the peak season, whose workload may be ten times higher than normal, thus increasing the cost of IT infrastructure. A system will be sitting idle for most of the year, outside of the peak season.

They need to plan for cost optimization and better user experience, which is another reason they may use the cloud to fulfill additional capacity and scale on-demand to reduce the cost. They need to ensure that systems are occupied while supporting the growth of new expertise.

Overall, an infrastructure architect needs to have a good understanding of data center operation and the components involved, such as heating, cooling, security, racking and stacking, server, storage, backup, software installation and patching, load balancers, and virtualization.

Network architect

Have you ever wondered how giant enterprises with multiple locations for offices or stores are connected? Here, the network architect comes into the picture, as they orchestrate an organization's network communication strategy and establish communication between IT resources, giving life to the IT infrastructure.

A network architect is responsible for designing the computer network, **Local Area Network (LAN)**, **Wide Area Network (WAN)**, internet, intranet, and other communication systems. They manage organizational information and network systems, and ensure low network latency and high network performance is available for users to increase their productivity. They establish secure connectivity between user workspaces and the internal network using **Virtual Private Network (VPN)** connectivity.

The network architect works closely with the infrastructure architect; sometimes you see this as an overlapping role to ensure all IT infrastructures are connected. They work with the security team and design the organization's firewall to protect against unethical attacks. They are responsible for monitoring and protecting the network via packet monitoring, port scanning, and putting an **Intrusion Detection System (IDS)** and **Intrusion Prevention System (IPS)** into place. You will learn more about IDS/IPS systems in *Chapter 8, Security Considerations*.

Overall, a network architect needs to have a good understanding of network strategies, network operations, secure connections using VPN, firewall configuration, network topology, load balance configuration, DNS routing, and IT infrastructure connectivity.

Data architect

Any solution design revolves around data, and it is mostly about storing, updating, and accessing it regardless of whether it is focused on customers or products. In the last decade, data growth has risen exponentially—not long ago, gigabytes of data were considered as big data, but now, even 100 terabytes of data are deemed to be normal—you can even get a 1-terabyte computer hard disk.

Traditionally, data was stored in a structured relational way. Now, most data is in an unstructured format generated from resources such as social media, the **Internet of Things (IoT)**, and application logs. There is a need to store, process, and analyze data to get useful insights, which is where the data architect role comes into the picture.

The data architect defines a set of rules, policies, standards, and models that govern the type of data that's used and collected in the organization database; they design, create, and manage the data architecture in an organization. A data architect develops data models and data lake designs to capture the business's **key performance indicators (KPIs)**, and enable data transformation. They ensure consistent data performance and data quality across the organization.

The primary customers for a data architect are as follows:

- Business executives using **Business Intelligence (BI)** tools for data visualization
- Business analysts using a data warehouse for greater data insight
- Data engineers performing data wrangling using **Extract, Transform, and Load (ETL)** jobs
- Data scientists for machine learning
- Development teams for application data management

To fulfill organizational needs, a data architect is responsible for the following:

- Selection of database technology
- Structured and unstructured data store choice
- Streaming and batch data processing
- A data lake as the centralized datastore
- A relational database schema for application development
- Data warehousing for data analysis and BI tools
- Datamart design
- Data security and encryption
- Data compliance

You will learn more about data architectures in *Chapter 13, Data Engineering for Solution Architecture*. Overall, the data architect needs to be aware of different database technologies, BI tools, data security, and encryption to make the right selection. As machine learning is becoming more prominent among enterprises, the emergence of dedicated machine learning architect roles is expected.

Machine learning architect

As we know, **artificial intelligence** (**AI**) and **machine learning** (**ML**) have been a hot topic for quite some time now, and more companies are pivoting to implement ML in their enterprise solutions stacks. The public cloud has accelerated organizations' adoption of ML, with easily accessible infrastructure and tools. ML helps to tackle customer problems in many ways, including to develop personalization, provide forecasts, and detect fraud. In addition to that, ML can solve many daily challenges for IT leaders, software architects, and solution architects, such as automation of security, infrastructure, disaster recovery, and monitoring of solutions. This has contributed to the rise of ML architect roles, which carry the following responsibilities at a very high level:

- Applying systems thinking to implement/adopt ML in the enterprise software stack
- Identifying and analyzing tools for ML and AI implementation
- Architecting the information/data architecture for ML
- Modifying the current software stack and tools to make way for ML integration
- Operationalizing ML with continuous monitoring and improvements

An ML architect creates an AI/ML solution architecture by applying architecture best practices while considering the performance optimization, security, compliance, reliability, cost optimization, and operational excellence of the AI/ML solution design. It's not the case that every problem can be solved with AI/ML, and ML architects should understand how ML solutions fit in an agile enterprise environment. They must put together AI/ML architecture design by providing a detailed understanding of design pillars, advanced design patterns, antipatterns, and the cloud-native aspect of modern AI/ML tech stack design. You will learn more about ML in *Chapter 14, Machine Learning Architecture*.

Security architect

Security should be the top priority of any organization; there are multiple instances when large and well-established organizations have gone out of business due to a security breach. Organizations not only lose customer trust but also experience legal complications due to security incidents. There are various industry compliance certifications, such as **Organizational Security** (**SOC2**), **Finance Data** (**PCI**), and **HealthCare data** (**HIPAA**), that are in place to ensure organization and customer data security, which a company needs to adhere to, depending on the nature of their application.

Looking at the critical nature of security, organizations need to research and design the most robust security architecture for their projects, and that's where a security architect is necessary. A security architect works closely with all teams within the organization and external vendors to make sure security is a high priority. A security architect's responsibilities include the following:

- Designing and deploying the implementation of the network and computer security in the organization
- Understanding the company's technology and information systems, and safeguarding the security of the computers in the organization
- Working with a variety of settings, such as securing company networks and websites
- Planning vulnerability testing, risk analysis, and security audits
- Reviewing and approving the installation of a firewall, VPN, and router, and scanning the server
- Testing final security processes and making sure they work as expected
- Providing technical guidance to the security teams
- Making sure applications comply with industry standards as required
- Making sure data is secure with the required accessibility and encryption

Security architects are expected to understand, design, and guide all aspects of security related to data, network, infrastructure, and applications with a variety of tools and techniques. You will learn more about security and compliance in *Chapter 8, Security Considerations*.

DevOps architect

As a system gets more complex, there is more potential for human error, which can lead to an additional effort being required, increased cost, and even reducing quality. Automation is the best way to avoid failure and improve overall system efficiency. Automation is not optional—if you want to be agile and move faster, automation is a must.

Automation can be applied anywhere, whether it is testing and deploying applications, spinning up infrastructure, or even ensuring security. Automation plays a critical role, and a DevOps architect role is to automate everything, wherever possible. DevOps is a combination of practices and tools that assist in delivering an application at a faster pace.

It allows the organization to serve its customers better and stay ahead of the competition.

In DevOps, the development team and operational team work together in parallel. For a software application, a DevOps architect defines **continuous integration and continuous deployment (CI/CD)**. In CI, automated builds and test runs happen before the development team merges its code changes into a central repository. CD expands upon CI by deploying all code changes to a production environment after the build and test stage.

The DevOps architect automates infrastructure deployment, known as **Infrastructure as Code**, which is highly prevalent in the cloud environment. DevOps can utilize tools such as **Chef** and **Puppet** for instructed automation, or use cloud-native tools if the workload is in a cloud environment. They may choose to automate infrastructure using script such as **Ansible** and **Terraform**. Infrastructure automation provides excellent flexibility for the development team in the aid of experimentation, and enables the operations team to create replica environments.

For smooth operation, a DevOps architect plans monitoring and alerting with automated communication in the event of issues or any significant changes. Any security incidents, deployment failures, or infrastructure failures can be monitored automatically, and alerts can be sent to the respective mobile devices or email accounts of a team when required.

The DevOps architect also plans for disaster recovery through different deployment methods. Organizational **Recovery Point Objective (RPO)** is the volume of data loss that an organization can tolerate. **Recovery Time Objective (RTO)** suggests how much time the application can take to recover and start functioning again. You will learn more about DevOps in *Chapter 12, DevOps and Solution Architecture Framework*.

Understanding a solution architect's responsibilities

Now we have broken down the various roles of a solution architect, we will next take a look at the details of the responsibilities of a solution architect. A solution architect is a technical leader in a customer-facing role, which comes with many responsibilities. The primary responsibility of a solution architect is to convert organization business visions into a technical solution and work as a liaison between businesses and technical stakeholders. A solution architect uses broad technological expertise and business experience to ensure the success of the solution's delivery.

A solution architect's responsibilities may differ slightly based on the nature of the organization. Often, in a consulting organization, a solution architect may be dedicated to a particular project and customer, while in a product-based organization, a solution architect may be working with multiple customers to educate them on a product and review their solution design.

A solution architect carries various responsibilities at different stages of the application development cycle, even before the project is kicked off. During the project incubation phase, the solution architect works with business stakeholders to prepare and evaluate the **request for response (RFR)** document. Once a project is kicked off, the solution architect analyzes the requirements to decide on the feasibility of technical implementation, while defining non-functional requirements such as scalability, high availability, performance, and security. A solution architect understands various project constraints and makes the technology selection by developing a proof of concept. Once development starts, the solution architect mentors the development team and adjusts both technical and business needs. After the application has launched, the solution architect makes sure that the application performs as per the defined non-functional requirements, and identifies the next iteration based on user feedback. You will learn more about the solution architect role at various stages of the product development life cycle in this section. Overall, a solution architect holds the following primary responsibilities detailed in *Figure 2.2*.

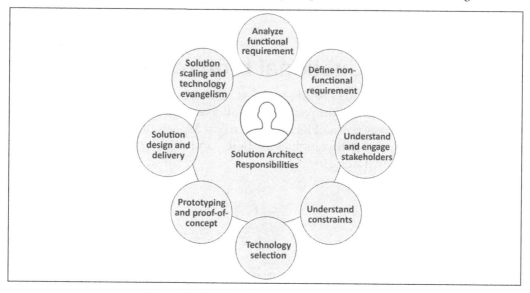

Figure 2.2: Solution architect's responsibility model

As shown, there are various significant responsibilities for a solution architect. In the upcoming sections, you will learn about the various aspects of the solution architect's responsibilities.

Analyzing user requirements

Business requirements are at the center of any solution design, and they are defined in raw terms when a project starts. It is necessary to engage a diverse set of groups from the beginning, which includes the technical capability to identify requirements.

The business stakeholder defines requirements, and multiple adjustments are warranted when it comes to the technological evolution of the project. To save effort, it is necessary to engage solution architects while defining the user requirement documentation.

The solution architect designs the application, which may impact the overall business outcome. This makes requirement analysis a critical skill that a solution architect should possess. A good solution architect needs to have the skills of a business analyst and the ability to work with a diverse set of stakeholders.

Solution architects bring a broad range of business experience with them—they are not only technical experts but also have a good knowledge of the business domain. They work closely with the product manager and other business stakeholders to understand all the aspects of requirements. A good solution architect helps the product team uncover hidden requirements, which a non-technical stakeholder may not have thought about from an overall solution perspective.

Defining non-functional requirements

Non-functional requirements (NFRs) may not be visible to users and customers directly, but their absence may impact the overall user experience in a negative way, and hamper the business. NFRs include critical aspects of the system, such as performance, latency, scalability, high availability, and disaster recovery. The most common NFRs are shown in *Figure 2.3*.

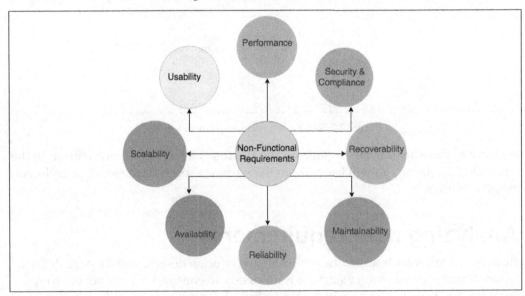

Figure 2.3: NFRs in a solution design

Consider the following NFRs:

- **Performance**:
    - What will the application load time be for users?
    - How can we handle network latency?

- **Security and compliance**:
    - How can we secure an application from unauthorized access,
    - Protect an application from malicious attacks,
    - And adhere to local laws and audit requirements?

- **Recoverability**:
    - How can we recover an application from an outage,
    - And minimize recovery time in the event of an outage?
    - How can we recover lost data?

- **Maintainability**:
    - How can we ensure application monitoring and alerts?
    - How can we ensure application support?

- **Reliability**:
    - How can we make sure the application performs consistently,
    - And inspect and correct glitches?

- **Availability**:
    - How can we ensure the high availability of an application,
    - And make an application fault-tolerant?

- **Scalability**:
    - How can we meet the increasing demand for resources?
    - How can we achieve a good scale for a sudden spike in utilization?

- **Usability**:
    - How can we simplify an application's use,
    - Achieve a seamless user experience,
    - And make the application accessible to a diverse set of users?

Depending on the nature of the project, however, there may be certain NFRs that are suitable only for that particular project (for example, voice clarity for a call center solution).

You will learn more about these attributes in *Chapter 3, Attributes of the Solution Architecture.*

The solution architect becomes engaged in a project from a very early stage, which means they need to design a solution by gauging requirements across the stakeholders within an organization. The solution architect needs to ensure consistency in solution design across system components and requirements. The solution architect is responsible for defining NFRs across groups and different components since they make sure that the desired usability of a solution is achieved across the board.

NFRs are an integral and essential aspect of solution design, which tends to slip when teams are too focused on business requirements, which can impact the user experience. A good solution architect has the primary responsibility of conveying the importance of NFRs and ensuring that they are implemented as part of solution delivery.

Engaging and working with stakeholders

A stakeholder is anyone who has an interest in the project, whether directly or indirectly. As well as the customer and user, it may also be the development team, sales, marketing, infrastructure, network, support team, or the project funding group. Stakeholders can also be internal or external to the project. Internal stakeholders include the project team, sponsors, employees, and senior management; external stakeholders include customers, suppliers, vendors, partners, shareholders, auditors, and the acting government of a country.

Stakeholders often have a different understanding of the same business problem as per the context they find themselves in; for example, a developer may look at a business requirement from a coding perspective, while an auditor may look at it from one of compliance and security. A solution architect needs to work with all technical and non-technical stakeholders.

Solution architects possess excellent communication skills and negotiation techniques, which help them to ascertain the optimal path for a solution while keeping everyone on board. A solution architect works as a liaison between technical and non-technical resources and fills the communication gap. Often, those communication gaps between a businessperson and the technical team become a reason for failure. The businessperson tries to look at things from more of a feature and functionality perspective, while the development team strives to build a more technically compatible solution, which may sometimes lean toward the non-functional side of the project.

The solution architect needs to make sure both teams are on the same page, and that the suggested features are also technically compatible. They mentor and guide the technical team as required and put their perspective into simple language that everyone can understand.

Handling various architecture constraints

Architecture constraints are one of the most challenging attributes of solution design. A solution architect needs to manage architectural constraints carefully and be able to negotiate between them to find an optimal solution. Often, these constraints depend on each other, and emphasizing one limitation can inflate others. The most common constraints are presented in *Figure 2.4*.

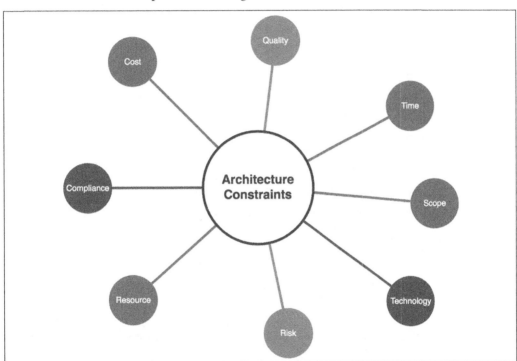

Figure 2.4: Architectural constraints in a solution design

As shown, solution design helps us understand the following attributes of an application:

- **Cost:**
    - How much funding is available for solution implementation?
    - What is the expected ROI?

- **Quality**:
    - How closely should outcomes match functional and non-functional requirements?
    - How can we ensure and track the quality of the solution?

- **Time**:
    - When should the output be delivered?
    - Is there any flexibility regarding delivery time?

- **Scope**:
    - What is the exact expectation from business and customer requirements?
    - How does the requirement gap need to be handled and accommodated?

- **Technology**:
    - What technology can be utilized?
    - What flexibility does using legacy versus new technologies provide?
    - Should we build in-house, or source from a vendor?

- **Risk**:
    - What can go wrong, and how can we mitigate it?
    - What is the risk tolerance of stakeholders?

- **Resource**:
    - What is required to complete solution delivery?
    - Who will work on the solution's implementation?

- **Compliance**:
    - What are the local legal requirements that might impact the solution?
    - What are the audit and certification requirements?

There could be more specific constraints related to a project, such as the way in which data is stored in a country due to government regulation, and opting for in-house development due to security concerns. Handling constraints can be very tricky.

A solution architect needs to balance constraints and analyze the trade-off of each; for example, saving costs by reducing resources may impact the delivery timeline.

Achieving a schedule with limited resources may affect quality, which in turn increases cost due to unwanted bug fixes. So, finding the balance between cost, quality, time, and scope is significant. **Scope creep** is one of the most challenging situations that a solution architect may be faced with, as it can negatively impact all other constraints and increase the risks of solution delivery.

It is essential for a solution architect to understand all the aspects of every constraint and to be able to identify any resulting risk. They must put risk mitigation plans into place and find a balance between them. Handling any scope creep can help a lot in delivering the project on time.

Making technology selections

Technology selection is the key aspect of a solution architect's role, and may involve the most complexity. There is a broad range of technologies available, and a solution architect is required to identify the right ones for the solution. The solution architect needs to have breadth and depth in their knowledge of technologies to make the best decision, since the chosen technology stack can impact the overall delivery of the product.

Each problem can have multiple solutions and an available range of technologies. To make the right selection, a solution architect needs to keep functional requirements and NFRs in mind, and define selection criteria while making a technology decision. The selected technology needs to consider different perspectives, whether the goal is the ability to integrate with other frameworks and APIs, or to meet performance requirements and security needs.

A solution architect should be able to choose the technology that not only satisfies current requirements but also scales for future needs.

Developing a proof of concept and a prototype

Creating a prototype is probably the most fun part of being a solution architect. To choose a proven technology, a solution architect needs to develop a **proof of concept (POC)** in various technology stacks to analyze their fit for the functional and non-functional requirements of the solution. The solution design POC is when a solution architect is trying to figure out the building blocks of the solution.

The idea of developing a POC is to evaluate technology with a subset of critical functional implementations, which can help us to decide on a technology stack based on their capabilities. It has a short life cycle and is limited to being reviewed by experts within a team or organization.

After evaluating multiple platforms using a POC, the solution architect may proceed with prototyping to a technology stack. A prototype is developed for demonstration purposes and given to the customer so that it can be used to secure funding. POCs and prototyping are far from being production-ready; solution architect builds have limited functionality, which can prove to be a challenging aspect of solution development.

Designing solutions and staying through delivery

Solution architects work on solution design after understanding different aspects of functional requirements, NFRs, solution constraints, and technology selection. In an agile environment, this is an iterative approach where the requirements may change over time and need to accommodate the solution design.

The solution architect needs to design a future-proof solution, which should have strong building blocks and be flexible enough to adjust to changes that can occur due to user demands or technology enhancements. For example, if the user demands increase ten times, then an application should be able to scale and accommodate user demands without significant changes to the architecture. Similarly, if new technology, such as ML or blockchain, gets introduced to solve a problem, your architecture should be able to accommodate them; for example, using AI to build a recommendation system on top of existing data for an e-commerce application.

However, the solution architect needs to be careful about drastic changes to the requirements and apply a risk mitigation plan. For future-proof design, you can take the example of a loosely coupled microservice architecture based on RESTful APIs. These architectures can be extended to new requirements and have the ability to integrate easily. You will learn more about different architecture designs in *Chapter 6, Solution Architecture Design Patterns*.

Figure 4.5 contains a flowchart that shows the solution delivery life cycle. The solution architect is involved in all the phases of solution design and delivery.

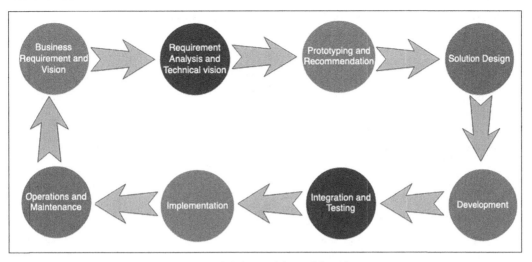

Figure 2.5: Solution delivery life cycle

As shown, the solution delivery life cycle includes the following, with the ways in which a solution architect is involved:

- **Business Requirement and Vision**: A solution architect works with business stakeholders to understand their vision.

- **Requirement Analysis and Technical Vision**: Analysis of the requirements, defining a technical vision in order to execute the business strategy.

- **Prototyping and Recommendation**: Makes a technology selection by developing POC and showcasing prototypes.

- **Solution Design**: A solution architect develops solution designs in line with an organization's standards and in collaboration with other impacted groups.

- **Development**: Works with the development team on solution development, and as a bridge between the business and technical team.

- **Integration and Testing**: Makes sure that the final solution is working as expected with all functional and non-functional requirements.

- **Implementation**: Works with the development and deployment team for smooth implementation and guides them through any issues.

- **Operation and Maintenance**: Ensures logging and monitoring are in place and guides the team on scaling and disaster recovery as required.

The overall life cycle is an iterative process. Once the application goes into production and customers start using it, more requirements may be discovered from customer feedback, which will drive the product vision for future enhancements.

The solution architect has major ownership during solution design, in which they do the following:

- Document solution standards
- Define high-level design
- Define cross-system integration
- Define different solution phases
- Define an implementation approach
- Define a monitoring and alert approach
- Document the pros and cons of design choices
- Document audit and compliance requirements

Solution architects are not only responsible for solution design: they also help project managers with resource and cost estimation, defining the project's timeline and milestones, the project's release, and its support plan. The solution architect works through different phases of the solution life cycle, from design to delivery and launch. The solution architect helps the development team overcome obstacles and hurdles by providing expertise and a broad understanding.

Ensuring post-launch operability and maintenance

The solution architect plays an integral role after the solution's launch with respect to product operability. To handle the increasing user base and product utilization, a solution architect should know how to scale the product to meet demands and ensure high availability without impacting the user experience.

In unforeseen events such as outages, a solution architecture guides infrastructure, IT support, and software deployment teams to execute a disaster recovery plan for business process continuation. The solution architect satisfies the organization's **Recovery Point Objectives (RPOs)** and **Recovery Time Objectives (RTOs)**. RPOs define how much data loss an organization can tolerate in terms of the volume of data lost during the outage interval—for example, a loss of 15 minutes of data. RTOs define how much time the system should take to get back up and running. You will learn more about RTOs and RPOs in *Chapter 12, DevOps and Solution Architecture Framework*.

In the event of performance issues due to an increase in demand, the solution architect helps scale the system horizontally to mitigate application bottlenecks, or vertically to alleviate database bottlenecks. You will learn more about different scaling mechanisms and self-healing in *Chapter 9, Architectural Reliability Considerations.*

The solution architect plans to accommodate any new requirements in an existing product that arise from usage patterns or for any other reason. They can make changes to NFRs based on monitoring user behavior; for example, users may leave a page if it takes more than 3 seconds to load. The solution architect works through this and guides the team in handling issues that may occur post-release.

Working as a technology evangelist

Being an evangelist is the most exciting part of the solution architect role. The solution architect increases product and platform adoption by spreading the word through public forums. They write blogs about solution implementation and conduct workshops to showcase the potential benefits and the use of technology platforms.

They build mass support for technologies and help establish a standard. A solution architect should be passionate about technology. They should be an excellent public speaker and possess excellent writing skills to perform the technology evangelist role.

Solution architects in an agile organization

In the last half decade, you may have seen the rapid adoption of the **agile methodology**. In this competitive market, an organization needs to be proactive to rapid changes, and bring output to the customer very quickly. Fast innovation and release can only be possible if organizations are adapting quickly and respond to change faster to accommodate user demand, which means there must be flexibility built into every part of the organization and solution architecture.

To be successful in an agile environment, a solution architect needs an agile mindset, and must adopt a rapid delivery method by continuously working with stakeholders to fulfill their needs. First, let's understand a little bit more about the agile methodology. This is a vast topic, and in this section, we will see a high-level overview.

Why the agile methodology?

Agile can create and respond to changes to make a profit in a fast-moving business environment. In today's competitive environment, where technology is moving fast (which results in a high probability of changes and customer demand), agile is the answer to coping with this situation and gaining a competitive edge.

Nowadays, all successful organizations are customer-driven: they take frequent feedback from end users on their products and use that feedback to expand their user base. Agile helps gather feedback from users to continuously adapt it to new software releases, and most of the time everything has a high priority. To deal with this situation, you need agile.

Executive management provides funding and seeks transparency. They demand productive output to increase ROI, and a solution architect wants to win their confidence by showing incremental development of the product. To create transparency for a project and keep track of its budget and delivery timeline, you need agile. When you continuously want to engage your stakeholders by showing them a demonstration of the product, and when development and testing are part of the same cycle, you need agile.

The preceding scenarios are situations where the agile methodology is required to keep the organization ahead with robust delivery and customer feedback.

Agile is *able to quickly move* in a timebox manner, which means you timebox activities in a short cycle and take an iterative approach for product development, instead of working on the entire product to develop and deliver it in one go. The agile methodology advocates seeking continuous feedback by keeping customers and stakeholders engaged closely, involving them in every phase of product development, adapting feedback into requirements, evaluating market trends, and working with them to prioritize the stakeholders. Then, the development team take up the prioritized requirements, conduct technical analyses, design, develop, test, and deliver.

Everyone works as a unified team toward one goal and breaks the silo mindset, with agile thinking helping the technical team to understand the requirements from the customer's perspective and respond to changes quickly and efficiently. This is the reason why most companies want to go agile. The agile methodology is fast and easy to adopt using many tools that are available on the market, such as **JIRA**, **VersionOne**, and **Rally**. You may face some initial challenges while developing agile thinking, but the benefits very much outweigh any challenges that an organization may face when moving toward adopting the agile methodology.

Agile manifesto

Applying any form of agile requires a clear understanding of the four values stated in the agile manifesto. Let's understand these values:

- **Individuals and interactions over processes and tools**: Processes and tools always help complete the project. Project stakeholders, who are a part of the project, know how to implement the plan and how to deliver the successful result with the help of tools for project delivery. But the primary responsibility for project delivery is the *people* and their collaboration.

- **Working software over comprehensive documentation**: Documentation is always an essential process for any product's development. In the past, many teams only worked to collect and create a repository for documents, such as high-level design, low-level design, and design change, which later help to achieve qualitative and quantitative descriptions of the product.

  - With the agile methodology, you focus on the deliverable. Therefore, according to this manifesto, you need documentation. However, you also need to define how much documentation is vital to the continuous delivery of the product. Primarily, the team should focus on delivering software incrementally throughout the product's life cycle.

- **Customer collaboration over contract negotiation**: Earlier, when organizations worked on a fixed bid or time and material projects, the customer was always involved in the first and the last stages of the software life cycle—they were outsiders who were not involved in product development. By the time they finally got a chance to see the product after launch, the market trends had changed, and they lost the market.

  - Agile believes that customers share equal responsibility for the product's launch, and that they should be involved in every step of development. They are part of the demonstration, giving feedback based on new market trends or consumer demand. Since the business is now part of the development cycle, these changes can be attained by being agile and having continuous customer collaboration.

- **Responding to change when following a plan**: In the current fast-paced market in which customers demands change with new market trends, businesses also keep on changing. It is vital to make sure there is a balance between frequently changing the requirements and welcoming the changes with agile, since sprint cycles vary from one to three weeks. Responding to change means that should anything change in the specification, then the development team will accept the change and show the deliverable in sprint demonstrations to keep winning the confidence of the customers. This manifesto helps the team understand the value of *welcoming changes*.

The **agile manifesto** is a tool that is used to establish basic guidelines for adopting an agile methodology. These values are the core of all agile techniques. Let us understand the agile process in more detail.

Agile process and terminology

Let's get familiar with the most common agile terms and how they bind together. Here, you will learn about the agile **scrum** process, which is widely adopted. The agile scrum process has a small sprint cycle of one to three weeks, depending on the project's stability, but the most common is a two-week **sprint cycle**, which can also be called a development cycle.

These sprints are development cycles where the team will analyze, develop, test, and deliver a working feature. The team takes an iterative approach and creates a working building block of the product as the project progresses with each sprint. Each requirement is written as a user story that keeps a customer persona in mind, and makes the requirement clearly visible.

The agile scrum team has varied roles. Let's understand the most common ones, and how the solution architect collaborates with them:

- **Scrum Team**: This consists of the product owner, Scrum Master, and development team. Analysts, technical architects, software engineers, software testers, and deployment engineers are part of the development team.
- **Scrum Master**: A person in this role facilitates all scrum ceremonies (which you will learn about in the next section), keeps the team motivated, and removes impediments for the team. The Scrum Master works with the solution architect to remove any technical blockers and get technical clarification for business requirements.
- **Product owner**: This is a businessperson who is a customer advocate. The product owner understands market trends and can define priorities within the business. The solution architect works with the product owner to understand the business' vision and keep it aligned with the technical view.
- **Development team**: Product implementation is carried out, with the team also being responsible for the project's delivery. They are a cross-functional team that is committed to continuous and incremental delivery. The solution architect needs to work closely with the development team for smooth product implementation and delivery.

Scrum ceremonies

The sprint cycle includes multiple activities that are performed to manage development, which are often called scrum ceremonies. Those scrum ceremonies are as follows:

- **Backlog grooming**: Grooming is a timebox meeting in which the product owner, solution architect, and business meet to discuss backlog stories, prioritize them, and create a consensus for sprint deliverables.

- **Sprint planning**: In sprint planning, the Scrum Master facilitates groomed stories that are assigned to the scrum team based on the team's capacity.

- **Sprint Daily Standup**: The Daily Standup is a very efficient way of collaborating, where all team members meet in one place and discuss their latest day's workload, what plans they have for the day, and whether they are facing any problems. This meeting is meant to be short and straightforward, at around 15 minutes in length. The Standup is the platform that the solution architect uses to collaborate with the development team.

- **Sprint demonstration**: During demonstrations, all stakeholders gather and review the team's work of what they have done in a sprint. Based on this, the stakeholder accepts and rejects the user stories. The solution architect makes sure that the functional and non-functional requirements have been met. During this meeting, teams collect feedback from the product owners and solution architect and look at what changes were made.

- **Sprint retrospect**: The retrospect is conducted at the end of each sprint cycle and is where the team inspects and adopts best practices. The team identifies things that went well, along with what they should continue to improve, as well as things that they can do better in the next sprint. Sprint retrospect helps the organization apply continuous improvements while working on their delivery.

Agile tools and terms

Let's learn about some agile tools that help drive team metrics and project progress:

- **Planning poker**: Planning poker is one of the most popular estimation techniques in the agile methodology, where the Scrum Master conducts a planning poker session to estimate user stories when a sprint starts. During this activity, each user story will be evaluated based on its complexity. Team members use comparative analysis to give story points for each user story, which helps the team understand how much effort is required to complete the user stories.

- **Burndown chart**: A burndown chart is used to monitor sprint progress and to help the team understand how much work is pending. The Scrum Master and the team always follow the burndown chart to make sure there is no risk in the sprint, and reuse that information to improve the estimation next time.

- **Product backlog**: The product backlog contains a collection of requirements in the form of user stories and epics. The product owner continuously updates the backlog and prioritizes requirements during sprint grooming. An epic is a high-level requirement, and product owners write a user story to refine them. The development team breaks down these user stories into a task, which is an executable action item.

- **Sprint board**: The sprint board contains a collection of user stories listed for the active sprint. The sprint board provides transparency, as anyone can look at the project's progress for that particular sprint cycle. The team refers to the board on a daily standup to determine overall work progress and remove any obstructions.

- **Definition of Done**: This means all user stories should pass the *Done* criteria that have been set up by the solution architect and product owner in collaboration with stakeholders. Some of these criteria are as follows:

  - The code must be peer reviewed
  - The code should be unit tested
  - Enough documentation has been generated to explain code flow and API design
  - Code quality is to an acceptable standard as defined by the team and organization
  - Code writing is to an acceptable standard as defined by the team and organization

Agile versus waterfall

Waterfall is one of the oldest and most traditional software development methodologies that organizations used to follow. In this section, you will learn about the difference between waterfall and agile and why organizations need to move over to agile. We are not going to look at the details of the waterfall process; instead, we will point out the key differences:

- Agile methodologies help change mindsets from the traditional method to an agile mindset. The motivation for this is to move from the waterfall method to agile methods in order to achieve maximum business value and win customer confidence.

This makes agile an advocate for customer collaboration at each step, while also providing transparency. The waterfall method tends to be more project- and document-centric, where customers were involved at the end phase.

- The waterfall method is more helpful for the project when all requirements are unambiguous and the sequence of their deliverables is also known, which helps remove any unpredictability as requirements are very straightforward. The agile methodology is helpful for companies that want to keep up with the market trend and have increased pressure from the customer. They need early releases for their products and have to be adaptive to changes in the requirements.

- Agile projects are delivered in a small iterative manner with the highest quality and to achieve business value. Many agile teams work in parallel across the sprint to provide a shippable solution for the product at the end of every sprint cycle. As every sprint has a small deliverable and keeps building on top of previous releases, the customer continuously gets to see a working model of the product. Waterfall has a long cycle, and stakeholders get to see the final product at the end, which means there isn't much scope left to accommodate changes.

- The agile process ensures the team is progressing toward its goals, and that the project will be completed on time by putting checkpoints in at every sprint cycle. In traditional waterfall methods, there is no frequent checkpoint that can ensure that the team is on the right path and verify whether the project will be completed on time, which may cause ambiguity.

- In the agile methodology, the customer always collaborates with the product owner and the team. This collaboration ensures that they observe and review the small, shippable product. Agile also ensures that work is being done, enabling progression to be shown to stakeholders. However, in the waterfall method, there is no such customer interaction until the project ends.

Agile is the most adaptive methodology, since fast-moving technologies and businesses are becoming unpredictable and need high team productivity. Agile supports inspecting and adapting cycles, which creates a balance between demand and control.

Agile architecture

What comes to mind when thinking about the solution architect in an agile model? There are many myths, such as thinking that the solution architecture is a very complex activity, and with agile you will be asked to submit your design right away or in the next sprint cycle. Another myth is that the agile architecture will not be robust to such architecture design and development, or that testing is not possible.

A solution architect in an agile environment needs to follow an iterative re-architect concept by inspecting and adapting the approach. It's about choosing the right solution for enterprises, communicating well, taking continuous feedback, and modeling in an agile way. The development team needs a solid foundation and the ability to adapt to changing requirements; they need guidance and mentoring from a solution architect.

The foundation of the agile architecture should be reducing the cost of changes, reducing unnecessary requirements by challenging them, and creating a framework to reverse incorrect requirements rapidly. The agile architect builds prototypes to minimize risk and plans for change by understanding them. They design the prototype while balancing the needs of all stakeholders and creating a loosely coupled architecture that can easily integrate with other modules.

Agile architecture advocates designing decoupled and extendable interfaces, automation, rapid deployment, and monitoring. Solution architects can build decoupled designs using microservice architecture and rapid deployment using test framework automation with a continuous deployment pipeline. You will learn more about various loosely coupled architecture patterns in *Chapter 6, Solution Architecture Design Patterns*.

Summary

In this chapter, you have learned how the solution architect fits into an organization, and how different kinds of solution architect roles may coexist within one. There are generalist solution architect roles, such as the enterprise solution architect, solution architect, technical architect, cloud architect, and architect evangelist. The generalist solution architect has a broad knowledge of technology and may develop in-depth expertise in a particular area. The specialist solution architect dives deep into other required areas of the project. The specialist solution architect possesses in-depth knowledge of their area of expertise, with some of the most common specialist solution architect roles being the network architect, data architect, security architect, infrastructure architect, and DevOps architect.

You have also seen solution architect responsibilities in great detail. Solution architects wear multiple hats; they work with stakeholders across the organization, analyze functional requirements, and define non-functional requirements. The solution architect ensures consistency and standards across the organization, and provides technology recommendations and solution prototypes. The solution architect handles various project constraints, such as cost, quality, scope, and resources, and finds a balance between them.

The solution architect helps the project manager to estimate costs and the resources required and to define a timeline while being present throughout the project from design to launch. During the project's implementation, the solution architect makes sure that the stakeholder's expectations have been met and works as a liaison between the technical and business teams. The solution architect engages in post-launch application monitoring, alerts, security, disaster recovery, and scaling.

The benefits of the agile methodology have also been covered. We took a brief overview of this, exploring the roles, tools, and terminology, and how agile differs from the traditional waterfall method. You learned about the traits of agile architecture and how solution architects should make their architecture more flexible and agile.

In the next chapter, you will learn about the different attributes of the solution architecture that you should consider while designing a solution. These attributes include architecture security, scalability, availability, reliability, fault tolerance, extensibility, portability, interoperability, operational excellence, performance efficiency, cost optimization, and self-healing.

Join our book's Discord space

Join the book's Discord workspace for a monthly *Ask me Anything* session with the authors: https://packt.link/SAHandbook

3
Attributes of the Solution Architecture

The solution architecture needs to consider multiple attributes and design applications. Solution design may have a broad impact across numerous projects in an organization, which demands a careful evaluation of the various properties of the architecture while also striking a balance between them. This chapter will provide a holistic understanding of each attribute, and how they are interrelated and coexist in solution design.

There may be more attributes than covered here, depending on the solution's complexity, but in this chapter, you will learn about the common characteristics that can be applied to most aspects of solution design. You can also view them as **non-functional requirements** (**NFRs**), which fulfill an essential aspect of design. It is the responsibility of a solution architect to look at all the attributes and make sure that they satisfy the desired requirements and fulfill customer expectations.

In this chapter, we will cover the following topics:

- Scalability and elasticity
- High availability and resiliency
- Fault tolerance and redundancy
- Disaster recovery and business continuity
- Extensibility and reusability
- Usability and accessibility

- Portability and interoperability
- Operational excellence and maintainability
- Security and compliance
- Cost optimization and budgets

Scalability and elasticity

Scalability has always been a primary factor while designing a solution. If you ask any enterprise about their existing and new solutions, most of the time they like to plan ahead for scalability. **Scalability** means giving your system the ability to handle growing workloads, and it can apply to multiple layers, such as the application server, web app, and database.

As most applications nowadays are web-based, let's also talk about elasticity. This is not only about growing out your system by adding more capabilities, but also shrinking it to save on unnecessary costs. Especially with the adoption of the public cloud, it has become easy to grow and shrink your workload quickly, with elasticity now replacing scalability. Traditionally, there are two modes of scaling:

- **Horizontal scaling**: Horizontal scaling is becoming increasingly popular as computing power has become an exponentially cheaper commodity in the last decade. In horizontal scaling, the team adds more servers to handle increasing workloads:

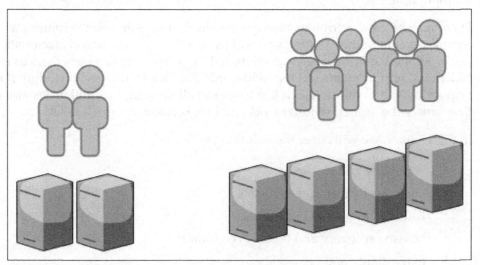

Figure 3.1: Horizontal scaling

As an example, take the diagram shown in *Figure 3.1*; let's say your application is capable of handling *1,000 requests per second* with *two server instances*. As your user base grows, the application starts receiving *2,000 requests per second*, which means you may want to double your application instances to four to handle the increased load.

- **Vertical scaling**: This has been around for a long time. It is a practice in which the team adds additional computer storage capacity and memory power to the same instance in order to handle increasing workloads. As shown in *Figure 3.2*, during vertical scaling, you will get a larger instance — rather than adding more new instances — to handle the increased workload:

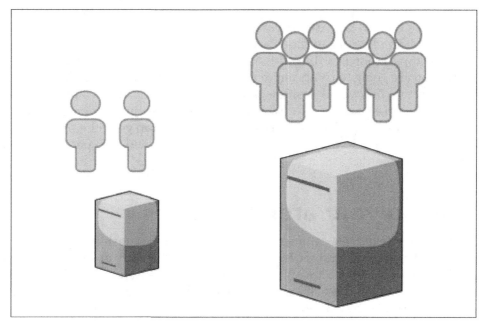

Figure 3.2: Vertical scaling

The vertical scaling model may not be as cost-effective, however; when you purchase hardware with more computing power and memory capacity, the cost increases exponentially. You want to avoid vertical scaling after a certain threshold unless it is absolutely required to handle increasing workload. Vertical scaling is most commonly used to scale relational database servers. However, you need to think about database sharding here. If your server hits the limits of vertical scaling, a single server cannot grow beyond a certain memory and computing capacity.

The capacity dilemma in scaling

Most businesses have a peak season when users are most active and the application has to handle additional load to meet demands. Take the classic example of an e-commerce website selling a variety of products, such as clothes, groceries, electronic items, and merchandise. Such sites have regular traffic throughout the year, but get 10 to 20 times more traffic in the shopping season; for example, Black Friday and Cyber Monday in the US, or Boxing Day in the UK, will see such spikes. This pattern creates an interesting problem for capacity planning, where your workload is going to increase drastically for a couple of months in the year.

In the traditional on-premises data center, additional hardware can take between four and six months before it becomes application-ready, which means a solution architect has to plan for capacity. Excess capacity planning means your IT infrastructure resources will be sitting idle for most of the year, and less capacity means you are going to compromise user experience during significant sales events, thus impacting the overall business significantly. This means a solution architect needs to plan elastic workloads, which can grow and shrink on demand. The public cloud makes capacity planning very easy, where you can get more resources — such as computer storage capacity — instantly, for a limited time period, as per an organization's needs.

Scaling your architecture

Let's continue with the e-commerce website example by considering a modern three-tier architecture, and see how we can achieve elasticity at a different layer of the application. Here, we are only targeting the elasticity and scalability aspects of architecture design. You will learn more about this in *Chapter 6, Solution Architecture Design Patterns. Figure 3.3* shows a three-tier architecture diagram of the AWS cloud tech stack.

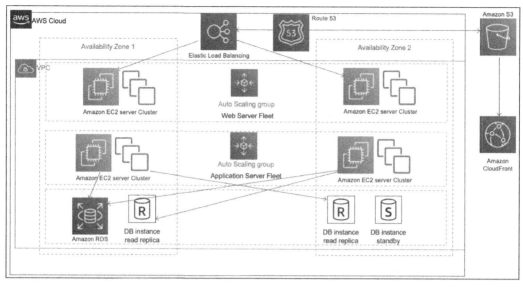

Figure 3.3: Scaling three-tier architecture

You can see a lot of components in this figure, including the following:

- Virtual server (Amazon Elastic Cloud Compute)
- Database (Amazon RDS)
- Load balancer (Amazon Elastic Load Balancer)
- DNS server (Amazon Route53)
- CDN service (Amazon CloudFront)
- Network boundary (VPC) and object store (Amazon S3)

As can be seen in *Figure 3.3*, there is a fleet of web and application servers behind the load balancer. In this architecture, the user sends an application request to the load balancer, which routes traffic to the web server. As user traffic increases, auto-scaling adds more servers in the web and application fleet. When there is low demand, it removes additional servers. Here, auto-scaling can add or remove servers based on the chosen matrix-like CPU utilization and memory utilization; for example, you can configure it such that when CPU utilization goes beyond 60%, add three new servers; if it goes below 30%, you can then remove two existing servers.

In addition to servers, scaling storage is another important aspect due to the growing size of data flow. This is especially the case for static content, such as images and videos, growing rapidly in size; this warrants more focus on storage scaling than has ever been done before. In the next section, you will learn about static content scaling.

Static content scaling

The web layer of the architecture is mostly concerned with displaying and collecting data and passing it to the application layer for further processing. In the case of an e-commerce website, each product will have multiple images—and perhaps even videos—to show a product's texture and demos, which means the website will have a great amount of static content with a read-heavy workload since, most of the time, users will be browsing products. In addition to that, users may upload multiple images and videos for product review.

Storing static content in a web server means consuming lots of storage space, and as product listings grow you have to worry about storage scalability. The other problem is that static content (such as high-resolution images and videos) requires large file sizes, which may cause significant load latency on the user's end. The web tier needs to utilize the **Content Distribution Network (CDN)** to solve this issue by applying content caching at edge locations.

CDN providers (such as Akamai, Amazon CloudFront, Microsoft Azure CDN, and Google CDN) provide edge locations across the globe where static content can be cached from the web server to available videos and images near the user's location, reducing latency. You will learn more about caching in *Chapter 6, Solution Architecture Design Patterns*.

To scale the static content storage, it is recommended to use object storage, such as Amazon S3, or an on-premise custom origin, which can grow independently of memory and computer capabilities. Additionally, scaling storage independently with popular object storage services, such as Amazon S3, saves on cost. These storage solutions can hold static HTML pages to reduce the load of web servers and enhance user experience by reducing latency through the CDN.

Server fleet elasticity

The application tier collects user requests from the web tier and performs the heavy lifting of calculating business logic and talking to the database. When user requests increase, the application tier needs to scale to handle them, and then shrink back as demands decrease. In such scenarios, users are tied to the session, where they may be browsing from their mobile and purchasing from their desktop.

Performing horizontal scaling without handling user sessions may cause a bad user experience, as it will reset their shopping progress.

Here, the first step is to take care of user sessions by decoupling them from the application server instance, which means you should consider maintaining the user session in an independent layer, such as a NoSQL database; these databases are *key-value pair stores*, where you can store semi-structured data. NoSQL databases are best suited for semi-structured data where data entries vary in their schema. For example, one user can enter their name and address while setting up a user profile. In contrast, another user can enter more attributes, such as phone number, gender, marital status in addition to name and address. As both users have different sets of attributes, NoSQL data can accommodate them and provide faster search. Key-value databases such as Amazon DynamoDB are highly partitionable and allow horizontal scaling at scales that other types of databases cannot achieve.

Once you start storing your user session in NoSQL databases such as Amazon DynamoDB or MongoDB, your instance can scale horizontally without impacting the user experience. You can add a load balancer in front of a fleet of application servers, which can distribute the load among instances; with the help of auto-scaling, you can automate the addition or removal of instances on demand.

Database scaling

Most applications use relational databases to store their transactional data. The main problem with relational databases is that they cannot scale horizontally until you plan for other techniques—such as sharding—and modify your application accordingly. This will be a lot of work.

When it comes to databases, it is better to take preventive care and reduce their load. Using a mix of storage methods, such as storing user sessions in separate NoSQL databases, storing static content in an object store, and applying an external cache, helps to offload the master database. It's better to keep the master database node for writing and updating data and use an additional read replica for all read requests.

The Amazon RDS engine provides up to six read replicas for relational databases, and Oracle plugins can live-sync data between two nodes. Read replicas may have milliseconds of delay while syncing with the master node, and you need to plan for that while designing your application. It is recommended to use a caching engine such as Memcached or Redis to cache frequent queries and thus reduce the load on the master node.

If your database starts growing beyond its current capacity, then you need to redesign and divide the database in to shards by applying partitions.

Here, each shard can grow independently, and the application needs to determine a partition key to store user data in a respective shard. For example, if the partition key is user_name, then usernames starting from A to E can be stored in one shard, names starting from F to I can be stored in the 2nd partition, and so on. The application needs to direct user records to the correct partition as per the first letter of their name.

So, as you can see, scalability is a significant factor while designing a solution architecture, and it can impact the overall project budget and user experience significantly if it's not planned properly. A solution architect always needs to think in terms of elasticity while designing applications and optimizing workloads for the best performance and least cost.

A solution architect needs to evaluate different options such as CDNs for static content scaling and load balancing, autoscaling options for server scaling, and various data storage options for caching, object stores, NoSQL stores, read replicas, and sharding.

In this section, you have seen discovered the various methods of scaling and how to inject elasticity into the different layers of your architecture. Scalability is an essential factor to ensure that there is high application availability to make your application resilient. We will learn more about high availability and resiliency in the next section.

High availability and resiliency

The one thing an organization doesn't want to see is *downtime*. Application downtime can cause a loss of business and user trust, which makes high availability one of the primary factors while designing the solution architecture. The requirement of application uptime varies from application to application.

If you have an external-facing application with a large user base, such as an e-commerce website or social media platform, then 100% uptime becomes critical. In the case of an internal application (accessed by an employee, such as an HR system or an internal company), a blog can tolerate some downtime. Achieving high availability is directly associated with cost, so a solution architect must always plan for high availability, as per the application requirements, to avoid over-architecting.

To achieve a **high availability** architecture, it is better to plan workloads in the isolated physical location of the data center so that, should an outage occur in one place, then your application replica can operate from another location.

As shown in the architecture diagram in *Figure 3.4*, you have a web and application server fleet available in two separate availability zones (which represent the different physical locations of the data centers).

The load balancer helps distribute the workload between two availability zones in case **Availability Zone 1** goes down due to a power or network outage. **Availability Zone 2** can handle user traffic, and your application will be up and running.

In the case of the database, you have a standby instance in **Availability Zone 2**, which will failover and become the primary instance in the event of an issue in **Availability Zone 1**. Both the master and standby instances continuously synchronize data.

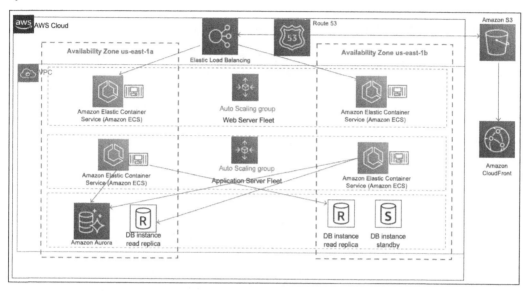

Figure 3.4: High availability and resilience architecture

The other important factor is the architecture's resiliency. When your application is in trouble and you are facing an intermittent issue, then apply the principle of self-healing, which means your application should be able to recover itself without human intervention.

For your architecture, resiliency can be achieved by monitoring the workload and taking proactive action. As shown in *Figure 3.4*, the load balancer will be monitoring the health of instances. If any instance stops receiving the request, the load balancer can take out the bad instances from the server fleet and tell autoscaling to spin up a new server as a replacement. The other proactive approach is to monitor the health of all instances (such as CPU and memory utilization and spinning up new instances as soon as a working instance starts to reach a threshold limit), such as by ensuring CPU utilization is higher than 70%, or that memory utilization is more than 80%.

The attributes of high availability and resiliency can help in terms of cost by achieving elasticity. For example, if server utilization is low, you can take out some servers and save on cost of having this excess capacity.

The high availability architecture goes hand-in-hand with self-healing, where you can make sure that your application is up and running, but you also need to have quick recovery to maintain the desired user experience.

While high availability ensures your system is up and available for users, it is also essential to maintain performance where fault tolerance comes into play. Let us now turn to the subjects of fault tolerance and redundancy.

Fault tolerance and redundancy

In the previous section, you learned that fault tolerance and high availability have a close relationship to each other. High availability means your application is available to the user, but perhaps with degraded performance. Suppose you need four servers to handle users' traffic. For this, you put two servers in two different physically isolated data centers. If there is an outage in one data center, then user traffic can be served from another data center. But now you have only two servers, which means only 50% of the original capacity is available, and users may experience performance issues. In this scenario, your application has 100% high availability, but is only 50% fault tolerant.

Fault tolerance is about handling workload capacity if an outage occurs, without compromising system performance. A full fault-tolerant architecture involves high costs due to increased redundancy. Whether your user base can live with degraded performance for the period of application recovery depends on your application's criticality.

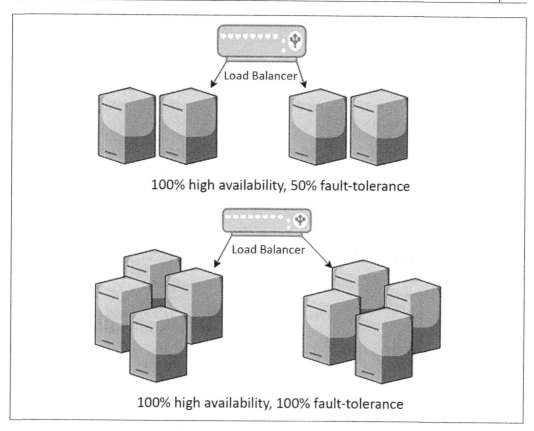

Figure 3.5: Fault-tolerance architecture

As shown in *Figure 3.5*, your application needs four servers to handle the full workload by distributing them into two different zones. In both scenarios, you are maintaining 100% high availability. To achieve 100% fault tolerance, you need full redundancy and have to maintain the double count of the servers so that the user doesn't encounter any performance issues during the outage of one zone. By keeping the same number of servers, a fault tolerance of only 50% is achieved.

While designing the application architecture, a solution architect needs to determine the nature of the application's user and whether a fault tolerance of 100% is required, which will inevitably come with a cost implication. For example, an e-commerce website may need 100% fault tolerance, as degraded performance directly impacts business revenue. At the same time, the internal payroll system, which employees use at the end of the month to check their salary slips, can tolerate reducing performance for a short period.

For business continuity, it is required to plan for uncertainty, which can cause system downtime and hamper overall availability. Disaster recovery helps to mitigate this risk by ensuring the system is available in unforeseen events. Let's learn more about disaster recovery planning in the next section.

Disaster recovery and business continuity

In the previous section, you learned about using high availability and fault tolerance to handle application uptime. There may be a situation when the entire region where your data center is located goes down due to massive power grid outages, earthquakes, or floods, but your global business should continue running. In such situations, you must have a disaster recovery plan where you will plan your business continuity by preparing sufficient IT resources in an entirely different region, perhaps even in different continents or countries.

When planning disaster recovery, a solution architect must understand an organization's **Recovery Time Objective (RTO)** and **Recovery Point Objective (RPO)**. RTO is a measure of how much downtime a business can sustain without any significant impact; RPO indicates how much data loss a business can tolerate. Reducing RTO and RPO means incurring greater cost, so it is essential to understand whether the business is mission-critical and needs minimal RTO and RPO. For example, a stock trading application cannot afford to lose a single data point, or a railway signaling application cannot be down, as human life depends on it.

The following architecture diagram in *Figure 3.6* shows a multi-site disaster recovery architecture where the primary data center location is in Ireland, Europe, and the disaster recovery site is in Virginia, USA, hosted on the AWS public cloud. In this case, a business can continue operating, even if something happens to the entire European region or to the public cloud. The fact that the disaster recovery plan is based on a multi-site model to achieve minimal RTO and RPO means minimal to no outage, and no data loss.

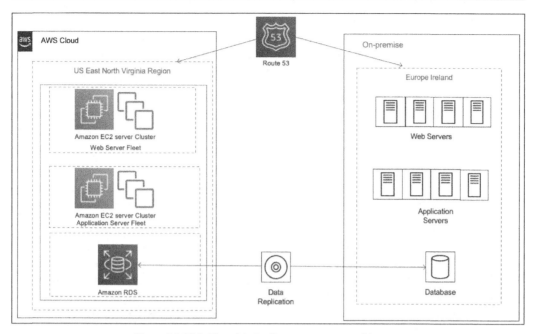

Figure 3.6: Hybrid multi-site disaster recovery architecture

The following are the most common disaster recovery plans, all of which you will learn about in *Chapter 12, DevOps and Solution Architecture Framework*:

- **Backup and Store**: This plan is the least costly but has the maximum RTO and RPO. In this plan, all the server's machine images and database snapshots should be stored in the disaster recovery site. In the event of a disaster, the team will try to restore the disaster site from a backup.

- **Pilot Lite**: In this plan, all the server's machine images are stored as a backup, and a small database server is maintained in the disaster recovery site with continual data synchronization from the main site. Other critical services, such as Active Directory, may be running in small instances. In the event of a disaster, the team will try to bring up the server from the machine image and scale up a database. Pilot Lite is a bit more costly but has lower RTO and RPO than Backup and Store.

- **Warm Standby**: In this plan, all the application servers and the database server (running at low capacity) instances in the disaster recovery site and continue to sync up with the leading site. In the event of a disaster, the team will try to scale up all the servers and databases. Warm Standby is costlier than the Pilot Lite option, but has lower RTO and RPO.

- **Multi-Site**: This plan is the most expensive and has a near-zero RTO and RPO. In this plan, a replica of the leading site is maintained in a disaster recovery site with equal capacity and that actively serves user traffic. In the event of a disaster, all traffic will be routed to an alternate location.

Often, organizations choose a less costly option for disaster recovery, but it is essential to perform regular testing to make sure the failover is working. The team should make operational excellence a routine checkpoint to make sure there is business continuity in the event of disaster recovery.

Extensibility and reusability

Businesses evolve as they grow, where applications not only scale to handle an increased user base but also keep adding more features to stay ahead and attain a competitive edge. A solution design needs to be extendable and flexible enough to modify an existing feature or add new functionality. To modularize their application, organizations often want to build a platform with a group of features and launch them as separate applications. This is only possible with reusable design.

To achieve solution extensibility, a solution architect needs to use a loosely coupled architecture wherever possible. At a high level, creating a RESTful- or queue-based architecture can help develop loosely coupled communication between different modules or across applications. You will learn more about the other kinds of architecture in *Chapter 6, Solution Architecture Design Patterns*. In this section, we will take a simple example to explain the concept of architecture flexibility.

Figure 3.7 shows an API-based architecture in an e-commerce application. Here, you have independent services, such as product catalog, order, payment, and shipping being utilized by an end user application in a pick-and-choose manner. Mobile and browser applications are used by the customer to place an online order. These applications need a product catalog service to browse the product on the web, an order service to place an order, and a payment service to make a payment.

The product catalog and order service, in turn, communicate with the shipping service to send ordered items to the customer's doorstep. On the other hand, brick-and-mortar stores use Point of Sale systems, where a customer representative scans barcodes, places orders on behalf of the customer, and takes payment. Here, no shipping service is required, as the customer picks up the item in-store.

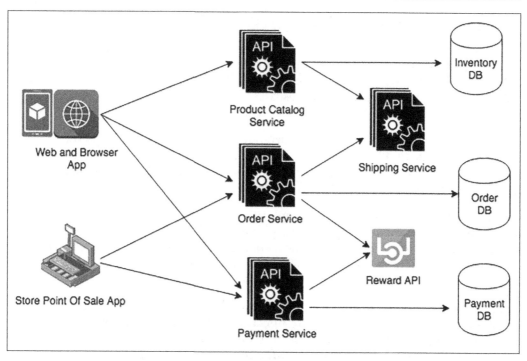

Figure 3.7: Extensible API-based architecture

From *Figure 3.7*, you can see the Reward API, which is used for third-party API integration. This architecture allows you to extend the current design to integrate the Reward API for customer retention, and to attract new customers by providing benefits when they purchase an item. Here, you can see how payment services are reutilized by both online and store ordering. Another service can reuse this if the organization wants to take payments for a gift card service, food services, and so on.

Extensibility and reusability are not limited to the service design level—it goes deep into the actual API framework level, where software architects should use **object-oriented analysis and design (OOAD)** concepts, such as inheritance and containership, to create an API framework. This can be extended and reutilized to add more features to the same service.

You may create a very feature-rich product, but it may not find wide appeal with users until they find it easy to navigate and access. Your application's usability and accessibility play a significant role in product success. Let's learn more about this in the next section.

Usability and accessibility

You want your users to have a seamless experience when browsing through the application. It should be so smooth that they don't even notice how easily they are able to find things—without any difficulties whatsoever. You can do this by making your application highly usable. User research and testing are essential aspects when it comes to defining usability that can satisfy user experience.

Usability is how quickly the user can learn navigation logic when using your application for the first time. It's about how quickly they can bounce back if they make a mistake and are able to perform the task efficiently. Complex and feature-rich applications have no meaning if they can't be used effectively.

Often, when you are designing your application, you want to target a global audience or significant geographic region. Your user base should be diverse in terms of technical amenities and physical abilities. You want your application to be accessible to everyone, regardless of whether a user has a slow internet connection, uses an old device, or they have physical limitations.

Accessibility is about inclusion, making your application usable by everyone. While designing an application, a solution architect needs to make sure it can be accessed over a slow internet connection and is compatible with a diverse set of devices. Sometimes, they may have to create a different version of the application altogether to achieve that.

Accessibility design should include design components, such as voice recognition and voice-based navigation, screen magnifiers, and an ability to read content aloud. Localization helps the application become available in a language that's specific to a region; for example, Spanish, Mandarin, German, Hindi, or Japanese.

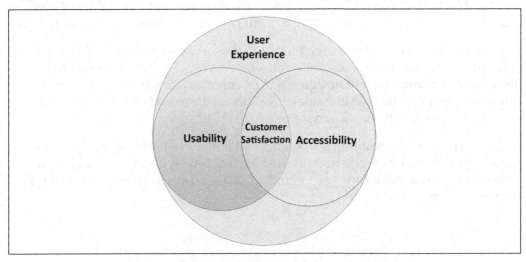

Figure 3.8: Customer satisfaction with usability and accessibility

As shown in *Figure 3.8*, customer satisfaction is a component of both usability and accessibility. You must know your users to achieve usability and accessibility — where accessibility is a component of usability — as they go hand in hand. Before starting the solution design process, a solution architect should work alongside a product owner to research users by conducting interviews, surveys, and gathering feedback on the mock frontend design. You need to understand the users' limitations and empower them with supporting features during application development.

When the product is launched, the team should plan for A/B testing by routing a small portion of user traffic to new features and understanding user reactions. A/B testing is a method of comparing two versions of an application against each other to determine which one performs better. After launch, the application must have a mechanism to collect continuous feedback (by providing a feedback form or by launching customer support) to make the design better.

A system cannot work alone long-term. To make the application feature-rich and simplified for user interactions the solution architect must consider its operability with other applications. Let's look at portability and interoperability in the next section.

Portability and interoperability

Interoperability is about the ability of one application to work with others through a standard format or protocol. Often, an application needs to communicate with the various upstream systems to consume data and downstream systems to supply data, so it is essential to establish that communication seamlessly.

For example, an e-commerce application needs to work with other applications in the supply chain management ecosystem. This includes enterprise resource planning applications to keep a record of all transactions, transportation life cycle management, shipping companies, order management, warehouse management, and labor management.

All applications should be able to exchange data seamlessly to achieve an end-to-end feature from customer order to delivery. You will encounter similar use cases everywhere, whether it is a healthcare application, manufacturing application, or telecom application.

A solution architect needs to consider application interoperability during design by identifying and working with various system dependencies. An interoperable application saves a lot in terms of cost, as it depends on systems that can communicate in the same format without any data messaging effort. Each industry has its standard size for data exchange that it needs to be understood and adhered to.

In general, for software design, the architect may choose a popular format, such as JSON or XML for different applications, so that they can communicate with each other. In modern RESTful API design and microservice architecture, both formats are supported out of the box.

System portability allows your application to work across different environments without the need for any changes, or with only minimal changes. Any software application must work across various operating systems and hardware to achieve higher usability. Since technology changes rapidly, you will often see that a new version of a software language, development platform, or operating system is released. Today, mobile applications are an integral part of any system design, and your mobile apps need to be compatible with major mobile operating systems platforms, including iOS, Android, and Windows.

During the design phase, the solution architect needs to choose a technology that can achieve the desired portability of the application. For example, if you are aiming to deploy your application across different operating systems, programming languages such as Java may be a good choice, as it is often supported by all operating systems, and your application will work on a different platform without needing to be ported across. For mobile applications, an architect may choose a JavaScript-based framework such as React Native, which can provide cross-platform mobile app development.

Interoperability enriches system extensibility, and portability increases the usability of an application. Both are critical attributes of architecture design and may add additional exponential costs if they're not addressed during solution design. A solution architect needs to carefully consider both aspects, as per industry requirements and system dependencies.

Operational excellence and maintainability

Operational excellence can be a great differentiator for your application by providing an on-par service to customers with minimal outage and high quality. It also helps the support and engineering teams increase productivity by applying proactive operational excellence. Maintainability goes hand-in-hand with operational excellence. Easily maintainable applications help reduce costs, avoid errors, and let you gain a competitive edge.

A solution architect needs to design for operation, which means the design should include how the workload will be deployed, updated, and operated in the long term.

It is essential to plan for logging, monitoring, and alerting to capture all incidents and take quick action for the best user experience. Apply automation wherever possible, whether deploying infrastructures or changing the application code to avoid human error.

Including deployment methods and automation strategy in your design is very important, as this can accelerate the time to market for any new changes without impacting existing operations. Operational excellence planning should consider security and compliance elements, as regulatory requirements may change over time and your application must adhere to them in order to operate.

Maintenance can be proactive or reactive; for example, once a new version of an operating system becomes available, you can modernize your application to switch platforms immediately, or monitor system health and wait until the end of the life of the software before making any changes. In any case, changes should be made in small increments with a rollback strategy. To apply these changes, you can automate the entire process by setting up a **continuous integration** and **continuous deployment** (CI/CD) pipeline. For the launch, you can plan for A/B or blue-green deployment.

For operational readiness, architecture design should include the appropriate documents and knowledge-sharing mechanisms—for example, creating and maintaining a runbook to document routine activity, and creating a playbook that can guide your system process through issues. This allows you to act quickly in the event of an incident. You should use *root cause analysis* for post-incident reporting to determine why the issue occurred and make sure it doesn't happen again.

Operational excellence and maintenance are an ongoing effort; every operational event and failure is an opportunity to learn and help improve your operation by learning from previous mistakes. You must analyze the operation's activities and failures, do more experimentation, and make improvements. You will learn more about operational excellence in *Chapter 10, Operational Excellence Considerations*.

Security and compliance

Security is one of the most essential attributes of solution design. Many organizations are compromised by security breaches, which results in a loss of customer trust and damage to your business' reputation. Industry-standard regulations, such as PCI for finance, HIPAA for health care, GDPR for the European Union, and SOC compliance, enforce security safeguards to protect consumer data while providing standard guidance to the organization. Depending on your industry and region, you must comply with local legislation by adhering to compliance needs.

Primarily, application security needs to be applied in the following aspects of solution design:

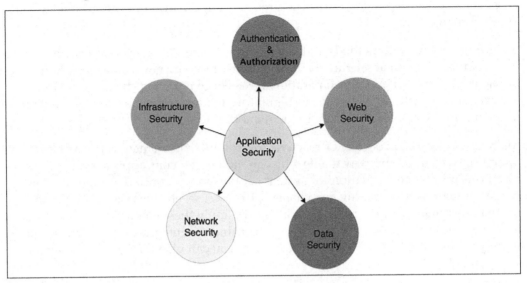

Figure 3.9: Security aspects in solution design

Let's take a look at the different security aspects. You will dive deep into each component in *Chapter 8, Security Considerations*.

Authentication and authorization

Authentication means specifying who can access the system, while **authorization** is applied to activities that a user can perform after getting inside the system or application. Solution architects must consider the appropriate authentication and authorization system while creating a solution design. Always start with the least privileged and provide further access as required by the user role.

If your application is for corporate internal use, you may want to allow access through a federated organizational system, such as Active Directory, SAML 2.0, or LDAP. If your application is targeting mass user bases, such as those that exist on social media websites or gaming apps, then you can allow them to authenticate through OAuth 2.0 and OpenID access, where users can utilize their other IDs, such as Facebook, Google, Amazon, and Twitter.

It is important to identify any unauthorized access and take immediate action to mitigate security threats; this warrants continuously monitoring and auditing the access management system. You will learn about application security in *Chapter 8, Security Considerations*.

Web security

A web application is often exposed to the internet and is vulnerable to external attacks. Solution design must consider preventing attacks, such as **cross-site scripting (XSS)** and **SQL injection**. These days, the **Distributed Denial of Service (DDoS)** method of attack is causing trouble for organizations. To prevent this, the appropriate tools are required, and an incident response plan needs to be put in place.

Solution architects should plan to use a **Web Application Firewall (WAF)** to block malware and SQL injection attacks. A WAF can be used to prevent traffic from a country where you don't have a user base or to block malicious IP addresses. A WAF, in combination with a CDN, can help to prevent and handle DDoS attacks.

Network security

Network security helps prevent overall IT resources inside an organization and application from being open to external users. Solution design must plan to secure the network, which can help prevent unauthorized system access, host vulnerabilities, and port scanning.

Solution architects should plan for minimal system exposure by keeping everything behind a corporate firewall and avoiding internet access wherever possible. For example, the web server shouldn't be exposed to the internet; instead, only the load balancer should be able to talk to the internet. For network security, plan to utilize an **Intrusion Detection System (IDS)** and an **Intrusion Prevention System (IPS)** and put them in front of network traffic.

Infrastructure security

If you are maintaining your own data center, then the physical security of the infrastructure is very important if you wish to block physical access to your server on the part of any unauthorized user. However, if you are leasing a data center or using a private cloud, then this can be handled by a third-party vendor. Logical access to the server must be secured by network security, which is done by configuring the appropriate firewall.

Malicious attacks are common, which is the primary reason for data center security breaches. Security infrastructure becomes very important, managing who can access data, and protect it from any vulnerabilities. From your application hosting data center to the company HR system and global location, you need to ensure every level of IT infrastructure is secure.

Data security

Data is one of the most critical components that need to be secured. After all, you are putting layers of security at the access, web, application, and network levels to secure your data. Data can be exchanged between two systems, so it must be *secure in transit*, or it may be *secure at rest* (sitting in a database or some storage unit).

Solution design needs to plan data-in-transit security with **Secure Socket Layer/ Transport Layer Security (SSL/TLS)** and security certification. Data at rest should be secured using various encryption mechanisms, which may be symmetric or asymmetric. The design should also plan to secure the encryption key with the right key management approach, as per application requirements. Key management can be achieved by using a hardware security module or services provided by cloud vendors. Rules of least privilege using identification and authorization management should be applied to define who can access what data.

While ensuring security, it is essential to have a mechanism to identify any security breach as soon as it occurs to enable a swift response. Adding automation to every layer to monitor, and get an immediate alert for, any violation must be part of the solution design. DevSecOps is becoming a trend in most organizations since it applies best practices to automating security needs and security responses during the software development part of the life cycle. You will learn more about DevSecOps in *Chapter 12, DevOps and Solution Architecture Framework*.

To comply with the relevant legislation, solution design needs to include an audit mechanism. For finance, regulatory compliance such as the **Payment Card Industry Data Security Standard (PCI DSS)** is strictly required to gain the log trails of every transaction in the system, which means all activity needs to be logged and sent to the auditor when required. Any **Personal Identifiable Information (PII)** data, such as customer email IDs, phone numbers, and credit card numbers, needs to be secured by applying encryption and limited access for any application storing PII data.

In on-premise environments, it is the customer organization's responsibility to secure the infrastructure and application, and also to get the appropriate certification for compliance. However, in the public cloud, environments such as AWS ease this burden, as infrastructure security and compliance are taken care of by the cloud vendor. The customer shares responsibility for the security of the application and makes sure it's compliant by completing the required audit.

Cost optimization and budget

Every solution is limited by budget, with investors looking for maximal ROI. The solution architect needs to consider cost-saving during architecture design.

Cost should be optimized from pilot creation to solution implementation and launch. Cost optimization is a continuous effort and should be a continuous process. Like any other constraint, cost-saving comes with a trade-off; it should make a point of determining whether other components, such as the speed of delivery and performance, are more critical.

Often, cost increases due to the over-provision of resources and overlooking the cost of procurement. The solution architect needs to plan optimal resources to avoid excessive underutilization. At the organization level, there should be an automated mechanism to detect ghost resources, where team members may create development and test environments that are no longer be in use after the completion of the implementation task. Often, ghost resources go unnoticed and cause costs to overrun. Organizations need to keep a record of their IT inventory by applying automated discovery, which ensures that all IT inventory is tracked and logged into a central database with their current health and operating status.

During technology selection, it is essential to evaluate *build versus source cost*. Sometimes, it's better to use a third-party tool when your organization doesn't have the expertise on hand and the cost of the build will be high, for example, sourcing log analysis and business intelligence tools. Also, we need to determine the ease of learning and the complexity of implementation when selecting a technology for solution implementation. From an IT infrastructure perspective, we need to evaluate capital expenditure versus operation expenditures, as maintaining a data center requires high capital investment upfront to meet unforeseen scaling demands. Since multiple choices are available, solution architects can select options from the following: public, private, and multi-cloud. Alternatively, they can take a hybrid approach.

Like all components, cost needs to be automated, and alerts need to be set up against budget consumption. Cost needs to be planned and divided between the organizational unit and the workload so that responsibilities can be shared with all groups. The team needs to continuously look at cost optimization by optimizing operation support and workload as more historical data is collected. You will learn more about cost optimization in *Chapter 11, Cost Consideration*.

Summary

In this chapter, you learned about the various solution architecture attributes that need to be considered while creating a solution design. You learned about two modes of scalability, vertical and horizontal, and how to scale various layers of the architecture, including the web layer, application servers, and databases.

You also learned how to apply elasticity to your workload using autoscaling so that it can grow and shrink on demand. This chapter also provided insights into designing a resilient architecture, and the methods used to achieve high availability. Furthermore, this helped you understand fault tolerance and redundancy so that you can make your application performant, as per your user's expectations, and plan for disaster recovery for the continuation of your business in the case of unforeseen events.

You then learned about the importance of making your architecture extendable and accessible and how architecture portability and interoperability help reduce costs and increase the adoption of your application. This chapter ended by explaining methods to apply operational excellence and security, and save on costs at every layer of your architecture, and how those attributes should be considered right from the beginning of the solution design process. You will look at each component in more detail later in this book.

In the next chapter, you will learn about the principle of solution architecture design. We will focus on how to design the solution architecture while bearing in mind various attributes that were explained in this chapter.

Join our book's Discord space

Join the book's Discord workspace for a monthly *Ask me Anything* session with the authors: https://packt.link/SAHandbook

4

Principles of Solution Architecture Design

In the previous chapter, you learned about the attributes of solution architecture. Those attributes are essential properties that a solution architect needs to keep in mind while creating a solution design. In this chapter, you will learn about the principles of solution architecture design, which incorporate various attributes during solution design.

This chapter throws light on the most important and common design principles. However, there could be more design aspects based on product complexity and industry domain. As you move forward on your learning path of becoming a solution architect in this book, these design principles and attributes will be further applied in order to create various design patterns in *Chapter 6, Solution Architecture Design Patterns*.

You will learn about the following topics in this chapter:

- Scaling workloads
- Building a resilient architecture
- Design for performance
- Using replaceable resources
- Think loose coupling
- Think service not server
- Using the right storage for the right requirements

- Think data-driven design
- Overcoming architectural constraints
- Adding security everywhere
- Applying automation everywhere

In this chapter, you will not only learn about designing scalable, resilient, and performant architecture, but you will also learn how to protect your application by applying security, overcoming architectural constraints, and applying changes along with the test and automation approach. These principles will help you to apply thinking in the right way by using a data-driven approach.

Scaling workloads

In the *Scalability and elasticity* section of *Chapter 3, Attributes of the Solution Architecture*, you learned about different modes of scaling and how to scale static content, a server fleet, and a database at a high level. Now, let's look at various types of scaling that can be used to handle workload spikes.

Scaling could be predictive if you are aware of your workload, which is often the case; or it could be reactive if you get a sudden spike or if you have never handled that kind of load before.

For example, the following **Auto Scaling group** has a maximum of six instances and a minimum size of three instances. During regular user traffic, three servers will be up and running to handle the workload, but to handle a traffic spike, the number of servers can reach six. Your server fleet will increase based on the scaling policies you define to adjust the number of instances. For example, you can choose to add one server when CPU utilization goes beyond 60% in the existing servers' fleet, but doesn't spin up more than six servers.

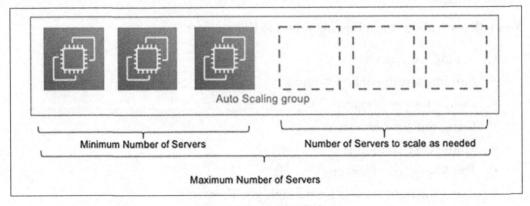

Figure 4.1: Server Auto Scaling

Regardless of scaling being reactive or predictive, you need to monitor the application and collect the data in order to plan your scaling needs. Let's dive deep into these patterns.

Predictive scaling

Predictive scaling is the best-case approach that any organization wants to take. Often, you can collect historical data of application workloads. For example, an e-commerce website such as Amazon may have a known traffic spike pattern, and you need predictive scaling to avoid any latency issues. Traffic patterns may include the following:

- Weekends have three times more traffic than a weekday
- Daytime has five times more traffic than at night
- Shopping seasons, such as Thanksgiving or Boxing Day, have 20 times more traffic than regular days
- Overall, the holiday season in November and December has 8 to 10 times more traffic than during other months

You may have collected the previous data based on monitoring tools that are in place to intercept the user's traffic, and based on this, you can predict the scaling requirements. Scaling may include planning to add more servers when workload increases, or to add additional caching. The above example of an e-commerce workload tends toward higher complexity and provides lots of data points to help us to understand overall design issues. For such complex workloads, predictive scaling becomes more relevant.

Predictive auto-scaling is a variation on scaling that is becoming very popular, where historical data and trends can be fed to prediction algorithms, and you can predict in advance how much workload is expected at a given time. Using this expected data, you can set up the configuration to scale your application.

To better understand predictive auto-scaling, look at the following metrics dashboard from the AWS predictive auto-scaling feature.

This graph has captured historical CPU utilization data of the server, and based on that, has provided the forecasted CPU utilization:

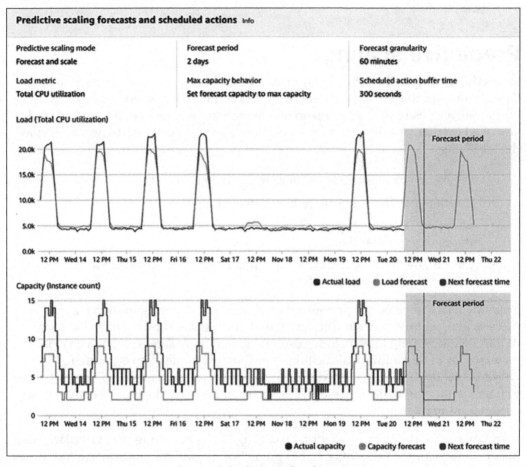

Figure 4.2: Predictive scaling forecast

In the following screenshot, an algorithm is suggesting how much minimum capacity you should plan in order to handle the traffic, based on the forecast:

Start time ▲	Min capacity ▼	Max capacity ▼
2018-11-20 08:55:00 UTC-0800	7	15
2018-11-20 09:55:00 UTC-0800	9	15
2018-11-20 11:00:00 UTC-0800	9	15
2018-11-20 12:00:00 UTC-0800	9	15
2018-11-20 13:00:00 UTC-0800	8	15
2018-11-20 14:00:00 UTC-0800	7	15
2018-11-20 15:00:00 UTC-0800	5	15
2018-11-20 16:00:00 UTC-0800	3	15
2018-11-20 17:00:00 UTC-0800	2	15
2018-11-20 18:00:00 UTC-0800	2	15

Scheduled scaling actions (32) — ‹ 1 2 3 4 ›

Figure 4.3: Predictive scaling capacity plan

You can see that there is a variation in the minimum capacity at different times of the day. Predictive scaling helps you to best optimize your workload based on predictions, while predictive auto-scaling helps to reduce latency and avoid an outage, as adding new resources may take some time. If there is a delay in adding additional resources to handle website traffic spikes, it may cause a request flood and false high traffic, as users tend to send repeated requests when they encounter slowness or outages.

In this section, you learned about predictive auto-scaling, but sometimes, due to a sudden spike in the workload, you require reactive scaling. We will learn about this in the next section.

Reactive scaling

With the use of a machine learning algorithm, predictive scaling is becoming more accurate, but sometimes you may have to deal with sudden traffic spikes, and will therefore depend upon reactive scaling. This unexpected traffic that may arrive could be even 10 times the volume of regular traffic; this usually happens due to a sudden demand or, for example, a first attempt to run sales events, where we're not sure about the level of incoming traffic.

Let's take an example where you are launching a flash deal on your e-commerce website. You will have a large amount of traffic on your home page, and from there, the user will go to the flash deal product-specific page. Some users may want to buy the product; therefore, they will go to the add to cart page.

In this scenario, each page will have a different traffic pattern, and you will need to understand your existing architecture and traffic patterns, along with an estimate of the desired traffic. You also need to understand the navigation path of the website. For example, the user has to log in to buy a product, which can lead to more traffic on the login page.

To plan for the scaling of your server resources for traffic handling, you need to determine the following patterns:

- Determine web pages, which are read-only and can be cached.
- Which user queries need to read just that data, rather than write or update anything in the database?
- Does a user query frequently, requesting the same or repeated data, such as their own user profile?

Once you understand these patterns, you can plan to offload your architecture in order to handle excessive traffic. To offload your web-layer traffic, you can move static content, such as images and videos, to content distribution networks from your web server. You will learn more about the *Cache Distribution* pattern in *Chapter 6, Solution Architecture Design Patterns*.

At the server fleet level, you need to use a load balancer to distribute traffic, and you need to use auto-scaling to increase or shrink several servers in order to apply horizontal scaling.

To reduce the database load, use the right database for the right requirements—a NoSQL database for storing user sessions and reviewing comments, a relational database for the transaction, and the application of caching to store frequent queries.

In this section, you learned about the scaling patterns and methods that are used to handle the scaling needs of your application in the form of *predictive scaling* and *reactive scaling*. In *Chapter 6, Solution Architecture Design Patterns*, you will learn about the details of the different types of design patterns, and how to apply them in order to be able to scale your architecture.

Building a resilient architecture

Design for failure and nothing will fail. Having a resilient architecture means that your application should be available for customers while also recovering from failure. Making your architecture resilient includes applying best practices to recover your application from increased loads due to more user requests, malicious attacks, and architectural component failure. Resiliency needs to be used in all architectural layers, including infrastructure, application, database, security, and networking. A resilient architecture should recover within the desired amount of time.

To make your architecture resilient, you need to define the time of recovery and consider the following points:

- Identify and implement redundant architectural components wherever required.

- Identify and implement backup and disaster recovery plans within a defined **Recovery Time Objective (RTO)** and **Recovery Point Objective (RPO)**

- Understand when to fix versus when to replace architectural components. For example, fixing a server issue might take longer than replacing it with the same machine image.

Security is one of the most important aspects of application resiliency. From the security perspective, the **Distributed Denial of Service (DDoS)** attack has the potential to impact the availability of services and applications. The DDoS attack usually puts fake traffic in your server and makes it busy, meaning that legitimate users are unable to access your application. This can happen at the network layer or the application layer. You will learn more about DDoS attacks and mitigation in *Chapter 8, Security Considerations*.

It's essential to take a proactive approach to prevent DDoS attacks. The first rule is to keep as much of the application workload as possible in the private network and not expose your application endpoints to the internet wherever possible.

To take early action, it is essential to know your regular traffic and have a mechanism in place to determine substantial suspicious traffic at the application and network packet levels.

Exposing your application through the **content distribution network (CDN)** will provide the inbuilt capability, and adding the **Web Application Firewall (WAF)** rule can help to prevent unwanted traffic. During a DDoS attack, Scaling should be your last resort, but be ready with an auto-scaling mechanism to enable you to scale your server in the case of such an event.

To achieve resiliency at the application level, the first thing that comes to mind is redundancy, which leads to making your application highly available by spreading the workload across geographic locations. To achieve redundancy, you can have a redundant server fleet at a different rack in the same data center and in a different region. If servers are spread across different physical locations, the first level of traffic routing can be handled using the **Domain Name System (DNS)** server before it reaches the load balancer:

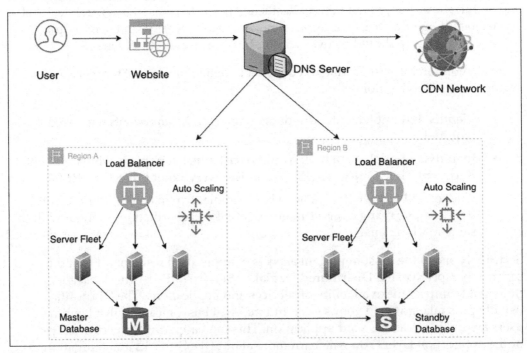

Figure 4.4: Application architecture resiliency

As you can see in the preceding architecture, resiliency needs to be applied in all the critical layers that affect the application's availability to implement the design of failure. To achieve resiliency, the following best practices need to be applied in order to create a redundant environment:

- Use the DNS server to route traffic between different physical locations so that your application will still be able to run in the case of an entire region failure.

- Use the CDN to distribute and cache static content such as videos, images, and static web pages near the user location so that your application will still be available in case of a DDoS attack or local **point of presence (PoP)** location failure.

- Once traffic reaches a region, use a load balancer to route traffic to a fleet of servers so that your application should still be able to run even if one location fails within your region.

- Use auto-scaling to add or remove servers based on user demand. As a result, your application should not get impacted by individual server failure.

- Create a standby database to ensure the high availability of the database, meaning that your application should be available in the event of a database failure.

In the preceding architecture, if any components fail, you should have a backup to recover it and achieve architecture resiliency. The load balancer and routers at the DNS server perform a health check to make sure that the traffic is only routed to healthy application instances. You can configure this to perform a shallow health check, which monitors local host failures, or deep health checks, which can also take care of dependency failure. However, a deep health check takes more time and is more resource-intensive than a shallow health check. You will learn more about resilient architecture in *Chapter 9, Architectural Reliability Considerations*.

At the application level, it is essential to avoid **cascade failure**, where the failure of one component can bring down the entire system. There are different mechanisms available to handle cascading, such as applying timeout, traffic rejection, implementing the **idempotent operation**, and using circuit-breaking patterns. You will learn more about these patterns in *Chapter 6, Solution Architecture Design Patterns*.

Design for performance

With the availability of fast internet, customers are seeking high-performance applications with minimal load time. Organizations have noticed that a direct revenue impact is proportional to application performance, and slowness in application load time can significantly impact customer engagement. Modern-era companies are setting a high expectation when it comes to performance, which results in high-performance applications becoming a necessity in order to stay in the market.

Like resiliency, the solution architect needs to consider performance at every layer of architecture design. The team needs to put monitoring in place to continue to perform effectively and work to improve upon it continuously. Better performance means increased user engagement and increases in the return on investment— high-performance applications are designed to handle application slowness due to external factors such as a slow internet connection. For example, you may have designed your blog web page to load within 500 milliseconds where there is good internet availability. However, where the internet is slow, you can load text first and engage the user with content while images and videos are still loading.

In an ideal environment, as your application workload increases, automated scaling mechanisms start handling additional requests without impacting application performance. But in the real world, your application latency goes down for a short duration when scaling takes effect. In a real-world situation, it's better to test your application for performance by increasing the load and understand if you can achieve the desired concurrency and user experience.

At the server level, you need to choose the right kind of server depending upon your workload. For example, choose the right amount of memory and compute to handle the workload, as memory congestion can slow down application performance, and eventually, the server may crash. For storage, it is important to choose the right **input/output operations per second (IOPS)**. For write-intensive applications, you need high IOPS to reduce latency and to increase disk write speed.

To achieve higher performance, apply caching at every layer of your architecture design. Caching makes your data locally available to users or keeps data in-memory in order to serve an ultra-fast response. The following are the considerations that are required to add caching to various layers of your application design:

- Use the browser cache on the user's system to load frequently requested web pages
- Use the DNS cache for quick website lookup
- Use the CDN cache for high-resolution images and videos that are near the user's location
- At the server level, maximize the memory cache to serve user requests
- Use cache engines such as Redis and Memcached to serve frequent queries from the caching engine
- Use the database cache to serve frequent queries from memory
- Take care of cache expiration and cache eviction at every layer

As you can see, keeping your application performant is one of the essential design aspects and is directly related to organizational profitability. The solution architect needs to think about performance when creating a solution design and should work relentlessly to keep improving the performance of the application. In *Chapter 7, Performance Considerations*, you will dive deeper to learn techniques to optimize your application for better performance.

Using replaceable resources

Organizations make a significant capital investment in hardware, and they develop the practice of updating them with a new version of the application and configuration. Over time, this leads to different servers running in varied configurations, and troubleshooting them becomes a very tedious task. Sometimes, you have to keep running unnecessary resources when they are not needed, as you are not sure which server to shut down.

The inability to replace servers makes it challenging to roll out and test any new updates in your server fleet. These problems can be solved by treating your server as a replaceable resource, which enables you to move more quickly to accommodate changes such as upgrading applications and underlying software.

That is why, while designing your application, always think of immutable infrastructure.

Creating immutable infrastructure

Immutable means, during application upgrades, that you will not only replace software but hardware, too. Organizations make a significant capital investment in hardware and develop the practice of updating them with a new version of the application and configuration.

To create replaceable servers, you need to make your application stateless and avoid the hardcoding of any server IP or database DNS name. Basically, you need to apply the idea of treating your infrastructure as software instead of hardware, and not apply updates to the live system. You should always spin up new server instances from the golden machine image, which has all the necessary security and software in place.

Creating immutable infrastructure becomes more viable with the use of a virtual machine, where you can create a golden image of your virtual machine and deploy it with the new version, rather than trying to update an existing version. This deployment strategy is also beneficial for troubleshooting, where you can dispose of the server that has an issue and spin up a new server from a golden image.

You should take a backup of logs for root cause analysis before disposing of the server with issues. This approach also ensures consistency across the environment, as you are using the same baseline server image to create all of your environment.

Canary testing is one of the popular methods for ensuring that all changes are working as intended in the production environment before rolling out to broader users. Let's now learn more about canary testing.

Canary testing

Canary testing is one of the popular methods that is used to apply rolling deployment with immutable infrastructure. It helps you to ensure that old-version production servers are replaced safely with new servers without impacting end users. In canary testing, you deploy your software update in a new server and route a small amount of traffic to it.

If everything goes well, you will keep increasing traffic by adding more new servers, while disposing of old servers. Canary deployment gives you a safe option to push your changes in the live production environment. If something goes wrong, only small numbers of users are impacted, and you have the option of immediate recovery by routing traffic back to the old servers.

The solution architect needs to think ahead to use replaceable resources for deployment. They need to plan session management and avoid server dependency on hardcoded resources ahead of time. Always treat resources as replaceable and design your applications to support hardware changes.

The solution architect needs to set a standard to use various rolling deployment strategies, such as A/B testing or blue/green deployment. Treat your server like cattle, not like a pet; when this principle is applied to the replacement of problematic IT resources, quick recovery is ensured, and troubleshooting time is reduced.

Think loose coupling

A traditional application builds a tightly integrated server where each server has a specific responsibility. Often, applications depend upon other servers for completeness of functionality.

As shown in the following diagram, in a tightly coupled application, the web server fleet has a direct dependency on all application servers and vice versa:

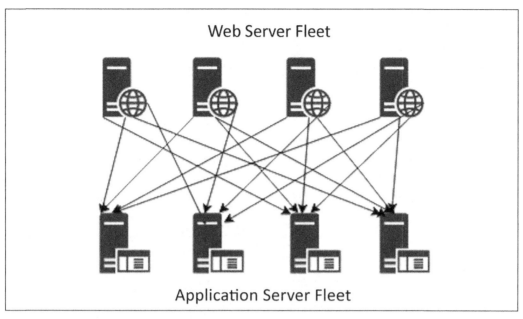

Figure 4.5: Tightly coupled architecture

In the preceding architecture diagram, if one application server goes down, then all web servers will start receiving errors, as the request will route to an unhealthy application server, which may cause a complete system failure. In this case, if you want to scale by adding and removing servers, it requires lots of work, as all connections need to be set up appropriately.

With loose coupling, you can add an intermediate layer such as a load balancer or a queue, which automatically handles failures or scaling for you.

In the following architecture diagram, there is a load balancer between the web server and the application server fleet, which makes sure to always serve user requests from a healthy application server:

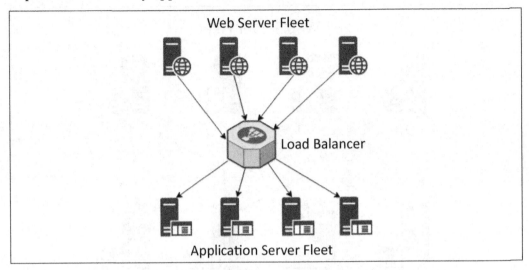

Figure 4.6: Load balancer-based, loosely coupled architecture

If one of the application servers goes down, the load balancer will automatically start directing all the traffic to the other three healthy servers. Loosely coupled architecture also helps you to scale your servers independently and replace unhealthy instances gracefully. It makes your application more fault-tolerant as an error radius is limited to a single instance only.

For a queue-based, loosely coupled architecture, take an example of an image-processing website, where you need to store an image, and then process it for encoding, thumbnails, and copyright. The following architecture diagram has queue-based decoupling. You can achieve loose coupling of systems by using queues between systems and exchanging messages that transfer jobs.

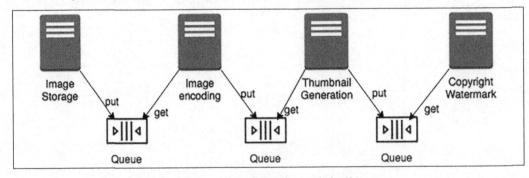

Figure 4.7: Queue-based, loosely coupled architecture

Queue-based decoupling enables the asynchronous linking of systems, where one server is not waiting for a response from another server and is working independently. This method lets you increase the number of virtual servers that receive and process the messages in parallel. If there is no image to process, you can configure auto-scaling to terminate the excess servers.

In a complex system, a loosely coupled architecture is achieved by creating a **service-oriented architecture (SOA)**, where independent services contain a complete set of functionalities and communicate with each other over a standard protocol. In modern design, microservice architecture is becoming highly popular, which facilitates the decoupling of an application component. The loosely coupled design has many benefits, from providing scalability and high availability to ease of integration.

In the next section, you will learn more about SOA, and you will also dive deep into the details of this topic in *Chapter 6, Solution Architecture Design Pattern*.

Think service not server

In the previous section, you learned about loose coupling and how important it is for our architecture to be loosely coupled for scalability and fault tolerance. Developing service-oriented thinking will help to achieve a loosely coupled architecture (as opposed to a server-oriented design, which can lead to hardware dependency and a tightly coupled architecture). SOA helps us to achieve ease of deployment and maintenance for your solution design.

When it comes to service-oriented thinking, solution architects always tend toward SOA. The two most popular SOAs are based on **Simple Object Access Protocol (SOAP)** services and **Representational State Transfer (RESTful)** services. In SOAP-based architecture, you format your message in XML and send it over the internet using the SOAP protocol, which builds on top of the HTTP.

In a RESTful architecture, you can format a message in XML, JSON, or plain text, and send it over a simple HTTP. However, RESTful architecture is comparatively more popular as it is very lightweight and much more straightforward than SOAP.

When talking about SOA nowadays, microservice architecture is increasingly popular. Microservices are independently scalable, which makes it easier to expand or shrink one component of your application without impacting others.

As you can see in the following diagram, in a monolithic architecture, all components are built in a single server and tied up with a single database, which creates a hard dependency, whereas in a microservice architecture, each component is independent, with its own framework and database, which allows them to be scaled independently:

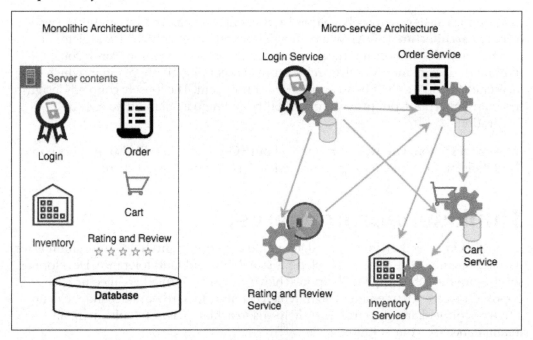

Figure 4.8: Monolithic and microservice architectures

In the preceding diagram, you can see an example of an e-commerce website where customers can log in and place an order, assuming the items they want are available, by adding items to the cart. To convert a monolithic architecture to a microservice-based architecture, you can create applications that are made of small independent components, which constitute smaller parts to iterate.

Taking the *modularization approach* means that the *cost, size, and risk of change* reduces. In the preceding case, each component is created as a service. Here, the **Login** service can independently scale to handle more traffic, as the customer may log in frequently to explore the product catalog and order status, while the **Order** service and the **Cart** service may have less traffic, as a customer may not place the order very often.

Solution architects need to think of microservices while designing a solution. The clear advantage of services is that you have a smaller surface area of code to maintain and services are self-contained. You can build them with no external dependencies. All prerequisites are included in the service, which enables loose coupling and scaling, and reduces the blast radius in case of failure.

Using the right storage for the right requirements

For decades, organizations have been using traditional relational databases and trying to fit everything there, whether it is key/value-based user session data, unstructured log data, or analytics data for a data warehouse. However, the truth is, the relational database is meant for transaction data, and it doesn't work very well for other data types—it's like using a Swiss Army knife, which has multiple tools that work but to a limited capacity; if you want to build a house, then the knife's screwdriver will not be able to perform a heavy lift. Similarly, for specific data needs, you should choose the right tool that can do the heavy lifting, and scale without compromising performance.

Solution architects need to consider multiple factors while choosing the data storage to match the right technology. Here are the important ones:

- **Durability requirement**: How should data be stored to prevent data corruption?
- **Data availability**: Which data storage system should be available to deliver data?
- **Latency requirement**: How fast should the data be available?
- **Data throughput**: What is the data read and write need?
- **Data size**: What is the data storage requirement?
- **Data load**: How many concurrent users need to be supported?
- **Data integrity**: How is the accuracy and consistency of data maintained?
- **Data queries**: What will be the nature of the queries?

In the following table, you can see different types of data with examples and appropriate storage types to use. Technology decisions need to be made based on storage type, as shown here:

Data Type	Data Example	Storage Type	Storage Example
Transactional, structured schema	User order data, financial transaction	Relational database	Amazon RDS, Oracle, MySQL, Amazon Aurora PostgreSQL, MariaDB, Microsoft SQL Server

Key/value pair, semi-structured, unstructured	User session data, application log, review, comments	NoSQL	Amazon DynamoDB, MongoDB, Apache HBase, Apache Cassandra, Azure Tables
Analytics	Sales data, supply chain intelligence, business flow	Data warehouse	IBM Netezza, Amazon Redshift, Teradata, Greenplum, Google BigQuery
In-memory	User home page data, common dashboard	Cache	Redis cache, Amazon ElastiCache, Memcached
Object	Image, video	File-based	SAN, Amazon S3, Azure Blob Storage, Google Storage
Block	Installable software	Block-based	NAS, Amazon EBS, Amazon EFS, Azure Disk Storage
Streaming	IoT sensor data, clickstream data	Temporary storage for streaming data	Apache Kafka, Amazon Kinesis, Spark Streaming, Apache Flink
Archive	Any kind of data	Archive storage	Amazon Glacier, magnetic tape storage, virtual tape library storage
Web storage	Static web contents such as images, videos, and HTML pages	CDN	Amazon CloudFront, Akamai CDN, Azure CDN, Google CDN, Cloudflare
Search	Product search, content search	Search index store and query	Amazon Elastic Search, Apache Solr, Apache Lucene
Data catalog	Table metadata, data about data	Metadata store	AWS Glue, Hive metastore, Informatica data catalog, Collibra data catalog
Monitoring	System log, network log, audit log	Monitor dashboard and alert	Splunk, Amazon CloudWatch, SumoLogic, Loggly

As you can see in the preceding table, there are various properties of data, such as structured, semi-structured, unstructured, key/value pair, and streaming. Choosing the right storage helps to improve not only the performance of the application but also its scalability. For example, you can store user session data in the NoSQL database, which will allow application servers to scale horizontally and maintain user sessions at the same time.

While choosing storage options, you need to consider the temperature of the data, which could be hot, warm, or cold:

- For hot data, you are looking for sub-millisecond latency and the required cache data storage. Examples of hot data include stock trading and making product recommendations in runtime.

- For warm data, such as financial statement preparation or product performance reporting, acceptable latency might vary from seconds to minutes, and you should use a data warehouse or a relational database.

- For cold data, such as storing 3 years of financial records for audit purposes, you can plan latency in hours, and store it in archive storage.

Choosing appropriate storage as per the data temperature also saves costs in addition to achieving the performance SLA. As any solution design revolves around handling the data, so a solution architect always needs to understand their data thoroughly and then choose the right technology.

In this section, we have covered a high-level view of data to get an idea of using the proper storage according to the nature of the data. You will learn more about data engineering in *Chapter 13, Data Engineering for Solution Architecture*. Using the right tool for the right job helps to save costs and improve performance, so it's essential to choose the right data storage for the right requirements.

Think data-driven design

Any software solution revolves around the collection and management of data. Take the example of an e-commerce website; the software application is built to showcase product data on the website and encourage the customers to buy them. It starts by collecting customer data when they create a login, adding a payment method, storing order transactions, and maintaining inventory data as the product gets sold. Another example is a banking application, which is about storing customer financial information and handling all financial transaction data with integrity and consistency. For any application, the most important thing is to handle, store, and secure data appropriately.

In the previous section, you have learned about different kinds of data types, along with the storage needs, which should help you to apply data thinking in your design. Solution design is heavily influenced by data and enables you to apply the right design-driven solution by keeping data in mind. While designing a solution, if your application needs ultra-low latency, then you need to use cache storage such as **Redis** or **Memcached**. If your website needs to improve its page load time with an attractive high-quality image, then you need to use a content distribution network such as Amazon CloudFront or Akamai to store data near the user location. Similarly, to improve your application performance, you need to understand if your database will be read-heavy (such as a blog website) or write-heavy (such as a survey collection) and plan your design accordingly.

It's not just application design, but operational maintenance and business decisions all revolve around data. You need to add monitoring capabilities to make sure that your application, and in turn, your business, is running without any issues. For application monitoring, you collect log data from the server and create a dashboard to visualize the metrics.

Continuous data monitoring and sending alerts in the case of issues help you to recover quickly from failure by triggering the auto-healing mechanism. From a business perspective, collecting sales data helps you to run a marketing campaign to increase the overall business revenue. Analyzing review sentiment data helps to improve the customer experience and retain more customers, which is critical for any business. Collecting overall order data and feeding it to the machine learning algorithm helps you to forecast future growth and maintain the desired inventory.

As a solution architect, you are not only thinking about application design, but also about the overall business value proposition. It's about other factors around the application, which can help to increase customer satisfaction and maximize the return on your investment. Data is gold and getting insights into data can make a tremendous difference to an organization's profitability.

Overcoming architectural constraints

Earlier, in *Chapter 2, Solution Architects in an Organization*, you learned about the various constraints that a solution architecture needs to handle and balance. The major limitations are cost, time, budget, scope, schedule, and resources. Overcoming these constraints is one of the significant factors that needs to be considered while designing a solution. You should look at the limitations as challenges that can be overcome rather than obstacles, as challenges always push you to the limit of innovation in a positive way.

A solution architect needs to make suitable trade-offs while considering the constraints. For example, a high-performance application results in more cost when you need to add additional caching in multiple layers of architecture. However, sometimes cost is more important than performance, primarily if a system is used by the internal employees, which doesn't directly impact revenue. Sometimes, the market is more important than launching a fully featured product, and you need to make the trade-off between scope versus speed. In such scenarios, you can take the **minimum viable product** (MVP) approach; you will learn more details about this in the next section.

Technology constraints become evident in a large organization, as bringing changes across hundreds of systems will be challenging. When designing applications, you need to use the most common technique that is used across the organization, which will help to remove the everyday challenges. You also need to make sure that the application is upgradable in order to adopt new technology, and be able to plug in components that are built on a different platform.

A RESTful service model is pretty popular when teams are free to use any technology for their development. The only thing they need to provide is a URL with which their services can be accessed. Even legacy systems such as mainframes can be integrated into the new system using an API wrapper around it and overcome technology challenges.

Throughout this book, you will learn more about handling various architectural constraints. Taking an agile approach helps you to overcome constraints and build a customer-centric product. In design principles, take everything as a challenge and not an obstacle. Consider any constraint as a challenge and find a solution to solve it.

Taking the minimum viable product approach

For a successful solution, always put the customer first, while also taking care of architectural constraints. Think backward from the customers' needs, determine what is critical for them, and plan to put your solution delivery in an agile way. One popular method of prioritized requirement is **MoSCoW**, where you divide customer requirements into the following categories:

- **Mo (Must have)**: Requirements that are very critical for your customers, without which the product cannot launch
- **S (Should have)**: Requirements that are the most desirable to the customer, once they start utilizing the application

- **Co (Could have)**: Requirements that are nice to have, but their absence will not impact upon the desired functionality of the application
- **W (Won't have)**: Requirements that customers may not notice if they are not there

You need to plan an MVP for your customer with must-have requirements and go for the next iteration of delivery with should-have requirements. With this phased delivery approach, you can thoroughly utilize your resources and overcome the challenges of time, budget, scope, and resources. The MVP approach helps you to determine customer needs. You are not trying to build everything without knowing if the features you've built have added value for the customer. This customer-focused approach helps to utilize resources wisely and reduces the waste of resources.

In the following diagram, you can see the evaluation for a truck manufacturing delivery, where the customer wants a delivery truck that gets delivered initially, and you evolve the process based on the customer's requirements:

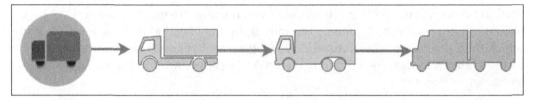

Figure 4.9: MVP approach to building the solution

Here, once a customer gets the first delivery truck, which is fully functioning, they can determine if they need a more significant load to handle, and based on that, the manufacturer can build a 6-wheel, a 10-wheel, and finally, an 18-wheel truck trailer. This stepwise approach provides working products with essential features that the customers can use, and the team can build upon it, as per customer requirements.

You can see how the MVP approach helps to utilize limited resources in an efficient way, which helps to buy more time and clarify the scope, in comparison to an approach where we turn up the first time with an 18-wheel truck, only to find out we only needed a 6-wheeler. In terms of the other factors, when you put the working product in the customer's hands early, it gives you an idea of where to invest. As your application has already started generating revenue, you can present use cases to ask for more resources as required.

Adding security everywhere

Security is one of the essential aspects of solution design; any gap in security can have a devastating effect on business and the organization's future.

The security aspect can have a significant impact on solution design, so you need to understand your security needs even before starting the application design. Security needs to be included in platform readiness at the hardware level and in application development at the software level. The following are the security aspects that need to be considered during the design phase:

- **Physical security of data center**: All IT resources in data centers should be secure from unauthorized access

- **Network security**: The network should be secure to prevent any unauthorized server access

- **Identity and Access Management (IAM)**: Only authenticated users should have access to the application, and they can do the activity as per their authorization

- **Data security in transit**: Data should be secure while traveling over the network or the internet

- **Data security at rest**: Data should be secure while stored in the database or any other storage

- **Security monitoring**: Any security incident should be captured, and the team alerted to act

Application design needs to balance security requirements such as encryption, and other factors such as performance and latency. Data encryption always has a performance impact as it adds a layer of additional processing because data needs to be decrypted in order to be utilized. Your application needs to accommodate the overhead of additional encryption processing without impacting overall performance. So, while designing your application, think of use cases where encryption is really required. For example, if the data is not confidential, you don't need to encrypt it.

The other aspect of application design to consider is regulatory compliance for adherence to local law. Compliance is essential if your application belongs to a regulated industry such as healthcare, finance, or the federal government. Each compliance has its requirement, which commonly includes the protection of data and the recording of each activity for audit purposes. Your application design should include comprehensive logging and monitoring, which will fulfill the audit requirement.

In this section, you have learned to apply security thinking while designing and keeping any regulatory needs in mind. Security automation is another factor, which you should always implement along with your design, so as to reduce and mitigate any security incidents. However, you have a high-level overview here. You will learn more details in *Chapter 8, Security Considerations*.

Applying automation everywhere

Most accidents happen due to human error, which can be avoided by **automation**. Automation not only handles jobs efficiently but also increases productivity and saves costs. Anything identified as a repeatable task should be automated to free up valuable human resources so that team members can spend their time on more exciting work and focus on solving a real problem. It also helps to increase team morale.

When designing a solution, think about what can be automated. Think to automate any repeatable task. Consider the following components to be automated in your solution:

- **Application testing**: You need to test your application every time you make any changes to make sure that nothing breaks. Also, manual testing is very time-consuming and requires lots of resources. It's better to think about automating repeatable test cases to speed up deployment and product launch. Automate your testing on a production scale and use rolling deployment techniques, such as canary testing and A/B testing, to release changes.

- **IT infrastructure**: You can automate your infrastructure by using *infrastructure as code* scripting, for example, Ansible, Terraform, and Amazon CloudFormation. The automation of infrastructure allows environments to be created in minutes compared to days. The automation of infrastructure as code helps to avoid configuration errors and creates a replica of the environment.

- **Logging, monitoring, and alerting**: Monitoring is a critical component, and you want to monitor everything every time. Also, based on monitoring, you may want to take automated action such as scaling up your system or alerting your team to act. You can monitor the vast system only by using automation. You need to automate all activity monitoring and logs to make sure that your application is running smoothly, and that it is functioning as desired.

- **Deployment automation**: Deployment is a repeatable task that is very time-consuming and delays the last-minute launch in many real-time scenarios. Automating your deployment pipeline by applying **continuous integration and continuous deployment (CI/CD)** helps you to be agile and iterate quickly on product features with a frequent launch. CI/CD helps you to make small incremental changes to your application.

- **Security automation**: While automating everything, don't forget to add automation for security. If someone is trying to hack your application, you want to know immediately and act quickly.

You want to take preventive action by automating any incoming or outgoing traffic in your system boundary and alert any suspicious activity.

Automation provides peace of mind by making sure the product is functioning without a glitch. While designing an application, always makes sure to think from an automation perspective and consider that as a critical component. You will learn more about automation in the coming chapters.

Summary

In this chapter, you learned about the various principles of solution architecture design that you need to apply when creating a solution design. These principles help you to take a multi-dimensional look into architecture and consider the important aspects for the success of the application.

You started the chapter with predictive and reactive patterns of scaling, along with the methodology and benefits. You also learned about building a resilient architecture that can withstand failure and recover quickly without impacting the customer experience.

Designing flexible architecture is the core of any design principle, and you learned about how to achieve a loosely coupled design in your architecture. SOA helps to build an architecture that can be easily scaled and integrated. You also learned about the microservice architecture, and how it is different from the traditional monolithic architecture, and its benefits.

You learned about the principle of data-focused design, as pretty much all applications revolve around data. You learned about different data types, with the example of storage and associated technology. Finally, you learned the design principle of security and automation, which applies everywhere and in all components.

As cloud-based services and architecture are becoming standard, in the next chapter, you will learn about cloud-native architecture and develop a cloud-oriented design. You will learn about different cloud migration strategies and how to create an effective hybrid cloud. You will also learn about the popular public cloud providers, with which you can explore cloud technologies further.

Join our book's Discord space

Join the book's Discord workspace for a monthly *Ask me Anything* session with the authors: https://packt.link/SAHandbook

5

Cloud Migration and Hybrid Cloud Architecture Design

Today's organizations need to be more agile to respond to customer demands, which requires the ability to quickly scale up to millions of customers and scale down as needed without impacting the budget. Organizations need to continuously acquire new customers, delighting them while working in a fiercely competitive environment. Cloud migration could be the answer for achieving agility and speed. The cloud enables frequent application releases and reduces costs by applying automation and data center consolidation.

So far, you have learned about various aspects of solution architecture, architecture attributes, and architecting principles. Now everyone is talking about the cloud and organizations are looking to move their workloads into the cloud to optimize operational costs. Public clouds such as **Amazon Web Services (AWS)**, **Microsoft Azure**, and **Google Cloud Platform (GCP)** are becoming the primary destinations to host applications, so it's important to learn about the proposition and methods to migrate to the cloud. In this chapter, you will learn about the various aspects of the cloud and develop cloud thinking, which will also help you understand the upcoming chapters better.

As you learned in *Chapter 1, The Meaning of Solution Architecture*, cloud computing refers to the on-demand delivery of IT resources over the web, and you pay as you utilize resources. The public cloud helps you acquire technologies such as compute, storage, networks, and databases on an as-needed basis, instead of buying and maintaining your own data centers.

With cloud computing, the cloud vendor manages and maintains the technology infrastructure in a secure environment and organizations access these resources over the web to develop and run their applications. An IT resource's capacity can go up or down instantly and organizations only pay for what they use.

Now, the cloud is becoming essential for every enterprise strategy. Almost every organization decreases its spending by moving into the public cloud, and on top of saving costs, they convert upfront capital expenditure into operational expenditure. A lot of startups born in the last decade started in the cloud and were fueled by *cloud infrastructure* for rapid growth. As enterprises move to the cloud, they must focus on cloud migration strategy and hybrid cloud.

In this chapter, you will learn about the various strategies of cloud migration and hybrid cloud by covering the following topics:

- Benefits of cloud native architecture
- Creating a cloud migration strategy
- Choosing a cloud strategy
- Steps for cloud migration
- Creating a hybrid cloud architecture
- Taking a multi-cloud approach
- Designing a cloud native architecture
- Popular public cloud choices

By the end of this chapter, you will have learned about the benefits of the cloud and be able to design cloud native architecture. You will understand different cloud migration strategies and steps. You will also learn about hybrid cloud design and popular public cloud providers.

Benefits of cloud native architecture

In recent years, technology has been changing rapidly and new companies have been born in the cloud world, disrupting old and long-standing organizations. Rapid growth is possible because of no upfront cost being involved when organizations use the cloud, and there is less risk in experimentation due to the *pay-as-you-go* model of the cloud compared to paying the upfront cost of hosting your own server.

The *cloud native approach* helps employees in an organization develop innovative thinking and implement their ideas without waiting for the long cycle of infrastructure.

With the cloud, customers don't need to plan excess capacity in advance to handle their peak season, such as the holiday shopping season for retailers; they have the elasticity to provision resources to meet demand instantly. This significantly helps reduce costs and improve the customer's experience. For any organization to stay in the competition, they have to move fast and innovatively.

With the cloud, enterprises are not only able to get their infrastructure quickly across the globe but can also access a wide variety of technologies that were never available before. These include access to cutting edge technologies such as the following:

- Big data and analytics
- Machine learning and artificial intelligence
- Robotics
- **Internet of Things (IoT)**
- Blockchain
- Quantum computing

Also, to achieve scalability and elasticity, these are some of the reasons that can trigger an initiative for cloud migration and hybrid cloud strategy:

- The data center needs a technology refresh
- The data center's lease is ending
- The data center has run out of storage and compute capacity
- Modernization of an application
- Leverage cutting-edge technologies
- Need to optimize IT resources to save on operational costs
- Disaster recovery planning and operational resilience
- Utilizing a content distribution network for the website
- Reduce upfront capital expenditures and eliminate maintenance costs
- Increase workforce efficiency and productivity
- Improve business agility

Every organization has a different strategy, and one size does not fit all when it comes to cloud adoption. The frequent use cases are putting development and testing environments in the cloud to add agility for developers so that they can move faster. As hosting web applications is becoming more economical and more straightforward with the cloud, organizations are using the cloud for digital transformation by hosting their websites and digital properties in the cloud.

For application accessibility, it is essential to not only build an application for the web browser but to ensure it is accessible through *smart mobiles* and *tablets*. The cloud is helping with such transformations. Data processing and analytics is another area where enterprises are utilizing the cloud since it is less expensive and faster to collect, store, analyze, and share data with the cloud.

Building a solution architecture for the cloud is slightly different than it is for regular enterprise architecting. While moving to the cloud, you have to develop cloud thinking and understand how to leverage the in-built capabilities of the cloud. For cloud thinking, you follow the *pay-as-you-go* model. You need to make sure that you optimize your workload properly and run your servers only when it's required.

You need to think about how to optimize costs by starting the server for your workload when needed and choosing the right strategy for the workload, which always needs to be running. In the cloud, the solution architect needs to have a holistic view of each component regarding performance, scaling, high availability, disaster recovery, fault tolerance, security, and automation.

The other areas of optimization are **cloud native monitoring** and **alerting mechanisms**. You may not need to bring your existing third-party tool from on-premise to the cloud as you can utilize native cloud monitoring better and get rid of costly third-party licensing software. Also, now, you get to have deployment capabilities to any part of the world in minutes, so don't restrict yourself to a particular region and utilize the global deployment model to build better high-availability and disaster recovery mechanisms.

The cloud provides excellent deals for automation; *you can pretty much automate everything*. Automation not only reduces errors and speeds up time to market; it also saves lots of cost by utilizing human resources efficiently and freeing them up from performing tedious and repetitive tasks. The cloud works on a *shared responsibility model* where cloud vendors are responsible for securing physical infrastructure. However, the security of an application and its data is entirely the customer's responsibility. Therefore, it's important to lock down your environment and keep tabs on security by utilizing cloud native tools for monitoring, alerts, and automation.

Throughout this book, you will learn about the cloud perspective of solution architecture and get an in-depth understanding of cloud architecture. Before defining your cloud strategy, let's learn about some popular public cloud choices that you should know.

Popular public cloud choices

Since the cloud is the norm now, there are many cloud providers on the market that provide cutting-edge technology platforms that are competing to get market share.

The following are the major cloud providers (at the time of writing):

- **AWS**: AWS is one of the oldest and largest cloud providers. AWS provides IT resources such as compute power, storage, databases, and other services on a need basis over the internet with a pay-as-you-go model. AWS not only offers IaaS; it has a broad range of offerings in PaaS and SaaS. AWS provides multiple offerings in cutting-edge technologies in the area of machine learning, artificial intelligence, blockchain, **Internet of Things (IoT)**, and a comprehensive set of significant data capabilities. You can host almost any workload in AWS and combine services to design an optimal solution.

- **Microsoft Azure**: Also known as Azure and like any cloud provider, it provides IT resources such as compute, network, storage, and databases over the internet to its customers. Like AWS, Azure also provides IaaS, PaaS, and SaaS offerings in the cloud, which include a range of services from computing, storage, data management, content distribution networks, containers, big data, machine learning, and IoT. Also, Microsoft has wrapped its popular offerings in the cloud through Microsoft Office, Microsoft Active Directory, Microsoft SharePoint, MS SQL Server, and so on.

- **GCP**: GCP provides cloud offerings in the area of computing, storage, networking, and machine learning. Like AWS and Azure, it has a global network of data centers available as infrastructure as a service for its customers to consume IT resources over the internet. In terms of compute, GCP offers Google Cloud Functions for the serverless environment, which you can compare with AWS Lambda functions in AWS and Azure Functions in Azure. Similarly, GCP offers multiple programming languages for application development with containers so that you can deploy application workloads.

There are many other cloud vendors available, such as Alibaba Cloud, Oracle Cloud, and IBM Cloud, but the major markets are captured by the aforementioned cloud providers. The choice of which cloud provider to use is up to the customer, which can be impacted by the availability of the functionality they are looking for or based on their existing relationship with providers. Sometimes, large enterprises choose a multi-cloud strategy to utilize the best providers. In the next section, you will learn about various strategies for cloud migration.

Creating a cloud migration strategy

As we mentioned in the previous section, there could be various reasons for cloud migration, and those play an essential role in your cloud journey. Your cloud strategy helps you to determine a migration strategy and prioritize applications.

In addition to primary business drivers for cloud migration, you could have more reasons related to the data center, business, application, team, and workload for cloud migration.

Cloud adoption is not just about choosing the platform, security design, and operation, but you also need to consider people, processes, and culture in addition to technology. For cloud migration success, you first need to align leaders and earn commitment from teams by upskilling them. You need to define the vision across the organization to ensure a successful cloud transition.

Often, migration projects adopt multiple strategies and utilize different tools accordingly. The migration strategy will influence the time it takes to migrate and how the applications are grouped for the migration process. The following diagram shows some of the commonly used strategies for migrating existing applications to the cloud:

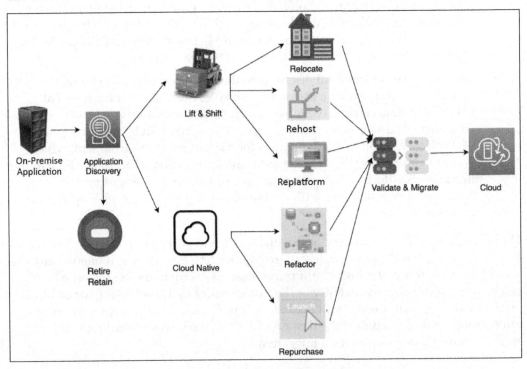

Figure 5.1: Cloud migration strategy

As shown in the preceding diagram, you can do a **Lift & Shift** of the server or application from the source environment to the cloud. Migrating a resource only needs minimal changes for it to work in the cloud. To take a more **Cloud Native** approach, you can refactor your application to fully utilize the cloud native feature, for example, converting monolithic applications into microservices.

If your application is a legacy application and cannot be moved, or it is not cloud compatible, you may want to retire it and replace it with a cloud native SaaS product or third-party solution.

An organization can take a mix of migration strategies; for example, if an application-hosted OS is at its end of life, then you need to upgrade the OS. You can take this opportunity to migrate to the cloud for better flexibility. In this case, most likely, you will choose the **replatform** method to recompile your code into a new version of the OS and validate all its features. After you've finished testing, you can migrate the application to the OS hosted in the infrastructure provided by the cloud. If you want to buy a new platform, for example, replacing your old CRM solution with SaaS-based solutions provided by Salesforce, you can choose a **retire and repurchase** strategy. If you want to rebuild your application from monolithic to microservices to add more agility, you may decide to **refactor**.

Your business objectives will drive your decision to migrate applications and define the strategy for migration as per their priority. For example, when cost efficiency is the main driver, the migration strategy typically involves mass migration with a heavy focus on the **Lift and Shift** approach. However, if the main goal is to enable agility and innovation, the cloud native approach (such as rearchitecting and refactoring) plays a key role in the cloud migration strategy. Let's learn learn more about each strategy in the following subsections.

Lift and Shift migration

Lift and Shift is the fastest mode of migration, as you need minimal work to move your application. However, it does not take advantage of the cloud native features. Let's look at the most common migration strategies, that is, **rehost**, **replatform**, and **relocate**, which are often utilized to do lift and shift with minimal changes needing to be made to the application.

Rehost

Rehost is fast, predictable, repeatable, and economical, which makes it the most preferred method for migrating to the cloud. Rehost is one of the quickest cloud migration strategies, where the server or application is lifted and shifted from the source on-premises environment to the cloud. Minimal changes may be made to the resources during the migration process.

Customers often use rehost to migrate their applications to the cloud quickly and then focus on optimization when the resources are running in the cloud. This technique allows them to realize the cost benefits of using the cloud.

Customers typically use the rehost technique for the following:

- A temporary development and testing environment
- For when servers are running packaged software, such as SAP and Microsoft SharePoint
- When an application doesn't have an active roadmap

While rehost is intended to be applied to packaged software and helps us move quickly into the cloud, you may need to upgrade underlying application platforms such as operating systems. In such a situation, you can use the replatform approach of cloud migration.

Replatform

When an operating system, server, or database version gets to its end of life, then it can trigger a cloud migration project, for example, upgrading the operating system of your web server from Microsoft Windows 2003 to Microsoft Windows 2008/2012/2016 or upgrading your Oracle database engine, and so on. The replatform strategy involves upgrading the platform as a part of the cloud migration project but without changing application architecture. You can decide to update your operating system or application to a newer release as part of the migration.

When using the replatform migration strategy, you may need to reinstall your application on the target environment, which triggers application changes. This requires thorough testing on your application after replatforming to ensure and validate its post-migration operational efficiency.

The following common reasons warrant the use of the replatform technique:

- Changing the operating system from 32-bit to 64-bit
- Changing the database engine
- Updating the latest release of the application
- Upgrading the operating system from Windows 2008 to Windows 2012 or 2019
- Upgrading the Oracle database engine from Oracle 8 to Oracle 19C/21C
- To get the benefits of managed services that are available from cloud vendors such as managed storage, databases, application deployment, and monitoring tools

Replatform helps you advance your application's underlying platform while migrating to the cloud. You can simply relocate your application to the cloud if it was deployed in containers or VMware. Now, let's learn more about the relocate strategy.

Relocate

You may deploy your application using containers or VMware appliances in your on-premise data center. You can move such workloads to the cloud using the accelerate migrations strategy known as **relocate**. Relocate helps you move hundreds of applications in days. You can quickly relocate applications based on VMware and container technologies to the cloud with minimal effort and complexity.

The relocation strategy does not require much upfront developer investment or an expensive test schedule since it provides the agility and automation you expect from the cloud. You need to determine existing configurations and use **VMotion** or **Docker** to relocate your servers to the cloud. VMotion is known for live migration. It's a VMware technology that enables a virtual instance to be moved from one physical host server to another without any interruption in the service.

Customers typically use the relocating technique for the following reasons:

* Workloads have been deployed in a container
* Applications have been deployed in VMware appliances

VMware Cloud (VMC) on AWS not only migrates applications, but it migrates thousands of virtual machines, from individual applications to entire data centers. While migrating your application to the cloud, you may want to take the opportunity to rebuild and rearchitect your entire application to make it more cloud native. The cloud native approach allows you to use the full capability of the cloud. Let's learn more about the cloud native approach.

The cloud native approach

When your team decides to move to cloud native, in the short term, it seems like more upfront work and slower migration to the cloud. This is a bit costly, but it pays off in the long term when you start using all the cloud benefits with an agile team to innovate.

You will see a drastic decrease in costs over time with the cloud native approach as you can optimize your workload for the right price while keeping performance intact with the *pay-as-you-go* model. Cloud native includes containerizing your application by rearchitecting it as a microservice or opting for a purely serverless approach.

For your business needs, you may want to replace the entire product with a *ready-to-use* SaaS offering, for example, replacing on-premise sales and HR solutions with Salesforce and Workday SaaS offerings. Let's learn more about the refactor and repurchase methods for the cloud native migration approach.

Refactor

The refactor method involves rearchitecting and rewriting an application before migrating it to the cloud to make it a cloud native application. In refactoring, you change the application to a more modular design, such as monolithic to microservice. Cloud native applications are applications that have been designed, architected, and built to perform efficiently in a cloud environment. The benefits of these cloud-inherent capabilities include *scalability*, *security*, *agility*, and *cost-efficiency*. Refactoring to microservices helps organizations to create small independent teams that can take complete ownership, thus increase the speed of innovation.

Refactoring requires more time and resources to recode the application and rearchitecture it before it can be migrated. This approach is commonly used by organizations that have extensive cloud experience or a highly skilled workforce. An alternative option for refactoring is to migrate your application to the cloud and then optimize it. You can use cloud native serverless technologies to reduce the admin overhead that comes with modular design.

Common examples of refactoring include the following:

- Changing platforms, such as AIX to UNIX
- Database transition from traditional to cloud databases
- Replacing middleware products
- Rearchitecting the application from monolithic to microservice
- Rebuilding application architecture such as containerizing or making it serverless
- Recoding application components
- Data warehouse modernization to connect organizations to customers

Sometimes, you may find a large effort being made to rebuild an application. As an architect, you should evaluate if purchasing the SaaS product helps you get a better **return on investment (ROI)**. Let's explore the repurchase strategy in more detail.

Repurchase

When your IT resources and projects are migrated to the cloud, you may need servers or applications, which require you to purchase a cloud-compatible license or release. For example, the current on-premises license for your application might not be valid when you run the application in the cloud.

There are multiple ways to address such scenarios of licensing. You can purchase a new license and continue to use your application in the cloud, or you can drop the existing application and replace it with another one in the cloud.

This replacement could be a SaaS offering of the same application.

Common examples of repurchase include the following:

- Replacing the application with SaaS such as Salesforce CRM or Workday HR
- Purchasing a cloud-compatible license

The cloud may not be the answer to all of your problems and sometimes, you will find a legacy application that may not benefit from cloud migration or discover rarely used applications that can be retired. Let's learn about the *retain or retire strategy* in more detail.

Retain or retire

When you are planning a cloud migration, it may not be necessary to move all applications. You may need to retain some applications due to technology constraints; for instance, there may be legacy applications coupled with an on-premise server that cannot move. On the other hand, you may want to retire some applications and use cloud native capabilities, for example, third-party application monitoring and alerting systems. Let's learn more about the retain or retire strategy.

Retain

You might encounter a few applications in your on-premises environment that are essential for your business but are not suitable for migration because of technical reasons, such as the OS/application not being supported on a cloud platform. In such situations, your application cannot be migrated to the cloud, but you can continue running it in your on-premises environment.

For such servers and applications, you may need to perform only the initial analysis to determine their suitability for cloud migration. However, the server or application may still have dependencies with applications that are migrated. Therefore, you may have to maintain the connectivity of these on-premises servers to your cloud environment. You will learn more about on-premises to cloud connectivity in the *Creating a hybrid cloud architecture* section of this chapter.

Some typical workload examples for retention are as follows:

- A legacy application where the customer doesn't see the benefit of moving to the cloud
- The operating system or application support is not available in the cloud, such as AS400 and a mainframe application

You may want to retain complex legacy systems as on-premise and prioritize them so that they can be moved at a later point; however, during discovery, often, organizations find applications that are not in use anymore but are still sitting around and consuming infrastructure space. You can choose to retire such applications. Let's explore more about the retiring strategy.

Retire

While migrating to the cloud, you may discover the following:

- Rarely used applications
- Applications consuming an excessive amount of server capacity
- Applications that may not be required due to cloud incompatibility

In such a situation, you may want to retire the existing workload and take a fresh approach, which is more cloud native.

A retirement strategy can be applied to hosts and applications that are soon going to be decommissioned. This can also be applied to unnecessary and redundant hosted applications. Depending on your business needs, such applications can be decommissioned on-premises without even migrating to the cloud. Hosts and applications that are commonly suited for retirement include the following:

- On-premise servers and storage for disaster recovery purposes
- Server consolidation to resolve redundancies
- Duplicate resources due to mergers and acquisitions
- Alternative hosts in a typical high-availability setup
- Third-party licensed tools such as workload monitoring and automation, which is available as in-built capabilities in the cloud

Most migration projects employ multiple strategies, and there are different tools available for each strategy. The migration strategy will influence the time it takes to migrate and how the applications are grouped for the migration process. Cloud migration is a good time to examine your overall inventory and get rid of the ghost server running under the developer's desk and going unaccounted for. In this section, you learned about various cloud strategies. Let's take a quick look at comparing them in the next section.

Choosing a cloud strategy

Choosing the right migration strategy for cloud adoption as per your business drivers is critical. It would be best to consider various constraints such as financial, resource, time, and skill. You can compare the effort required for the different strategies covered in the previous section in the following table:

Migration Strategy	Description	Time and Cost	Optimization Opportunities
Refactor	Re-architect application into more modularized such as monolithic to microservice	▭	▭
Replatform	Migrate application to upgraded platform without changing core architecture, such traditional database to cloud or higher operating system version	▭	▭
Repurchase	Replacing your current enviroment by purchasing a cloud-based solution	▭	▭
Rehost	Quickly lift and shift your applications to the cloud without architecture changes	▭	▭
Retain	Leaving the application on-premises for now at least	▭	NA
Relocate	Quickly relocate applications to the cloud without changing them, such as container-based applications	▭	NA
Retire	Identify the assests that are no longer useful and remove them entirely	NA	NA

To reduce the cloud migration risk, it's always recommended to take a phased approach when migrating applications to the cloud. First, prioritize business functionality and then optimize applications to realize the difference in cost-saving, performance improvement, and resource productivity. Try to migrate first, and in subsequent phases, you can go for optimization. For example, if you are migrating an application that uses an MS SQL database and replacing it with a cloud native database such as Amazon Aurora, the best approach is to migrate the application in the first phase, followed by migrating the database while monitoring risk and application stability in the second phase. You can choose to optimize your application in subsequent steps by using a cloud native serverless tech stack such as AWS Lambda and Amazon DynamoDB.

The migration strategy should be defined so that it can be executed quickly by allowing teams to work independently. The cloud migration strategy can impact other organizational factors such as building engineering functions within the organization rather than outsourcing. You can build a DevOps culture in the organization by automating the entire code testing and deployment pipeline.

Often, the customer sees the typically unseen advantage of optimizing the workload and tightening security while running application discovery to prepare for migration. There are multiple phases involved in cloud migration. In the next section, you will learn about the steps for cloud migration.

Steps for cloud migration

In the previous section, you learned about different migration strategies and grouped your application in order to apply the appropriate migration technique. These strategies are also known as the 7 R's (retain, retire, relocate, rehost, repurchase, replatform, and refactor), and some or all of them could be part of your cloud journey.

Since you may need to perform and manage multiple applications in the cloud, it's better to set up a cloud **Center of Excellence (CoE)** and standardize this process with a cloud migration factory. The cloud CoE includes experienced people from various IT and business teams across the organization that act as a dedicated cloud team focused on accelerating the building of cloud expertise in the organization. The cloud migration factory defines migration processes and tools, as well as the steps that need to be taken, as shown in the following diagram:

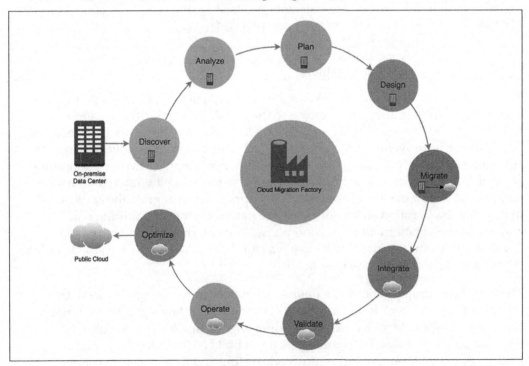

Figure 5.2: Cloud migration steps

As shown in the previous diagram, the cloud migration steps include the following:

- **Discover**: Discovery of cloud migration portfolios and on-premise workloads
- **Analyze**: Analyze discovered data and workloads
- **Plan**: Plan migration to the cloud and define the migration strategy
- **Design**: Design the application as per the migration strategy
- **Migrate**: Execute the migration strategy
- **Integrate**: Integrate with dependencies
- **Validate**: Validate functionality after migration
- **Operate**: Plan to operate in the cloud
- **Optimize**: Optimize your workload for the cloud

One of the initial steps of a cloud migration project is to assess and prioritize the applications for migration. To accomplish this, you need to get a complete inventory of the IT assets in your environment to determine which servers, applications, and business units are suitable for migrating to the cloud, prioritize the migration plan, and determine a migration strategy for these applications. Let's drill down into each step and learn more about them.

Discovering your workload

In the discovery phase of your migration project, you discover and capture detailed data about your *cloud migration portfolio*, for example, the scope of your migration project. You identify servers and applications in your portfolio, as well as their interdependencies and current baseline performance metrics. In addition to that, workload discovery includes understanding the existing storage, such as the database and file system, networking configurations, security and compliance needs, application release frequency, DevOps model, escalation path, operating system maintenance and patching, licensing requirements, as well as other associated assets.

Then, you analyze the gathered information to determine application connectivity and capacity requirements, which can guide you in designing and architecting the target cloud environment and identifying the cost. To consider all factors you need to have cross-functional discussions with other business units, from IT to marketing and program management, which helps in aligning changes to support cloud migration processes.

Detailed discovery can also help in identifying any issues in the current state of the application that might need mitigation before you migrate to the cloud. While analyzing the discovery data, you will also determine an appropriate migration method for your application.

Portfolio discovery is the process of identifying all the IT assets that are involved in your cloud migration project, including servers and applications, their dependencies, and performance metrics.

You will also need to gather business details about your resources, such as the **Net Present Value (NPV)** of the resource, the refresh cycle of the application, the roadmap of the application, and the business criticality of the server or application. These details will help you determine your migration strategy and create a migration plan. In most organizations, these details are maintained across multiple business units and teams. Therefore, during the process of discovery, you may have to interact with various teams, such as business, development, data center, network, and finance.

It is essential to understand that your discovery landscape will depend on various factors:

- What has already been migrated to the cloud?
- What application dependencies are there, along with resources and assets?
- What are the business drivers for cloud migration?
- What is the estimated duration for the entire migration project?
- How many phases is the migration process going to happen in?

One of the top challenges of a migration project is *determining interdependencies among applications*, particularly since they pertain to **input/output (I/O)** operations and communications. Cloud migration becomes even more challenging as organizations expand due to mergers, acquisitions, and growth. Organizations often do not have complete information about the following:

- The inventory of the number of servers
- Server specifications such as the type and version of OS, RAM, CPU, and disk
- Server utilization and performance metrics
- Server dependencies
- Overall networking details

Performing thorough portfolio discovery helps in answering questions such as the following:

- Which applications, business units, and data centers are good candidates for migration?
- How suitable are the applications for migrating to the cloud?

- What known or unknown risks are associated with migrating an application to the cloud?
- How should the applications be prioritized for migration?
- Which other IT assets is the application dependent on?
- What are the best migration strategies for the application?
- Is it better to have some downtime for the application than to perform a live migration due to its dependencies and risks?

Several tools are available in the market that can help automate the discovery process and provide more detailed information in a variety of formats. These tools can be classified based on various characteristics, such as deployment type, operation, support, and type of data discovered and reported.

Most of the available solutions can be broadly classified into two categories:

- **Agent-based solutions**: They require their software client to be installed on a server to gather the necessary details.
- **Agentless solutions**: They may be able to capture this information without any additional installations.

Some solutions perform *port scanning* to probe a server or host for open ports, while others perform *packet scanning*, which often involves capturing and analyzing network packets to decode the information. The tools also vary based on the granularity of the data that's discovered, the storage types, and the reporting options. For example, some tools can provide a higher stack of intelligence beyond the network and can also determine the type of applications running.

The complexity of the discovery process depends on the organization's workload and if it already has a well-maintained inventory in place. Discovery processes are typically run for at least a couple of weeks to gather more holistic information about your environment. Once you discover all the necessary information, you need to analyze it. Let's look at the analysis step in more detail.

Analyzing the information

To identify server and application dependencies, you need to analyze the network connectivity data, port connections, system, and process information on the hosts. Depending on your tool, you can visualize all the contacts from a server to identify its dependencies, or you can run queries to list all the servers running a specific process, using a particular port, or talking to a specific host.

To group your servers and applications for migration scheduling, you need to identify patterns in your host configurations. Often, some prefixes are embedded in the server hostnames to signify their association with a particular workload, business unit, application, or requirement. Some environments might also use tags and other metadata to associate such details with the host.

To right-size your target environment, you can analyze the performance metrics for your servers and applications:

- If a server is *over-provisioned*, you can revise your right-size mapping information. You can also optimize this process by leveraging the utilization data for the server/application instead of the server specifications.

- If a server is *under-provisioned*, you might assign a higher priority to the server to migrate to the cloud.

Depending on the environment, the type of data that's captured during the discovery process might vary. The data analyzed for migration planning is to determine target network details such as firewall configuration, workload distribution, and the phases in which the application will be migrated.

You can combine this insight with the availability of your resources and business requirements to prioritize your cloud migration workload. This insight can help you in determining the number of servers to be included as part of each cloud migration sprint.

Based on the discovery and analysis of your cloud migration portfolio, you can determine an appropriate cloud migration strategy for your applications. For instance, servers and applications that are less complex and run on a supported OS might be suitable candidates for a lift and shift strategy. Servers or applications that run on an unsupported OS might need further analysis to determine an appropriate strategy.

In a cloud migration project, discovery, analysis, and planning are tightly integrated. You perform a full discovery of your cloud migration portfolio and analyze the data to create a migration plan. By the end of the analysis phase, based on your analysis and the details you've gathered from business owners, you should be able to do the following for each server/application that is part of your cloud migration portfolio:

- Choose a migration strategy for the server/application, depending on your organization's cloud adoption strategy. You may be limited to specific choices within retain, retire, relocate, repurchase, rehost, replatform, and refactor.

- Assign a priority for migrating the resources to the cloud. Eventually, all the resources that are part of the cloud migration portfolio may migrate to the cloud, but this priority will determine the urgency of that migration. A higher-priority resource might move earlier in the migration schedule.

- Document the business driver for migrating the resources to the cloud, which will drive the need and priority for migrating the resources to the cloud.

Planning utilizes the information collected in the discovery and analysis phase to create migration waves. Waves are logical groupings of resources that can be sequentially deployed into production and test/dev environments during cloud migration. Let's look at migration planning in more detail.

Creating a migration plan

The next phase in your migration project is *planning cloud migration*. You will use the information you gathered during the portfolio discovery phase to create an efficient migration plan. By the end of this phase in your migration project, you should be able to create an ordered backlog of applications that can migrate to the cloud.

The main goals of the migration planning phase include the following:

- Choosing a migration strategy
- Defining the success criteria for the migration
- Determining the right size of the resources in the cloud
- Determining a priority for applications to migrate to the cloud
- Identifying migration patterns
- Creating a detailed migration plan, checklist, and schedule
- Creating migration sprint teams
- Identifying tools for migration

In preparation for the migration planning phase, you must perform a detailed discovery of all the IT assets that are part of your cloud migration portfolio. The target destination environment in the cloud is also architected before the planning phase. Migration planning includes determining the cloud account structure and creating a network structure for your application. It is also essential to understand hybrid connectivity with the target cloud environment. Hybrid connectivity will help you plan for applications that might have dependencies on resources that are still running on-premise.

The order of application migration can be determined through three high-level steps:

1. Evaluate each application across several business and technical dimensions associated with a potential migration to accurately quantify the environment.

2. Identify the dependencies for each application with qualifications such as locked, tightly coupled, and loosely coupled to identify any dependency-based ordering requirements.

3. Determine the desired prioritization strategy of the organization to determine the appropriate relative weighting of the various dimensions.

The initiation of an application or server migration depends on two factors:

*   First, the prioritization strategy of your organization and the application priority. Your organization might place varying emphasis on a few dimensions, such as maximizing ROI, minimizing risk, ease of migration, or another custom dimension.

*   Second, the insight gained through the portfolio discovery and analysis phase can help you identify application patterns that match its strategy.

For example, if the organizational strategy is to minimize the risk, then business criticality will have more weight in identifying the applications. If ease of migration is the strategy, applications that can be migrated using rehost will have higher priority, as rehost is a more straightforward process than other strategies. The outcome of planning should be an ordered list of applications that can be used to schedule the cloud migration.

The following are the planning aspects of migration:

1. Gather baseline performance metrics for your applications before migration. Performance metrics will help you design or optimize your application architecture in the cloud quantitatively. You might have captured most of these performance details during the discovery phase.

2. Create test plans and user acceptance plans for your applications. These plans will help in determining the outcome (success or failure) of the migration process.

3. You also need to have cutover strategies and rollback plans that define how and where the applications will continue to run based on the outcome of the migration.

4. Operations and management plans will be useful for determining the ownership of roles during migration and post-migration. You can leverage **Responsible, Accountable, Consult, Inform (RACI)** matrix spreadsheets to define these roles and responsibilities for your application that span the entire cloud migration journey.

5. Identify points of contact within the application team that can provide timely support in case of escalations. Close collaboration across the teams will ensure the successful completion of the migration as per the schedule (sprint).

If your organization has some of these processes already documented for your existing on-premises environment, for example, change control process, test plans, and run books for operations and management, you might be able to leverage them.

You need to compare performance and cost before, during, and after migration, which can be an indication that they are not currently capturing enough of the right **Key Performance Indicators (KPIs)** to enable this insight. The customer needs to identify and begin achieving useful KPIs so that there is a baseline to compare against during and after migration. The KPI approach in migration has a twofold goal. First, it needs to define the capabilities of your existing application and then compare them with the cloud infrastructure.

When the new products are added to the catalog or a new service is launched, it increases your company revenue, and that's a count against company KPIs. Generally, IT metrics include the quality of the product and the number of bugs that are reported for an application. A **Service-Level Agreement (SLA)** defined for fixing a critical bug, system downtime, and performance metrics includes system resource utilization values such as memory utilization, CPU utilization, disk utilization, and network utilization.

You can use a continuous delivery methodology such as **Scrum** to efficiently migrate applications to the cloud. With the help of the Scrum methodology, you can create multiple sprints and add your applications to the sprint backlogs based on prioritization. You can sometimes combine many applications and create waves that follow a similar migration strategy and are possibly related to each other. Typically, you would maintain a constant duration across sprints and vary the application based on factors such as sprint team size and the complexity of the application.

If you have small teams that have in-depth knowledge about the applications that need to be migrated, then you can use weekly sprints, where each sprint consists of the discover/analyze, plan/design, and migrate phases, with a final cutover on the last day of the sprint. However, as the team iterates through the sprints, the workload in each sprint can increase because the teams have now gained experience in the migration process and can incorporate the feedback from previous sprints to make the current sprint more efficient with continuous learning and adaptation.

If you are migrating a complex application, you could also use the entire week for just the plan/design phase and perform the other phases in separate sprints. Tasks that you perform within the sprint and their deliverables can vary, depending on factors such as complexity and team size. The key is to get value from the sprint.

You can create multiple teams to assist in the migration process, depending on various factors such as your product backlog, migration strategy, and organizational structure. Some customers create groups focused on each migration strategy such as a rehost team, a refactor team, and a replatform team. You could also have a team specialized in optimizing your application architecture in the cloud. The multi-team strategy is the preferred model for organizations that have a large number of applications to be migrated to the cloud.

The team can be divided into the following segments:

- First, the team can validate the essential components to ensure your environment (dev, test, or prod) is working, adequately maintained, and monitored.
- The integration team will determine the application configuration and also find the dependencies, which will help reduce the waste that's made by another team.
- The lift and shift migration sprint team migrates large applications that don't require refactoring or replatforming. The team will use automation tools to deliver small amounts of incremental value after every sprint.
- The replatform migration sprint team focuses on application architecture changes in order to migrate applications to the cloud, for example, modernizing application design for microservices or updating the operating system to the latest version.
- The refactor migration sprint team is responsible for managing various migration environments such as production, testing, and development. They make sure all the environments are scalable and functioning as required by monitoring them closely.
- The innovation migration sprint team works collaboratively with groups such as the foundation and transition team to develop a package solution that can be used by other groups.

It's recommended that you run a pilot migration project while planning and continuously building a product backlog so that these adaptations and lessons learned can be incorporated into the new plan. It's best to target non-production migration waves first in the pilot phase. The successful results of the pilot project and sprint can also be used to help secure stakeholder buy-in for the cloud transformation program.

Designing the application

During the design phase, your focus should be on successfully migrating applications and making sure your application design meets the required success criteria and is up to date after it has been migrated to the cloud. For example, if you are maintaining user sessions in the on-premise application server (so that it can scale horizontally), make sure that a similar architecture is implemented in the cloud after the migration, which defines the success criteria.

It is essential to understand that the primary goal of this phase is to ensure that your application has been designed to meet the migration success criteria. You need to identify opportunities that enhance your application, and they can be accomplished and achieved during the optimization phase.

For migration, first, you need to have a complete understanding of your organization's foundational architecture on-premises and in the cloud, which includes the following:

- User account
- Network configuration
- Network connectivity
- Security
- Governance
- Monitoring

Knowledge of these components will help you to create and maintain a new architecture for your application. For example, if your application handles sensitive information such as **Personally Identifiable Information** (**PII**) and has control access, this means your architecture needs a specific network setting to meet compliance needs.

During the design phase, you will identify the architecture gap and enhance your architecture as per your application requirements. When you have multiple accounts, each account may have some level of relationship or dependency; for example, you can have a security account to ensure that all your resources are compliant with company-wide security guidelines.

When thinking about your application's network design, you need to consider the following:

- Network packet flows entering the boundaries of your application
- External and internal traffic routing

- Firewall rules for network protection
- Application isolation from the internet and other internal applications
- Overall network compliance and governance
- Network log and flow audit
- Separation of application risk levels, as per their exposure to data and users
- DDoS attack protection and prevention
- Network requirements for production and non-production environments
- SaaS-based multi-tenancy application access requirements
- Network boundaries at the business unit level in an organization
- Billing and implementation of the shared services model across the business unit

You can consider hybrid connectivity options with an on-premise system, depending on your connectivity needs. To build and maintain a secure, reliable, performant, and cost-optimized architecture in the cloud, you need to apply best practices. Review your cloud foundational architecture against the cloud best practices before migrating to the cloud.

Chapter 4, Principles of Solution Architecture Design, highlights common architectural design patterns that you can consider when migrating your application to the cloud. It is important to emphasize here that the primary goal of the design phase in the migration process is to design your application architecture so that it meets the migration success criteria identified in the planning phase. Your application can be further optimized during the optimization phase of the migration project.

In the process of migrating to the cloud, you can design your application architecture so that it benefits from the global cloud infrastructure and increases the proximity to your end users, mitigates risk, improves security, and addresses data residency constraints. Systems that are expected to grow over time should be built on top of a scalable architecture that can support growth in users, traffic, or data with no drop in performance.

For applications that need to maintain some state information, you could make specific components of the architecture stateless. If there are any layers in the architecture that need to be stateful, you could leverage techniques such as session affinity to be still able to scale such components. Leverage a distributed processing approach for applications that process vast amounts of data.

Another approach to reducing the operational complexity of running applications is using serverless architectures. These architectures can also reduce costs because you are neither paying for underutilized servers nor provisioning redundant infrastructure to implement high availability. You will learn more about serverless architecture in *Chapter 6, Solution Architecture Design Patterns*.

The following diagram shows a migration design from on-premises to the AWS cloud, starting with the on-premises design:

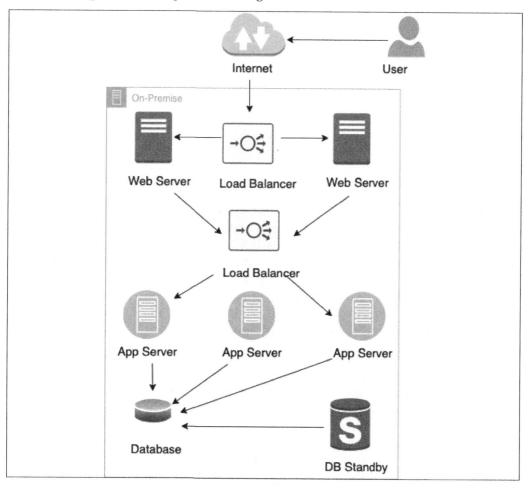

Figure 5.3: On-premise architecture mapping

Now we transition to an AWS cloud design:

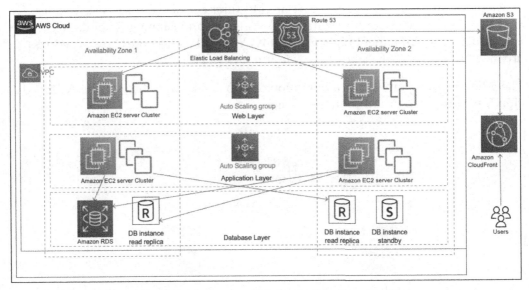

Figure 5.4: On-premise to AWS cloud architecture mapping

In the preceding diagram, as part of the cloud migration strategy, it was determined to rehost the web servers and introduce auto-scaling to provide the elasticity that can help meet spikes in demand. Elastic load balancers are also added to distribute the incoming traffic to the web server instances. The application servers were migrated using refactor, and the platform for the database tier changed from the traditional database to a cloud native **Amazon RDS**. The entire architecture is distributed across multiple availability zones to provide high availability, and the database replicates to a standby instance in the second availability zone.

As an output of your design phase, you should create a detailed design document for the architecture of your application in the cloud. The design document should include details such as the user account that the application must migrate to, network configuration, and a list of users, groups, and applications that need access to the data held by this application. The design document should clearly articulate application hosting details and application-specific requirements for backup, licensing, monitoring, security, compliance, patching, and maintenance. Ensure that you create a design document for each application. You will need it during the migration validation phase to perform a basic cloud functionality check and an application functionality check.

Performing application migration to the cloud

The migration execution step brings your plans to fruition. In the execution phase, you need to define a set of steps and configurations, as you will repeat them during the dev/test and production waves. Before executing migration, ensure that you have a migration plan and that you have identified the sprint teams and migration waves and schedules, have created a prioritized backlog, and have notified all the application stakeholders about the migration schedule, timelines, and their roles and responsibilities.

You must also ensure that the target environment in the cloud has already been set up with the foundational architecture and core services. You might have some application-specific pre-steps, such as performing a backup or sync before migration, shutting down the servers, or unmounting disks and devices from the server. Make sure you put in place your essential components, such as networking and firewall rules, authentication and authorization, and accounts. All need to be configured appropriately. You need to test your applications on the infrastructure to make sure that they have access to required servers, load balancers, databases, authentication servers, and so on. You need to pay special attention to application logging and monitoring to measure performance comparisons.

Make sure you have good network connectivity with the cloud environment during the migration process. A good estimate of the amount of data that needs to be migrated also helps you properly estimate the time it will take to migrate your data to the cloud, given other factors such as bandwidth and network connectivity. You also need to understand the tools that are available to perform the migration. Given the number of devices that are available in the market, you might have to narrow down the selection criteria based on your requirements and other constraints.

As you know, rehost is often the fastest way to migrate your application to the cloud. When the application is running in the cloud, you can further optimize it to leverage all the benefits that the cloud has to offer. By quickly migrating your applications to the cloud by applying the lift and shift approach, you may start realizing the cost and agility benefits sooner.

Depending on the migration strategy, you typically migrate the entire server, including the application and the infrastructure that the application is running on, or just the data that belongs to an application. Let's look at how to migrate data and servers.

Data migration

Cloud data migration refers to the process of moving existing data to a new cloud storage location. Most applications will require data storage throughout their progression into the cloud. Storage migration typically aligns with one of two approaches, but organizations may perform both at the same time:

- First, a single lift-and-shift move. This may be required before new applications can be started up in the cloud.

- Second, a hybrid model weighted toward the cloud, which results in newly architected cloud native projects with some legacy on-premises data. The legacy data stores may shift toward the cloud over time.

However, your approach to migrating data will vary. It depends on factors such as the amount of data, network and bandwidth constraints, the data classification tier (such as backup data, mission-critical data, data warehouses, or archive data), and the amount of time you can allocate for the migration process.

If you have extensive archives of data or data lakes in a situation where bandwidth and data volumes are unrealistic, you might want to lift and shift the data from its current location straight into a cloud provider's data centers. You can do this either by using dedicated network connections to accelerate network transfers or by physically transferring the data over the hard drive.

If your data stores can gradually migrate over time, or when new data is aggregating from many non-cloud sources, consider methods that provide a friendly interface to the cloud storage service. These migration services can leverage or complement existing installations such as backup and recovery software or a **Storage Area Network (SAN)**.

For a small-scale database, one-step migration is the best option, which requires you to shut down the application for from a couple of hours to a few days as per the complexity of the workload. During the downtime, all information from the database is extracted and migrated to the destination database in the cloud. Once the database has been migrated, it needs to be validated with the source database for no data loss. After that, a final cutover can be completed.

In the other case, if a system requires minimal downtime, a two-step migration process is more commonly used for databases of any size:

- In the first step, information is extracted from the source database.

- In the next step, data is migrated while the database is still up and running. You can configure **change data capture (CDC)** to ensure all data is migrated and the application is in a working state during migration.

In the entire process, there is no downtime. After the migration task has been completed, you can perform functionality and performance tests for connectivity to external applications or any other criteria as needed.

During this time, because the source database is still up and running, changes will need to be propagated or replicated before the final cutover. At this point, you would schedule downtime for the database, usually a few hours, and synchronize the source and destination databases. After all the change data has been transferred to the target database, you should perform data validation to ensure a successful migration and finally route application traffic to a new cloud database.

You might have mission-critical databases that cannot have any downtime. Performing such zero-downtime migrations requires detailed planning and the appropriate data replication tools. You will need to use continuous data replication tools for such scenarios. It is important to note here that source database latency can be impacted in the case of synchronous replication as it waits for data to be replicated everywhere before responding to the application while the replication is happening.

You can use asynchronous replication if your database downtime is only for a few minutes. With zero-downtime migration, you have more flexibility regarding when to perform the cutover since the source and target databases are always in sync.

Server migration

There are several methods you can use to migrate a server to the cloud:

- The host or **OS cloning** technique involves installing an agent on the source system that will clone the OS image of the system. A snapshot is created on the source system and then sent to the target system. This type of cloning is used for a one-time migration. With the **OS Copy** method, all operating system files are copied from the source machine and hosted on a cloud instance. For the OS copy method to be effective, the people and/or tool that executes the migration must understand the underlying OS environment.

- The **disaster recovery** replication technique deploys an agent on the source system that's used to replicate data to the target. However, the data is replicated at the file system or block level. A few solutions continuously replicate the data to target volumes, offering a continuous data replication solution. With the **Disk Copy** method, the disk volume is copied in its entirety. Once the disk volume has been captured, it can be loaded into the cloud as volumes, which can then be attached to a cloud instance.

- For virtual machines, you could use agentless techniques to export/import your VM into the cloud. With the **VM Copy** method, the on-premise virtual machine image is copied. If the on-premise servers are running as virtual machines, such as VMware or OpenStack, then you can copy the VM image and import it into the cloud as a *machine image*. One main benefit of this technique is that you can have server backup images that can be launched over and over again.

- With the **User Data Copy** method, only the application's user data is copied. Once the data has been exported from the original server, you can choose one of three migration strategies—*repurchase, replatform, or refactor*. The user data copy method is only viable for those who know the application's internals. However, because it only extracts user data, the user data copy method is an OS-agnostic technique.

- You can containerize your application and then redeploy it in the cloud. With the containerization method, both the application binary and user data are copied. Once the application binary and user data have been copied, it can be run on a container runtime that is hosted on the cloud. Because the underlying platform is different, this is an example of the replatform migration strategy.

Several migration tools in the market can help you migrate your data and/or server to the cloud. Each major public cloud provides its own tool for migration; however, you can also use other popular cloud migration tools such as CloudEndure, NetApp, Dynatrace, Carbonite, Microfocus, and so on. Some tools take a disaster recovery strategy for migration, and some disaster recovery tools also support continuous replication to facilitate live migrations. There are some that specialize in forklifting your servers, performing database migrations across platforms, or database schema conversion. The tool must be able to support business processes that you are comfortable with, and you must have the operational staff to manage it.

Integration, validation, and cutover

Migration, integration, and validation go hand in hand as you want to do continuous validation while performing various integration with your application in the cloud. The team starts by performing the necessary cloud functionality checks to ensure that the application is running with proper network configuration (in the desired geolocation) with some designated traffic flow. Instances can start or stop as desired when the basic cloud functionality check is complete. You need to validate that the server configuration (such as RAM, CPU, and hard disk) is the same as intended.

Some knowledge of the application and its functionality is required to perform these checks. When the primary check is complete, then you can perform integration tests for the application.

These integration tests include checking integration with external dependencies and applications; for example, to make sure the application can connect to Active Directory, **Customer Relationship Management (CRM)**, patch or configuration management servers, and shared services. When integration validation is successful, the application is ready for cutover.

During the integration phase, you integrate the application and migrate it to the cloud with external dependencies to validate its functionality. For example, your application might have to communicate with an Active Directory server, a configuration management server, or shared services resources that are all external to the application. Your application may also need to be integrated with external applications that belong to your clients or vendors, such as a supplier receiving a feed from your APIs after a purchase order placement.

When the integration process is complete, you need to validate the integration by performing unit tests, smoke tests, and **user acceptance tests (UATs)**. The results from these tests help you get approval from the application and business owners. The final step of the integration and validation phase includes a sign-off process from the application and business owner of the application, which will allow you to cut over the application from on-premises to the cloud.

The final phase of the cloud migration factory is the **cutover process**. In this phase, you take the necessary steps to redirect your application traffic from the source on-premise environment to the target cloud environment. Depending on the type of data or server migration (one-step, two-step, or zero-downtime migration), the steps in your cutover process may vary. Some factors to consider when determining a cutover strategy include the following:

- Acceptable downtime for the application
- The frequency of the data update
- Data access patterns such as read-only or static data
- Application-specific requirements such as database syncs, backups, and DNS name resolutions
- Business constraints, such as the day or time during which the cutover can happen and the criticality of the data
- Changing management guidelines and approvals

Live migration is most popular for business-critical workload migration. Let's learn more about it.

Live migration cutover

The following diagram illustrates a cutover strategy for live zero-downtime migration. In this method, the data is continuously replicated to the destination, and you perform most of the functional validation and integration testing at the destination while the application is still up and running:

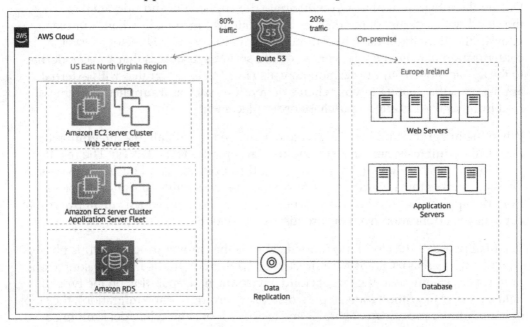

Figure 5.5: Live migration cutover using blue-green deployment

In the replication process, the source on-premise database and target cloud database are always in sync. When all the integration and validation tests are completed successfully and the application is ready for cutover, you can take a **blue-green approach** to do the cutover. The idea behind blue-green deployment is that your blue environment is your existing production environment carrying live traffic. In parallel, you provision a green environment, which is identical to the blue environment other than the new version of your code. You will learn more about blue-green deployments in *Chapter 12, DevOps and Solution Architecture Framework.*

Initially, the application continues to run both on-premises and in the cloud, resulting in traffic being distributed between the two sides. You can increase traffic to cloud applications gradually until all the traffic is directed to the new application, thus resulting in a cutover with no downtime.

The other most commonly used cutover strategies involve some downtime. You schedule downtime for the application, pause the traffic, take the application offline, and perform the final sync by applying the CDC process.

After the final sync, it might be a good idea to perform a quick smoke test on the destination side. At this point, you can redirect the traffic from the source to the application running in the cloud, thus completing the cutover. Data is most critical to sync and cutover during migration as it changes continuously when an application is live. You can use data migration tools such as AWS **Database Migration Service (DMS)** and Oracle GoldenGate to perform one-time data migration of CDC data.

Operating the cloud application

The operation phase of the migration process helps you to allow, run, use, and operate applications in the cloud to the level agreed upon with the business stakeholders. Most organizations typically already have guidelines defined for their on-premises environments. This operational excellence procedure will help you identify the process changes and training that will allow operations to support the goals of cloud adoption.

Let's discuss the differences between deploying complex computing systems in a data center versus deploying them in the cloud. In a data center environment, the burden of building out the physical infrastructure for a project falls on the company's IT department. This means you need to make sure that you have the appropriate physical environmental safeguards for your servers, such as power and cooling, so that you can physically safeguard these assets, and that you have maintained multiple redundant facilities at various locations to reduce the chances of a disaster.

The downside of the data center approach is that it requires significant investment; it can be challenging to secure the resources that are necessary if you wish to experiment with new systems and solutions.

In a cloud computing environment, this changes dramatically. Instead of your company owning the physical data center, the physical data center is managed by the cloud provider. When you want to provision a new server, you ask your cloud provider for a new server with a certain amount of memory, disk space, data I/O throughput rate, processor capability, and so on. In other words, computing resources become a service that you can provision, and de-provision as needed.

The following are the IT operations that you would want to address in the cloud:

- Server patching
- Service and application logging
- Cloud monitoring
- Event management
- Cloud security operations

- Configuration management
- Cloud asset management
- Change management
- Business continuity with disaster recovery and high availability

IT organizations typically follow standards such as **Information Technology Infrastructure Library (ITIL)** and **Information Technology Service Management (ITSM)** for most of these operations. ITSM organizes and describes the activities and processes involved in planning, creating, managing, and supporting IT services, while ITIL applies best practices to implement ITSM. You need to modernize your ITSM practices so that they can take advantage of the agility, security, and cost benefits provided by the cloud.

In traditional environments, the development team and the IT operations team work in their silos. The development team gathers the requirements from business owners and develops builds. System administrators are solely responsible for operations and for meeting uptime requirements. These teams generally do not have any direct communication during the development life cycle, and each team rarely understands the processes and requirements of the other team. Each team has its own set of tools, processes, and approaches, which often leads to redundant and sometimes conflicting efforts.

In a **DevOps** (short for **development and operations**) approach, both the development team and the operations team work collaboratively during the build and deployment phases of the software development life cycle, sharing responsibilities, and providing continuous feedback. DevOps is a methodology that promotes collaboration and coordination between developers and operational teams to deliver products or services continuously. The software builds are tested frequently throughout the build phase in production-like environments, which allows for the early detection of defects or bugs.

This approach is beneficial in organizations where the teams rely on multiple applications, tools, technologies, platforms, databases, devices, and so on in the process of developing or delivering a product or service. You will learn more about DevOps in *Chapter 12, DevOps and Solution Architecture Framework*.

Application optimization in the cloud

Optimization is a very important aspect of operating in the cloud, and this is a continuous process of improvement. In this section, you will learn about the various optimization areas. There are chapters dedicated to each optimization consideration in this book. The following are the major optimization areas:

- **Performance**: Optimize for performance to ensure that a system is architected to deliver efficient performance for a set of resources, such as instances, storage, databases, and space/time. You will learn more about architecture performance considerations in *Chapter 7, Performance Considerations*.

- **Security**: Continuously review and improve security policies and processes for the organization to protect data and assets in the AWS cloud. You will learn more about architecture security considerations in *Chapter 8, Security Considerations*.

- **Reliability**: Optimize applications for reliability to achieve high availability and defined downtime thresholds for applications, which will aid in recovering from failures, handling increased demand, and mitigating disruptions over time. You will learn more about architecture reliability considerations in *Chapter 9, Architectural Reliability Considerations*.

- **Operational excellence**: Optimize operational efficiency and the ability to run and monitor systems to deliver business value and to improve supporting processes and procedures continually. You will learn more about architecture operational considerations in *Chapter 10, Operational Excellence Considerations*.

- **Cost**: Optimize the cost efficiency of an application or a group of applications, while considering fluctuating resource needs. You will learn more about architecture cost considerations in *Chapter 11, Cost Considerations*.

As a quick overview of some of the major elements to consider, to optimize costs, you need to understand what is currently being deployed in your cloud environment and the price of each of those resources. By using detailed billing reports and enabling billing alerts, you can proactively monitor your costs in the cloud.

Remember that, in the public cloud, you pay for what you use. Therefore, you will be able to reduce costs by turning off instances when they are not needed. By automating your instance deployment, you can also tear down and build up the instance entirely as required.

As you offload more, you need to maintain, scale, and pay for less infrastructure. Another way to optimize costs is by designing your architecture for *elasticity*. Make sure you right-size your resources, use auto-scaling, and adjust your utilization based on price and need. For example, it might be more cost-efficient for an application to use more small instances than fewer large instances.

Several application architectural modifications can help you improve the performance of your application. One way to improve the performance of your web servers is to offload your web page through caching. You can write an application that lets you cache images, JavaScript, or even full pages to provide a better experience to your users.

You can design n-tier and service-oriented architectures to scale each layer and module independently, which will help optimize performance. You will learn more about this architecture pattern in *Chapter 6, Solution Architecture Design Patterns*.

Customers may want to retain a workload on-premise during cloud migration due to a phased approach or inability to migrate to the cloud due to application complexity or licensing issues. In such scenarios, you need to build a hybrid cloud where the on-premise workload can interact with the cloud workload and exchange information seamlessly. Let's learn more details on creating hybrid cloud architecture.

Creating hybrid cloud architecture

The value of the cloud is growing, and many large enterprises are moving their workload to the cloud. However, often, it's not possible to move entirely to the cloud in one day, and for most customers, this is a journey. Those customers seek a hybrid cloud model where they maintain a part of the application in an on-premise environment that needs to communicate with the cloud module.

In a hybrid deployment, you need to establish connectivity between the resources running in the on-premises environment and the cloud environment. The most common method of hybrid deployment is between the cloud and existing on-premises infrastructure to extend and grow an organization's infrastructure into the cloud while connecting cloud resources to the internal system. The common causes of setting up a hybrid cloud may include the following:

- You want to have operating legacy applications in an on-premise environment while you refactor and deploy in the cloud with a blue-green deployment model.

- A legacy application such as a mainframe may not have a compatible cloud option and has to continue running on-premise. You need time to refactor the tech stack.

- You need to keep part of the application on-premise due to compliance requirements.

- To speed up migration, keep the database on-premise and move the application server to the cloud.

- The customer wants to have more granular control of part of the application.

- Data ingestion in the cloud from on-premise for the cloud's **Extract, Transform, Load (ETL)** pipeline.

Public cloud vendors provide a mechanism for integrations between a customer's existing infrastructure and the cloud so that customers can easily use the cloud as a seamless extension of their current infrastructure investments. These hybrid architecture functionalities allow customers to do everything, from integrating networking, security, and access control to powering automated workload migrations and controlling the cloud from their on-premises infrastructure management tools.

Taking the example of the AWS cloud, you can establish a secure connection to the AWS cloud using a VPN. Since a VPN connection is set up over the internet, there may be latency issues due to multiple router hops from third-party internet providers. You can have your fiber optics private line go to the AWS cloud for better latency using AWS Direct Connect.

As shown in the following diagram, with AWS Direct Connect, you can establish high-speed connectivity between your data center and the AWS cloud to achieve a low-latency hybrid deployment:

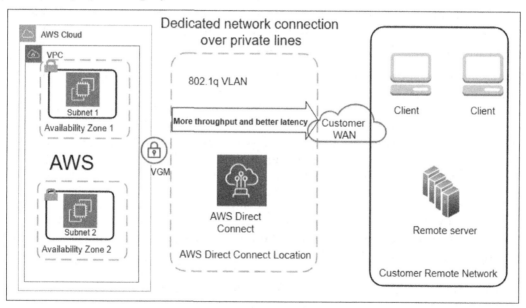

Figure 5.6: Hybrid cloud architecture (on-premises to cloud connectivity)

As shown in the preceding diagram, **AWS Direct Connect Location** establishes the connectivity between the on-premises data center and the AWS cloud. This helps you achieve the customer need of having dedicated fiber-optic lines to an AWS Direct Connect location; the customer can opt for this fiber optic line from a third-party vendor such as AT&T, Verizon, T-Mobile or Comcast in the USA. AWS has a directly connected partner in each region of the world.

At the AWS Direct Connect location, the customer's fiber-optic line is connected to an AWS private network, which provides dedicated end-to-end connectivity from the data center to the AWS cloud. These optic lines can provide speeds of up to 10 GB/s. To secure traffic over direct connect, you can set up a VPN, which will apply IPSec encryption to the traffic flow. As more cloud offerings become available in the market from prominent vendors, organizations may choose to take a multi-cloud approach. Let's learn more details about the multi-cloud strategy.

Taking a multi-cloud approach

Before the cloud existed, organizations used multiple vendors to use the best of the breed and avoid vendor lock-in. As more public cloud players come into the market, organizations are looking to create a multi-cloud approach. A multi-cloud approach is about utilizing two or more public cloud providers to serve organization infrastructure and technology needs. The multi-cloud strategy could be a mix of major public cloud providers such as AWS, GCP, Microsoft Azure, Oracle Cloud, IBM, and so on. Organizations can choose to share their workload between different clouds based on their geographical availability, technical capabilities, and cost. They can also combine multi-cloud with on-premise.

One of the major advantages of a multi-cloud strategy is having vendor flexibility. With multi-cloud, you get the advantage of choosing between vendors and retain your negotiation power, agility, and flexibility. In the event of a missed SLA, you have the option to switch over to a better cloud provider. Another advantage is being able to plan disaster recovery in the same region when one cloud provider has an outage; you can rely on other providers. Each cloud provider has its strength, and you can pick the services best available across the cloud.

While the multi-cloud approach provides a competitive advantage to organizations, it also comes with its challenges. One of the most prominent challenges is skill set. You need to have people who understand multiple clouds while creating a workload hosting strategy and, more than that, need to replicate teams to dive deep into each cloud tech stack. You could consider hiring a consultant or outsourcing your cloud management to global system integrators who have a pool of human resources across the cloud.

The other major challenge is coordinating data availability, security, and performance across multiple clouds.

While each cloud vendor provides in-built security, cross-region applications, and cloud native tools for performance, this area pretty much become the organization's responsibility when it comes to the cloud. You need to implement consistent data management across the cloud, taking data from one cloud and feeding it to another, and ensuring consistent performance.

As you can see, the multi-cloud approach has its advantages and disadvantages, so you need to think when choosing a multi-cloud strategy. Once you have started your cloud journey, you may want to build cloud native applications. Let's learn more about building cloud native architecture.

Designing cloud native architecture

You learned about the cloud native approach earlier in this chapter from a migration point of view, where the focus was on refactoring and rearchitecting applications when migrating to the cloud. Each organization may have a different opinion on cloud native architecture but, at the center of it, becoming cloud native is all about utilizing all the cloud capabilities in the best way possible. True cloud native architecture is about designing your application so that it can be built in the cloud from its foundations.

Cloud native doesn't mean hosting your application on the cloud platform; it's about leveraging services and features provided by the cloud. This may include the following:

- Containerizing your monolithic architecture in a microservice and creating a CI/CD pipeline for automated deployment.
- Building a serverless application with technology such as AWS Lambda **Function as a Service (FaaS)** and Amazon DynamoDB (a managed NoSQL database in the cloud).
- Creating a serverless data lake using Amazon S3 (a managed object storage service), AWS Glue (a managed Spark cluster for ETL), and Amazon Athena (a managed Presto cluster for ad hoc queries).
- Using a cloud native monitoring and logging service, for example, Amazon CloudWatch.
- Using a cloud native auditing service, for example, AWS CloudTrail.

The following architecture is an example of a cloud native serverless architecture for a micro-blogging application:

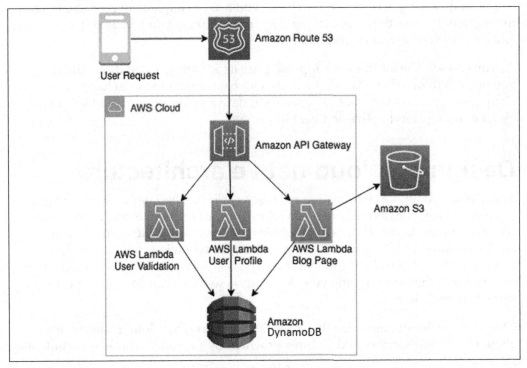

Figure 5.7: Cloud native micro-blogging application architecture

The preceding diagram depicts utilizing cloud native serverless services in the AWS cloud. Here, Amazon Route 53, which manages the DNS service, is routing user requests. Lambda manages function as a service to handle the code for **User Validation**, **User Profile**, and **Blog Page**. All the blog assets are stored in Amazon S3, which manages object storage services, and all user profile data is stored in Amazon DynamoDB, which is managed by the NoSQL store.

As users send requests, AWS Lambda validates the user and looks at their profile to ensure they have a subscription in Amazon DynamoDB; after that, it picks blog assets such as pictures, videos, and a static HTML writeup from Amazon S3 and displays them to the user. This architecture can be scaled in an unlimited manner as all services are cloud native managed services, and you are not handling any infrastructure.

Crucial factors such as high availability, disaster recovery, and scalability are taken care of by these cloud native services so that you can focus on your feature development. In terms of cost, you will only pay if a request goes to a blogging application. If no one is browsing for the blog at night, you don't pay anything for hosting your code; you only pay a nominal fee for storage.

The benefit of cloud native architecture is that it enables fast-paced innovation and agility in the team. It simplifies building out a complex application and infrastructure. As system administrators and developers, you focus strictly on designing and building your networks, servers, file storage, and other computing resources, and leave the physical implementation to your cloud computing provider. Cloud native architecture provides several benefits:

- **Fast scale-out, on-demand**: You can request the resources you need when you need them. You only pay for what you use.

- **Replicate quickly**: Infrastructure-as-code means you can build once and replicate more. Instead of building your infrastructure by hand, you can structure it as a series of scripts or applications. Building your infrastructure programmatically gives you the ability to build and rebuild it on demand, when needed for development or testing.

- **Tear up and tear down easily**: In the cloud, services are provided on-demand, so it's easy to build up a large experimental system. Your system may include a cluster of scalable web and application servers, multiple databases, terabytes of capacity, workflow applications, and monitoring. You can tear it all down as soon as the experiment is completed and save costs.

There are many more examples in the area of storage, networking, and automation for building cloud native architecture. You will learn more about this architecture in *Chapter 6, Solution Architecture Design Patterns*.

Summary

In this chapter, you learned how the cloud is becoming the most popular mainstream application hosting and development environment for enterprises. At the beginning of this chapter, you learned about cloud thinking and how it's related to solution architecture design. Since more organizations are looking to move into the cloud, this chapter focused on various cloud migration strategies, techniques, and steps.

You learned about various cloud strategies, as per the nature of workload and migration priorities. Migration strategies include the ability to rehost and replatform your application for Lift and Shift and take the cloud native approach by refactoring and rearchitecting your application to take advantage of cloud native capabilities.

You may find some unused inventory during application discovery and retire it. If you choose to not migrate a certain workload, then retain the application as is on-premises.

Then, you learned about the steps involved in cloud migration, which help you discover your on-premise workload, analyze collected data, and create a plan to decide on which migration strategy to take.

During the design phase, you create a detailed implementation plan and execute that during the migration steps, where you learned to set up connectivity with the cloud and move your application from on-premise to the cloud.

After that, you learned about how to integrate, validate, and operate your workload into the cloud after migration and apply continuous optimization for cost, security, reliability, performance, and operational excellence. The hybrid cloud architecture is an integral part of the migration process, so you learned how to establish connectivity between on-premise and the cloud by looking at an architecture example of the AWS cloud. At the end of this chapter, you learned about significant cloud providers and their offerings.

In the next chapter, you will dive deep and learn more about various architecture design patterns, along with the reference architecture. You will learn about architecture patterns such as multi-tier, service-oriented, serverless, and microservices.

Further reading

To learn more about the major public cloud providers, please refer to the following links:

- **Amazon Web Services (AWS)**: https://aws.amazon.com
- **Google Cloud Platform (GCP)**: https://cloud.google.com
- **Microsoft Azure**: https://azure.microsoft.com
- **Oracle Cloud Infrastructure (OCI)**: https://www.oracle.com/cloud/
- **Alibaba Cloud:** https://us.alibabacloud.com
- **IBM Cloud**: https://www.ibm.com/cloud

Almost every cloud provider extends their learning credentials to new users, which means you can sign up with your email and try their offerings out before you choose which one to go with.

Join our book's Discord space

Join the book's Discord workspace for a monthly *Ask me Anything* session with the authors: https://packt.link/SAHandbook

6
Solution Architecture Design Patterns

Have you ever wondered how large enterprises design scalable systems? Before starting application development, solution architects worked across organizations and weighed multiple options to develop architecture design to handle the business need. There are multiple ways to design a solution. A solution architect needs to take the right approach based on user requirements along with the architecture constraints of cost, performance, scalability, and availability. In this chapter, you will learn about various solution architecture patterns along with reference architectures and how to apply them in real-world scenarios.

In the previous chapters, you learned about the attributes and principles of solution architecture design. This chapter is both exciting and essential as you will be able to apply your learning to various architecture design patterns. In this chapter, you will gain an understanding of some of the significant solution architecture patterns, such as layered, event-driven, microservice, loosely coupled, service-oriented, and RESTful architectures.

You will learn the advantages of various architectural designs and examples that demonstrate when to utilize them. You will also gain an understanding of architecture design anti-patterns in addition to the following architecture design patterns:

- Building an *n*-tier layered architecture
- Creating a multi-tenant SaaS-based architecture
- Building stateless and stateful architecture designs

- Understanding service-oriented architecture
- Building a serverless architecture
- Creating a microservice architecture
- Building a queue-based architecture
- Creating an event-driven architecture
- Building a cache-based architecture
- Understanding the circuit breaker pattern
- Implementing the bulkheads pattern
- Creating a floating IP pattern
- Deploying an application with a container
- Database handling in application architecture
- Avoiding anti-patterns in solution architecture

By the end of the chapter, you will know how to optimize your solution architecture design and apply best practices, making this chapter the center point and core of your learning.

Building an n-tier layered architecture

In *n*-tier architecture (also known as **multitier architecture**), you need to apply the principle of loosely coupled design (refer to *Chapter 4, Principles of Solution Architecture Design*) and attributes of scalability and elasticity (refer to *Chapter 3, Attributes of the Solution Architecture*). In multilayer architecture, you divide your product functions into multiple layers, such as presentation, business, database, and services, so that each layer can be implemented and scaled independently.

With multitier architecture, it is easy to adopt new technologies and make development more efficient. This layered architecture provides the flexibility to add new features in each layer without disturbing the features of other layers. In terms of security, you can keep each layer secure and isolated from the others, so if one layer gets compromised, the other layers won't be impacted. Application troubleshooting and management also become manageable as you can quickly pinpoint where the issue is coming from and which part of the application needs to be troubleshot.

The most common architecture in multilayer design is **three-tier architecture**, so let's learn more about it. The following diagram shows an architecture that allows you to interact with a web application from the browser and perform the required functions, for example, ordering your favorite T-shirt or reading a blog and leaving a comment:

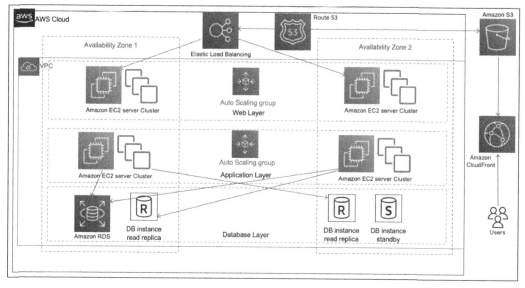

Figure 6.1: Three-tier website architecture

In the preceding architecture, you have the following three layers:

- **Web Layer**: The web layer is the user-facing part of the application. End users interact with the web layer to collect or provide information.

- **Application Layer**: The application layer mostly contains business logic and acts upon information received from the web layer.

- **Database Layer**: All kinds of user data and application data are stored in the database layer.

Let's take a look at these layers in more detail.

The web layer

The web layer is also known as the **presentation tier**. The web layer provides a user interface that helps the end user to interact with the application. The web layer is your user interface (in this case, the website page), where the user enters information or browses for it. Web developers may build a presentation tier user interface in technologies such as HTML, CSS, AngularJS, ReactJS, **JavaServer Pages (JSP)**, and **Active Server Pages (ASP)**. This tier collects the information from the user and passes it to the application layer.

The web layer is user-facing, so organizations spend most of their time improving the user experience. Many organizations have dedicated **User Experience (UX)** teams that conduct research in various areas to understand how users interact with applications.

Also, the solution architect needs to make sure architecture design includes UX input and page load performance. There should be seamless information flow between the web layer and application layer to return the correct information to users within the expected timeframe, such as user login, profile loading, and so on. Let look at more details on the application layer.

The application layer

The application layer is also known as the **logic tier**, as this is the core of the product where all the business logic resides. The presentation tier collects the information from the user and passes it to the logic tier to process it and get a result. For example, on an e-commerce website such as www.amazon.com, users can enter a date range on the order page of the website to find their order summary. In return, the web layer passes the data range information to the application layer. The application layer processes the user input to perform business logic such as the count of orders, the sum of amounts, and the number of items purchased. This returns information to the web layer to render it for the user.

Generally, in three-tier architecture, all algorithms and complex logic live in the application tier, including creating a recommendation engine or showing personalized pages to the user as per their browsing history. You may add layers such as a domain layer, data access layer, or presentation layer to make a 4- or 5-tier architecture. Developers may choose to implement this layer in a server-side programming language, for example, C++, Java, .NET, or Node.js. The application layer is the center of system design and requires most of the design effort. Most of the application features depend on logic built at the application layer. The application layer performs logic on the data, which is stored in the database layer. Let's look at the database layer in more detail.

The database layer

The database layer, which is also known as the **data tier**, stores all the information related to user profiles and transactions. Essentially, it contains any data that needs to persist in being stored in the data tier. This information is sent back to the application layer for logic processing and then, eventually, it renders to the user in the web layer. For example, if the user is logged in to a website with their user ID and password, then the application layer verifies the user credentials with information stored in the database. If the credentials match the stored information, the user is allowed to log in and access the authorized area of the website.

The architect may choose to build a data tier in relational databases, for example, PostgreSQL, MariaDB, Oracle Database, MySQL, Microsoft SQL Server, Amazon Aurora, or Amazon RDS. The architect may also add a NoSQL database such as Amazon DynamoDB, MongoDB, or Apache Cassandra.

The data tier is not only used to store transaction information but also to hold user session information and application configuration. To meet performance needs, an architect might decide to add caching databases such as Memcached and Redis. You will learn more about various databases in *Chapter 13, Data Engineering for Solution Architecture*.

The data tier needs special attention in terms of security. You need to make sure to protect user information by applying data encryption at rest and in transit. In the *n*-tier layered architecture diagram, you will notice that each layer has its own auto scaling configuration, which means it can be scaled independently. Also, each layer has a network boundary, which means having access to one layer doesn't allow access to other layers. You will learn more about security considerations in *Chapter 8, Security Considerations*.

When designing multitier architecture, you need to consider how many layers should be added to your design. For example, the solution architect may decide to break down the application layer into a business layer, service layer, and persistent layer. However, each layer requires its fleet of servers and network configurations. So, adding more layers means increasing the cost and management overhead, whereas keeping fewer layers means creating a tightly coupled architecture. The architect needs to decide on the number of tiers based on application complexity and user requirement. For example, you may want to add additional tiers such as a data access layer for database access logic and keep the data storage layer for the database engine. You can add more layers to reduce complexity by defining logical separation, which can help to increase the maintainability of the general application and the ability to scale and achieve performance.

Creating a multi-tenant SaaS-based architecture

In the previous section, you learned about multitier architecture, which is also called a **single tenancy** when built for a single organization. Multi-tenant architecture is becoming more popular as organizations adopt the digital revolution while keeping the overall application and operational cost low. The **Software-as-a-Service (SaaS)** model is built on a multi-tenant architecture, where a single instance of the software and the supporting infrastructure serve multiple customers. In this design, each customer shares the application and database, with each tenant isolated by their unique configuration, identity, and data. They remain invisible to each other while sharing the same product.

As multi-tenant SaaS providers own everything from the hardware to the software, SaaS-based products offload an organization's responsibilities to the maintenance and updates of the application, as this is taken care of by the SaaS provider.

Each customer (tenant) can customize their user interface using a configuration without any code changes. As multiple customers share a common infrastructure, they get the benefit of scale, which lowers the cost further. Some of the most popular SaaS providers are Salesforce CRM, the Jira tool, and Amazon QuickSight.

As shown in the following architecture diagram, there are two organizations (tenants) using the same software and infrastructure. The SaaS vendor provides access to the application layer by allocating a unique tenant ID to each organization. Each tenant can customize their user interface as per their business needs using a simple configuration:

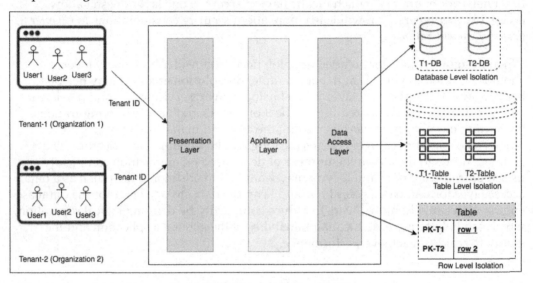

Figure 6.2: Multi-tenant SaaS architecture

As shown in the preceding architecture design, the presentation layer provides a user interface and the application layer holds the business logic. At the data access layer, each tenant will have data-level isolation with one of the following methods:

- **Database Level Isolation**: In this model, each tenant has its database associated with its tenant ID. When each tenant queries data from the user interface, they are redirected to their database. This model is required if the customer doesn't want a single shared database for compliance and security reasons.
- **Table Level Isolation**: This isolation level can be achieved by providing a separate table for each tenant. In this model, tables need to be uniquely assigned to each tenant, for example, with the tenant ID prefix. When each tenant queries data from the user interface, they are redirected to their tables as per their unique identifier.

- **Row Level Isolation**: In this isolation level, all tenants share the same table in a database. There is an additional column in a table where a unique tenant ID is stored against each row. When an individual tenant wants to access their data from the user interface, the data access layer of the application formulates a query based on the tenant ID to the shared table. Each tenant gets a row that belongs to their users only.

For enterprise customers, a careful assessment should be carried out, to understand whether a SaaS solution is the right fit for them based on their unique features' requirements. This is because often, a SaaS model has limited customization capabilities. Additionally, we need to find the cost value proposition if a large number of users need to subscribe. The cost comparison should be calculated based on the total cost of ownership when making a *build versus buy* decision. This is because building software is not the primary business of most organizations, so the SaaS model is becoming highly popular as organizations can focus on their business and let the experts handle the IT side of it.

Building stateless and stateful architecture designs

While designing a complex application such as an e-commerce website, you need to handle the user state to maintain activity flow, where users may be performing a chain of activities such as adding to the cart, placing an order, selecting a shipping method, and making a payment. Currently, users can use various channels to access an application, so there is a high possibility that they will be switching between devices; for example, adding items to the cart from their mobile and then completing checkout and payment from a laptop. In this situation, you would want to persist user activity across devices and maintain their state until the transaction is complete. Therefore, your architecture design and application implementation need to plan for user session management in order to fulfill this requirement.

To persist user states and make applications stateless, user session information needs to be stored in persistent database layers such as the NoSQL database. This state can be shared between multiple web servers or microservices. Traditionally, a monolithic application uses stateful architecture, where user session information is stored in the server itself rather than via any external persistence database storage.

The session storage mechanism is the main difference between stateless and stateful application designs. Since session information in a stateful application is local to the server, it cannot be shared between other servers and also doesn't support modern microservice architecture. You will learn more about microservice-based architecture in the *Creating a microservice architecture* section.

Often, a stateful application doesn't support horizontal scaling very well, as the application state persists in the server, which cannot be replaced. The stateful application works well early on when the user base was not very huge. However, as the internet becomes more popular, it is reasonable to assume that you will have millions of users active on a web application. Therefore, efficient horizontal scaling is important for handling such a large user base and achieving low application latency.

In a stateful application, state information is handled by the server, so once users establish a connection with a particular server, they have to stick with it until the transaction completes. You can put a load balancer in front of the stateful application, but to do that, you have to enable sticky sessions in a load balancer. A sticky session routes requests for a particular user session to the same physical machine that serviced the first request to ensure that the user session is not lost due to requests being routed to different servers. The load balancer has to route user requests to one server, where session information has been established. Enabling sticky sessions violates the load balancer's default round-robin request for the distribution method. Other issues may include lots of open connections to the server as you need to implement a session timeout for the client.

Your design approach should focus more on the shared session state using the stateless method, as it allows horizontal scaling. The following diagram shows an architecture that depicts a stateless application for a web application:

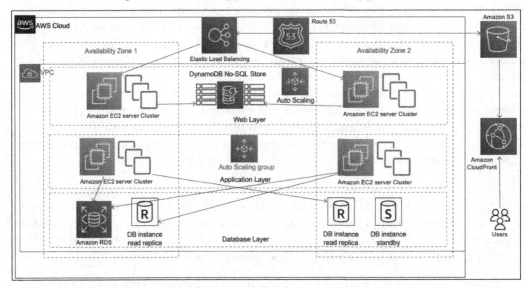

Figure 6.3: A stateless application architecture

The preceding architecture diagram is a three-tier architecture with a web, application, and database layer. To make applications loosely coupled and scalable, all user sessions are stored persistently in the NoSQL database, for example, Amazon DynamoDB.

You should use client-side storage, such as cookies, for the session ID. This architecture lets you use the scale-out pattern without having to worry about a loss of user state information. A stateless architecture removes the overhead to create and maintain user sessions and allows consistency across the application's modules. A stateless application has performance benefits too, as it reduces memory usage from the server side and eliminates the session timeout issue.

Adopting a stateless pattern can complicate tasks; however, with the right approach, you can achieve a rewarding experience for your user base. You can develop applications using the microservice approach with REST design patterns and deploy them in containers. For this, use authentication and authorization to connect users to the server.

You will learn more about the REST design pattern and microservices in the next section. As access to state information from multiple web servers focuses on a single location, you must use caution to prevent the performance of the data store from becoming a bottleneck.

Understanding service-oriented architecture

In **service-oriented architecture (SOA)** patterns, different application components interact with each other using a communication protocol over the network. Each service provides end-to-end functionality, for example, *fetching an order history*. SOA is widely adopted by large systems to integrate business processes, for example, taking your payment service from the main application and putting it as a separate solution.

In a general sense, SOAs take monolithic applications and spread some of those operations out into individual *services* that operate independently of each other. The goal of using an SOA is to loosen the coupling of your application's services. Sometimes, an SOA includes not just splitting services apart from one another but splitting resources into separate instances of that service. For instance, while some choose to store all of their company's data in a single database split by tables, an SOA would consider modularizing the application by function into separate databases altogether. This allows you to scale and manage throughput based on the individual needs of tables for each database.

SOA has multiple benefits, for example, the parallelization of development, deployment, and operation. It decouples the service so that you can optimize and scale each service individually.

However, it also requires more robust governance to ensure work performed by each service's team meets the same standard. With SOA, the solution could become complex enough to increase the overhead to balance that, so you need to make the right choice of tools and automation of service monitoring, deployment, and scaling.

There are multiple ways in which to implement SOA. Here, you will learn about the **Simple Object Access Protocol (SOAP)** web service architecture and **Representational State Transfer (REST)** web service architecture.

Originally, SOAP was the most popular messaging protocol, but it is a bit heavyweight as it entirely relies on XML for data interchange. Now, REST architecture is becoming more popular as developers need to build more lightweight mobile and web applications. Let's learn about both architectures and their differences in more detail.

SOAP web service architecture

SOAP is a messaging protocol that is used to exchange data in a distributed environment in XML format. SOAP is a standard XML where data is transported in an envelope format called a **SOAP envelope**, as shown in the following diagram:

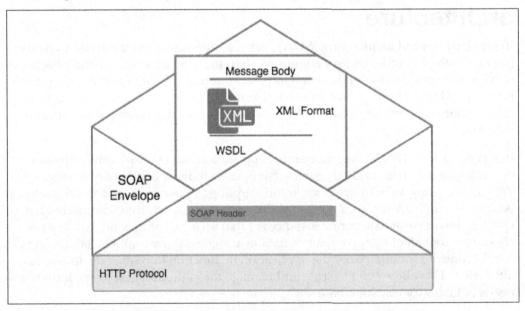

Figure 6.4: SOAP envelope for web service data exchange

As shown in the preceding diagram, a **SOAP envelope** contains two parts and these SOAP messages are formatted in XML and are typically sent using **HyperText Transfer Protocol (HTTP)**:

- **SOAP Header**: The SOAP header provides information on how a recipient of a SOAP message should process it. It contains authorization information to deliver the message to the right recipient and for data encoding.

- **Message Body**: The message body contains the actual message in the **Web Services Description Language (WSDL)** specification. WSDL is an XML format file that describes the **Application Programming Interface (API)** contract with the message structure, API operations, and the server's **Unique Resource Locator (URL)** address. Using a WSDL service, a client application can determine where a service is being hosted and what functionality it can perform.

The following code shows an example of a SOAP envelope XML. Here, you can see both the header and message wrapped up under the SOAP envelope:

```xml
<env:Envelope xmlns:env="http://www.w3.org/2003/05/soap-envelope">
<env:Header>
    <n:orderinfo xmlns:n="http://exampleorder.org/orderinfo">
       <n:priority>1</n:priority>
       <n:expires>2019-06-30T16:00:00-09:00</n:expires>
    </n:orderinfo>
  </env:Header>
  <env:Body>
    <m:order xmlns:m="http://exampleorder.org/orderinfo">
      <m:getorderinfo>
            <m:orderno>12345</m:oderno>
      </m:getorderinfo>
    </m:order>
  </env:Body>
```

SOAP commonly uses HTTP, but other protocols such as SMTP can be used.

In a SOAP-based web service, the service provider creates an API contract in the form of WSDL. WSDL lists all of the operations that web services can perform, such as providing order information, updating orders, deleting orders, and more. The service provider shares WSDL with the web service client team, using which the client generates an acceptable message format, sends data to the service provider, and gets the desired response. The web service client fills the values in the generated XML message and sends it across to the service provider with authentication details for processing. Let's look at a WSDL example:

```xml
<?xml version="1.0"?>
<definitions name="Order"
```

```
targetNamespace="http://example.com/order.wsdl"
        xmlns:tns="http://example.com/ order.wsdl"
        xmlns:xsd1="http://example.com/ order.xsd"
        xmlns:soap="http://schemas.xmlsoap.org/wsdl/soap/"
        xmlns="http://schemas.xmlsoap.org/wsdl/">

    <types>
        <schema targetNamespace="http://example.com/ order.xsd"
                xmlns="http://www.w3.org/2000/10/XMLSchema">
            <element name="PlaceOrder">
                <complexType>
                    <all>
                        <element name="itemID" type="string"/>
                    </all>
                </complexType>
            </element>
            <element name="ItemPrice">
                <complexType>
                    <all>
                        <element name="price" type="float"/>
                    </all>
                </complexType>
            </element>
        </schema>
    </types>

    <message name="GetOrderInfo">
        <part name="body" element="xsd1:GetOrderRequest"/>
    </message>

    <message name="GetItemInfo">
        <part name="body" element="xsd1:ItemPrice"/>
    </message>

    <portType name="OrderPortType">
        <operation name="GetOrderInfo">
            <input message="tns: GetOrderInfoInput "/>
            <output message="tns: GetOrderInfoOutput"/>
        </operation>
    </portType>

    <binding name="OrderSoapBinding" type="tns:OrderPortType">
```

```
        <soap:binding style="document" transport="http://schemas.
xmlsoap.org/soap/http"/>
        <operation name="GetOrderInfo">
            <soap:operation soapAction="http://example.com/GetOrderInfo
"/>
            <input>
                <soap:body use="literal"/>
            </input>
            <output>
                <soap:body use="literal"/>
            </output>
        </operation>
    </binding>

    <service name="OrderService">
        <documentation>My first Order</documentation>
        <port name="OrderPort" binding="tns:OrderBinding">
            <soap:address location="http://example.com/order"/>
        </port>
    </service>

</definitions>
```

At a high level, you can see six major elements are used to define an SOA contract in WSDL:

- types: It gives data type definition to explain messages exchanged.
- message: Message represents a definition of the data being transmitted. A message has logical parts, which are associated with a definition.
- portType: It is a set of operations and contains input message and output messages.
- binding: Binding defines a protocol and data format specifications for the operations and messages defined by a particular port type.
- port: It provides an address for binding by defining a single communication endpoint.
- service: It is used to aggregate a set of related ports.

A software architect defines the WSDL and message schema, which the development team uses to generate code for client and server skeleton in the programming language of their choice for business logic implementation. The overall intent of this section is to give an overview of SOAP-based architecture.

There are various resources available on the internet, such as W3Schools tutorials to dive deep into SOAP-based service implementation for the development team, that you can explore.

The following diagram shows details about a message exchange in a web service using SOAP. Here, the web service client sends the request to the service provider who hosts the web service, and receives the response with the desired result:

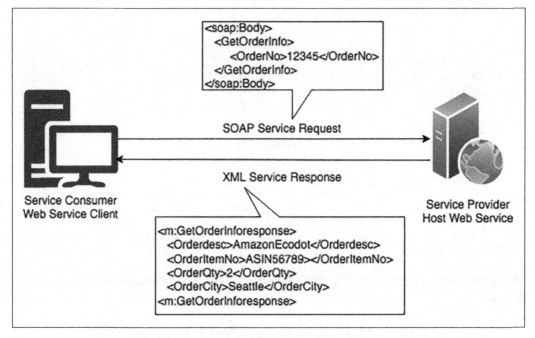

Figure 6.5: SOAP-based web service

In the preceding diagram, the client is an e-commerce website user interface. The user wants their order information and hence sends the SOAP message in XML format to the application server with the order number. The application server hosts the order service, which then responds with the customer's order details.

The implementation of a SOAP-based web service has high complexity and requires a lot of bandwidth, which can impact web application performance, such as page loading time, and any major changes in the server logic require all clients to update their code. REST was created to address SOAP-based web service problems and provide a more flexible architecture. Let's learn more about RESTful architecture and why it is becoming popular.

RESTful web service architecture

A **REST** or RESTful web service offers better performance due to its lightweight architecture. It allows different messaging formats such as JSON, plaintext, HTML, and XML, compared to SOAP, which only allows XML. REST is an architecture style that defines the standard for loosely coupled application design using the HTTP protocol for data transmission.

JavaScript Object Notation (JSON) is a more accessible format for data exchange in REST architecture. JSON is also lightweight and language-independent. It contains a simple key-value pair that makes it compatible with data structures defined in most programming languages.

REST focuses on the design principle for creating a stateless service. Like SOAP-based services, the web service client doesn't need to generate a complex client skeleton, but it can access the web server resources using the unique **Uniform Resource Identifier (URI)**. The client can access RESTful resources with the HTTP protocol and perform standard operations such as GET, PUT, DELETE, and POST on the resources. Let's take a look at the differences between REST and SOAP:

Attributes	REST	SOAP
Design	Architectural style with an informal guideline	Predefined rules with a standard protocol
Message Format	JSON, YAML, XML, HTML, plaintext, and CSV	XML
Protocol	HTTP	HTTP, SMTP, and UPD
Session State	Default stateless	Default stateful
Security	HTTPS and SSL	Web Services Security and ACID compliance
Cache	Cached API calls	Cannot cache API calls
Performance	Fast with fewer resources	Needs more bandwidth and compute power

Your choice of architecture design between REST and SOAP depends upon your organization's needs. The REST service offers an effective way to integrate with lightweight clients such as smartphones, while SOAP provides high security and is suitable for complex transactions. Let's learn about a reference architecture based on service-oriented design.

Building an SOA-based e-commerce website architecture

An e-commerce website such as www.amazon.com has users from all parts of the world and a huge catalog with millions of products. Each product has multiple images, reviews, and videos. Maintaining such a big catalog for a global user base is a very challenging task.

This reference architecture follows SOA principles. The services are operating as independently as possible from each other. This architecture can be implemented using either SOAP-based or RESTful web architecture:

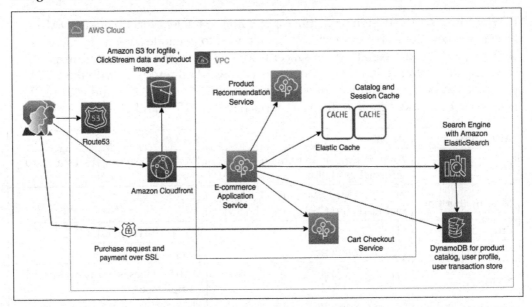

Figure 6.6: E-commerce website SOA

As shown in the preceding architecture diagram, we can take note of the following:

* When a user types a website address into the browser, the user request reaches out to the DNS server to load the website. The DNS requests for the website are routed by Amazon Route 53 to the server where the web applications are being hosted.

* The user base is global, and users continue browsing for products to purchase as the website has a large product catalog with static images and videos. A content distribution network such as Amazon CloudFront caches and delivers static assets to users.

- The catalog contents, such as static product images and videos, along with other application data, such as log files, are stored in Amazon S3.

- Users will browse the website from multiple devices, for example, they will add items in a cart from their mobile and then make a payment on a desktop. To handle user sessions, a persistent session store is required such as DynamoDB. In fact, DynamoDB is a NoSQL database where you don't need to provide a fixed schema, so it is a great storage option for product catalogs and attributes.

- To provide high performance and reduce latency, Amazon ElastiCache is used as a caching layer for the product to reduce read and write operations on the database.

- A convenient search feature is key for product sales and business success. Amazon CloudSearch helps to build scalable search capability by loading the product catalog from DynamoDB.

- A recommendation can encourage a user to buy additional products based on their browsing history and past purchases. A separate recommendation service can consume the log data stored on Amazon S3 and provide potential product recommendations to the user.

- The e-commerce application can also have multiple layers and components that require frequent deployment. AWS Elastic Beanstalk handles the auto-provisioning of the infrastructure, deploys the application, handles the load by applying auto scaling, and monitors the application.

In this section, you learned about SOA along with an architecture overview. Let's learn more about the critical aspect of modern architecture design with a serverless architecture.

Building a serverless architecture

In a traditional scenario, if you want to develop an application, you need to have a server where your desired operating system and required software can be installed. While you are writing your code, you need to make sure that your server is up and running. During deployment, you need to add more servers to keep up with user demand and add scaling mechanisms such as **auto scaling** to manage the desired number of servers to fulfill users' requests. In this entire situation, a lot of effort goes into infrastructure management and maintenance, which has nothing to do with your business problem.

Going serverless gives you the ability to focus on your application and write code for feature implementation without worrying about underlying infrastructure maintenance.

Serverless means there is no server required to host your code, which frees you up from auto scaling and decoupling overheads while providing a low-cost model. All heavy lifting of server management and scaling is taken care of by cloud providers.

A public cloud, such as AWS, provides several serverless services in the area of computer and data storage, which makes it easier to develop an end-to-end serverless application. When you talk about serverless, the first thing that comes to mind is AWS Lambda functions, which is a **Function as a Service (FaaS)** and is provided by the AWS cloud. To make your application service-oriented, Amazon API Gateway offers you the ability to put RESTful endpoints in front of your AWS Lambda functions and helps you to expose them as microservices. Amazon DynamoDB provides a highly scalable NoSQL database, which is an entirely serverless NoSQL data store, and Amazon **Simple Storage Service (S3)** provides serverless object data storage.

Let's take a look at an example of a reference serverless architecture in the following architecture diagram for the delivery of a secure survey:

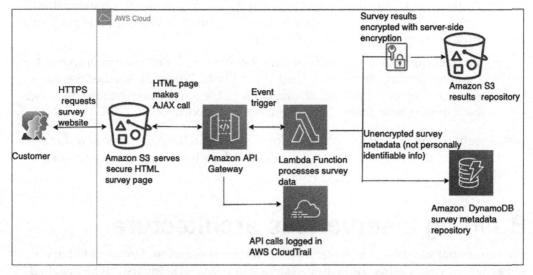

Figure 6.7: Serverless architecture for a secure survey delivery

In this example, a serverless architecture serves, delivers, and processes secure surveys, all on managed services:

1. First, a customer requests the website over HTTPS. The web page is served directly from Amazon S3.

2. The customer's survey is submitted via an AJAX call to Amazon API Gateway.

3. Amazon API Gateway logs this to Amazon CloudTrail. If a survey's results are lost, or if one of the AJAX calls includes malicious activity of some sort, these logs may be helpful in identifying and fixing the problem.

4. Amazon API Gateway then turns the AJAX call into an event trigger for an AWS Lambda function, which pulls the survey data and processes it.

5. The results of the survey are sent by the AWS Lambda function to an Amazon S3 bucket, where they are secured with *server-side encryption*.

6. Metadata from the survey, which does not include any personally identifiable information, is then written and stored in a DynamoDB table. This could be used for later queries and analysis.

Due to the increasing popularity of serverless architecture, you will see more reference architectures using serverless services as we move forward with this book. Also, now more frameworks become available to build and manage serverless applications, such as the AWS **Serverless Application Model (SAM)**. SAM is an open-source framework for building serverless applications that provides easy syntax to create functions, APIs, and databases for serverless applications.

You can define the application model using **YAML (Yet Another Markup Language)**. YAML is becoming highly popular and replacing JSON in many places due to its syntactical simplicity, easiness to learn, and being lightweight. During deployment, SAM transforms YAML configuration file syntax into AWS CloudFormation syntax, enabling you to build serverless applications faster.

The concept of microservices is also becoming popular with the adoption of RESTful-style architectures. Let's learn more about REST architectures and microservices in the next sections.

Creating a microservice architecture

Often, microservices are architected in REST-style web services and are independently scalable. This makes it easier to expand or shrink the relevant components of your system while leaving the rest untouched. A system that employs microservices can more easily withstand incidents where application availability can degrade gracefully to avoid any cascading failures. Your system becomes fault-tolerant, that is, built with failure in mind.

The clear advantage of microservices is that you have to maintain a smaller surface area of code. Microservices should always be independent. You can build each service with no external dependencies where all prerequisites are included, which reduces the inter-dependency between application modules and enables loose coupling.

The other overarching concept of microservices is **bounded contexts**, which are the blocks that combine together to make a single business domain. A business domain could be something like car manufacturing, bookselling, or social network interactions that involve a complete business process. An individual microservice defines boundaries in which all the details are encapsulated.

Scaling each service is essential while dealing with the large-scale access of applications, where different workloads have different scaling demands. Let's learn about some best practices for designing microservice architecture:

- **Create a separate data store**: Adopting a separate data store for each microservice allows the individual team to choose a database that works best for their service. For example, the team that handles website traffic can use a very scalable NoSQL database to store semi-structured data. The team handling order services can use a relational database to ensure data integrity and the consistency of transactions. This also helps to achieve loose coupling where changes in one database do not impact other services.

- **Keep servers stateless**: As you learned in the previous section, *Building stateless and stateful architecture designs*, keeping your server stateless helps in scaling. Servers should be able to go down and be replaced easily, with minimal or no need for storing state on the servers.

- **Create a separate build**: Creating a separate build for each microservice makes it easier for the development team to introduce new changes and improve the agility of the new feature release. This helps to make sure that the development team is only building code that is required for a particular microservice and not impacting other services.

- **Deploy in a container**: Deploying in a container gives you the tool to deploy everything in the same standard way. You can choose to deploy all microservices in the same way regardless of their nature using containers. You will learn more about container deployment in the *Deploying an application with a container* section.

- **Go serverless**: Try to use a serverless platform or a leveraging function with service capability, such as AWS Lambda, when your microservices are not too complex. Serverless architecture helps you to avoid infrastructure management overhead.

- **Blue-green deployment**: The better approach is to create a copy of the production environment. Deploy the new feature and route a small percentage of the user traffic to make sure the new feature is working as per the expectation in a new environment. After that, increase the traffic in the new environment until the entire user base is able to see the new feature. You will learn more about blue-green deployment in *Chapter 12, DevOps and Solution Architecture Framework.*

- **Monitor your environment**: Good monitoring is the difference between reacting to an outage and proactively preventing an outage with proper rerouting, scaling, and managed degradation. To prevent any application downtime, you want services to offer and push their health status to the monitoring layer, because what knows more about status than the service itself? Monitoring can be done in many ways, such as with plugins, or by writing to a monitoring API.

While microservice architectures have various advantages, a modular approach comes with the overhead of managing more infrastructure. You need to carefully choose the tools to help you manage and scale multiple modules in parallel. While designing microservice architecture, wherever possible, try to use serverless platforms, which will help mitigate infrastructure and operation overhead. Let's take a look at a microservice-based reference architecture for a real-time voting application.

Real-time voting application reference architecture

A microservice-based architecture is illustrated in the following diagram, representing a real-time voting application, where small microservices process and consolidate user votes. The voting application collects individual user votes from each mobile device and stores all the votes in a NoSQL Amazon DynamoDB database.

Finally, there is application logic in the AWS Lambda function, which aggregates all of the voting data cast by users to their favorite actor and returns the final results:

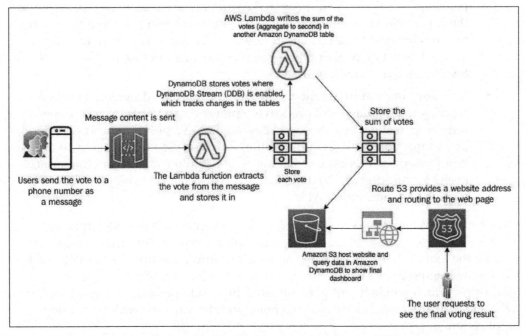

Figure 6.8: Microservice-based real-time voting application architecture

In the preceding architecture, the following things are happening:

1. Users text a vote to a phone number or a short code provided by a third party such as *Twilio*.

2. The third party is configured to send the content of the message to an endpoint created by Amazon API Gateway, which then forwards the response to a function built in AWS Lambda.

3. This function extracts the vote from the message content and writes the result and any metadata into a table in Amazon DynamoDB.

4. This table has DynamoDB Streams enabled, which allows you to track changes to your tables on a rolling basis.

5. After the update, DynamoDB Streams notifies a second AWS Lambda function, which has the application logic to aggregate the votes (to every second) and writes them back to another DynamoDB table. The second table only stores the sum of the votes for each category.

6. A dashboard to display a summary of votes is created using HTML and JavaScript and hosted as a static website in Amazon S3. This page uses the AWS JavaScript SDK to query the aggregate Amazon DynamoDB table and display the voting results in real time.

7. Finally, Amazon Route 53 is used as a DNS provider to create a hosted zone pointing to a custom domain name in the Amazon S3 bucket.

This architecture is not only microservice-based but also serverless. Using microservices, you can create applications made of small independent components, which constitute smaller parts to iterate. Microservice-based architecture means that the cost, size, and risk of change reduces, increasing the rate of change.

Message queues play a vital role in achieving accurate loose coupling and help to avoid application throttling. A queue allows secure and reliable communication between components. Let's learn more about queue-based architecture in the next section.

Building a queue-based architecture

In the previous section, you learned about microservice design using RESTful architecture. The RESTful architecture helps your microservice to be easily discoverable, but what happens if your service goes down? This is a contemporary architecture, where your client service waits for a response from the host service, which means that the HTTP request blocks the API. Sometimes, your information may be lost due to the unavailability of a downstream service. In such cases, you must implement some retry logic in order to retain your information.

A queue-based architecture provides a solution to this problem by adding message queues between services, which holds information on behalf of services. The queue-based architecture provides fully asynchronous communication and a loosely coupled architecture. In a queue-based architecture, your information is still available in the message. If a service crashes, the message can get the process as soon as the service becomes available. Let's learn some of the terminology of a queue-based architecture:

- **Message**: A message has two parts—the header and the body. The header contains metadata about the message, while the body contains the actual message.

- **Queue**: The queue holds the messages that can be used when required.

- **Producer**: A service that produces a message and publishes it to the queue.

- **Consumer**: A service that consumes and utilizes the message.

- **Message broker**: Helps to gather, route, and distribute messages between the producer and consumer.

Let's learn about some typical queue-based architecture patterns to get an idea of how they work.

Queuing chain pattern

A queuing chain pattern is applied when sequential processing needs to run on multiple systems that are linked together. Let's understand the *queuing chain pattern* using the example of an image-processing application. In an image-processing pipeline, sequential operations of capturing the image and storing it on a server, running a job to create different-resolution copies of the image, watermarking the image, and thumbnail generation are tightly linked to each other. A failure in one part can cause the entire operation to be disrupted.

You can use queues between various systems and jobs to remove a single point of failure and design true loosely coupled systems. The queuing chain pattern helps you to link different systems together and increase the number of servers that can process the messages in parallel. If there is no image to process, you can configure **auto scaling** to terminate the excess servers.

The following diagram shows a queuing chain pattern architecture. Here, the queue provided by AWS is called Amazon **Simple Queue Service (SQS)**:

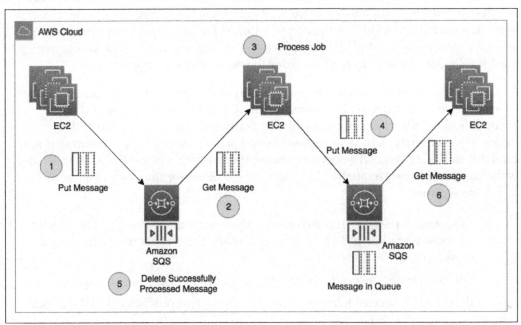

Figure 6.9: Queuing chain pattern architecture

The preceding architecture has the following steps:

1. As soon as the raw image is uploaded to the server, the application needs to watermark all of the images with the company's logo. Here, a fleet of Amazon EC2 servers is running batch jobs to watermark all the images and push the processed image into the Amazon SQS queue.

2. The second fleet of Amazon EC2 servers pulls the watermarked images from the Amazon SQS queue.

3. The second fleet of EC2 workers processes the image and creates multiple variations with different resolutions.

4. After encoding the images, the EC2 workers push the message into another Amazon SQS queue.

5. As the image is processed, the job deletes the message from the previous queue to make space.

6. The final fleet of EC2 servers gets encoded messages from the queue and creates thumbnails along with the copyright.

The benefits of this architecture are as follows:

*   You can use loosely coupled asynchronous processing to return responses quickly without waiting for another service acknowledgment.

*   You can structure the system through the loose coupling of Amazon EC2 instances or containers using Amazon SQS.

*   Even if the Amazon EC2 instance fails, a message remains in the queue service. This enables processing to be continued upon recovery of the server and creates a system that is robust to failure.

You may get fluctuations in application demand that can cause unexpected message loads. Automating your workload as per the queue message load will help you to handle any fluctuations. Let's learn more about using the *job observer pattern* to handle such automation next.

Job observer pattern

Queuing chain patterns help you design a loosely coupled architecture, but how will you handle workload spike? In case of request fluctuation, you need to adjust your processing power based on user demand, which can be addressed by the job observer pattern.

In the job observer pattern, you can create an auto scaling group, based upon the number of messages in the queue to process. The job observer pattern helps you to maintain performance through increasing or decreasing the number of server instances used in job processing.

The following diagram depicts the job observer pattern:

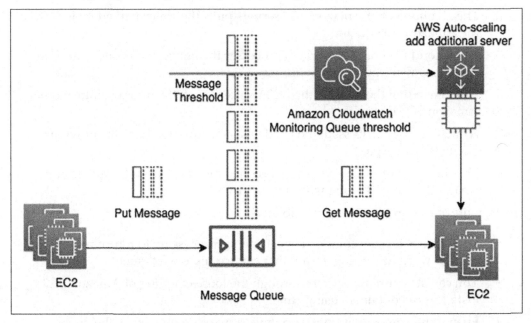

Figure 6.10: Job observer pattern architecture

In the preceding architecture, the first fleet of Amazon EC2 servers is on the left-hand side, running batch jobs and putting messages in the queue, for example, image metadata. The second fleet of EC2 servers on the right-hand side is consuming and processing those messages, for example, image encoding. As the message reaches a certain threshold, Amazon CloudWatch triggers auto scaling to add the additional server in the consumer fleet to speed up the job processing. Auto scaling also removes additional servers when the queue depth goes below the threshold.

The job observer pattern computes scale with job size, providing efficiency and cost savings. The job observer pattern architecture allows the job to be completed in a shorter timeframe. The process is resilient, which means job processing doesn't stop if a server fails.

While queue-based architecture provides loose coupling, it works mostly on the **Asynchronous Pull** method, where the consumer can pull messages from the queue when they are available.

Often, you need to drive communication between various architecture components where one event should trigger other events. Let's learn more about event-driven architecture in the next section.

Creating an event-driven architecture

Event-driven architecture helps you to chain a series of events together to complete a functional flow. For example, when you are making a payment to buy something on a website, you are expecting to get your order invoice generated and to get an email as soon as the payment is complete. Event-driven architecture helps to rope in all of these events so that making a payment can trigger another task to complete the order flow. Often, you will see message queues, which you learned about in the previous section, as the central point while talking about event-driven architecture. Event-driven architecture can also be based on the publisher/subscriber model or the event stream model.

Publisher/subscriber model

In the **publisher/subscriber (pub/sub)** model, when an event is published, a notification is sent to all subscribers, and each subscriber can take the necessary action as per their requirements of data processing. Let's take an example of a photo studio application, which enriches a photo with different filters and sends a notification to the user. The following architecture depicts a pub/sub model:

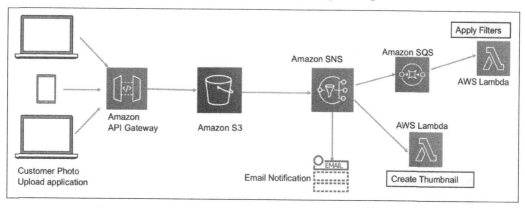

Figure 6.11: Photo studio application pub/sub event-driven architecture

In the preceding diagram, you will notice the following things:

1. The user first uploads the picture to an **Amazon S3** bucket using a web/ mobile application.

2. The **Amazon S3** bucket then sends a notification to Amazon **Simple Notification Service (SNS)**. **Amazon SNS** is a message topic with the following subscribers:

    • Here, the first subscriber is using the email service, and as soon as the photo upload is complete, an email is sent to the user

    • The second subscriber is using an **Amazon SQS** queue, which gets the message from the **Amazon SNS** topic and applies various filters in code written in AWS Lambda to improve the image quality

    • The third subscriber is using the direct **AWS Lambda** function, which creates the image thumbnail

In this architecture, Amazon S3 publishes the message to the SNS topic as a producer, which is consumed by multiple subscribers. Additionally, as soon as the message comes to SQS, it triggers an event for the Lambda function to process images.

Event stream model

In the event stream model, the consumer can read from the continuous flow of events coming from the producer. For example, you can use the event stream to capture the continuous flow of a clickstream log and also send an alert if there are any anomalies detected, as shown in the following architecture diagram:

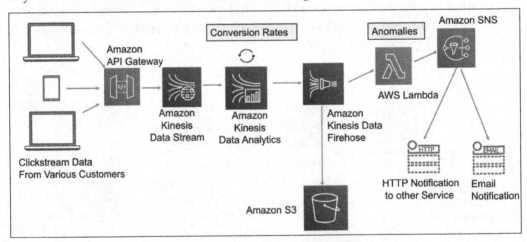

Figure 6.12: Clickstream analysis event stream architecture

Amazon Kinesis is a service that is used to ingest, process, and store continuous streaming data. In the preceding diagram, various customers clicking on e-commerce applications from web and mobile applications produce a stream of click events.

These clickstreams are sent to analytics applications using **Amazon API Gateway** for real-time analytics. In this analytics application, **Kinesis Data Analytics** calculates **Conversion Rates** over a certain period of time, for example, the number of people that ended up making a purchase in the last five minutes. After aggregating data in real time, **Amazon Kinesis Data Analytics** sends the results to **Amazon Kinesis Data Firehose**, which stores all the data files in **Amazon S3** storage for further processing as needed.

A Lambda function reads from the event stream and starts examining the data for **Anomalies**. As anomalies in the conversion rates are detected, the **AWS Lambda** function sends a notification on email for the campaign team to be notified. In this architecture, the event stream is occurring continuously, and **AWS Lambda** is reading from the stream for a specific event.

You should use event-driven architecture to decouple the producer and consumer and keep the architecture extendable so that a new consumer can be integrated at any time. This provides a highly scalable and distributed system with each subsystem having an independent view of events. However, you need to apply a mechanism to avoid duplicate processing and error message handling.

To achieve good application performance, caching is an important factor and it can be applied at every architecture layer and in pretty much any architecture component. Let's learn more about cache-based architecture in the next section.

Building a cache-based architecture

Caching is the process of temporarily storing data or files in an intermediary location between the requester and the permanent storage, for the purpose of making future requests faster and reducing network throughput. Caching increases the application speed and lowers the cost. It allows you to reuse previously retrieved data. To increase application performance, caching can be applied at various layers of the architecture, such as the web layer, application layer, data layer, and network layer.

Normally, the server's **random access memory (RAM)** and in-memory cache engines are utilized to support application caching. However, if caching is coupled to a local server, then the cache will not be persisting data, in case of a server crash. Now, most of the applications are in a distributed environment, so it's better to have a dedicated caching layer that should be independent of the application life cycle. If you applied horizontal scaling to your application, all servers should be able to access the centralized caching layer to achieve the best performance.

The following diagram depicts the mechanism of caching in various layers of solution architecture:

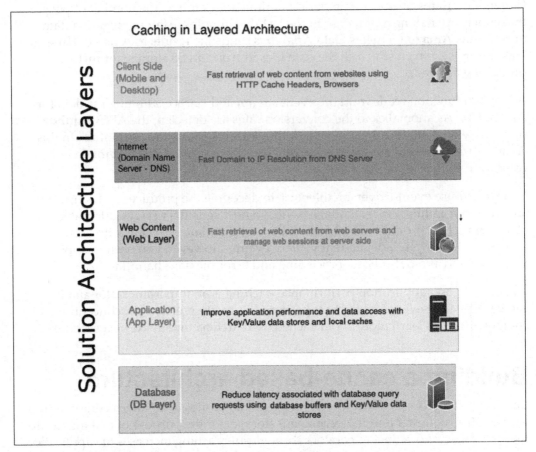

Figure 6.13: Caching at the architecture layers

As shown in the preceding diagram, the following are the caching mechanisms at each layer of architecture:

- **Client side**: Client-side caching is applied to user devices such as mobile and desktop. This caches the previously visited web content to respond faster to a subsequent request. Each browser has its own caching mechanism. HTTP caching makes the application faster by caching content at the local browser. The cache-control HTTP header defines browser caching policies for both the client request and server response. These policies define where the content should be cached and how long it will persist, which is known as **time to live (TTL)**. Cookies are another method used to store information at the client machine in order to respond to the browser faster.

- **DNS cache**: When a user types the website address over the internet, the public **Domain Name System (DNS)** server looks up the IP address. Caching this DNS resolution information will reduce the website's load time. DNS information can be cached to a local server or browser after the first request and any further requests to that website will be faster.

- **Web caching**: Much of the request involves retrieving web content such as images, video, and HTML pages. Caching these assets near to the user's location can provide a much faster response for a page load. This also eliminates disk read and server load time. A **content distribution network (CDN)** provides a network of edge locations where static content such as high-resolution images and videos can be cached. It's very useful for reading heavy applications such as games, blogs, e-commerce product catalog pages, and more. The user session contains lots of information regarding user preference and their state. It provides a great user experience to store the user's session in its own key-value store for quick user response.

- **Application caching**: At the application layer, caching can be applied to store the result of a complex repeated request to avoid business logic calculations and database hits. Overall, it improves application performance and reduces the load on the database and infrastructure.

- **Database caching**: Application performance highly depends upon speed and throughput provided by the database. Database caching allows you to increase database throughput significantly and lower data retrieval latency. A database cache can be applied in front of any kind of relational or non-relational database. Some database providers integrate caching, while applications handle local caching.

Redis and **Memcached** are the most popular caching engines. While Memcached is faster (it is good for low-structure data and stores data in a key-value format), Redis is a more persistent caching engine and is capable of handling complex data structures required for an application such as a gaming leaderboard; you will learn more details in the section *Memcached versus Redis* in this chapter. Let's learn about a few more caching design patterns.

Cache distribution pattern in a three-tier web architecture

Traditional web hosting architecture implements a standard three-tier web application model that separates the architecture into the presentation, application, and persistence layers.

As shown in the following architecture diagram, caching is applied at the web, application, and database layers:

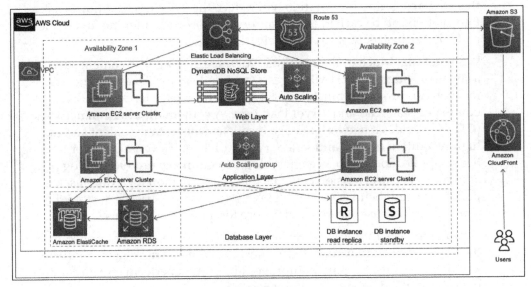

Figure 6.14: Cache distribution pattern architecture

One of the ways you can offload your web page is through caching. In caching patterns, your goal is to try to hit the backend as little as possible. You can write an application where you can cache images, JavaScript, or even full pages to provide a better experience for your users. As shown in the preceding diagram, caching is applied to the various layers of architecture:

- **Amazon Route 53** provides DNS services to simplify domain management and to help cache DNS-to-IP mapping.

- **Amazon S3** stores all static content such as high-resolution images and videos.

- **Amazon CloudFront** provides edge caching for high-volume content. It also uses these cache-control headers to determine how frequently it needs to check the origin for an updated version of that file.

- **Amazon DynamoDB** is used for session stores in which web applications cache to handle user sessions.

- **Elastic Load Balancing** spreads traffic to web server **Auto Scaling** groups in this diagram.

- **Amazon ElastiCache** provides caching services for the app, which removes the load from the database tier.

In general, you only cache static content; however, dynamic or unique content affects the performance of your application. Depending on the demand, you might still get some performance gain by caching the dynamic or unique content. Let's take a look at a more specific pattern.

Rename distribution pattern

When using a **CDN** such as Amazon CloudFront, you store frequently used data in an edge location near to the user for fast performance. Often, you set up **TTL** (**Time To Live**) in the CDN for your data, which means the edge location will not query back to the server for updated data until the TTL expires. TTL is the time that an object is stored in a caching system before it's deleted or refreshed. You may have situations where you need to update CDN cached content immediately, for example, if you need to correct the wrong product description.

In such a situation, you can't wait for the file's TTL to expire. The rename distribution pattern helps you to update the cache as soon as new changes are published so that the user can get updated information immediately. The following diagram shows the *rename distribution pattern*:

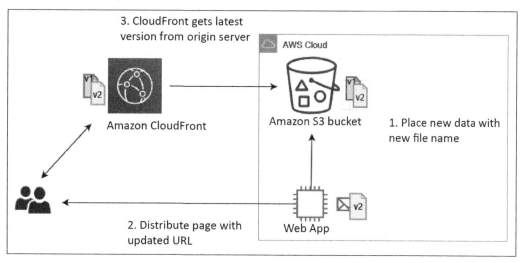

Figure 6.15: Rename distribution pattern architecture

As shown in the preceding diagram, using the rename distribution pattern with the cache distribution pattern helps to solve the update issue. With this pattern, instead of overwriting the file in the origin server and waiting for the TTL in CloudFront to expire, the server uploads the updated file with a new filename and then updates the web page with the new URL. When the user requests original content, CloudFront has to fetch it from the origin and can't serve the obsolete file that's already cached.

However, you have the option to invalidate the old file immediately, but that will cost more, so it's better to put a new version of the file for the CDN to pick immediately. Again, you have to update the URL in the application to pick up a new file, adding some overhead compared to the invalidation option. It would be best if you make a decision based on your business requirement and budget.

If you don't want to use a CDN for a user base distributed across a country, instead, you can use the proxy cache server. Let's learn more about it in the next section.

Cache proxy pattern

You can increase your application performance significantly by adding a cache layer. In a cache proxy pattern, static content or dynamic content is cached upstream of the web app server. As shown in the following architectural diagram, you have a caching layer in front of the web application cluster:

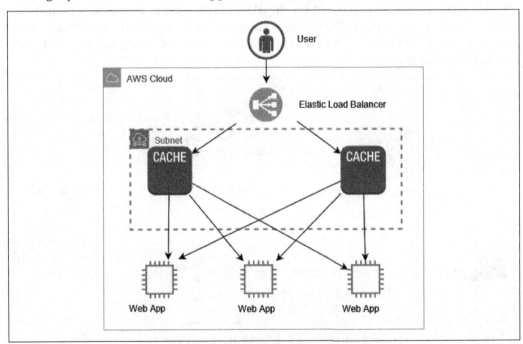

Figure 6.16: Cache proxy pattern architecture

In the preceding diagram, for high-performance delivery, cache content is delivered by the cache server. A few benefits of cache proxy patterns are as follows:

- Cache proxy patterns help you to deliver content using the cache, which means no modification is needed at the web server or application server level.

- They reduce the load of content generation for dynamic content in particular.
- You have the flexibility to set up a cache at the browser level such as in HTTP headers, URLs, cookies, and more. Alternatively, you can cache information in the cache layer if you don't want to store it at the browser level.

In the cache proxy pattern, you need to make sure that you maintain multiple copies of the cache to avoid the single point of failure. Sometimes, you may want to serve your static content from both the server and CDN, each of which requires a different approach. Let's deep dive into this hybrid situation in the next section.

Rewrite proxy pattern

Sometimes, you want to change the access destinations of static website content such as images and videos, but don't want to make changes to the existing systems. You can achieve this by providing a proxy server using rewrite proxy patterns. To change the destination of static content to other storage such as a content service or internet storage, you can use a proxy server in front of the web server fleet. As shown in the following architecture diagram, you have a proxy server in front of your application layer, which helps to change the content delivery destination without modifying the actual application:

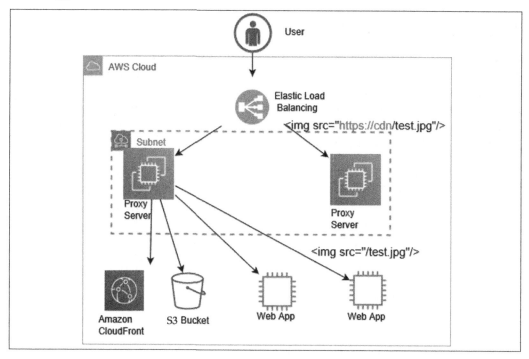

Figure 6.17: Rewrite proxy pattern architecture

As shown in the preceding diagram, to accomplish a rewrite proxy pattern, place the proxy server in front of the currently running system. You can construct a proxy server using software such as **Apache NGINX**. The following are the steps to build a rewrite proxy pattern:

1. Put a running proxy server on an EC2 instance, which is able to overwrite the content between the **load balancer** and the storage service such as **Amazon S3**, which stores the static content

2. Add to the proxy server rules for overwriting URLs within the content. These rules will help **Elastic Load Balancing (ELB)** to point to a new location, as shown in the preceding diagram, which redirects the proxy server rule from `https://cdn/test.jpg` to `/test.jpg`

3. As required, apply auto scaling to the proxy servers by configuring a number of minimum and maximum proxy servers as per the application load

In this section, you learned about various ways to handle caching for static content distribution over the network. However, caching at the application layer is very important for improving application performance for the overall user experience. Let's learn more about the app caching pattern to handle dynamic user data delivery performance.

App caching pattern

When it comes to applying caching to applications, you want to add a cache engine layer between your application servers and the database. The app caching pattern allows you to reduce the load on the database as the most frequent query is served from the caching layer. The *app caching pattern* improves overall application and database performance. As shown in the following diagram, you can see the caching layer applied between the application layer and the database layer:

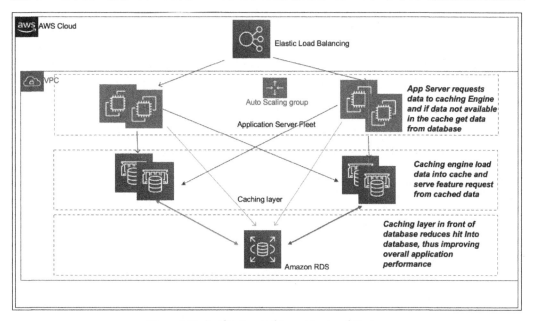

Figure 6.18: Application caching pattern architecture

As shown in the preceding diagram, based on your *data access pattern*, you can use either **lazy caching** or **write-through**. In lazy caching, the cache engine checks whether the data is in the cache and, if not, gets it from the database and keeps it in the cache to serve future requests. Lazy caching is also called the **cache aside pattern**.

In the **write-through** method, data is written in the cache and in the data store at the same time. If the data gets lost from the cache, then it can get it again from the database. Write-through is used mainly in application-to-application situations where users are writing a product review (which always needs to load on the product page). Let's learn more about the popular caching engines *Redis* and *Memcached*.

Memcached versus Redis

Redis and Memcached are two popular caching engines used in application design. Often, the Redis cache engine is required for more complex application caching needs such as creating a leaderboard for a game. However, Memcached is more high-performing and is helpful for handling heavy application loads. Each caching engine has its own pros and cons. Let's take a look at the major differences between them, which will help you to make a decision of which to use:

Memcached	Redis
Offers multithreading	Single-threaded
Able to use more CPU cores for faster processing	Unable to utilize multi-core processor, which results in comparatively slow performance
Supports key-value style data	Supports complex and advanced data structures
Lacks data persistence; loses the data stored in cache memory in the event of a crash	Data can persist using built-in read replicas with failover
Easy maintenance	More complexity involved owing to the need to maintain the cluster
Good to cache flat strings such as flat HTML pages, serialized JSON, and more	Good to create a cache for a gaming leaderboard, a live voting app, and more

Overall, if you need to decide which engine to use, base it on a use case that can justify using Redis or Memcached. Memcached is simple and has lower maintenance, and it is typically preferred when your cache doesn't need the advanced features that Redis offers. However, if you need the advantage of data persistence, advanced data types, or any of the other features listed, then Redis is the best solution.

When implementing caching, it's essential to understand the validity of data that needs to be cached. If the cache hit rate is high, that means the data is available in the cache when required. For a higher cache hit ratio, offload the database by reducing direct queries; this also improves the overall application performance. A cache miss occurs when data is not present in the cache, which increases the load in the database. The cache is not a large data store, so you need to set the TTL and evict the cache as per your application needs.

As you have seen in this section, there are multiple benefits of applying caches, including application performance improvement, the ability to provide predictable performance, and the reduction in database cost.

Let's learn about some more application-based architecture that demonstrates the principle of loose coupling and constraint handling.

Understanding the circuit breaker pattern

It's common for a distributed system to make a call to other downstream services, and the call could fail or hang without response. You will often see code that retries the failed call several times. The problem with a remote service is that it could take minutes or even hours to correct, and an immediate retry might end up in another failure. As a result, end users wait longer to get an error response while your code retries several times. This retry function would consume the threads, and it could potentially induce a cascading failure.

The circuit breaker pattern is about understanding the health of downstream dependencies. It detects when those dependencies are unhealthy and implements logic to gracefully fail requests until it detects that they are healthy again. The circuit breaker can be implemented using a persistence layer to monitor healthy and unhealthy requests over the past request interval.

If a defined percentage of requests observe an unhealthy behavior over the past interval or over a total count of exceptions, regardless of percentage, the circuit is marked as open. In such a situation, all requests throw exceptions rather than integrate with the dependency for a defined timeout period. Once the timeout period has subsided, a small percentage of requests try to integrate with the downstream dependency, to detect when health has returned. Once a sufficient percentage of requests are healthy again over an interval, or no errors are observed, the circuit closes again, and all the requests are allowed to integrate as they usually would thoroughly.

The implementation decisions involve the state machine to track/share the healthy/ unhealthy request counts. The states of services can be maintained in DynamoDB, Redis/Memcached, or another low-latency persistence store.

Implementing the bulkheads pattern

Bulkheads are used in ships to create separate watertight compartments that serve to limit the effect of failure, ideally preventing the ship from sinking. If water breaks through the hull in one compartment, the bulkheads prevent it from flowing into other compartments, limiting the scope of the failure.

The same concept is useful to limit the scope of failure in the architecture of large systems, where you want to partition your system to decouple dependencies between services. The idea is that one failure should not cause the entire system to fail, as shown in the following diagram:

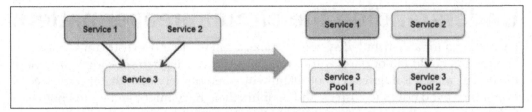

Figure 6.19: Bulkhead pattern

In the bulkhead pattern, it's better to isolate the element of the application into the pool for service, which has a high dependency; so, if one fails, others continue to serve upstream services. In the preceding diagram, **Service 3** is partitioned into two pools from a single service. Here, if **Service 3** fails, then the impact of either **Service 1** or **Service 2** depends on their dependency on the pool, but the entire system does not go down. The following are the major points to consider when introducing the bulkhead pattern in your design, especially for the shared service model:

- Save part of the ship, which means your application should not shut down due to the failure of one service.

- Decide whether less-efficient use of resources is okay. Performance issues in one partition should not impact the overall application.

- Pick a useful granularity. Don't make the service pools too small; make sure they are able to handle application load.

- Monitor each service partition performance and adhere to the SLA. Make sure all of the moving parts are working together and test the overall application when one service pool is down.

You should define a service partition for each business or technical requirement. You should use this pattern to prevent the application from cascading failure and isolating critical consumers from the standard consumer.

Often, legacy application servers have a configuration with hardcoded **Internet Protocol (IP)** addresses or **Domain Name Server (DNS)** names. Making any server change for modernization and upgrade requires making changes in the application and revalidating it. In these cases, you don't want to change the server address. Let's learn how to handle such a situation with a floating IP in the next section.

Creating a floating IP pattern

It's common that monolithic applications have lots of dependencies on the server where they are deployed. Often, application configuration and code have hardcoded parameters based on the server DNS name and IP address. Hardcoded IP configuration creates challenges if you want to bring up a new server in case of an issue with the original server. Additionally, you don't want to bring down the entire application for the upgrade, which may cause significant downtime.

To handle such a situation, you need to create a new server keeping the same server IP address and DNS name. This can be achieved by moving the network interface from a problematic instance to the new server. The network interface is generally based on a **Network Interface Card** (**NIC**), which facilitates communication between servers over a network. It can be in the form of hardware or software. Moving the network interface means that now your new server assumes the identity of the old server. With that, your application can live with the same DNS and IP address. It also allows easy rollback by moving the network interface to the original instance.

The public cloud (for example, AWS) made it easy by providing an **Elastic IP** (**EIP**) and **Elastic Network Interface** (**ENI**). If your instance fails and you need to push traffic to another instance with the same public IP address, then you can move the EIP address from one server to another, as shown in the following architecture diagram:

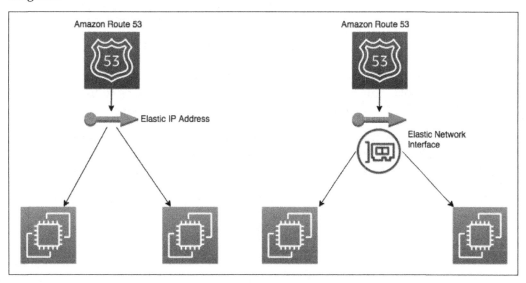

Figure 6.20: Floating IP and interface pattern

Since you are moving EIP, the DNS may not need to update. EIP can move your server's public IP across instances. If you need to move both public and private IP addresses, then use a more flexible approach such as ENI, as shown on the right of the preceding diagram. ENI can move across instances, and you can use the same public and private address for traffic routing or application upgrades.

So far, you have learned about multiple architecture patterns where applications are deployed in the virtual machine. However, in many cases, you may not be able to utilize the virtual machine fully. To optimize your utilization further, you can choose to deploy your application in containers. Containers are most suitable for microservice deployment. Let's learn more about container-based deployment in the next section.

Deploying an application with a container

As many programming languages are invented and technologies evolve, this creates new challenges. There are different application stacks that require different hardware and software deployment environments. Often, there is a need to run applications across different platforms and migrate from one to another platform. Solutions require something that can run anything everywhere and is consistent, lightweight, and portable.

Just as shipping containers standardized the transport of freight goods, software containers standardize the transport of applications. Docker creates a container that contains everything a software application would need to be able to run all of its files, such as filesystem structure, daemons, libraries, and application dependencies. Containers isolate software from its surrounding development and staging environments. This helps to reduce conflicts between teams running different software on the same infrastructure.

VMs isolate at the operating system level, and containers isolate at the kernel level. This isolation allows several applications to run on a single-host operating system, and yet still have their filesystem, storage, RAM, libraries, and, mostly, their own *view* of the system:

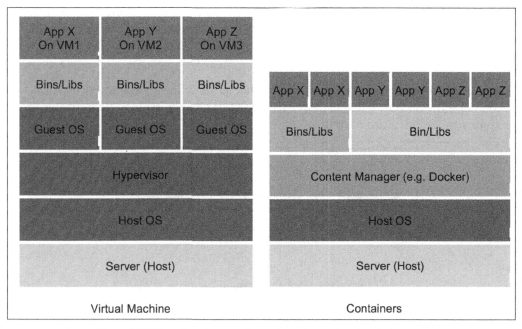

Figure 6.21: Virtual machines and containers for application deployment

As shown in the preceding diagram, multiple applications are deployed in a single virtual machine using containers. Each application has its runtime environment, so you can run many individual applications while keeping the same number of servers. Containers share a machine's operating system kernel. They start instantly and use less computing time and RAM. Container images are constructed from the filesystem layers and share standard files. Shared resourcing minimizes disk usage, and container image downloads are much faster. Let's take a look at why containers are becoming more popular, along with their benefits.

The benefit of containers

Customers often ask these questions when it comes to containers:

- Why do we need containers when we have instances?
- Don't instances already provide us with a level of isolation from the underlying hardware?

While the preceding questions are valid, several benefits accrue from using a system such as **Docker**. One of the key benefits of Docker is that it allows you to fully utilize your virtual machine resources by hosting multiple applications (on distinct ports) in the same instance.

Docker uses certain features of the Linux kernel, namely kernel namespaces and groups, to achieve complete isolation between each Docker process, as indicated in the following architecture diagram:

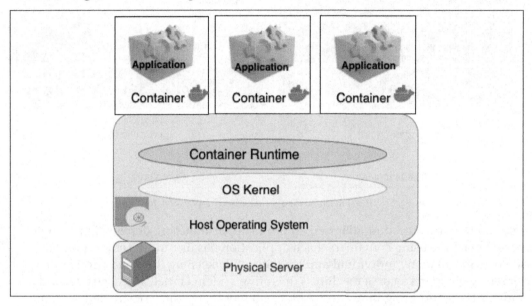

Figure 6.22: Container layer in application infrastructure

As shown in the preceding diagram, it's possible to run two or more applications that require different versions of the Java runtime on the same machine, as each Docker container has its version of Java and the associated libraries installed. In turn, the container layer in the application infrastructure makes it easier to decompose your applications into microservices that can run side by side on the same instance. Containers have the following benefits:

- **Portable runtime application environment**: Containers provide platform-independent capabilities, where you build your application once and deploy it anywhere regardless of the underlying operating system
- **Faster development and deployment cycles**: Modify the application and run it anywhere with quick boot time, typically within seconds
- **Package dependencies and application in a single artifact**: Package the code, library, and dependencies together to run the application in any operating system

- **Run different application versions**: Applications with different dependencies run simultaneously in a single server

- **Everything can be automated**: Container management and deployment are done through scripting, which helps to save cost and human error

- **Better resource utilization**: Containers provide efficient scaling and high availability and multiple copies of the same microservice container can be deployed across servers for your application

- **Easy to manage the security aspect**: Containers are platform-specific rather than application-specific

Container deployment is becoming very popular due to its benefits. There are multiple ways to orchestrate containers. Let's look at container deployment in more detail next.

Container deployment

Complex applications with multiple microservices can be quickly deployed using container deployment. The container makes it easier to build and deploy the application more quickly as the environment is the same. Build the container in development mode, push to test, and then release to production. For hybrid cloud environments, container deployment is very useful. Containers make it easier to keep environments consistent across microservices. As microservices aren't always very resource-consuming, they can be placed together in a single instance to reduce cost.

Sometimes, customers have short workflows that require a temporary environment setup. Those environments may be queue systems or continuous integration jobs, which don't always utilize server resources efficiently. Container orchestration services such as Docker and Kubernetes can be a workaround, allowing them to push and pop containers onto the instance.

Docker's lightweight container virtualization platform provides tools to manage your applications. Its standalone application can be installed on any computer to run containers. Kubernetes is a container orchestration service that works with Docker and another container platform. Kubernetes allows automated container provisioning and handles security, networking, and scaling aspects diligently.

Containers help the enterprise to create more cloud native workloads, and public cloud providers such as AWS extend services to manage Docker containers and Kubernetes.

The following diagram shows Docker's container management using Amazon **Elastic Container Service (ECS)**, providing a fully managed elastic service to automate the scaling and orchestration of Docker containers:

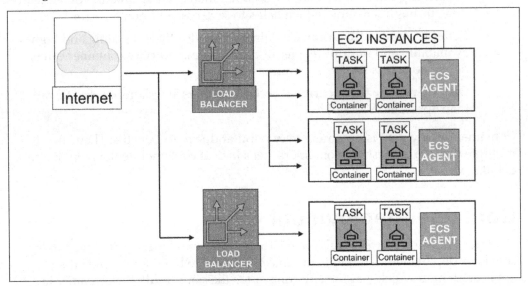

Figure 6.23: Container deployment architecture

In the preceding diagram, multiple containers are deployed in a single Amazon EC2 virtual machine, which is managed through Amazon ECS and facilitates the agent communication service and cluster management. All user requests are distributed using a load balancer among the containers. Similarly, AWS provides Amazon **Elastic Kubernetes Service (EKS)** to manage containers using Kubernetes.

Containers are a broad topic, and, as a solution architect, you need to be familiar with all of the available options. This section provides an overview of containers. However, you will need to deep dive further if you choose to utilize containers for your microservice deployment. Let's look at a container-based architecture in the next section.

Building container-based architecture

As you learned in the previous section, containerization helps create environments for repeatable and scalable applications. To start container adoption, you need to identify a pilot workload managed through container orchestrations. You can take existing microservice components and deploy them in containers. After identifying gaps and operational needs, you can define a migration strategy to move your workload to containers.

Like any other changes, container migrations come with challenges if your applications are not designed to run in a container environment. As applications often persist files to local storage and make stateful sessions, container migration needs to address these requirements.

For container platforms, you can make choices; you can choose Docker, OpenShift, Kubernetes, and so on. However, Kubernetes is becoming an increasingly popular open-source container orchestrator. Public cloud vendors such as AWS provide a platform to manage containers such as Amazon ECS for Docker and Amazon EKS for Kubernetes. These cloud services provide a control plane to choose various compute options to select self-managed nodes, managed nodes, or serverless options with AWS Fargate. The following architecture diagram shows running a stateful service on Amazon EKS in your programming languages of choice, such as Java or .NET. Given the architecture, you can manage the session state in a Redis database.

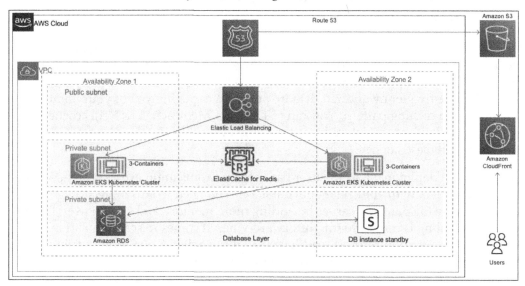

Figure 6.24: Deploying a stateful application on a container

As you can see in the preceding diagram, the container-based architecture includes the following components:

- An Amazon **virtual private cloud** (**VPC**) with one public subnet for the load balancer, and two private subnets for the application and database deployment

- An application load balancer to access the website that is running inside the containers

- An Amazon EKS cluster with a managed node group in Kubernetes. Those nodes run multiple application containers

- An Amazon ElastiCache Redis database to stores the user sessions state

The above architecture helps you to scale the application by saving the user sessions in a Redis database. This solution requires changing the application code, and there are situations where this is not an option.

As of now, you have learned about various architecture patterns focusing on application development. Everyone has to agree that data is an integral part of any architecture design, and most of the architecture revolves around collecting, storing, and processing the visualization of data. Let's learn more about handling data in application architecture in the next section.

Database handling in application architecture

Data is always at the center of any application development, and scaling data has always been challenging. Handling data efficiently improves application latency and performance. In the previous section, *Building cache-based architecture*, you learned how to handle frequently queried data by putting a cache in front of your database under the app caching pattern. You can put either a Memcached or Redis cache in front of your database, which reduces the many hits on the database and results in improving database latency.

In application deployment, as the user base of your application grows, you need to handle more data with your relational database. You need to add more storage or vertically scale the database server by adding more memory and CPU power. Often, horizontal scaling is not very straightforward when it comes to scaling relational databases. If your application is read-heavy, you can achieve horizontal scaling by creating a read replica. Route all read requests to database read replicas, while keeping the master database node to serve write and update requests. As a read replica has asynchronous replication, it can add some lag time. You should choose the read replica option if your application can tolerate some milliseconds of latency. You can use read replicas to offload reporting.

You can use database sharding to create a multi-master for your relational database and inject the concept of horizontal scaling. The sharding technique is used to improve writing performance with multiple database servers. Essentially, databases are prepared and divided with identical structures using appropriate table columns as *keys* to distribute the writing processes. As demonstrated in the following architecture diagram, the customer database can be divided into multiple shards:

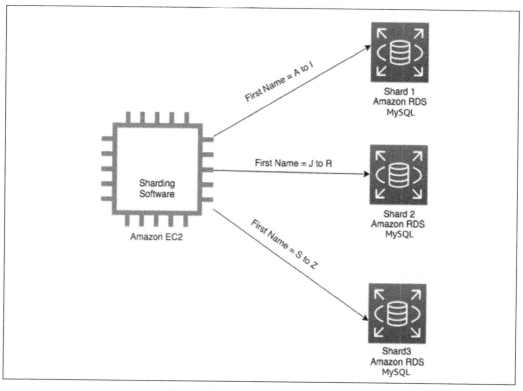

Figure 6.25: Relational database sharding

As shown in the preceding diagram, without *shards*, all data resides in one partition; for example, the user's first name starts with A to Z in one database. With sharding, data is split into large chunks called shards. For example, the users' first names beginning with A to I are in one database, J to R in another database, and S to Z in a third database. In many circumstances, sharding gives you higher performance and better operating efficiency.

 You can use Amazon RDS in sharding backend databases. Install sharding software such as MySQL combined with a Spider storage engine on an Amazon EC2 instance. Then, first, prepare multiple RDS databases and use them as the sharding backend databases.

However, what if your master database instance goes down? In that case, you need to maintain high availability for your database. Let's take a closer look at database failover.

High-availability database pattern

For the high availability of your application, it is critical to keep your database up and running all of the time. As horizontal scaling is not a straightforward option in the relational database, it creates additional challenges. To achieve high database availability, you can have a standby replica of the master database instance, as shown in the following diagram:

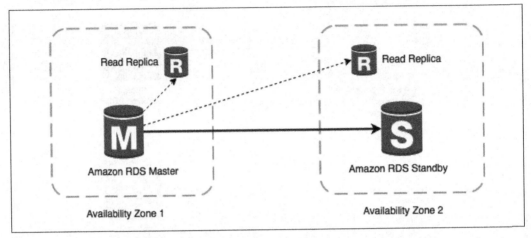

Figure 6.26: High-availability database pattern

As shown in the preceding diagram, if the master instance goes down, your application server switches over to the standby instance. A read replica takes the load off of the master instance to handle latency. Master and standby are located in different **availability zones**, so your application will still be up even when an entire availability zone is down. This architecture also helps to achieve zero downtime, which may be caused during the database maintenance window. When a master instance is down for maintenance, the application can failover to a secondary standby instance and continue serving user requests.

For the purpose of disaster recovery, you will want to define the database backup and archival strategy, depending on your application's **recovery point objective (RPO)** of how frequently you want to take backups. If your RPO is 30 minutes, it means your organization can only tolerate 30 minutes worth of data loss. In that case, you should take a backup every half an hour. While storing the backup, you need to determine how long the data can be stored for customer query purposes. You may want to store data for six months as an active backup and then in an archival store as per the compliance requirement.

Consider how quickly you might need to access your backup and determine the type of network connection needed to meet your backup and recovery requirements as per the company **recovery time objective (RTO)**.

For example, if your company's RTO is 60 minutes, it means you should have enough network bandwidth to retrieve and restore your backup within an hour. Also, define whether you are backing up snapshots of complete systems or volumes attached to systems.

You may also need to classify your data, for example, if it has customer-sensitive information such as email, addresses, personally identifiable information, and more. You need to define the data encryption strategy accordingly. You will learn more about data security in *Chapter 8, Security Considerations*.

You can also consider migrating from an RDBMS to a NoSQL database, depending upon your application's growth and complexity. NoSQL can provide you with greater scalability, management, performance, and reliability than most relational databases. However, the process of migrating to NoSQL from an RDBMS can be time-consuming and labor-intensive.

There is lots of data to process in any application, for example, clickstream data, application log data, rating and review data, social media data, and more. Analyzing these datasets and getting insight can help you to grow your organization exponentially. You will learn more about these use cases and patterns in *Chapter 13, Data Engineering for Solution Architecture*. As of now, you have learned about the best practices to design a solution architecture. Let's learn about some anti-patterns, which should be avoided, in the next section.

Avoiding anti-patterns in solution architecture

In this chapter, you have learned about a different way of designing solution architecture with various design patterns. Often, teams can drift away from best practices due to timeline pressure or the unavailability of resources. You always need to give special attention to the following architecture design anti-patterns:

- In an anti-pattern (an example of a poorly designed system), scaling is done reactively and manually. When application servers reach their full capacity with no more room, users are prevented from accessing the application. On user complaints, the admin finds out that the servers are at their full capacity and starts launching a new instance to take some of the load off. Unfortunately, there is always a few minutes' lag between the instance launch and its availability. During this period, users are not able to access the application. You should take a proactive approach and use auto scaling to add additional processing power when servers reach a certain threshold like 60% CPU utilization or 60% of memory utilization.

- With anti-patterns, automation is missing. When application servers crash, the admin manually launches and configures the new server and notifies the users manually. Detecting unhealthy resources and launching replacement resources can be automated, and you can even notify when resources are changed.

- With anti-patterns, the server is kept for a long time with hardcoded IP addresses, which prevents flexibility. Over time, different servers end up in different configurations and resources are running when they are not needed. You should keep all of the servers identical and should have the ability to switch to a new IP address. You should automatically terminate any unused resources.

- With anti-patterns, an application is built in a monolithic way, where all layers of the architecture including web, application, and data layers are tightly coupled and server dependent. If one server crashes, it brings down the entire application. You should keep the application and web layers independent by adding a load balancer in between. If one of the app servers goes down, the load balancer automatically starts directing all of the traffic to the other healthy servers.

- With anti-patterns, the application is server bound, and the servers communicate directly with each other. User authentication and sessions are stored in the server locally and all static files are served from the local server. You should choose to create a service-oriented RESTful architecture, where the services talk to each other using a standard protocol such as HTTP. User authentication and sessions should be stored in low-latency distributed storage so that the application can be scaled horizontally. The static asset should be stored in centralized object storage that is decoupled from the server.

- With anti-patterns, a single type of database is used for all kinds of needs. You are using a relational database for all needs, which introduces performance and latency issues. You should use the right storage for the right need, such as the following:

  - NoSQL to store the user session
  - Cache data store for low-latency data availability
  - Data warehouse for reporting needs
  - Relational database for transactional data

- With anti-patterns, you will find a single point of failure by having a single database instance to serve the application. Wherever possible, eliminate single points of failure from your architectures. Create a secondary server (standby) and replicate the data. If the primary database server goes offline, the secondary server can pick up the load.

- With anti-patterns, static content such as high-resolution images and videos are served directly from the server without any caching. You should consider using a CDN to cache heavy content near the user location, which helps to improve page latency and reduce page load time.

- With anti-patterns, you can find security loopholes that open server access without a fine-grained security policy. You should always apply the principle of least privilege, which means starting with no access and only giving access to the required user group.

The preceding points provide some of the most common anti-patterns. Throughout this book, you will learn the best practices of how to adopt them in solution design.

Summary

In this chapter, you learned about various design patterns by applying the techniques from *Chapter 3*, *Attributes of the Solution Architecture*, and *Chapter 4*, *Principles of Solution Architecture Design*. First, you built the architecture design foundation from a multilayer architecture with a reference architecture from three-tier web application architecture. You learned how to design a multi-tenant architecture on top of a three-tier architecture, which can provide a SaaS kind of offering. You learned how to isolate multi-tenant architecture at the database label, schema level, and table level as per customer and organization needs.

User state management is very critical for complex applications such as finance, e-commerce, travel booking, and more. You learned about the difference between stateful and stateless applications and their benefits. You also learned how to create a stateless application with a persistent layer of the database for session management. You learned about the two most popular SOA patterns, SOAP-based and RESTful-based patterns, along with their benefits. You looked at a reference architecture of an e-commerce website based on SOA and learned how to apply the principles of loose coupling and scaling.

You learned about serverless architecture and how to design a secure survey delivery architecture that is entirely serverless. You also learned about microservice architecture using the example of a serverless real-time voting application, which builds on the microservice pattern. For more loose coupling designs, you learned about the queuing chain and job observer patterns, which provide loosely coupled pipelines to process messages in parallel. You learned about the pub/sub and event stream models to design event-driven architecture.

It's not possible to achieve your desired performance without applying caching. You learned about various cache patterns to apply to caches at the client side, content distribution, web layer, application layer, and database layer.

You learned about architecture patterns to handle failure such as a circuit breaker to handle the downstream service failure scenario and the bulkhead pattern to handle complete service failure. You learned about floating IP patterns to change servers without changing their address in failure situations to minimize downtime.

You learned about the various techniques of handling data in an application and how to make sure your database is highly available to serve your application. Finally, you learned about various architecture anti-patterns and how to replace them using best practices.

While in this chapter you learned about various architecture patterns, in the next chapter, you will learn about architecture design principles for performance optimization. Additionally, you will deep dive into technology selection in the areas of computing, storage, databases, and networking, which can help to improve your application's performance.

Join our book's Discord space

Join the book's Discord workspace for a monthly *Ask me Anything* session with the authors: https://packt.link/SAHandbook

Performance Considerations

In this era of fast internet, users expect very high-performance applications. There have been experiments that show that every second of application load delay causes a significant loss in an organization's revenue. Therefore, the application's performance is one of the most critical attributes of solution design that can impact your product adoption growth.

In the previous chapter, you learned about various solution architecture design patterns that can be used to solve a complex business problem. In this chapter, you will understand the best practices to optimize your application for optimal performance. You will learn various design principles that you can use to optimize the solution architecture's performance. Here, performance needs to be optimized at every layer and in every component of the architecture.

You will understand how to choose the right technology at various layers of your architecture to improve your application's performance continuously. You will learn how to follow the best practices of performance optimization in this chapter. We will focus on the following topics in particular:

- Design principles for architecture performance
- Technology selection for performance optimization
- Performance monitoring

By the end of the chapter, you will understand important attributes of performance improvement, such as latency, throughput, and concurrency. You will be able to make better decisions regarding your choice of technology, which can help you to improve performance at the various layers of architecture, such as compute, storage, database, and networking.

Design principles for architecture performance

Architectural performance efficiency focuses on using application infrastructure and resources to meet increasing demand and technology evaluation. Technology vendors and open-source communities continuously work to improve the performance of applications. Often, large enterprises continue to work on legacy programming languages and technologies because of fear of changing and taking risks. As technology evolves, it often addresses critical performance issues, and the advancement of technology in your application helps improve application performance.

Many large public cloud providers, such as **Amazon Web Services (AWS)**, Microsoft Azure, and **Google Cloud Platform (GCP)**, offer technology as a service. This makes it easier to adopt complex technologies more efficiently with minimal effort—for example, you might use storage as a service to manage a massive amount of data or a NoSQL database as a managed service to provide high-performance scalability to your application.

Now organizations can utilize a **content distribution network (CDN)** to store heavy image and video data near user locations to reduce network latency and improve performance. With Edge locations, it becomes easier to deploy workloads closer to your user base, which helps to optimize application performance by reducing latency over the network.

As servers virtualize, you can be more agile and experiment with your application, and you can apply a high degree of automation. Agility helps you experiment and determine what technology and method are best suited for your application workload. For example, you can choose if your server deployment should go for virtual machines, containers, or use serverless with AWS Lambda, a **Function as a Service (FaaS)**. Let's look at some vital design principles to consider for your workload performance optimization.

Reducing latency

Latency can be a significant factor in your product adoption, as users are looking for faster applications. It doesn't matter where your users are located, you need to provide a reliable service for your product to grow. You may not achieve zero latency, but the goal should be to reduce the response time to within the user tolerance limit.

Latency is the time delay between the user sending a request and receiving the desired response.

The following diagram shows an example where it takes 600ms for a client to send a request to the server and 900ms for the server to respond, which introduces a total latency of 1.5 seconds (1500ms):

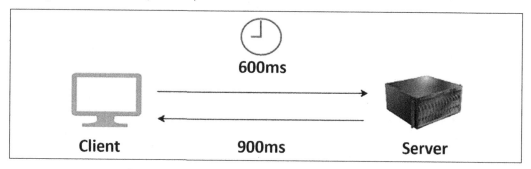

Figure 7.1: Request-response latency in a client-server model

Now, any application needs to access the internet to have a diverse set of global users. These users expect consistency in performance, regardless of their geographical location. It is sometimes challenging, as it takes time to move data over the network from one part of the world to another.

Network latency can be caused by various factors, such as the **network transmission medium**, **router hops**, and **network propagation**. Often, a request that is sent over the internet hops over multiple routers, which adds latency. Enterprises commonly use their fiber-optic line to set up connectivity between their corporate network and cloud, which helps avoid inconsistency.

In addition to the problems caused by the network, latency can occur in various components of the architecture. Your compute server can have latency issues at the infrastructure level due to memory and processor problems, where the data transfer between the CPU and RAM is *slow*. The disk can have latency due to slow read and write processes. Latency in a **hard disk drive (HDD)** is dependent on the time it takes to select a disk memory sector to come around and position itself under the head for reading and writing.

The disk memory sector is the physical location of data in the memory disk. In an HDD, data is distributed in memory sectors during write operations, as the disk is continuously rotating, so data can be written randomly. During the read operation, the head needs to wait for the rotation to bring it to the disk memory sector.

At the database level, latency can be caused by slow data reads and writes from the database due to hardware bottlenecks or slow query processing. Taking the database load off by distributing the data with partitioning and sharding can help to reduce latency.

There could be an issue with transaction processing from code that needs to be handled using garbage collection and multithreading at the application level. Achieving low latency means *higher throughput*, as latency and throughput are directly related, so let's learn more about throughput.

Improving throughput

Network throughput is the quantity of data sent and received at a given time. At the same time, latency is defined when the user initiates a request in the application and gets the response. When it comes to networks, *bandwidth* plays an important role.

 Bandwidth determines the maximum amount of data that can get transferred over the network.

Throughput and latency have a direct relationship as they work together. Lower latency means high throughput as more data can transfer in less time. To understand this better, let's take the analogy of a country's transportation infrastructure.

Let's say that highways with lanes are network pipelines and cars are data packets. Suppose a given highway has 16 lanes between 2 cities. Not all vehicles can reach the destination at the desired time; they may get delayed because of traffic congestion, lanes closing, or accidents. Here, latency determines how fast a car can travel from one city to another, while throughput tells us how many cars can reach their destinations. For a network, using full bandwidth is challenging because of errors and traffic congestion.

Network throughput is measured by the amount of data sent over the network in **bits per second (bps)**. Network bandwidth is the maximum size of the network pipeline that it can process. The following diagram illustrates the amount of data transferred between the client and the server:

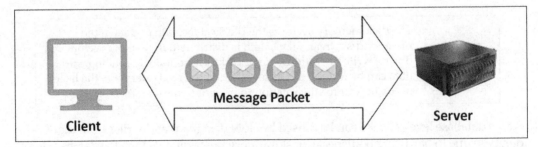

Figure 7.2: Throughput in a network

In addition to the network, throughput is applicable at the disk level. Disk throughput is determined by a factor of **input/output operations per second (IOPS)** and the amount of data requested (I/O size). Disk throughput is determined in **megabytes per second (Mbps)** using the following formula:

$$\text{Average I/O size} * \text{I/OPS} = \text{Throughput in MB/s}$$

So, if your disk IOPS is 20,000 and the I/O size is 4 KB (4,096 bytes), then the throughput will be 81.9 MB/s (20,000 x 4,096 and converted from bytes to megabytes).

I/O requests and disk latency have a direct relationship. **I/O** means write and read, respectively, while **disk latency** is the time taken by each I/O request to receive the response from the disk. Latency is measured in milliseconds and should be minimal. It is impacted by disk **revolutions per minute (RPM)**. **IOPS** is the number of operations that the disk can serve per second.

At the operating system level, throughput is determined by the amount of data transfer between the CPU and RAM per second. At the database level, throughput is determined by the number of transactions a database can process per second. At the application level, your code needs to handle transactions that can be processed every second by managing the application memory with the help of garbage collection handling and efficient use of the memory cache.

When you look at latency, throughput, and bandwidth, there is another factor called concurrency, which applies to the various components of architecture and helps to improve application performance. Let's learn more about concurrency.

Handling concurrency

Concurrency is a critical factor for solution design as you want your application to process multiple tasks at a time. For example, your application needs to handle multiple users simultaneously and process their requests in the background. Another example is when your web user interface needs to collect and process web cookie data to understand user interaction with the product while showing users their profile information and the product catalog. Concurrency is about doing multiple tasks at the same time.

People often get confused between parallelism and concurrency by thinking they are both the same thing; however, concurrency is different from parallelism. In parallelism, your application divides an enormous task into smaller subtasks, which it can process in parallel with a dedicated resource for each subtask. In concurrency, however, an application processes multiple tasks simultaneously by utilizing shared resources among the threads.

The application can switch from one task to another during processing, which means that the critical section of code needs to be managed using **locks** and **semaphores**.

As illustrated in the following diagram, concurrency is like a traffic light signal where the traffic flow switches between all four lanes to keep traffic going. As there is a single thread along which you should pass all traffic, processing in other lanes has to stop while traffic in one lane is in the *clearing process*. In the case of parallelism, there is a parallel lane available, and all cars can run in parallel without interrupting each other, as shown in the following diagram:

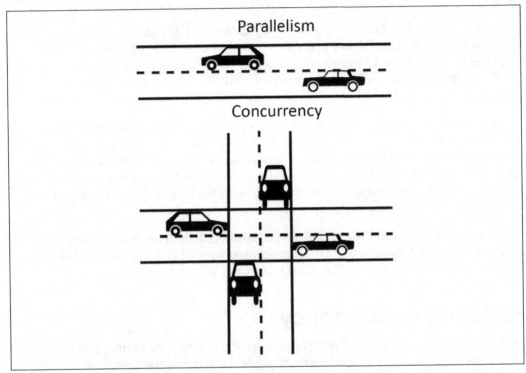

Figure 7.3: Concurrency versus parallelism

In addition to transaction processing at the application level, concurrency needs to apply at the network level where multiple servers share the same network resources. There is a need to handle many network connections for a web server when users try to connect to it over the network. It needs to process the active request and close the connection for the completed or timeout request. At the server level, you will see multiple CPUs assigned or a multicore processor. These help in handling concurrency as the server can handle more threads to complete various tasks simultaneously.

At the memory level, the shared memory concurrency model helps to achieve concurrency. In this model, the concurrent modules interact with each other using shared memory. It could be two programs running on the same server and sharing filesystems to read and write. Also, there could be two processors or processor cores sharing the same memory. The disk in your server can encounter concurrency situations where two programs try to write to the same memory block. Concurrent I/O helps to improve disk concurrency by allowing the disk to read and write a file simultaneously.

The database is always a central point of architecture design. Concurrency plays an essential role in data handling as the database should have the ability to respond to multiple requests simultaneously. Database concurrency is more complicated as one user might be trying to read a record while another user is updating it simultaneously. The database should only allow data viewing when it gets fully saved. Make sure that the data is completely committed before another user tries to update it. Caching can help to improve performance significantly; let's learn about some different cache types in architecture.

Applying caching

In *Chapter 6, Solution Architecture Design Patterns*, you learned how to apply caching at various levels of architecture in the *Cache-based architecture* section. Caching helps to improve application performance significantly. Although you learned the different design patterns to apply to the cache by adding an external caching engine and technology such as a CDN, it's essential to understand that almost every application component and infrastructure has a cache mechanism. Utilizing the caching mechanism at each layer can help reduce latency and improve the application's performance.

The CPU has its hardware cache at the server level, which reduces the latency when accessing data from the main memory. The CPU cache includes the instruction and data cache; the data cache stores copies of frequently used data. The cache is also applied at the disk level, but it is managed by operating system software (known as the **page cache**); however, the CPU cache is entirely managed by hardware. The disk cache originates from secondary storage, such as the HDD or **solid-state drive (SSD)**. Frequently used data is stored in an unused portion of the main memory (that is, the RAM as the page cache, which results in quicker access to content).

Often, the database has a cache mechanism that saves the results from the database to respond faster. The database has an internal cache that gets data ready in the cache based on the pattern of your use. They also have a query cache that saves data in the main server memory (RAM) if you make a query more than once. The query cache gets cleared in case of any changes in the data inside the table. If the server runs out of memory, the oldest query result gets deleted to make space.

You have a DNS cache at the network level, which stores the web domain name and corresponding IP address local to the server. DNS caching allows a quick DNS lookup if you revisit the same website domain name. The DNS cache is managed by the operating system and contains all recent visits to websites. You learned about client-side cache mechanisms such as the **browser cache** and various caching engines like **Memcached** and **Redis** in *Chapter 6, Solution Architecture Design Patterns.*

In this section, you learned about the original design factors, such as latency, throughput, concurrency, and caching, which need to be addressed for architecture performance optimization. Each component of the architecture (whether it is a network at the server level or an application at the database level) has a certain degree of latency and a concurrency issue that needs to be handled.

You should design your application for the desired performance, as improving performance comes with a cost. The specifics of performance optimization may differ from application to application. Solution architecture needs to direct the effort accordingly — for example, a stock-trading application cannot tolerate even sub-millisecond latency. On the other hand, an e-commerce website can live with a couple of seconds' latency. Let's learn about selecting technology for various architecture levels to overcome performance challenges.

Technology selection for performance optimization

In *Chapter 6, Solution Architecture Design Patterns,* you learned about various design patterns, including microservice, event-driven, cached-based, and stateless. An organization may choose a combination of these design patterns depending on their solution's design needs. You can have multiple approaches to architecture design depending on your workload. Once you finalize your strategy and start solution implementation, the next step is to optimize your application. To optimize your application, you need to collect data by performing load testing and defining benchmarking as per your application's performance requirements.

Performance optimization is a continuous improvement process, one in which you need to take cognizance of optimal resource utilization from the beginning of solution design to after the application's launch. You need to choose the right resources as per the workload or tweak the application and infrastructure configuration. For example, you may want to select a NoSQL database to store the session state for your application and store transactions in the relational database.

For analytics and reporting purposes, you can offload your production database by loading data from the application database to data warehousing solutions and create reports from there.

In the case of servers, you may want to choose a virtual machine or containers. You can take an entirely serverless approach to build and deploy your application code. Regardless of your approach and application workload, you need to choose the primary resource type: computing, storage, database, and network. Let's look at more details on how to select these resource types for performance optimization.

Making a computational choice

In this section, you will see the use of the term *compute* instead of *the server*, as nowadays software deployments are not limited to servers. A public cloud provider such as AWS has serverless offerings, where you don't need a server to run your application. One of the most popular FaaS offerings is AWS Lambda. Like AWS Lambda, other popular public cloud providers extend their offerings in the FaaS space—for example, Microsoft Azure has Azure Functions, and GCP offers Google Cloud Functions.

However, organizations still make the default choice to go for servers with virtual machines. Now, containers are also becoming popular as the need for automation and resource utilization is increased. Containers are becoming the preferred choice, especially in the area of microservice application deployment. The optimal choice of computing—whether you want to choose server instances, containers, or go for serverless—depends upon application use cases. Let's look at the various compute choices available.

Selecting the server instance

Nowadays, the term **instance** is getting more popular as virtual servers become the norm. These virtual servers provide flexibility and better use of resources. Particularly for cloud offerings, all cloud providers offer virtual servers, which can be provisioned with a mere click on a web console or API call. The server instance helps in automation and provides *infrastructure as code*, where everything can be automated everywhere.

As your workload varies, you might prefer one of the different kinds of processing unit choices available. Let's look at some of the most popular options for processing power:

- **The central processing unit (CPU)**: The CPU is one of the most popular computing processing choices. CPUs are easy to program, enable multitasking, and, most importantly, are versatile enough to fit anywhere, making them the preferred choice for general-purpose applications. The CPU's function is measured in GHz (gigahertz), which indicates that the clock rate of the CPU speed is in billions of cycles per second.

CPUs are available at a low cost; however, they cannot perform well for parallel processing as CPUs have the primary capabilities of sequential processing.

- **The graphical processing unit (GPU)**: As the name suggests, the GPU was designed initially to process graphics applications and provide massive processing power. As the volume of data grows, it needs to process data by utilizing **massively parallel processing (MPP)**. For large data processing use cases, such as machine learning, GPUs have become the obvious choice and are used in many compute-intensive applications. You may have heard of the **tera floating-point operation (TFLOP)** as a unit of computation power for GPUs. A teraflop refers to the processor's capability to calculate one trillion floating-point operations per second.

  GPUs consist of thousands of small cores, compared to CPUs, which have very few large cores. GPUs have a mechanism to create thousands of threads using CUDA programming, and each thread can process data in parallel, which makes processing super fast. GPUs are a bit costlier than CPUs. When it comes to processing capabilities, you will find that GPUs are in the sweet spot of cost and performance for an application that requires image analysis, video processing, and signal processing. However, they consume lots of power and may not work with a specific algorithm where more customized processors are required.

- **Field-programmable gate array (FPGA)**: FPGAs are very different from CPUs or GPUs. They are programmable hardware with a flexible collection of logic elements that can be reconfigured for the specific application, which can be changed after installation. FPGAs consume much less power than GPUs but are also less flexible. They can accommodate MPP and also provide a feature to configure them as CPUs. Overall, the FPGA cost is higher, as they need to be customized for each application and require a longer development cycle. FPGAs may perform poorly for sequential operations and are not very good for flops (floating-point operations).

- **Application-specific integrated circuit (ASIC)**: ASICs are purpose-built custom integrated circuit optimization for a specific application—for example, specific to the deep learning TensorFlow package, which Google provides as a **tensor processing unit (TPU)**. They can be custom designed for the applications to achieve an optimum combination of power consumption and performance. ASICs incur high costs because of the most extended development cycle, and you have to perform a hardware-level redesign for any changes.

The following diagram shows a comparison between the types of processing mentioned in the preceding list. Here, the ASIC is most efficient but takes a longer development cycle to implement. ASICs provide the most optimal performance but have the least flexibility to reutilize, while CPUs are very flexible and can fit many use cases:

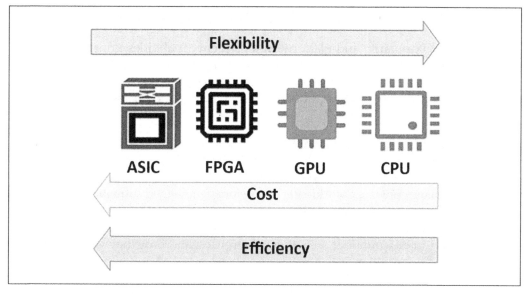

Figure 7.4: Comparison between CPUs, GPUs, FPGAs, and ASICs

As shown in the preceding diagram, from the cost perspective, CPUs are the cheapest, and ASICs are the costliest. Today, the CPU has become a commodity and is used everywhere for general-purpose devices to keep costs lower. The GPU has become famous for compute-intensive applications, and the FPGA has become the first choice where more customized performance is required. You will see these processing choices available from public cloud providers, such as AWS. In addition to CPUs, the **Amazon Elastic Cloud Compute (EC2)** offering provides a P-series instance that makes heavy use of the GPU. The F-series instance provides FPGAs for custom hardware acceleration.

In this section, you learned about the most popular computing choices. You may hear about other types of processors, such as the **accelerated processing unit (APU)**. The APU combines the CPU, GPU, and **digital signal processor (DSP)**, which is optimized to analyze analog signals and then requires high-speed data processing in real time. Let's learn more about other popular compute-type containers that are gaining popularity rapidly because of their capability to optimize the use of resources within the virtual machine.

Working with containers

In *Chapter 6, Solution Architecture Design Patterns*, you learned about container deployment and its benefits in the section titled *Deploying an application with a container*. The use of containers is becoming the norm for deploying complex microservice applications because of the ease of automation and resource utilization efficiency. There are various platforms available for container deployment.

Because of their popularity and platform-independent capabilities, containers become the first choice to build a cloud-agnostic platform. You can deploy containers in your on-premise data center and manage them through your cloud. Also, you can take a relocate approach to move a container from on-prem to the cloud without any changes.

You can build a multi-cloud platform with a container, and now each major public cloud vendor provides tools to manage a container environment spread over multiple platforms. For example, AWS provides **ECS Anywhere**, which enables you to run and manage container workloads on customer-managed infrastructure easily. Similarly, GCP provides **Google Anthos**, which gives you container management across on-premise and other cloud platforms. Let's learn about some of the most popular choices in the container area, their differences, and how they work together.

Docker

Docker is one of the most in-demand technologies. It allows you to package an application and its related dependencies together as a container and deploy it to any operating system platform. Docker provides platform-independent capabilities to a software application, making the overall software development, testing, and deployment process simplified and more accessible.

Docker container images are portable from one system to another over a local network or across the internet using Docker Hub. You can manage and distribute your container using a Docker Hub container repository. If you make any changes in the Docker image that cause issues in your environment, it's easy to revert to the working version of the container image, making overall troubleshooting easier.

Docker containers help you to build a more complex multilayer application. For example, suppose you need to run the application server, database, and message queue together.

In that case, you can run them side by side using a different Docker image and then establish communication between them. Each of these layers may have a modified version of libraries, and Docker allows them to run on the same computing machine without conflict.

When using Docker, the development team builds an application and packages it with required dependencies into a container image. This application image is run in a container on the Docker host. Like you manage code in a code repository such as GitHub, in the same way, a Docker image should be stored in a registry. Docker Hub is a public registry, and other public cloud vendors provide their own registries, such as **AWS ECR (Elastic Container Registry)** and **Azure Container Registry**. In addition, you can have a private registry on-premises for your own Docker images.

Public cloud providers, such as AWS, provide container management platforms, such as **Amazon Elastic Container Service (ECS)**. Container management helps to manage Docker containers on top of the cloud virtual machine, Amazon EC2. AWS also provides the serverless option of container deployment using Amazon Fargate, where you can deploy containers without provisioning virtual machines.

Complex enterprise applications are built based on microservices that may span across multiple containers. Managing various Docker containers as a part of one application can be pretty complicated. Kubernetes helps to solve the challenges of the multi-container environment; let's learn more about Kubernetes.

Kubernetes

Kubernetes can manage and control multiple containers in production environments with ease. You can consider Kubernetes as a container orchestration system. You can host a Docker container in bare metal (physical server) or a virtual machine node called a Docker host, and Kubernetes can co-ordinate across a cluster of these nodes.

Kubernetes makes your application self-healing by replacing unresponsive containers in the case of any application error. It also provides horizontal scaling capabilities and a blue-green deployment ability to prevent any downtime. Kubernetes distributes incoming user traffic load between the container and manages the storage shared by various containers.

As shown in the following diagram, Kubernetes and Docker work well together to orchestrate your software application. Kubernetes handles network communication between Docker nodes and Docker containers:

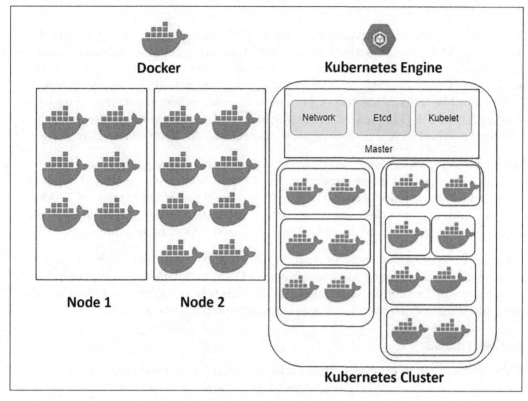

Figure 7.5: Docker and Kubernetes

Docker works as an individual piece of the application, and Kubernetes takes care of the orchestration to make sure all these pieces work together as designed. It's easier to automate overall application deployment and scaling with Kubernetes. In Docker, containers are hosted in nodes, and each Docker container in a single node shares the same IP space. In Docker, you need to manage the connections between containers by taking care of any IP conflict. Kubernetes solves this problem by having a master instance that keeps track of all nodes hosting containers.

Kubernetes's master node is responsible for assigning an IP address and hosting a key-value store for container configuration and a **kubelet** to manage the containers. The kubelet is the primary "node agent" that runs on each node and ensures that the containers defined in the pods are started and continue running. Docker containers are grouped into **pods**, where they share the same IP address. This entire setup is called a **Kubernetes cluster**.

While Kubernetes is quickly becoming popular, other options are available, such as **Docker Swarm**, which Docker itself builds. Docker Swarm is a **container orchestration tool**, which allows the user to manage multiple containers deployed across multiple host machines. However, Swarm doesn't have a web-based interface like Kubernetes and does not provide auto scaling and external load balancing.

Kubernetes is complex to learn. A public cloud provider, such as AWS, provides Amazon **Elastic Kubernetes Service (EKS)** to simplify the management of the Kubernetes cluster. OpenShift is another Kubernetes distribution managed by Red Hat and is offered as a **Platform as a Service (PaaS)**. Similarly, Microsoft Azure provides **Azure Kubernetes Service (AKS)** and GCP provides **Google Kubernetes Engine (GKE)**, offering a simple way to automatically deploy, scale, and manage Kubernetes.

Overall, containers add a layer of virtualization to the whole application infrastructure. While they are helpful in resource utilization, you may want to choose a bare-metal physical machine for your application deployment if it requires ultra-low latency.

Going serverless

In recent years, serverless computing has become possible because of the popularity of public cloud offerings by cloud providers such as Amazon, Google, and Microsoft. Serverless computing allows developers to focus on their code and application development without worrying about underlying infrastructure provisioning, configuration, and scaling. Serverless offerings abstract server management and infrastructure decisions from developers, and let them focus on their area of expertise and the business problem they are trying to solve. Serverless computing brings the relatively new concept of **Function as a Service (FaaS)**.

FaaS offerings are available using AWS Lambda, Microsoft Azure Functions, and Google Cloud Functions. You can write your code in the cloud editor, and AWS Lambda handles the computing infrastructure underneath to run and scale your function. You can design event-based architecture or RESTful microservices by adding an API endpoint using Amazon API Gateway and AWS Lambda functions. Amazon API Gateway is a managed cloud service that adds RESTful APIs and WebSocket APIs as frontends for the Lambda functions and enables real-time communication between applications. You can further break your microservice into small tasks that can be scaled automatically and independently.

In addition to focusing on your code, you never have to pay for idle resources in the FaaS model. Rather than scaling your entire service, you can scale the required functions independently with built-in availability and fault tolerance.

However, it could be a pretty daunting task if you have thousands of features to orchestrate, and predicting the auto scaling cost can be tricky. It is perfect for scheduling jobs, processing web requests, or queuing messages.

In this section, you learned about the various computing choices, looking at server instances, serverless options, and containers. You need to select these compute services based on your application's requirements. No rule forces you to choose a particular type of computing; it is all about your organization's choice of technology, the pace of innovation, and the nature of the software application.

However, in general, you can stick to a virtual or bare-metal machine for the monolithic application, and for complex microservices, you can choose containers. For simple task scheduling or events-based applications, you can go for serverless functions as an obvious choice. Many organizations have built complex applications entirely on serverless, which helped them reduce costs and achieve high availability without managing any infrastructure.

Let's learn about another important aspect of your infrastructure and how it can help you to optimize performance.

Choosing storage

Storage is one of the critical factors for your application's performance. Any software application needs to interact with storage for installation, logging, and accessing files. The optimal solution for your storage will differ based on the following factors:

Access methods	Block, file, or object
Access patterns	Sequential or random
Access frequency	Online (hot), offline (warm), or archival (cold)
Update frequency	**Write once read many (WORM)** or dynamic
Access availability	Availability of storage when required
Access durability	Reliability of data store to minimize any data loss
Access throughput	IOPS and data read/write per second in MBs.

These depend upon your data format and scalability needs. You first need to decide whether your data will be stored in block, file, or object storage. These are storage formats that store and present data in a different way. Let's look at this in more detail.

Working with block storage and storage area network

Block storage divides data into blocks and stores them as chunks of data. Each block has a unique ID that allows the system to place data wherever it is most easily accessible as blocks don't store any metadata about files. Hence, a server-based operating system manages and uses these blocks in the hard drive. Whenever the system requests data, the storage system collects the blocks and gives the result back to the user. Block storage deployed in a **storage area network (SAN)** stores data efficiently and reliably. It works well when a large amount of data needs to be stored and accessed frequently—for example, database deployment, email servers, application deployment, and virtual machines.

SAN storage is sophisticated and supports *complex, mission-critical applications*. It is a high-performance storage system that communicates block-level data between the server and storage; however, SAN is significantly costly and should be used for large-scale enterprise applications where low latency is required.

To configure your block-based storage, you must choose between an SSD and an HDD. HDDs are the legacy data storage system for servers and enterprise storage arrays. HDDs are cheaper, but they are slower and need more power and cooling. SSDs use semiconductor chips and are faster than HDDs. They are much more costly; however, as technology evolves, SSDs have become more affordable and gain popularity because of their efficiency and lower power and cooling requirements.

Working with file storage and network area storage

File storage has been around for a long time and is widely used. In file storage, data is stored as a single piece of information and is organized inside folders. When you need to access the data, you provide the file path and get the data files; however, a file path can grow complicated as files become nested under multiple folder hierarchies. Each record has limited metadata, including the filename, time of creation, and updated timestamps. You can take the analogy of a book library where you store books in drawers and keep a note of the location where each book is stored.

Network area storage (NAS) is a file storage system that is attached to the network and displays to the user where they can store and access their files. NAS also manages user privilege, file locking, and other security mechanisms that protect the data. NAS works well for file-sharing systems and local archives. When it comes to storing billions of files, NAS might not be the right solution, given that it has limited metadata information and a complex folder hierarchy. To store billions of files, you need to use object storage. Let's learn more about object storage and its benefits over file storage.

Working with object storage and cloud data storage

Object storage bundles data with a unique identifier and metadata that is customizable. Object storage uses a flat address space compared to the hierarchical addresses in file storage or addresses distributed over a chunk of blocks in block storage. Flat address space makes it easier to locate data and retrieve it faster regardless of the data storage's location. Object storage also helps the user to achieve unlimited scalability of storage.

Object storage metadata can have lots of details such as object name, size, timestamp, and so on, and users can customize it to add more information than tagging in file storage. Data can be accessed by a simple API call and is very cost-effective to store. Object storage performs best for high-volume, unstructured data; however, objects cannot be modified but only replaced, making it not a good use case for a database.

Cloud data storage, such as **Amazon Simple Storage Service (S3)**, provides an unlimited scalable object data store with high availability and durability. You can access data with a unique global identifier and metadata file prefix. The following diagram shows all three storage systems in a nutshell:

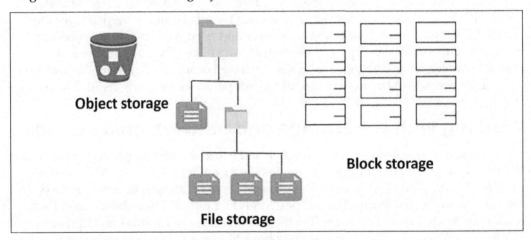

Figure 7.6: Data storage systems

As shown in the preceding diagram, block storage stores data in blocks. You should use block storage when your application needs very low latency and data storage access by a single instance. File storage stores data in a hierarchical folder structure and has little latency overhead. You should use the file storage system when a separate room needs to access multiple instances. Object storage stores data in buckets with a unique identifier for the object. It provides access over the web to reduce latency and increase throughput. You should use object storage to store and access static content, such as images and videos. You can store a high volume of data in the object store and perform big data processing and analysis.

Direct-attached storage (DAS) is another kind of data storage that is directly attached to the host server; however, it has very limited scalability and storage capacity. The **magnetic tape drive** is another popular storage system for backing up and archiving. Because of its low cost and high availability, magnetic tape drives are used for archival purposes but have high latency, making them unsuitable for use in direct applications.

Often, you will need to increase throughput and data protection for a mission-critical application, such as a transactional database, where data is stored in SAN storage; however, individual SAN storage may have limited volume and throughput. You can overcome this situation using a **redundant array of independent disks (RAID)** configuration. RAID is a way of storing data on multiple disks. It protects data loss from drive failure and increases disk throughput by striping various disks together.

RAID uses the technique of disk mirroring or disk striping, but for the operating system, RAID is a single logical disk. RAID has different levels to distinguish the configuration type. For example, RAID 0 uses disk striping and provides the best performance but has no fault tolerance, whereas RAID 1 is **disk mirroring**. It duplicates the data storage and provides no performance improvement for write operations but doubles the read performance. You can combine RAID 0 and RAID 1 to form RAID 10, also known as RAID 1+0. It helps to achieve the best of both with high throughput and fault tolerance. It requires a minimum of four disks and stripes data across mirrored pairs.

Select the storage solution that matches your access pattern to maximize performance. There are various options available with a cloud offering to choose from for your block, file, and object storage method. For example, the public cloud AWS provides **Amazon Elastic Block Store (EBS)** as a SAN type of storage in the cloud and **Amazon Elastic File System (EFS)** as a NAS type of storage in the cloud. Amazon S3 is very popular for object storage. Similarly, Microsoft Azure provides Azure Disk Storage for SAN, Azure Files for NAS, and Azure Blob for block storage. Different storage solutions allow you to choose your storage methods based on the access pattern, whether working in an on-premise environment or going cloud native.

Now that you have learned about the compute and storage choices necessary to achieve optimal performance, let's look at the next critical component of application development: the database. Choosing the right database for the right need will help you maximize your application performance and lower overall application latency. There are different types of databases available, and choosing the correct database is critical.

Choosing the database

Often, you will want to standardize a common platform and use a database for ease of management; however, you should consider using a different database solution as per your data requirements. Selecting the incorrect database solution can impact system latency and performance. The choice of a database can vary based on your application's requirements for availability, scalability, data structure, throughput, and durability. There are multiple factors to consider when choosing to use a database. For example, the access pattern can significantly impact the selection of database technology. It would be best if you optimized your database based on the access pattern.

Databases generally have a configuration option for workload optimization. You should consider the configuration for memory, cache, storage optimization, and so on. You should also explore the operational aspect of database technologies regarding scalability, backup, recovery, and maintenance. Let's look at the different database technologies that can be used to fulfill the database requirements of applications.

Online transactional processing

Most of the traditional relational databases are considered to use **online transactional processing** (OLTP). The transactional database is the oldest and most popular method of storing and handling application data. Some examples of relational OLTP databases are Oracle, Microsoft SQL Server, MySQL, PostgreSQL, Amazon RDS, and others. The data access pattern for OLTP involves fetching a small dataset by looking up its ID. A database transaction means that either all related database updates were completed or none of them were.

The relational model allows processing complex business transactions in an application, such as banking, trading, and e-commerce. It will enable you to aggregate data and create complex queries using multiple joins across tables. While optimizing your relational database, you need to consider including the following optimizations:

- A database server that includes computing, memory, storage, and networking
- Operating system-level settings, such as a RAID configuration of the storage volume, volume management, and block size
- Database engine configuration and partition as required
- Database-related options, such as schema, index, and view

Scaling can be tricky for the relational database as it can scale vertically and hit the upper limit of system capacity. For horizontal scaling, you have to read the replica for *read scaling* and partition for *write scaling*. In the previous chapter, you learned how to scale a relational database in the section titled *Database handling in the application architecture*.

OLTP databases are suitable for large and complex transactional applications; however, they don't scale well where a massive amount of data needs to aggregate and be queried. Also, with the internet boom, there is a lot of unstructured data coming from everywhere, and relational databases cannot handle unstructured data efficiently out of the box. In this case, the NoSQL database comes to the rescue. Let's learn more about how to handle a nonrelational database.

Nonrelational databases

There is a lot of unstructured and semistructured data produced by applications such as social media programs, the **Internet of Things (IoT)**, clickstream data, and logs, where you have a very dynamic schema. These data types may have different schemas for each set of records. Storing this data in a relational database could be a very tedious task. Everything has to be filed in a fixed schema, which can either cause lots of null values or data loss. The nonrelational or **NoSQL** database provides you with the flexibility to store such data without worrying about a fixed schema. Each record can have a variable number of columns and can be stored in the same table.

NoSQL databases can store a large amount of data and provide *low-access latency*. They are easy to scale by adding more nodes when required and can support horizontal scaling out of the box. They can be an excellent choice to store user session data and make your application stateless to achieve horizontal scaling without compromising user experience. You can develop a distributed application on top of the NoSQL database, which provides good latency and scaling, but query joining must be handled at the application layer. NoSQL databases don't support complex queries such as joining tables and entities.

There are various choices available for the NoSQL database, for example, Cassandra, HBase, and MongoDB, which you can install in a cluster of virtual machines; however, the public cloud-like AWS provides a managed NoSQL database called **Amazon DynamoDB**, which offers high throughput sub-millisecond latency with unlimited scaling.

You can use OLTP for a relational database, but it has limited storage capacity. It doesn't respond well to queries for large amounts of data and performs aggregations as required for data warehouses. Data warehousing needs are more analytical than transactional. The **online analytical processing (OLAP)** database satisfies the gap of the OLTP database to query a large dataset. Let's learn more about the OLAP database.

Online analytical processing

OLTP and NoSQL databases are helpful for application deployment but have limited capabilities for large-scale analysis. A query for a large volume of structured data for analytics purposes is better served by a data warehouse platform designed for faster access to structured data. Modern data warehouse technologies adopt the columnar format and use MPP, which helps to fetch and analyze data faster.

The columnar format avoids the need to scan the entire table when you need to aggregate only one column for data—for example, if you want to determine your inventory sales in a given month. There may be hundreds of columns in the order table, but you need to aggregate data from the purchase column only. With a columnar format, you will only scan the purchase column, which reduces the amount of data scanned compared to the row format and increases the query performance.

With MPP, you store data in a distributed manner between child nodes and submit a query to the leader nodes. Based on your partition key, the leader node will distribute queries to the child nodes, where each node picks up part of a query to perform parallel processing. The leader node then collects the subquery result from each child node and returns your aggregated result. This parallel processing helps you to execute the query faster and process a large amount of data quicker.

You can use this kind of processing by installing software such as IBM Netezza or Microsoft SQL Server on a virtual machine, or you can go for a more cloud-native solution, such as Snowflake. A public cloud, such as AWS, provides the petabyte-scale data warehousing solution Amazon Redshift, which uses the columnar format and MPP. You will learn more about data processing and analytics in *Chapter 13, Data Engineering for Solution Architecture*.

You need to store and search a large amount of data, especially when you want to find a specific error in your logs or build a document search engine. For this kind of capability, your application needs to create a data search functionality. Let's learn more about data search.

Building a data search functionality

Often, you will need to search a large volume of data to solve issues quickly or get business insights. Searching your application data will help you access detailed information and analyze it from different views. To search for data with low latency and high throughput, you need to have search engines as your technology choice.

Elasticsearch is one of the most popular search engine platforms and is built on top of the **Apache Lucene** library. Apache Lucene is a free and open-source software library that is the foundation of many popular search engines. The **ELK** (short for **Elasticsearch, Logstash, and Kibana**) Stack is easy to use to discover large-scale data and index it for searching automatically. Because of its properties, multiple tools have been developed around Elasticsearch for visualization and analysis. For example, **Logstash** works with Elasticsearch to collect, transform, and analyze a large amount of an application's log data. **Kibana** has an in-built connector with Elasticsearch that provides a simple solution for creating dashboards and analyzing indexed data.

Elasticsearch can be deployed in virtual machines and scale horizontally to increase capacity by adding new nodes to the cluster. The public cloud AWS provides the managed service **Amazon OpenSearch Service**, making it cost-effective and simple to scale and manage the Elasticsearch cluster in the cloud.

In this section, you learned about the various database technologies and where they are used. Your applications can use a combination of all database technologies for their different components to achieve optimal performance. For complex transactions, you need to use a relational OLTP database, and to store and process unstructured or semistructured data, you need to use a nonrelational NoSQL database. You should use a NoSQL database where very low latency is required over multiple geographical regions and where you need to handle complex queries at the application layer, such as in a gaming application. If you need to perform any large-scale analytics on structured data, use a data warehouse OLAP database. You can use a cache database to improve the performance efficiency of a database. You learned about Redis and Memcached in *Chapter 6, Solution Architecture Design Patterns*, in the section *Memcached versus Redis*.

Let's look at another critical component of your architecture, which is **networking**. Networking is the backbone of the entire application and establishes communication between the servers and the outside world. Let's learn about networking as regards application performance.

Improving network performance

In this era of fast internet availability in almost every corner of the world, it is expected that applications will have a global user reach. Any delay in the system's response time depends upon the request load and the distance of the end-user from the server. If the system is not able to respond to user requests promptly, it can have a ripple effect by continuing to engage all system resources and pile up a considerable request backlog, which will degrade the overall system performance.

To reduce latency, you should simulate the user's location and environment to identify any gaps. As per your findings, you should design the server's physical location and caching mechanism to reduce network latency; however, the network solution choice for an application depends upon the networking speed, throughput, and network latency requirements. An application to handle a global user base needs to have fast connectivity with its customers, and location plays an important role. Edge locations provided by the CDN help to localize the rich content and reduce overall latency.

In *Chapter 6, Solution Architecture Design Patterns*, you learned how to use a CDN to put data near your user's location in the section titled *Cache-based architecture*. There are various CDN solutions available with an extensive network of edge locations. You can use a CDN if your application is static-content-heavy, where you need to deliver large image and video content to your end-user. Some of the more popular CDN solutions are Akamai, Cloudflare, and Amazon CloudFront (provided by the AWS cloud). Let's look at some DNS routing strategies to achieve low latency if your application is deployed globally.

Defining a DNS routing strategy

To have global reach, you may be deploying your application in multiple geographical regions. When it comes to user request routing, you want to route their requests to the nearest and fastest available server for a quick response from your application. The DNS router provides the mapping between the domain names and the IP addresses. It ensures that the requests are served by the correct server when the user types in the domain name—for example, when you type amazon.com in your browser to do some shopping, your request is always routed to the Amazon application server DNS service.

The public cloud-like AWS provides a DNS service called **Amazon Route 53**, where you can define a different kind of routing policy as per your application's needs. Amazon Route 53 provides DNS services to simplify domain management and zone APEX support. The following are the most used routing policies:

- **Simple routing policy**: As the name suggests, this is the most straightforward routing policy and doesn't involve any complications. It is helpful to route traffic to a single resource—for example, a web server that serves content for a particular website.

- **Failover routing policy**: This routing policy requires you to achieve high availability by configuring active-passive failover. If your application goes down in one region, then all the traffic can be routed to another region automatically.

- **Geolocation routing policy**: If the user belongs to a particular location, you can use a geolocation policy. A geolocation routing policy helps to route traffic to a specific region.

- **Geoproximity routing policy**: This is like a geolocation policy, but you have the option to shift traffic to other nearby locations when needed.

- **Latency routing policy**: If your application runs in multiple regions, you can use a latency policy to serve traffic from the region where the lowest latency can be achieved.

- **Weighted routing policy**: A weighted routing policy is used for A/B testing, where you want to send a certain amount of traffic to one region and increase this traffic as your trial proves more and more successful.

Additionally, Amazon Route 53 can detect anomalies in the source and volume of DNS queries and prioritize requests from users that are known to be *reliable*. It also protects your application from a DDoS attack. Once traffic passes through the DNS server, in most cases, the next stop will be a load balancer, which will distribute traffic among a cluster of servers. Let's learn some more details regarding the load balancer.

Implementing a load balancer

The load balancer distributes network traffic across the servers to improve concurrency, reliability, and application latency. The load balancer can be *physical* or *virtual*. It would be best if you chose a load balancer based on your application's needs. Commonly, two types of load balancer can be utilized by the application:

- **Layer 4 or network load balancer**: Layer 4 load balancing routes packets based on information in the packet header—for example, source/destination IP addresses and ports. Layer 4 load balancing does not inspect the contents of a packet, which makes it less compute-intensive and therefore faster. A network load balancer can handle millions of requests per second.

- **Layer 7 or application load balancer**: Layer 7 load balancing inspects and routes packets based on the full contents of the packet. Layer 7 is used in conjunction with HTTP requests. The materials that inform routing decisions are factors such as HTTP headers, URI path, and content type. It allows for more robust routing rules but requires more compute time to route packets. The application load balancer can route the request to containers in your cluster based on their distinctive port number.

Depending on the environment, you can choose hardware-based load balancers, such as an F5 load balancer or a Cisco load balancer. You can also select a software-based load balancer, such as **Nginx**.

The public cloud provider AWS facilitates a managed virtual load balancer called **Amazon Elastic Load Balancing (ELB)**. ELB can be applied at layer 7 as an application load balancer and layer 4 as a network load balancer.

A load balancer is an excellent way of securing your application, making it highly available by sending a request to healthy instances. It works together with auto-scaling to add or remove instances as required. Let's look at auto-scaling and learn how it helps to improve overall performance and the high availability of your application.

Applying auto-scaling

You learned about auto-scaling in *Chapter 4, Principles of Solution Architecture Design*. You learned about predictive auto-scaling and reactive auto-scaling in the section titled *Design for scale*. The concept of auto-scaling became popular with the agility provided by the cloud computing platform. Cloud infrastructure allows you to quickly scale up or scale down your server fleet based on user or resource demand.

With a public cloud platform such as AWS, you can apply auto-scaling at every layer of your architecture. You can scale the web server fleet based on your requests in the presentation layer and at the application layer based on the server's memory and CPU utilization. You can also perform scheduled scaling if you know the traffic pattern when the server load increases. At the database level, auto-scaling is available for relational databases such as Amazon Aurora Serverless and Microsoft Azure SQL database. A NoSQL Database such as Amazon DynamoDB can be auto-scaled based on throughput capacity.

When auto-scaling, you need to define the number of desired server instances. You need to determine the maximum and minimum server capacity as per your application's scaling needs. The following screenshot illustrates the auto-scaling configuration from the AWS cloud:

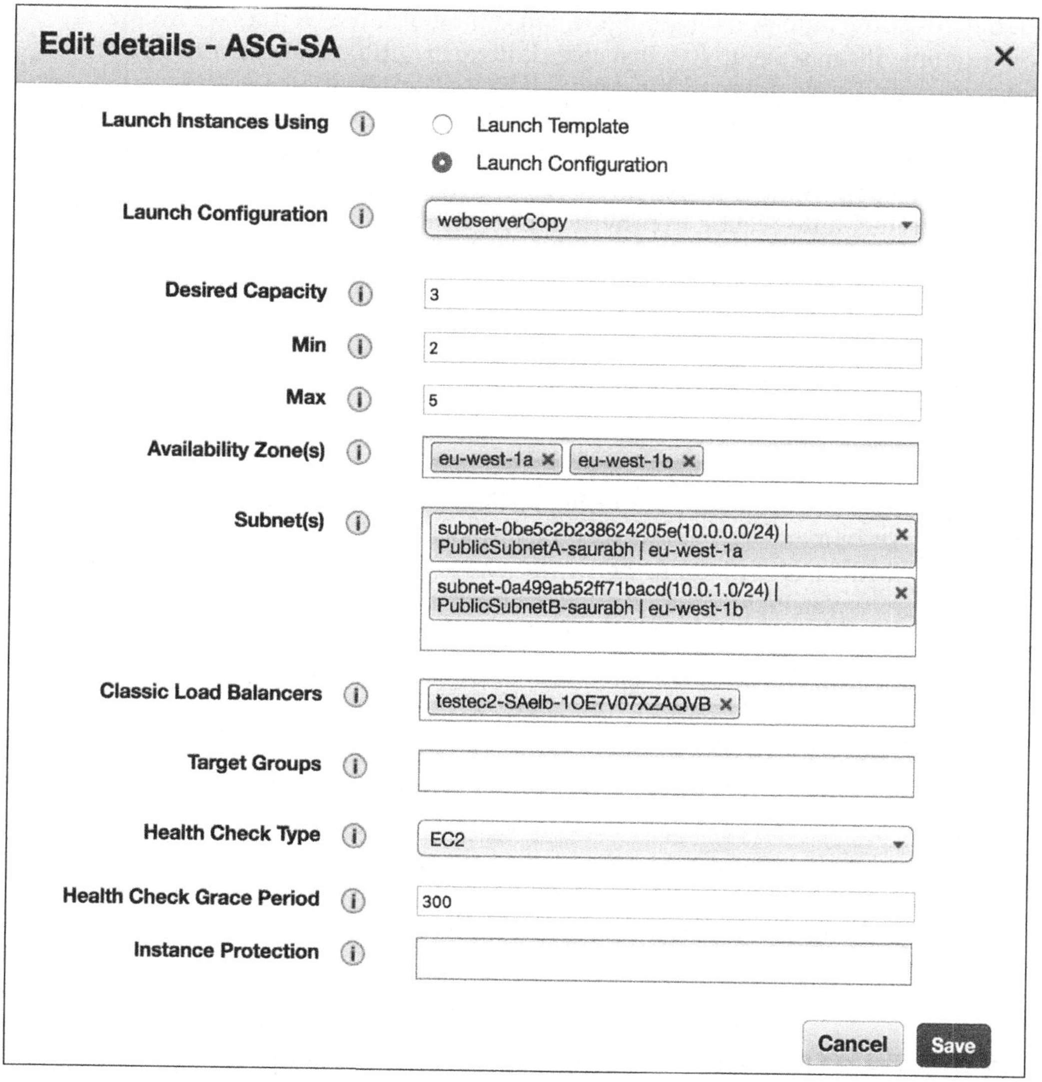

Edit details - ASG-SA   ✕

Launch Instances Using ⓘ	○ Launch Template
	● Launch Configuration
Launch Configuration ⓘ	webserverCopy ▼
Desired Capacity ⓘ	3
Min ⓘ	2
Max ⓘ	5
Availability Zone(s) ⓘ	eu-west-1a ✕ eu-west-1b ✕
Subnet(s) ⓘ	subnet-0be5c2b238624205e(10.0.0.0/24) | ✕ PublicSubnetA-saurabh | eu-west-1a subnet-0a499ab52ff71bacd(10.0.1.0/24) | ✕ PublicSubnetB-saurabh | eu-west-1b
Classic Load Balancers ⓘ	testec2-SAelb-1OE7V07XZAQVB ✕
Target Groups ⓘ	
Health Check Type ⓘ	EC2 ▼
Health Check Grace Period ⓘ	300
Instance Protection ⓘ	

Cancel   **Save**

Figure 7.7: Auto-scaling configuration

In the preceding auto-scaling configuration setting, if three web server instances are running, it can scale up to 5 instances if the CPU utilization of servers goes above 50% and scale down to 2 instances if the CPU utilization goes below 20%. In an unhealthy instance, the count will go below the desired capacity in a standard scenario. In such a case, the load balancer will monitor the instance health and use auto-scaling to provide new instances. The load balancer monitors instance health and will trigger auto-scaling to provision new instances as required.

Auto-scaling is a good feature to have, but make sure you set up your desired configurations to limit the cost of a change in CPU usage. In the case of unforeseen traffic due to a **distributed denial of service (DDoS)** attack, auto-scaling can significantly increase costs. It would help if you planned to protect your system from such kinds of events. You will learn more about this in *Chapter 8, Security Considerations*.

You need **high-performance computing (HPC)** to perform manufacturing simulation or human DNA analysis at the instance level. HPC performs well when you put all instances in the same network close to each other for low latency of data transfer between a cluster node. Between your data centers or the cloud, you can choose to use your private network, which can provide an additional performance benefit. For example, to connect your data center to the AWS cloud, you can use Amazon Direct Connect. Direct Connect provides 10 Gbps private fiber-optic lines, where network latency is much lower than sending data over the internet.

In this section, you have learned about various networking components that can help to improve application performance. You can optimize your application network traffic according to your user location and application demand. Performance monitoring is an essential part of your application, and you should do proactive monitoring to improve the customer experience. Let's learn more about performance monitoring.

Managing performance monitoring

Performance monitoring is essential when you are trying to understand any performance issue and reduce end-user impact proactively. You should define your performance baseline and raise the alarm to the team in the case of a threshold breach—for example, an application's mobile app load time should not be more than three seconds. Your alarm should be able to trigger an automated action to handle poorly performing components—for example, adding more nodes in a web application cluster to reduce the request load.

There are multiple monitoring tools available to measure application performance and overall infrastructure.

You can use a third-party tool, such as Splunk or the AWS-provided Amazon CloudWatch, to monitor any application. Monitoring solutions can be categorized into **active monitoring** and **passive monitoring** solutions:

- With active monitoring, you need to simulate user activity and identify any performance gap upfront. Application data and workload situations are constantly changing, which requires continuous proactive monitoring. Active monitoring works alongside passive monitoring as you run the known possible scenarios to replicate the user experience. You should run active monitoring across all dev, test, and prod environments to catch any issue before reaching the user.

- Passive monitoring tries to identify an unknown pattern in real time. For a web-based application, passive monitoring needs to collect essential metrics from the browser that can cause performance issues. You can gather metrics from users regarding their geolocation, browser types, and device types to understand the user experience and the geographic performance of your application. Monitoring is all about data, and it includes the ingestion, processing, and visualization of lots of data.

Performance always comes with a cost, and, as a solution architect, you need to think about the trade-offs to take the right approach. For example, an organization's internal applications, such as the timesheet and HR programs, may not need as high performance as external products, such as e-commerce applications. An application that deals with trading (for example) needs very high performance, which requires more investment. As per your application's needs, you can balance durability, consistency, cost, and performance. You will continue to learn about the various monitoring methods and tools in upcoming chapters and dive deep into monitoring and alerts in *Chapter 9, Architectural Reliability Considerations*.

Tracking and improving performance are complex tasks where you need to collect lots of data and analyze patterns. An access pattern helps you to make the right choice for performance optimization. Load testing is one method that allows you to tweak your application configuration by simulating user load and provides you with data to make the right decisions for your application architecture. Applying continuous active monitoring in combination with passive monitoring helps you to maintain consistent performance for your application.

Summary

In this chapter, you learned about the various architecture design principles that impact the performance of applications. You learned about latency and throughput at different layers of architecture and how they relate to each other.

For highly performant applications, you need to have low latency and high throughput at every architecture layer. Concurrency helps to process a large number of requests. You also learned the difference between parallelism and concurrency and gained insight into how caching can help to improve overall application performance.

Then you learned about choosing your technology and their working models, which can help achieve your desired application performance. While looking at the compute option, you learned about the various processor types and their differences to help you make the right choice when selecting server instances. You learned about containers and how they can help you to utilize the resources efficiently and at the same time help to improve performance. You also learned how Docker and Kubernetes work well with each other and fit into your architecture.

In the section on choosing storage, you learned about different kinds of storage, such as block, file, and object storage, and their differences. You also learned about the available storage choices in on-premise and cloud environments. Storage choice depends on multiple factors. You can enhance disk storage durability and throughput by putting multiple volumes in a RAID configuration.

In the section on choosing a database, you learned about the various database types, including relational, nonrelational, data warehouse, and data search. While looking at choosing your network, you learned about the different request routing strategies that can help you to improve network latency for your globally distributed user. You learned how load balancers and auto-scaling could help you manage many user requests without compromising application performance.

In the next chapter, you will learn how to secure your application by applying authentication and authorization. It will ensure that your data at rest and in transit and your application are protected from various kinds of threats and attacks. You will also learn about compliance requirements and how to satisfy them when designing your application. You will learn the details about security audits, alerts, monitoring, and automation.

Join our book's Discord space

Join the book's Discord workspace for a monthly *Ask me Anything* session with the authors: https://packt.link/SAHandbook

8

Security Considerations

Security is always at the center of architecture design. Many large enterprises suffer financial losses due to security breaches when their customer data gets leaked. Organizations can therefore not only lose customer trust but also the entire business. There are many industry-standard compliances and regulations out there to make sure your application is *secure* and protects customer-sensitive data. In the previous chapter, you learned about various performance-improvement aspects and technology choices for your architecture. In this chapter, you will gain an understanding of best practices to secure your application and make sure it is compliant with industry-standard regulations.

Security isn't just about getting through the outer boundary of your infrastructure. It's also about ensuring that your environments and their components are secured from each other. For example, in the server, you can set up a firewall that allows you to determine which ports on your instances can send and receive traffic, and where that traffic can come from. You can use firewall protection to reduce the probability that a security threat on one instance will not spread to other instances in your environment. Similar precautions are required for other services such as data and applications. Specific ways to implement security best practices are discussed throughout this chapter.

You will learn about the following best security practices in this chapter:

- Designing principles for architectural security
- Selecting technology for architectural security
- Security and compliance certifications
- The cloud's shared security responsibility model

You will learn about various design principles applicable to secure your solution architecture. Security needs to be applied at every layer and in every component of the architecture. You will get an understanding of the right technology to select to ensure your architecture is secure at every layer.

Designing principles for architectural security

Security is all about the ability to protect your system and information while delivering business value for your customers. You need to conduct an in-depth security risk assessment and plan a mitigation strategy for the continuous operation of your business. The following sections talk about the standard design principles that help you to strengthen your architectural security.

Implementing authentication and authorization control

The purpose of authentication is to determine if a user can access the system with the provided credentials of user ID and password, while authorization determines what a user can do once they are inside the system. You should create a centralized system to manage your users' authentication and authorization.

Centralized user management system helps you to keep track of users' activity so you can deactivate them if they are no longer a part of the system. You can define standard rules to onboard a new user and remove access for inactive users. The centralized system eliminates reliance on long-term credentials and allows you to configure other security methods such as password rotation and strength.

For authorization, you should start with the **principle of least privilege**—it means users should not have any access to begin with, and are assigned only the required access types according to their job role. Creating an access group according to job role helps to manage the authorization policy in one place and apply authorization restrictions across a large number of users. For example, you can restrict the development team to have full access to the dev environment and read-only access to the production environment. If any new developer joins, they should be added to this dev group, where all authorization policies are managed centrally.

Enabling **single sign-on** (SSO) with a centralized users repository helps to reduce the hassle of remembering multiple passwords for your user base and eliminates any risk of password leakage.

Large organizations use centralized user management tools such as **Active Directory (AD)** for employee authentication and authorization, to provide them access to internal enterprise applications such as the HR system, the expense system, the timesheet application, and so on.

In a customer-facing application, such as e-commerce and social media websites, you can use an OpenID authentication system to maintain a centralized system. You will learn about large-scale user management tools in more detail in the *OAuth and OpenID Connect* section of this chapter.

Applying security everywhere

Often, organizations have a main focus of ensuring the physical safety of their data center and protecting the outer networking layer from any attack. Instead of just focusing on a single outer layer, ensure that security is applied at every layer of the application.

Apply the **defense-in-depth (DiD)** approach, and put security at various layers of the application; for example, a web application needs to be secured from external internet traffic by protecting the **Enhanced Data rates for Global Evolution (EDGE)** network and **Domain Name System (DNS)** routing. Apply security at the load balancer and network layers to block any malicious traffic.

Secure every instance of your application by allowing only required incoming and outgoing traffic in the web application and database layer. Protect operating systems with antivirus software to safeguard against any malware attack. Apply both proactive and reactive measures of protection by putting an **intrusion detection system (IDS)** and **intrusion prevention system (IPS)** in front of your traffic flow and a **web application firewall (WAF)** to protect your application from various kinds of attacks. You will learn more details about the various security tools to use in the *Selecting technology for architectural security* section of this chapter.

Reducing the blast radius

While applying security measures at every layer, you should always keep your system isolated in a small pocket to reduce the blast radius. If attackers get access to one part of the system, you should be able to limit a security breach to the smallest possible area of the application. For example, in a web application, keep your load balancer in a separate network from other layers of the architecture, as that will be internet-facing. Further, apply network separation at the web, application, and database layers. In any case, if an attack happens in one layer, it will not expand to other layers of the architecture.

The same rules are applied to your authorization system to give the least privilege to users and provide only the minimum required access. Make sure to implement **multi-factor authentication (MFA)** so that even if there's a breach in user access, the attacker always needs a second level of authentication to get into the system.

Provide minimal access to ensure that you are not exposing the entire system and provide temporary credentials to make sure access is not open for a long time. Take caution when providing programmatic access by putting a secure token in place, with frequent key rotation.

Monitoring and auditing everything all the time

Put the logging mechanism for every activity in your system and conduct a regular audit. Audit capabilities are often required from various industry-compliance regulations. Collect logs from every component, including all transactions and each API call, to put centralized monitoring in place. It is a good practice to add a level of security and access limitation for a centralized logging account so that no one is able to tamper with it.

Take a proactive approach and have the alert capability to take care of any incident before the user gets impacted. Alert capabilities with centralized monitoring help you to take quick action and mitigate any incident. Monitor all user activity and application accounts to limit the security breach.

Automating everything

Automation is an essential way to apply quick mitigation for any security-rule violation. You can use automation to revert changes made against desired configurations and alert the security team—for example, if someone added admin users in your system and an open firewall to an unauthorized port or IP address. You can apply automation to remove such undesired changes in the system. Applying automation in security systems has become popular with the concept of DevSecOps. DevSecOps is about adding security to every part of application development and operation. You will learn more about DevSecOps in *Chapter 12, DevOps and Solution Architecture Framework*.

Create secure architectures and implement security control that is defined and managed as code. You can version-control your security as a code template, and analyze changes as required. Automated security mechanisms as software code help you scale security operations more rapidly, in a cost-effective way.

Protecting data

Data is at the center of your architecture, and it is essential to secure and protect it. Most of the compliance regulations in place are there to protect customer data and identity. Most of the time, any attack has the intention of stealing the user's data. You should categorize your data as per its sensitivity level and protect it accordingly. For example, customer credit card information should be the most sensitive data and needs to be handled with the utmost care. On the other hand, a customer's first name may not be that sensitive while the card number is sensitive information.

Create mechanisms and tools that minimize the need for direct access to data. Avoid manual processing of data by applying tool-based automation that eliminates human error, especially when handling sensitive data. Apply access restrictions to the data wherever possible to reduce the risk of data loss or data modification.

Once you categorize data sensitivity, you can use the appropriate encryption, tokenization, and access control to protect the data. Data needs to be protected not only at rest but also in motion—when transmitting over the network—as well. You will learn about various mechanisms to protect data in the *Data security* section of this chapter.

Responding to security incidents

Keep yourself ready for any security events. Create an incident management process as per your organizational policy requirements. Incident management can differ from one organization to another and from one application to another. For example, if your application is handling **Personally Identifiable Information** (**PII**) of your customers, you need a tighter security measure in your incident response. However, if the application is handling small amounts of sensitive data, such as an inventory management application, then it will have a different approach.

Make sure to simulate the incident response to see how your security team is recovering from the situation. Your team should use automation tools for speed of detection, investigation, and response to any security event. You need to set up the alert, monitor, and audit mechanisms to do **Root Cause Analysis** (**RCA**) to prevent such events from occurring again.

In this section, you learned about the general security principles to apply in your architecture for application security. In the next section, you will learn how to apply these principles using different tools and techniques.

Selecting technology for architectural security

The previous section was more focused on the general rules of application security to consider while creating an architecture design, but the question is: *How do we apply these rules to make the application secure during implementation?*. There are various tools and technologies available for each layer of your application to make it secure.

In this section, you will learn in detail about the multiple technology choices to apply in the area of user management and protection of the web, infrastructure, and data of your application. Let's start with the first area, user identity and access management.

User identity and access management

User identity and access management are vital parts of information security. You need to make sure only authenticated and authorized users are able to access your system resources in a defined manner. User management could be a daunting task as your organization and product adoption grows. User access management should differentiate and manage access to an organization's employees, vendors, and customers.

Enterprise or corporate users could be the organization's employees, contractors, or vendors. Those are specialist users who have a special privilege to develop, test, and deploy the application. In addition to that, they require access to another corporate system to do their daily job—for example, an **Enterprise Resource System (ERP)**, a payroll system, an HR system, a timesheet application, and so on. As your organization grows, the number of users can grow from hundreds to thousands.

The end users are the customers who use your applications and have minimal access to explore and utilize the desired feature of the application—for example, players of a gaming application, users of social media applications, or customers of an e-commerce website. The count of these users could be from thousands to millions as the popularity of your product or application grows. The other factor is that user count can grow exponentially, which can add challenges. You need to take special care of security when exposing the application to external-facing internet traffic to protect it from various threats.

Let's talk about corporate user management first. You need to have a centralized repository where you can enforce security policies such as strong password creation, password rotation, and MFA for better user management. The use of MFA provides another means of validating someone's identity, if a password may have already been compromised. Popular MFA providers include Google Authenticator, Gemalto, YubiKey, RSA SecurID, Duo, and Microsoft Authenticator.

From a user-access perspective, **role-based authentication (RBA)** simplifies user management; you can create user groups as per the user's role and assign an appropriate access policy. As illustrated in the following diagram, you have three groups—admin, developer, and tester—with the corresponding access policy applied to the individual group. For example, an admin can access any system, including production, while developer access is limited to the dev environment, and the tester can only access the test environment:

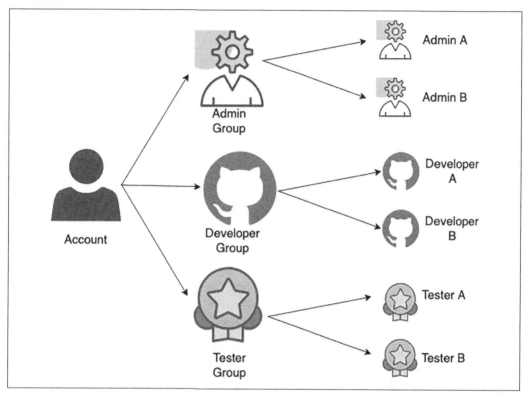

Figure 8.1: User group organization

As shown in the preceding diagram, when any new user joins the team, they get assigned to the appropriate group as per their role. In this way, each user has a defined set of standard access. The user group also helps to update access in case a new development environment gets introduced, and all developers need to have access to that.

SSO (Single Sign-On) is the standard process to reduce any security lapses and help to automate the system. SSO provides users with a login to the different corporate systems, using a single user ID and password. **Federated Identity Management (FIM)** allows users to access the system without a password with a pre-authenticated mechanism. Let's look at some more details.

Federated identity management and single sign-on

FIM (Federated identity management) provides a way to connect the identity management system when user information is stored in the third-party **identity provider (IdP)**. With FIM, the user only provides authentication information to the IdP, which in turn already has a trusted relationship with the service.

As illustrated in the following diagram, when a user logs in to access a service, the service provider gets credentials from the IdP, rather than getting them directly from the user:

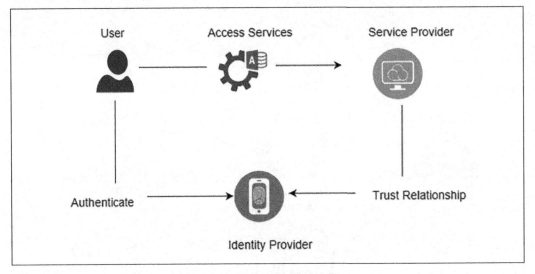

Figure 8.2: FIM authentication flow

SSO allows the use of a single sign-on, with which the user can access multiple services. Here, a service provider could target an environment where you want to log in—for example, a **Customer Relationship Management (CRM)** application or your cloud application. An IdP could be a corporate AD. Federation allows authentication similar to an SSO but without a password, as the federation server knows users and allows them to access information.

There are various techniques available to implement FIM and SSO. Let's look at some of the popular **Identify and Access Management (IAM)** choices available.

Kerberos

Kerberos is an authentication protocol that allows two systems to identify each other in a secure way and helps to implement SSO. It works in the client-server model and uses a ticket system for user identity.

Kerberos has a **Key Distribution Center (KDC)**, which facilitates authentication between two systems. The KDC consists of two logical parts—the **Authentication Server (AS)** and the **Ticket-Granting Server (TGS)**.

Kerberos stores and maintains the secret keys of each client and server in the datastore. It establishes a secure session between two systems during their communication and identifies them with the stored secret key. The following diagram illustrates the architecture of Kerberos authentication:

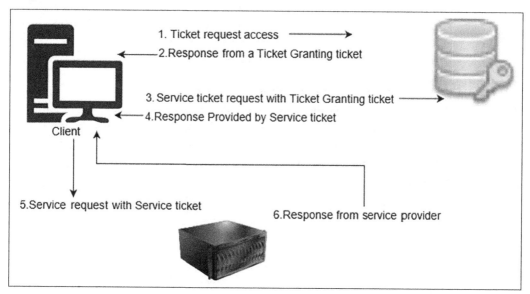

Figure 8.3: Kerberos authentication

As shown in the preceding diagram, when you want to access a service, the following steps are involved:

1. The client sends an access ticket request to the AS as a plaintext request. This request contains the client ID, TGS ID, IP address, and authentication time.

2. The AS checks if your information is available in the KDC database. Once the AS has found your information, it establishes a session between the client request and the TGS. The AS then replies to the client with the **Ticket-Granting Ticket (TGT)** and the TGS session key.

3. Now, the TGS session key asks for a password, and, given the correct password, a client can decrypt the TGS session key. However, it cannot decrypt the TGT since the TGS secret key is not available.

4. Now, the client sends the current TGT to the TGS with the authenticator. The TGS contains the session key along with the client ID and **Service Principal Name (SPN)** of the resource the client wants to access.

5. Now, the TGS again checks if the requested service address exists in the KDC database. If it does, the TSG will then encrypt the TGT and send a valid session key for the service to the client.

6. The client forwards the session key to the service to prove that the user has access, and the service grants access.

While Kerberos can be very useful, it is an open-source protocol, and generally large enterprises like to use more managed software with robust support, such as AD. Let's look at the working mechanism of one of the most popular user management tools, Microsoft AD, which is based on the **Lightweight Directory Access Protocol (LDAP)**.

Microsoft Active Directory

AD (Active Directory) is an identity service developed by Microsoft for users and machines. AD has a domain controller, also known as **Active Directory Domain Services (AD DS)**, which stores the user's and the system's information, their access credentials, and their identity. The following diagram illustrates a simple flow of the necessary authentication process:

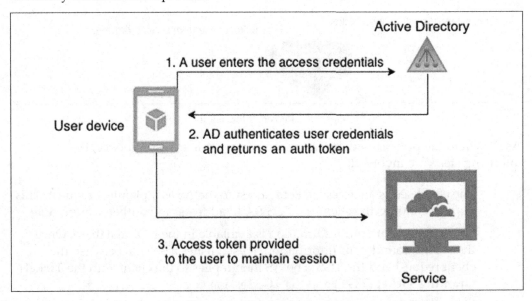

Figure 8.4: AD authentication flow

As shown in the preceding diagram, the user login is managed by AD or any resource on the domain networks. Users first send the request to the domain controller with their credentials and communicate with the **Active Directory Authentication Library (ADAL)**. The ADAL verifies the user credentials and sends back an access token with a continuous session for the requested service.

LDAP (**Lightweight Directory Access Protocol**) is the standard protocol that handles the tree-like hierarchical structure of information stored in directories. **Active Directory Lightweight Directory Services (AD LDS)** provides an LDAP interface to the directory of users and systems. For file encryption and network traffic encryption, **Active Directory Certificate Services (AD CS)** provides the key infrastructure functionality. **Active Directory Federation Services (ADFS)** provides access mechanisms for external resources such as web app logins for a large number of users.

As many organizations have started using cloud services, let's learn about the active directory service provided by AWS cloud.

Amazon Web Services Directory Service

Amazon Web Services (AWS) Directory Service helps to connect AWS resources in your account with an existing on-premises user management tool such as AD. It helps to set up a new user management directory in the AWS cloud. AWS Directory Service facilitates a secure connection to the on-premises directory. After establishing the connection, all users can access cloud resources and on-premises applications with their already existing credentials.

AWS AD Connector is another service that helps you to connect the existing Microsoft AD to the AWS cloud. You don't need any specific directory synchronization tool. After setting up an AD connection, users can utilize their existing credentials to log on to AWS applications. Admin users can manage AWS resources, using AWS IAM.

AD Connector helps to enable MFA by integrating with your existing MFA infrastructure, such as YubiKey, a Gemalto token, an RSA token, and so on. For a smaller user base (fewer than 5,000 users), AWS provides Simple AD, which is a managed directory powered by *Samba 4 Active Directory Compatible Server*. Simple AD has common features such as user accounts management, user group management, SSO based on Kerberos, and user group policies.

Google Identity federation with Active Directory

Google cloud uses Google Identity for user authentication and authorization. It allows easy user management by federating user identities from the existing identity management system in AD. To implement federation, you can use Google Cloud Directory Sync to synchronize users and groups from an AD service to the Google Cloud domain directory. You can also use ADFS AD for federated authentication within the existing environment.

In this section, you have learned a high-level overview of AD and managed AD services provided by Microsoft and Amazon. The other directory services provided by major technology companies include Okta, Centrify, Ping Identity, and Oracle **Identity Cloud Service (IDCS)**.

Security Assertion Markup Language

Earlier in this section, under *Federated identity management and single sign-on*, you learned about IdPs and SPs. To access a service, the user gets validated from the IdP, which in turn has a trusted relationship with the SP. **Security Assertion Markup Language (SAML)** is one of the mechanisms to establish a trusted relationship between an IdP and an SP. SAML uses **extensible markup language (XML)** to standardize communication between an IdP and an SP. SAML enables SSO, so users can use a single credential to access multiple applications.

A SAML assertion is an XML document that the IdP sends to the service provider with user authorization. The following diagram illustrates the flow of the SAML assertion:

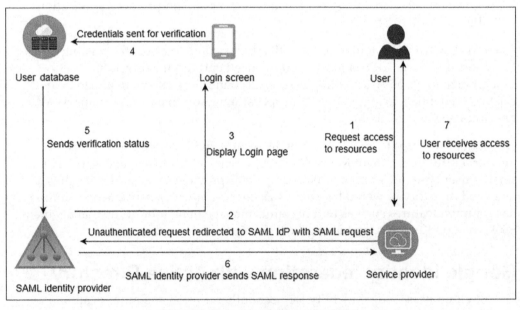

Figure 8.5: User authentication using SAML

As mentioned in the preceding diagram, the following steps are taken to implement user authentication using SAML:

1. A user sends a request to access the service—for example, the Salesforce CRM application—as a service provider.

2. The service provider (a CRM application) sends a SAML request with the user information to the SAML IdP.

3. The SAML IdP pops up the SSO login page, where users enter authentication information.

4. The user access credential goes to the identity store for validation. In this case, the user identity store is an *AD*.

5. The user identity store sends the user validation status to the SAML IdP, with whom the identity store has a trusted relationship.

6. The SAML IdP sends a SAML assertion to the service provider (a CRM application) with information pertaining to user verification.

7. After receiving the SAML response, the service provider allows application access to the user.

Sometimes, service providers can act as an IdP as well. SAML is very popular for establishing a relation between any identity store and service provider. All modern identity store applications are SAML 2.0-compatible, which allows them to communicate with each other seamlessly. SAML allows user identity to be federated and enables SSO for enterprise users.

However, for large user bases such as social media and e-commerce websites, **OAuth** (short for **Open Authorization**) and **OpenID** are more suitable. Let's learn more about OAuth and **OpenID Connect (OIDC)**.

OAuth and OpenID Connect

OAuth is an open standard authorization protocol that provides secure access to an application. OAuth provides secure access delegation. OAuth doesn't share password data but uses the authorization token to establish the identity between service providers and consumers. Users of an application provide access to their information without giving login credentials. While OAuth is mainly for authorization, many organizations have started adding their own mechanisms for authentication. **OIDC** defines the authentication standard on top of **OAuth authorization**.

Large technology companies such as Amazon, Facebook, Google, and Twitter allow users to share information in their accounts with third-party applications. For example, you can log in to a new photo app using your Facebook login and authorize the new app to access only your Facebook photo information.

The following diagram illustrates an OAuth access delegation flow:

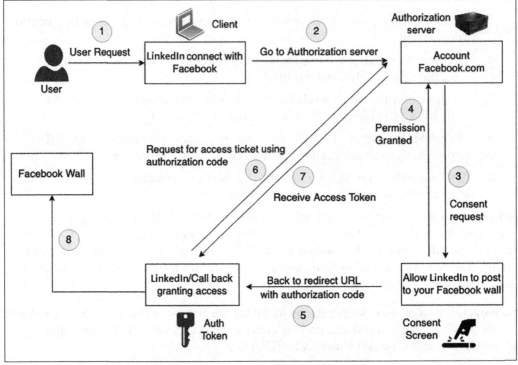

Figure 8.6: User access delegation with OAuth 2.0

As shown in the preceding diagram, the authentication flow follows these steps:

1. In this scenario, you want the LinkedIn app to get your profile photo from Facebook.

2. The LinkedIn app requests authorization to access Facebook profile photos.

3. The authorization server (which is your Facebook account in this case) creates and displays a consent screen to you.

4. You provide your consent to the request for the LinkedIn app to access only your Facebook profile photos.

5. After getting your approval, the authorization Facebook server sends an authorization code back to the requesting LinkedIn app.

6. The LinkedIn app then requests an access token from the authorization server (Facebook account) using the authorization code.

7. The authorization server identifies the LinkedIn app and checks the validity of the authentication code. If the access token is validated, the server issues an access token to the LinkedIn app.

8. The LinkedIn app can now access resources such as Facebook profile photos using the access token.

OAuth 2.0, which is faster than OAuth 1.0 and more comfortable to implement, is now most commonly used. **JSON Web Token (JWT)** is a simple and accessible token format that can be used with OAuth and is popular with OpenID.

JSON Web Token

A JWT has a JSON structure that has information about expiration time, issuer, subject, and so on. It is more robust than **Simple Web Token (SWT)** and simpler than SAML 2.0. You can see a JWT in the following screenshot:

Figure 8.7: Sample JWT

As shown in the preceding screenshot, JWTs consist of three parts separated by dots, as you can see in the **Encoded** section:

- Header: The header consists of two parts: the type of the token, which is JWT, and the signing algorithm being used, such as HS256 or RSA.

- Payload: The payload contains the claims. Claims are statements about the user and any additional data.

- Signature: The signature verifies the message wasn't changed along the way. It can also verify the sender of the JWT.

JSON has a simpler structure than XML, and is also smaller in size, making JWT more compact than SAML. JWT is a good choice to pass information into HTML and HTTP environments.

In this section, you learned about the most common user management tools and services. However, there are various other protocols and services available for user authentication and authorization. Implementation of the protocols mentioned previously can be complicated, and there is a large amount of packaged software available that makes the job easier.

Amazon Cognito is a user access management service provided by AWS that includes standard-based authorization such as SAML 2.0, OIDC, and OAuth 2.0, along with an enterprise user directory that provides the ability to connect with AD. Okta and Ping Identity provide enterprise user management and the ability to communicate with various service provider tools in one place.

Once your application is exposed to the internet, there are always various kinds of attacks that are bound to happen. Let's learn about some of the most common attacks, and how to set up the first layer of defense for web-layer protection.

Handling web security

As user demand is changing to require 24/7 availability of services, businesses are evolving to go into online mode and adopting web application models. Web applications also help a company to gain a global customer base. Businesses such as online banking and e-commerce websites are always available, and they deal with customers' sensitive data such as payment information and payer identity.

Now, web applications are central to any business, and these applications are exposed to the world. Web applications can have vulnerabilities, which makes them exposed to cyber-attacks and data breaches. Let's explore some common web vulnerabilities and how to mitigate them.

Web app security vulnerabilities

A web application is prone to security breaches as hackers orchestrate cyber-attacks from different locations and by various methods. A web application is more vulnerable to theft than a physical store location. Just as you lock and protect your physical shop, in the same way, your web app needs to protect itself from unwanted activity. Let's explore some standard methods of attack that can cause security vulnerabilities in your web application.

Denial of service and distributed denial of service attacks

A **Denial of Service (DoS)** attack attempts to make your website unreachable to your users. To achieve a successful DoS attack, the attacker uses a variety of technologies that consume network and system resources, thus interrupting access for legitimate users. The attacker uses multiple hosts to orchestrate the attack against a single target.

A **Distributed Denial of Service (DDoS)** attack is a type of DoS attack where multiple compromised systems (typically infected with *Trojans*) are used to target a single system. Victims of a DDoS attack find that all their systems are maliciously used and controlled by the hacker in the distributed attack. As illustrated in the following diagram, a DDoS attack happens when multiple systems exhaust the bandwidth of resources of a targeted system:

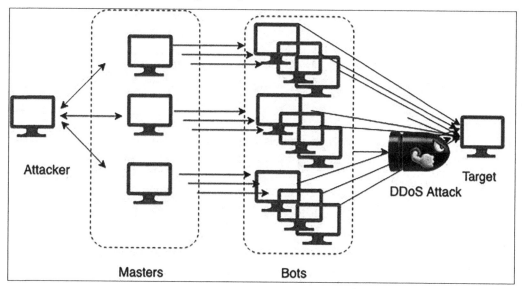

Figure 8.8: DDoS attack

The general concept of a DDoS attack is to leverage additional hosts to amplify the requests made to the target, rendering them overprovisioned and unavailable. A DDoS attack is often the result of multiple compromised systems, whereby a botnet puts a flood of traffic in the targeted system.

The most common DDoS attack happens at the application layer, using either a DNS flood or a **Secure Sockets Layer (SSL)** negotiation attack. In DNS floods, attackers exhaust the resources of a DNS server with too many requests. During SSL negotiations, attackers send a large amount of unintelligible data for computationally expensive SSL decryption. The attacker can perform other SSL-based attacks on the server fleet and overburden it with unnecessary task processing.

At the infrastructure layer, a typical DDoS attack happens in the form of the following:

- **User Datagram Protocol (UDP) reflection**: With UDP reflection, attackers spoof the target server's IP address and make a request that returns amplified significant responses from a hacked reflector server.

- **SYN floods**: With SYN floods, attackers exhaust the target server's **Transmission Control Protocol (TCP)** service by creating and abandoning high numbers of connections, blocking legitimate users from accessing the server.

Often, attackers try to get sensitive customer data, and for that purpose, they use a different kind of attack called **SQL injection (SQLi)** attacks. Let's learn more about them.

SQL injection attacks

As the name suggests, in an SQLi attack, attackers inject malicious **Structure Query Language (SQL)** to get control of an SQL database and fetch sensitive user data. The attacker uses SQLi to gain access to unauthorized information, take control of an application, add new users, and so on.

Take an example of a loan-processing web application. You have loanId as a field that customers can use to get all information related to their loan finance. The typical query will look like this: SELECT * FROM loans WHERE loanId = 117. If proper care is not taken, attackers can execute a query such as SELECT * FROM loans WHERE loanId = 117 or '1=1' and get access to the entire customer database, as this query will always return the true result.

The other common method to hack user data through script injection is **cross-site scripting (XSS)** where a hacker impersonates a legitimate user. Let's learn more about it.

Cross-site scripting attacks

You must have encountered phishing emails that have links impersonating a website known to you. Clicking on these links may lead to compromised data through XSS. With XSS, the attacker attaches their code to a legitimate website and executes it when the victim loads the web page. The malicious code can be inserted in several ways, such as in a URL string or by putting a small amount of JavaScript code on the web page.

In an XSS attack, the attacker adds a small code snippet at the end of the URL or client-side code. When you load the web page, this client-side JavaScript code gets executed and steals your browser cookies.

These cookies often contain sensitive information, such as the access token and authentication to your banking or e-commerce websites. Using these stolen cookies, the hacker can get into your bank account and take your hard-earned money.

Cross-site request forgery attacks

A **Cross-Site Request Forgery (CSRF)** attack takes advantage of user identity by creating confusion. It typically tricks the user with a transaction activity in which the state gets changed—for example, changing the password of a shopping website or requesting a money transfer to your bank.

It is slightly different than an XSS attack as, with CSRF, the attacker tries to forge the request rather than insert a code script. For example, the attacker can forge a request to transfer a certain amount of money from the user's bank and send that link in an email to the user. As soon as users click on that link, the bank gets a request and transfers the money to the attacker's account. CSRF has minimal impact on the individual user account, but it can be very harmful if attackers are able to get into the admin account.

Buffer overflow and memory corruption attacks

A software program writes data in a temporary memory area for fast processing, which is called a **buffer**. With a buffer overflow attack, an attacker can overwrite a portion of the memory connected with the buffer. An attacker can deliberately cause a buffer overflow and access connected memory, where an application executable may be stored. The attacker can replace the executable with the actual program and take control of the entire system. Buffer overflow attacks can cause memory corruption with unintentional memory modification, which the hacker can use to inject code.

Looking at the overall application, there are more security threats that exist at the infrastructure layer, network layer, and data layer. Let's explore some standard methods to mitigate and prevent security risks at the web layer.

Web security mitigation

Security needs to be applied to every layer, and special attention is required for the web layer due to its exposure to the world. For web protection, important steps include keeping up with the latest security patches, following the best software development practices, and making sure proper authentication and authorization are carried out. There are several methods to protect and secure web applications; let's explore the most common methods.

Web application firewalls

WAFs are necessary firewalls that apply specific rules to HTTP and HTTPS traffic (that is, port 80 and 443). WAFs are software firewalls that inspect your web traffic and verify that it conforms to the norms of expected behavior. WAFs provide an additional layer of protection from web attacks.

WAF rate limiting is the ability to look at the amount or type of requests sent to your service and define a threshold that caps how many requests are allowed per user, session, or IP address. Approved and un-approved lists allow you to allow or block users explicitly. AWS WAF helps you to secure your web layer by creating and applying rules to filter web traffic. These rules are based on conditions that include HTTP headers, user geolocation, malicious IP addresses, or custom **Uniform Resource Identifiers (URIs)**, and so on. AWS WAF rules block common web exploits such as XSS and SQLi.

AWS WAF provides a centralized mechanism in the form of rules that can be deployed across multiple websites. This means that you can create a single set of rules for an environment that has various websites and web applications running. You can reuse rules across applications instead of recreating them.

Overall, WAF is a tool that applies a set of rules to HTTP traffic. It helps to filter web requests based on data such as IP addresses, HTTP headers, HTTP bodies, or URI strings. It can be useful for mitigating DDoS attacks by offloading illegitimate traffic. Let's learn more about DDoS mitigation.

DDoS mitigation

Resilient architecture can help to prevent or mitigate DDoS attacks. A fundamental principle in keeping your infrastructure secure is reducing the potential number of targets that an attacker can hit. In short, if an instance doesn't need to be public, then don't make it public. An application-layer attack can spike monitoring metrics such as network utilization for your **content distribution network (CDN)**, load balancer, and server metrics due to HTTP flood. You can apply various strategies to minimize the attack surface area:

- Wherever possible, try to reduce the number of necessary internet entry points. For example, open incoming internet access to your load balancer, not web servers.
- Hide any required internet entry points from untrusted end users so that they cannot access them.
- Identify and remove any non-critical internet entry points — for example, expose file-share storage for vendors to upload data with limited access, rather than exposing it to worldwide internet traffic.

- Isolate the access point and apply a specific restrictions policy for end user traffic compared to application management traffic.
- Create a decoupled internet entry point to minimize the attack surface.

Your primary goal is to mitigate DDoS attacks at the edge location of the CDN. It's more challenging and costly to handle DDoS attacks if they get through to your application servers. The following diagram illustrates a DDoS mitigation example for an AWS cloud workload:

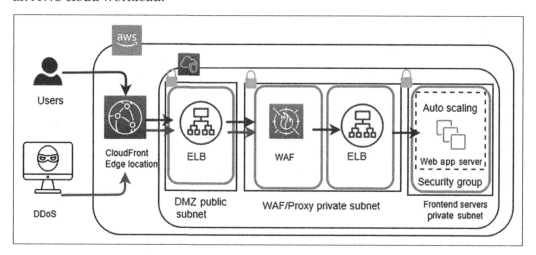

Figure 8.9: DDoS WAF sandwich mitigation strategy

The preceding diagram illustrates a **WAF sandwich architecture**, where the WAF appliance is staged between two load balancers to handle a DDoS attack. Frequent DDoS attacks come from attacking strategies such as SYN floods and UDP reflection, which Amazon CloudFront prevents by only accepting well-formed connections before the attacking strategy can reach your application servers. CDNs such as Amazon CloudFront help to tackle DDoS attacks by isolating them at a geographically isolated location and preventing the traffic from affecting other locations. Network firewall security helps you to control incoming and outgoing traffic at an individual server level.

As mentioned in the previous section, WAFs are used to protect web applications against exploit attacks such as XSS and SQLi attacks. In addition to this, WAFs also help to detect and prevent DDoS attacks at the web application layer.

To handle a DDoS attack, you can apply either horizontal or vertical scaling. You can take advantage of scaling in the following way:

1. First, select the right server size and configuration for your web application.

2. Second, apply a load balancer to distribute traffic among the fleet of servers and add auto-scaling to add/remove servers as required.

3. Finally, use the CDN and DNS server, as they are built to handle traffic at scale.

Scaling for DDoS attacks is an excellent example of why it's essential to set reasonable maximum counts for your servers. A DDoS attack could scale your servers out to a count that would be extremely costly, while still potentially not being able to avoid becoming unavailable. Having reasonable maximum limits for expectations of regular traffic spikes would prevent a DDoS attack from costing your company too much money.

In this section, you learned about various security risks and vulnerabilities at the web layer and some standard methods to protect them. As security needs to be applied to every layer, let's explore more about the protection of the infrastructure layer.

Securing an application and its infrastructure

In the previous section, you learned about securing the web layer. As security needs to be applied at every layer of your workload, let's learn about securing the application and network layers.

Application and operating system hardening

It is not possible to entirely eliminate vulnerabilities in your application, but you can limit system attacks by hardening your application's operating system, filesystem, and directory. Once attackers can get into your application, they can get root access and orchestrate an attack on the entire infrastructure. It is essential to limit attacks to the application level by restricting the directory by *hardening permission*. At the process level, restrict memory and CPU utilization to prevent a DoS attack.

Set the right permission at the file, folder, and file partition levels, which is the only requirement for the application to execute. Avoid giving root privilege to the application or its users. You should create a separate directory with only required access for each application so only the required user has application access. Don't use common access for all applications.

Automate application restart by using tools and avoid a manual approach, whereby users need to log in to the server to start.

You can use process control tools such as **DAEMON Tools** and **Supervisord** to automate an application restart. For a Linux operating system, a utility such as **systemd** or **System V init** scripts help to start/stop the application.

Software vulnerabilities and secure code

It is always recommended to apply the latest security patch to your operating system provided by your operating system vendor. This helps to fill any security holes in the system and protect your system from vulnerabilities where attackers are able to steal your security certificate or run arbitrary code. Make sure to integrate secure coding best practices into your software development process, as recommended by the **Open Web Application Security Project (OWASP)**, details about which can be found here: https://owasp.org/www-project-top-ten/.

Keeping your system up to date with the latest security patch is very important. It is better to automate the process of the most recent patch installation as soon as it becomes available. However, sometimes, running a security patch may break your working software, so it's better to set up a **Continuous Integration and Continuous Deployment (CI/CD)** pipeline with automated test and deployment. You will learn more about the CI/CD process in *Chapter 12, DevOps and Solution Architecture Framework*.

The AWS cloud provides a system manager tool that allows you to apply security patches and monitoring of your server fleet in the cloud. You can use a tool such as **auto-updates** or **unattended-upgrades** to automate security patch installation.

Network, firewall, and trusted boundary

When it comes to protecting your infrastructure, securing the network comes into consideration first. The physical security of your IT infrastructure in the data center is to be taken care of by providers. In the case of cloud-like AWS providers, they take the utmost care of the physical security of your infrastructure. Let's talk about ensuring network security, which is your responsibility as an application owner.

To understand it better, let's take an example from a public cloud provider such as AWS. You can apply the same example to your on-premises or private cloud network infrastructure as well.

As illustrated in the following diagram, you should apply security at every layer and define trusted boundaries around each layer, with minimal access:

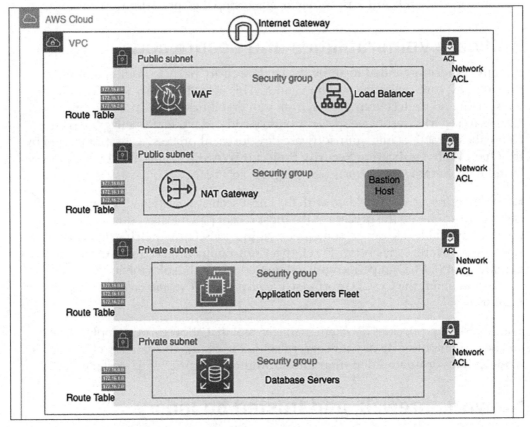

Figure 8.10: Network configuration for infrastructure security

In the preceding diagram, the load balancer is in a public subnet, which can accept internet traffic and distribute it to the application server fleet. WAF filter traffic is based on set rules and protects your application from various attacks, as you learned in the previous section. The application server fleet and database servers are in a private subnet, which means direct internet access is not reachable to expose them to the public internet. Let's dive deep into the preceding architecture diagram and walk through each layer, as follows:

- Amazon **Virtual Private Cloud (VPC)** provides you with logical network isolation of your infrastructure. Amazon VPC is your network environment in the cloud. It's where you will launch many of your resources. It's designed to provide greater control over the isolation of your environments and their resources from each other. You can have multiple VPCs in each account or region.

- When you create a VPC, you specify its set of IP addresses with **Classless Inter-Domain Routing (CIDR)** notation. CIDR notation is a simplified way of showing a specific range of IP addresses. For example, 10.0.0.0/16 covers all IPs from 10.0.0.0 to 10.0.255.255, providing 65,535 IP addresses to use.

- Subnets are segments or partitions of a network divided by the CIDR range. They create trusted boundaries between private and public resources. Rather than defining your subnets based on the application or functional tier (web/app/data), you should organize your subnets based on internet accessibility. A subnet allows you to define clear, subnet-level isolation between public and private resources.

- In this environment, all of your resources that require direct access to the internet (public-facing load balancers, **Network Address Translation (NAT)** instances, bastion hosts, and so on) would go into the public subnet, while all other instances (such as database and application resources) would go into your private subnet. Use subnets to create layers of separation between *tiers* of resources, such as putting your application instances and your data resources into separate private subnets.

- The majority of resources on AWS can be hosted in private subnets, using public subnets for controlled access to and from the internet as necessary. Because of this, you should plan your subnets so that your private subnets have substantially more IPs available compared to your public subnets.

- While subnets can provide a fundamental element of segregation between resources using **Network Access Control List (NACL)** rules, security groups can give an even more fine-grained level of traffic control between your resources, without the risk of overcomplicating your infrastructure and wasting or running out of IPs.

- A routing table contains a set of rules, called **routes**. Routes determine which application servers are to receive network traffic. For better security, use a custom route table for each subnet.

- Security groups are the virtual firewalls that control inbound and outbound traffic for one or more instances from the CIDR block range, or another security group, as designated resources. As per the principle of least privilege, deny all incoming traffic by default and create rules that can filter traffic based on TCP, UDP, and **Internet Control Message Protocol (ICMP)** protocols.

- An NACL is an optional virtual firewall that controls inbound and outbound traffic at the subnet level. An NACL is a stateless firewall that is compared to the security group, which is stateful. This means that if your incoming request is allowed, then the outbound request does not have to be inspected or tracked. While stateless, you have to define both inbound and outbound traffic rules explicitly.

- Internet traffic is routed through an **internet gateway** (**IGW**) to make a subnet public. By default, internet accessibility is denied for internet traffic in your environment. An IGW needs to be attached to your VPC, and the subnet's route table should define the rules to the IGW.

- A private subnet blocks all incoming and outgoing internet traffic, but servers may need outgoing internet traffic for software and security patch installation. A NAT gateway enables instances in a private subnet to initiate outbound traffic to the internet and protects resources from incoming internet traffic.

- A bastion host acts like a jump server, which allows access to other resources in the private subnet. A bastion host needs to be hardened with tighter security so that only appropriate people can access it. To log in to the server, always use *public-key cryptography* for authentication rather than a regular user ID and password method.

Many organizations typically collect, store, monitor, and analyze network flow logs for various purposes, including troubleshooting connectivity and security issues and testing network access rules. You need to monitor traffic flow to your system VPC, which includes recording incoming and outgoing traffic information from your network. **VPC Flow Logs** enables you to capture that information, along with accepted and rejected traffic information for the designated resource to understand traffic patterns better.

Flow logs can also be used as a security tool for monitoring traffic that is reaching your instance. You can create alarms to notify you if certain types of traffic are detected. You can also create metrics to help you to identify trends and patterns. You can create a flow log for a VPC, a subnet, or a network interface. If you create a flow log for a subnet or VPC, each network interface in the VPC or subnet is monitored.

As you can see, there are multiple layers for security available at the network layer that can help to protect your infrastructure. Keeping resources in their isolated subnet helps to reduce the blast radius. If an attacker can penetrate one component, you should be able to restrict them to limited resources. You can use an IDS and an IPS in front of your infrastructure to detect and prevent any malicious traffic. Let's learn more about them.

Intrusion detection system and intrusion prevention system

An IDS detects any cyber-attack happening through network traffic by recognizing an attack pattern. An IPS goes a step further and helps to stop malicious traffic proactively.

The IPS sits behind the firewall and provides a layer of analysis for dangerous content such as malicious packets dropping, blocking traffic from the source address, and connection resetting.

The IPS has two major detection methods, signature-based detection and statistical anomaly-based detection, for finding exploits. **Signature-based detection** is based on a dictionary of uniquely identifiable patterns of each exploit. Each exploit signature is stored in a continuously growing dictionary of signatures to determine a pattern. **Statistical anomaly detection** defines a baseline performance parameter. It takes samples of network traffic randomly and compares them to the baseline performance level. If network traffic activity is outside the parameters, the IPS takes action.

You need to determine the applicability of the IDS/IPS system as per your application's requirements. An IDS can be host-based or network-based.

Host-based IDS

In an IDS, a host- or agent-based IDS is running on each host of your environment. It can review the activity within that host to determine if an attack has occurred and has been successful. It can do this by inspecting logs, monitoring the filesystem, monitoring network connections to the host, and so on. The software or agent then communicates with a central/command application about the health or security of the host it is monitoring.

The pros of host-based solutions include that they can deeply inspect the activity inside each host. They can horizontally scale as far as required (each host gets its own agent), and do not need to impact the performance of running applications. The cons include the additional configuration management overheads that can be introduced if managing agents on many servers, which are burdensome for an organization.

As each agent is operating in isolation, widespread/coordinated attacks can be harder to detect. To handle coordinated attacks, the system should respond immediately across all hosts, which requires the host-based solution to play well with the other components, such as the operating system and the application interface, deployed on the host.

Network-based IDS

A network-based IDS inserts an appliance into the network, through which all traffic is routed and inspected for attacks.

The pros include a simple/single component that needs to be deployed and managed away from the application hosts. Also, it is hardened or monitored in a way that might be burdensome across all hosts. An individual/shared view of security exists in a single place so that the big picture can be inspected for anomalies/attacks.

However, a network-based IDS includes the performance hit of adding a network hop to applications. The need to decrypt/re-encrypt traffic to inspect it is both a massive performance hit and a security risk that makes the network appliance an attractive target. Any traffic that the IDS is unable to decrypt cannot inspect/detect anything.

An IDS is a detection and monitoring tool and does not act on its own. An IPS detects, accepts, and denies traffic based on set rules. IDS/IPS solutions help to prevent DDoS attacks due to their anomaly-detection capabilities that make them able to recognize when valid protocols are used as an attack vehicle. An IDS and an IPS read network packets and compare contents to a database of known threats. Continuous auditing and scanning are required for your infrastructure to proactively secure it from any attack, so let's learn more about this.

In this section, you learned all about securing your infrastructure from various types of attacks. The goal of these attacks is to get hold of your data. You should secure your data in such a way that an attacker is not able to acquire sensitive information even after getting hold of the data. Let's learn about data protection using security at the data layer, encryption, and backup.

Data security

In today's digital world, every system revolves around data. Sometimes, this data may contain sensitive information such as customer health records, payment information, and government identity. Securing customer data to prevent any unauthorized access is most important. There are many industries that place stress on data protection and security.

Before architecting any solution, you should define basic security practices as per the application objective, such as complying with regulatory requirements. There are several different approaches used when addressing data protection. The following section describes how to use these approaches.

Data classification

One of the best practices is to classify your data, which provides a way to categorize and handle organizational data based on levels of sensitivity.

According to data sensitivity, you can plan data protection, data encryption, and data access requirements.

By managing data classification as per your system's workload requirements, you can create the data controls and level of access needed for the data.

For example, content such as a user rating and review is often public, and it's fine to provide public access, but user credit card information is highly sensitive data that needs to be encrypted and put under very restricted access.

At a high level, you can classify data into the following categories:

- **Restricted data**: This contains information that could harm the customer directly if it got compromised. Mishandling of restricted data can damage a company's reputation and impact a business adversely. Restricted data may include customer PII data such as social security numbers, passport details, credit card numbers, and payment information.

- **Private data**: Data can be categorized as confidential if it contains customer-sensitive information that an attacker can use to plan to obtain their restricted data. Confidential data may include customer email IDs, phone numbers, full names, and addresses.

- **Public data**: This is available and accessible to everyone, and requires minimal protection—for example, customer ratings and reviews, customer location, and customer username if the user made it public.

You can have a more granular category depending on the type of industry and the nature of the user data. Data classification needs to balance data usability versus data access. Setting different levels of access, as mentioned previously, helps to restrict only the necessary data and make sure sensitive data is not exposed. Always avoid giving direct human access to data and add some tools that can generate a read-only report for users to consume in a restrictive manner.

Data encryption at rest

Data at rest means it is stored somewhere such as a **storage area network (SAN)** or **network-attached storage (NAS)** drive, or in cloud storage. All sensitive data needs to be protected by applying symmetric or asymmetric encryption, explained in this section, with proper key management.

Data encryption is a method to protect your data whereby you convert your data from plaintext to encoded ciphertext format using an encryption key. To read these ciphertexts, they first need to be decrypted using the encryption key, and only authorized users will have access to those decryption keys.

Commonly used key-based encryption falls into one of two categories of cryptography:

- **Symmetric-key encryption**: With symmetric encryption algorithms, the same key is used to encrypt and decrypt the data. Each data packet is self-encrypted with a secret key. Data is encrypted while saving and decrypted during retrieval. Earlier, symmetric encryption used to be applied as per the **Data Encryption Standard (DES)**, which used a 56-bit key. Now, the **Advanced Encryption Standard (AES)** is heavily used for symmetric encryption, which is more reliable as it uses a 128-bit, 192-bit, or 256-bit key.

- **Asymmetric-key encryption**: With the help of asymmetric algorithms, two different keys can be used, one to encrypt and one to decrypt. In most cases, the encryption key is a public key and the decryption key is a private key. Asymmetric key encryption is also known as **public-key encryption**. The public and private keys are *unidentical*, but they are paired together. The private key is only available to one user, while the public key can be distributed across multiple resources. Only the user who has a private key can decrypt the data. **Rivest–Shamir–Adleman (RSA)** is one of the first and most popular public key encryption algorithms used to secure data transmissions over a network.

Data encryption and decryption come with a performance price as it adds an additional layer for processing. You need to make a careful trade-off while choosing data for encryption. You may want to apply encryption only where it's really necessary to avoid performance and key management overhead.

If you are encrypting your data with an AES 256-bit security key, it's become almost impossible to break the encryption. The only way to decrypt is by getting your hands on the encryption key, which means you need to secure your code and keep it in a safe place. Let's learn about some essential management methods to safeguard your encryption key.

Encryption key management

Key management involves controlling and maintaining your encryption key. You need to make sure that only authorized users can create and access the encryption key. Any encryption key management system handles storage, rotation, and destruction of the key in addition to access management and key generation. Key management differs depending on whether you are using a symmetric or asymmetric algorithm. The following methods are popular for key management.

Envelope encryption

Envelope encryption is a technique to secure your data encryption key. Data encryption keys are symmetric keys to increase the performance of data encryption. Symmetric encryption keys work with an encryption algorithm such as AES and produce ciphertext that you can store safely, as it is not readable by a human. However, you need to save the symmetric encryption data key along with data to use it for data decryption, as needed. Now, you need to further protect the data key in isolation, which is where envelope encryption helps you to protect it. Let's understand it in more detail with the help of the following diagram:

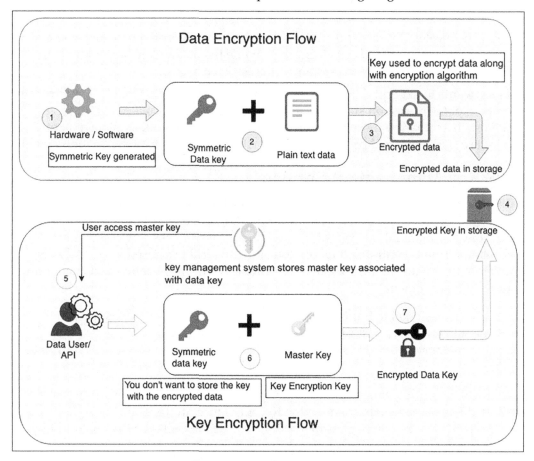

Figure 8.11: Envelope encryption

The preceding diagram illustrates the following flow to explain envelope encryption:

1. The symmetric key is generated from software or hardware.
2. The generated symmetric data key is used to encrypt plaintext data.

3. The key encrypts data using an algorithm such as AES and generates encrypted ciphertext data.

4. The encrypted data is stored in targeted storage.

5. As the data key needs to be stored with ciphered data, the data key needs to be encrypted further. The user gets the customer master key stored in the key management systems to encrypt the data key.

6. The data key is encrypted using the master key. Your master key is the main encryption key as it encrypts the data encryption key. Only the master key can encrypt multiple data keys, and it is securely stored in the key management systems, with restricted access.

7. The master key encrypts the data key, and the encrypted data key is stored along with ciphered data in storage, while the master key is securely stored in the key management system with restricted access.

If a user wants to decrypt data, then they first need a master key that has, in turn, an encrypted data encryption key. This master key can be stored in a separate access system such as a hardware security module or software-based key management service provided by cloud providers such as AWS. Let's look into this in more detail.

AWS Key Management Service

AWS **Key Management Service (KMS)** uses envelope encryption whereby a unique data key encrypts customer data, and KMS master keys encrypt data keys. You can bring your key material to AWS KMS and manage user access, key distribution, and rotation from a centralized place. You can also disable unused keys, and a low number of keys helps to improve the performance of the application and encourage better key management.

AWS KMS is designed to limit access and protect master keys. KMS helps you to implement key security best practices by never storing plaintext master keys on disk or in memory. KMS also gracefully rotates the master keys to secure your data further.

AWS KMS is a multitenancy key management module; a customer wants to have a dedicated key management module due to compliance. In the same line, other cloud vendors provide a key management system, such as the GCP-provided Cloud Key Management, and Microsoft provides Azure Key Vault.

Sometimes, customers want to have their key management system due to industry regulatory reasons for multi-tenancy. They can choose to store the key in an HSM in such a situation. Cloud providers such as AWS also provide stores, such as AWS CloudHSM. You can choose your own HSM vendor as well. Let's explore HSM in more depth.

Hardware security module

A **hardware security module (HSM)** is a device that is designed to secure encryption keys and associated cryptographic operations. An HSM is designed with physical mechanisms to protect the keys, which includes tamper detection and response. In case of any key tampering, the HSM destroys the keys and prevents any security compromise.

An HSM includes logical protections to limit access controls. Logical separation helps the HSM appliance administrator to manage the device securely. Access restriction applies rules for users who can connect it to the network and provision the IP address. You can create a separate role for everyone, including security officers, appliance admins, and users.

As the loss of a key can make your data useless, you need to make sure of high availability for your HSM by maintaining at least two HSMs in different geographic locations. You can use other HSM solutions, such as SafeNet or Voltage. To protect your key, choose a managed HSM provided by cloud services such as AWS CloudHSM or CipherCloud.

Data encryption in transit

Data in transit means data in motion and transferred over the network. You may encrypt data at rest in the source and destination, but your data transfer pipeline needs to be secure when transferring data. When transferring data over an unencrypted protocol such as HTTP, it can get leaked by an attack such as an **eavesdropping attack** or **man-in-the-middle (MITM)** attack.

In an eavesdropping attack, the attacker captures a small packet from a network and uses it to search for any other type of information. A MITM attack is a tampering-based attack, where the attacker secretly alters the communication to start communicating on behalf of the receiver. These kinds of attacks can be prevented by transferring data over SSL, using a strong protocol such as **Transport Security Layer (TSL)**.

You will observe that most websites now use HTTPS protocol for communication, which encrypts data using SSL. By default, HTTP traffic is unprotected. SSL/TLS protection for HTTP traffic (HTTPS) is supported by all web servers and browsers. HTTP traffic is also applicable to service-oriented architectures such as **Representational State Transfer (REST)**- and **Simple Object Access Protocol (SOAP)**-based architectures.

SSL/TSL handshakes use certificates to exchange a public key using asymmetric encryption and then use the public key to exchange a private key using symmetric encryption. A security certificate is issued by an acceptable **Certification Authority (CA)** such as Verisign. Procured security certificates need to be secured using a **Public Key Infrastructure (PKI)**. The following is a standard SSL handshake with RSA key exchange:

1. **Client Hello**: The client sends a message to the server to communicate with the client via SSL. Information includes the SSL version number, cipher settings, and user session-specific data.

2. **Server Hello**: Server sends information back to the client, which requires using SSL. The server confirms the SSL version number and certificate with the public key.

3. **Authentication and pre-master secret**: The client authenticates the server certificate with the details such as common name, date, and issuer. The client creates the pre-master secret for the session as per their cipher, encrypts with the server's public key, and sends the encrypted pre-master secret to the server.

4. **Decryption and master secret**: The server uses its private key to decrypt the pre-master secret. Both the server and client perform steps to generate the master secret with the agreed cipher.

5. **Encryption with session key**: Both the client and server exchange messages to inform that future messages will be encrypted. It is called a shared secret. Once shared, the client and server exchange messages to confirm message encryption and decryption. From there, both protect their communication for the rest of the session.

Non-web transmission of data over the network should also be encrypted, and this includes **Secure Shell (SSH)** and **Internet Protocol Security (IPsec)** encryption. SSH is most prevalent while connecting to servers, and IPsec is applicable to securing corporate traffic transferred over a **virtual private network (VPN)**. File transfer should be secured using **SSH File Transfer Protocol (SFTPS)** or **FTP Secure (FTPS)**, and email server communication needs to be secured by **Simple Mail Transfer Protocol Secure (SMTPS)** or **Internet Message Access Protocol (IMAP)**.

In this section, you learned about various methods to secure data at rest and in motion with different cryptographic techniques. Data backup and recovery is an important aspect of protecting your data in the case of any unforeseen incidents. You will learn more about data backup in *Chapter 9, Architectural Reliability Considerations*, in the *Disaster recovery planning* section.

There are many governing bodies available that publish compliance, which is a set of checklists to ensure customers' data security. Compliance also makes sure that organizations comply with industry and local government rules. Let's learn more about various compliance measures in the next section.

Security and compliance certifications

There are many compliance certifications depending on your industry and geographical location to protect customer privacy and secure data. For any solution design, compliance requirements are among the critical criteria that need to be evaluated. The following are some of the most popular industry-standard compliances:

- Global compliance includes certifications that all organizations need to adhere to, regardless of their region. These include ISO 9001, ISO 27001, ISO 27017, ISO 27018, SOC 1, SOC 2, SOC 3, and CSA STAR for cloud security.

- The US government requires various kinds of compliance to handle the public sector workload. These include FedRAMP, DoD SRG Level-2, 4, and 5, FIPS 140, NIST SP 800, IRS 1075, ITAR, VPAT, and CJIS.

- Industry-level compliance of an application applies to a particular industry. These include PCI DSS, CDSA, MPAA, FERPA, CMS MARS-E, NHS IG Toolkit (in the UK), HIPAA, FDA, FISC (in Japan), FACT (in the UK), Shared Assessment, and GLBA.

- Regional compliance certification applies to a particular country or region. These include EU GDPR, EU Model Clauses, UK G-Cloud, China DJCP, Singapore MTCS, Argentina PDPA, Australia IRAP, India MeitY, New Zealand GCIO, Japan CS Mark Gold, Spain ENS and DPA, Canada Privacy Law, and US Privacy Shield.

As you can see, there are many compliance certifications available from different regulatory bodies as per industry, region, and government policy. We are not going into the details of compliance, but you need to evaluate your application with compliance requirements before starting your solution design. Compliance requirements influence the overall solution design heavily. You need to decide what kind of encryption is required, as well as the logging, auditing, and location of your workload based on your compliance needs.

Logging and monitoring help to ensure robust security and compliance. Logging and monitoring are essential. If an incident occurs, your team should be notified immediately and be ready to respond to incidents. You are going to learn more about monitoring and alert methods in *Chapter 10, Operational Excellence Considerations*.

There are several compliance industries depending on your application geolocation, industry, and government rules. You learned about the various categories of compliance and some common compliance standards appropriate for each group. Many organizations are moving to the cloud, so it's vital to understand security in the cloud.

The cloud's shared security responsibility model

As the cloud is becoming the norm and many organizations are moving their workload to a public cloud such as AWS, **Google Cloud Platform** (**GCP**), and Azure, the customer needs to understand the cloud security model. Security in the cloud is a joint effort between the customer and the cloud provider. Customers are responsible for what they implement using cloud services and for the applications connected to the cloud. In the cloud, customer responsibility for application security needs depends upon the cloud offerings they are using and the complexity of their system.

The following diagram illustrates a cloud security model from one of the largest public cloud providers (AWS), and it's pretty much applicable to any public cloud provider, such as Azure, GCP, Oracle, IBM, or Alibaba:

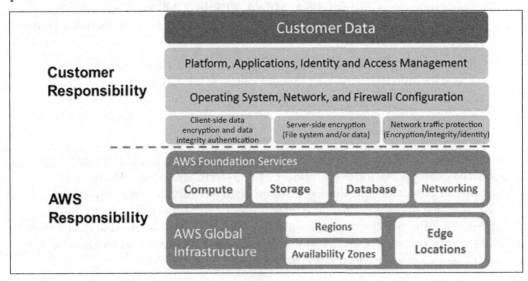

Figure 8.12: AWS cloud shared security responsibility model

As shown in the preceding diagram, AWS handles the security of the cloud, specifically the physical infrastructures that host your resources.

This includes the following:

- **Data centers**: Non-descript facilities, 24/7 security guards, two-factor authentication, access logging and review, video surveillance, and disk degaussing and destruction
- **Hardware infrastructure**: Servers, storage devices, and other appliances that rely on AWS services
- **Software infrastructure**: Host operating systems, service applications, and virtualization software
- **Network infrastructure**: Routers, switches, load balancers, firewalls, cabling, and so on. Also includes continuous network monitoring at external boundaries, secure access points, and redundant infrastructure

The customer handles the **security in the cloud**, which includes the following:

- **Server's operating system**: The operating system installed on the server could be vulnerable to attacks. Patching and maintenance of the operating system is the customer's responsibility, as software applications depend heavily upon it.
- **Application**: Every application and its environments, such as dev, test, and prod, are maintained by the customer. So, handling password policies and access management is the customer's responsibility.
- **Operating system/host-based firewalls**: Customers need to protect their entire system from external attacks. However, the cloud provides security in that area, but customers should consider an IDS or an IPS to add an extra layer of security.
- **Network configuration and security group**: The cloud provides tools to create a network firewall, but it depends on the application requirements as to which traffic needs to be stopped or allowed to go through. Customers are responsible for setting up firewall rules to secure their systems from external and internal network traffic.
- **Customer data and encryption**: Data handling is the customer's responsibility, as they are more aware of the data protection that's needed. The cloud provides tools to apply for data protection by using various encryption mechanisms, but it's the customer's responsibility to apply those tools and secure their data.

The public cloud also provides various compliance certifications that apply to the hardware portions managed by them. To make your application compliant, you need to handle and complete audits for application-level complaints. As a customer, you get an additional advantage by inheriting security and compliance provided by the cloud provider.

Try to automate security best practices wherever possible. Software-based security mechanisms improve your ability to scale more rapidly, cost-effectively, and securely. Create and save a custom baseline image of a virtual server, and then use that image automatically on each new server you launch. Create an entire infrastructure that is defined and managed in a template to replicate best practices for the new environment.

The cloud provides all kinds of tools and services to secure your application in the cloud, along with in-built security at the IT infrastructure level. However, it's up to the customer how they want to utilize those services and make their application secure in the cloud. The overall cloud provides better visibility and centralized management for your IT inventory, which helps to manage and secure your system.

Security is the priority for any solution, and a solution architect needs to make sure their application is secure and protected from any attack. Security is a continuous effort. Each security incident should be treated as an improvement opportunity for the application. A robust security mechanism should have authentication and authorization controls. Every organization and application should automate responses to security events and protect infrastructure at multiple levels.

Summary

In this chapter, you learned about various design principles to apply security best practices for your solution design. These principles include key considerations during solution design to protect your application by putting in the appropriate access control, data protection, and monitoring. You need to apply security at every layer. Starting with user authentication and authorization, you learned about applying security at the web layer, application layer, infrastructure layer, and database layer. Each layer is vulnerable to a different kind of attack, and you learned various methods to protect your application with the available technology choices.

For user management, you learned about using FIM and SSO to handle corporate users, and various methods for implementation of user authentication and authorization. These choices include enterprise management services such as Microsoft's AD and AWS Directory Service. You also have options to handle millions of users, using OAuth 2.0.

At the web layer, you learned about various attack types such as **DDoS**, **SQLi**, and **XSS**. You learned about how to protect those attacks, using different DDoS prevention techniques and network firewalls. You learned various techniques to protect code at the application layer and ensure the security of your infrastructure. You dived deep into different network components and methods to build trusted boundaries to limit the attack radius.

You learned about data protection by putting proper data classification in place and tagged your data as confidential, private, or public data. You learned about symmetric and asymmetric algorithms and how they differ from each other. You learned about using key management to protect the public/private encryption key. Data can be in motion or sitting in storage. You learned about how to protect data in both modes. In the end, you learned about various compliance and shared security responsibility models applicable to a cloud workload.

While this chapter is about applying security best practices, reliability is another essential aspect of any solution design. To make your business successful, you need to create a reliable solution that should always be available and able to handle workload fluctuation. In the next chapter, you will learn about the best practices to make your application reliable with the available technology choices. You will learn various disaster recovery and data replication strategies to make your application more reliable.

Join our book's Discord space

Join the book's Discord workspace for a monthly *Ask me Anything* session with the authors: https://packt.link/SAHandbook

9
Architectural Reliability Considerations

Application reliability is one of the essential aspects of architecture design. A reliable application helps to win customer trust by making it available whenever the customer needs it. As all kinds of businesses are now online, high availability has become one of the mandatory criteria for online applications. Users want to browse your application anytime and complete tasks such as shopping and banking at their convenience. Reliability is one of the essential recipes for any business to be successful.

Reliability means the ability of the system to recover from failure. It's about making your application fault-tolerant so that it can recover without impacting the customer experience. A reliable system should be able to recover from any infrastructure failure or server failure. Your system should be prepared to handle any situation that could cause disruption.

In this chapter, you will learn various design principles applicable to making your solution reliable. When assessing reliability, you need to consider every component of the architecture. You will understand how to choose the right technology to ensure your architecture's reliability at every layer. You will learn the following best practices for reliability in this chapter:

- Design principles for architectural reliability
- Technology selection for architectural reliability
- Improving reliability with the cloud

By the end of this chapter, you will have learned about various disaster recovery techniques and data replication methods to ensure the high availability of your application and the continuation of business processes.

Design principles for architectural reliability

The goal of reliability is to contain the impact of any failure in the smallest area possible. By preparing your system for the worst-case scenarios, you can implement various mitigation strategies for the different components of your infrastructure and applications.

 Before a failure occurs, you should thoroughly test your recovery procedures.

The following are the standard design principles that help you to strengthen your system's reliability. You will find that all reliability design principles are closely related and complement each other.

Making systems self-healing

System failure needs to be predicted in advance, and in the case of failure incidence, you should have an automated response for system recovery, called system self-healing. Self-healing is the ability of the solution to recover from failure automatically. A self-healing system detects failure proactively and responds to it gracefully with minimal customer impact. Failure can happen in any layer of your entire system, including hardware failure, network failure, or software failure. Usually, data center failure is not an everyday event, and more granular monitoring is required for frequent failures such as database connection and network connection failures. The system needs to monitor the failure and act to recover.

To make system self-healing, first, you need to identify **Key Performance Indicators (KPIs)** for your application and business. These KPIs may include the number of requests served per second or page load latency for your website at the user level. You can define maximum CPU utilization at the infrastructure level, such as it should not go above 60% and memory utilization *should not go beyond 50%* of the total available **Random-Access Memory (RAM)**.

As you defined your KPIs, you should put the monitoring system to track failures and notify you as your KPIs reach the threshold. You should apply automation around monitoring so that the system can self-heal in the event of any incidents. For example, add more servers when CPU utilization reaches near 50% — proactive monitoring helps prevent failures.

Applying automation

Automation is the key to improving your application's reliability. Try to automate everything from application deployment and configuration to the overall infrastructure. Automation provides you with agility where your team can move fast and experiment more often. You can replicate the entire system infrastructure and the environment with a single click to try a new feature.

You can plan the auto-scaling of your application based on a schedule, for example, an e-commerce website may have more user traffic on weekends. You can also automate scaling based on the user request volume to handle the unpredictable workload. Use automation to launch independent and parallel jobs that will provide greater accuracy when combined with the results from the individual job.

Frequently, you need to apply the same configuration that you have on your development environment to **Quality Assurance (QA)** environments. There may be multiple QA environments for each testing stage, which includes functional testing, UAT, and stress testing environments. Often, a QA tester discovers a defect caused by wrongly configured resources, which could introduce a further delay in the test schedule. Most importantly, you cannot afford to have a configuration error in production servers.

To reproduce precisely the same configuration, you may need to document step-by-step configuration instructions. Repeating the same steps to configure each environment manually can be error-prone. There is always a chance of human error, such as a typo, for example, in a database name. The solution to this challenge is to automate these steps by creating a script. The automation script itself can be the documentation.

As long as the script is correct, it is more reliable than manual configuration. It is undoubtedly reproducible. Detecting unhealthy resources and launching replacement resources can be automated, and you can notify the IT operations team when resources are changed. Automation is a fundamental design principle that needs to apply everywhere in your system.

Creating a distributed system

Monolithic applications have low reliability when it comes to system uptime, as a tiny issue in a particular module can bring down the entire system. Dividing your application into multiple small services reduces the *impact area*. One part of the application shouldn't impact the whole system, and the application can continue to serve critical functionality. For example, in an e-commerce website, an issue with the payment service should not affect the customer's ability to place orders, as payment can be processed later.

At the service level, scale your application horizontally to increase system availability. Design a system to use multiple smaller components working together rather than a single monolithic system to reduce the impact area. In a distributed design, requests are handled by different system components, and the failure of one component doesn't impact the functioning of other parts of the system. For example, on an e-commerce website, the failure of warehouse management components will not impact the customer placing the order.

However, the communication mechanism can be complicated in a distributed system. You need to take care of system dependencies by utilizing the circuit breaker pattern. As you learned regarding the circuit breaker pattern in *Chapter 6, Solution Architecture Design Patterns*, the basic idea is simple. You wrap a protected function call in a circuit breaker object, which monitors for failures and takes automated action to mitigate it.

Monitoring and adding capacity

Resource saturation is the most common reason for application failure. Often, you will encounter the issue where your applications start rejecting requests due to CPU, memory, or hard disk overload. Adding more resources is not always a straightforward task, as you should have additional capacity available when needed.

In a traditional on-premises environment, you need to calculate server capacity based on the assumption in advance. Workload capacity prediction becomes more challenging for a business such as a shopping website and any online business. Online traffic is very unpredictable and fluctuates heavily driven by global trends. Usually, procuring hardware can take anywhere between 3 to 6 months, and it's tough to guess capacity in advance. Ordering excess hardware will incur an extra cost as a resource is sitting idle, and a lack of resources will cause the loss of business due to application unreliability.

You need an environment where you don't need to guess capacity, and your application can scale on demand.

A public cloud provider such as **Amazon Web Services (AWS)** provides **Infrastructure as a Service (IaaS)**, facilitating the on-demand availability of resources.

In the cloud, you can monitor system supply and demand. You can automate the addition or removal of resources as needed. It allows you to maintain the level of resources that will satisfy demand without over-provisioning or under-provisioning.

Performing recovery validation

When it comes to infrastructure validation, most of the time, organizations focus on validating a happy path where everything is working. Instead, you should validate how your system fails and how well your recovery procedures work. Validate your application, assuming everything fails all the time. Don't just expect that your recovery and failover strategies will work. Make sure to test them regularly, so you're not surprised if something does go wrong.

A simulation-based validation helps you to uncover any potential risks. You can automate a possible scenario that could cause your system to fail and prepare an incident response accordingly. Your validation should improve application reliability in such a way that nothing will fail in production.

Recoverability is sometimes overlooked as a component of availability. To improve the system's **Recovery Point Objective (RPO)** and **Recovery Time Objective (RTO)**, you should back up data and applications along with their configuration as a machine image. You will learn more about RTO and RPO in the next section. Suppose a natural disaster makes one or more of your components unavailable or destroys your primary data source. In that case, you should be able to restore the service quickly and without losing data. Let's talk more about specific disaster recovery strategies to improve application reliability and associated technology choices.

Technology selection for architectural reliability

Application reliability often looks at the availability of the application to serve users. Several factors go into making your application highly available. However, **fault tolerance** refers to the built-in redundancy of an application's components. Your application may be highly available but not be 100% fault-tolerant. For example, if your application needs four servers to handle the user request, you divided them between two data centers for high availability. If one site goes down, your system is still highly available at 50% capacity, but it may impact user performance expectations. However, if you create equal redundancy in both sites with four servers each, your application will not be only highly available but will be 100% fault-tolerant.

Suppose your application is not 100% fault-tolerant. In that case, you want to add automated scalability, defining how your application's infrastructure will respond to increased capacity needs to ensure your application is available and performing within your required standards. To make your application reliable, you should be able to restore services quickly and without losing data. Going forward, we are going to address the recovery process as disaster recovery. Before going into various disaster recovery scenarios, let's learn more about the RTO/RPO and data replication.

Planning the Recovery Time Objective and Recovery Point Objective

Business applications need to define service availability in the form of a **Service-Level Agreement** (**SLA**). Organizations define SLAs to ensure application availability and reliability for their users. You may want to define an SLA, saying your application should be 99.9% available in a given year, or that the organization can tolerate downtime of 43 minutes per month, and so on. The defined SLA primarily drives the RPO and RTO for an application.

The RPO is the amount of data loss an organization can tolerate in a given period of time. For example, my application is acceptable if it loses 15 minutes' worth of data. For example, if you are processing customer orders every 15 minutes for fulfillment, then you can tolerate reprocessing that data in case of any system failure at order fulfillment application. The RPO helps to define a data backup strategy. The RTO is about application downtime and how much time the application should take to recover and function normally after an incidence of failure. The following diagram illustrates the difference between the RTO and RPO:

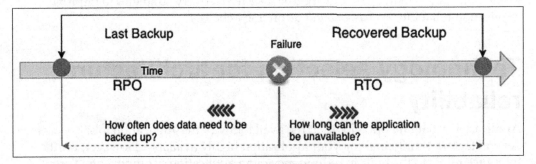

Figure 9.1: RTO and RPO

In the preceding diagram, suppose the failure occurs at 10 A.M., and you took the last backup at 9 A.M.; in the event of a system crash, you would lose 1 hour of data. When you restore your system, there is an hour's worth of data loss, as you have been taking data backups every hour.

In this case, your system RPO is 1 hour, as it can tolerate living with an hour's worth of data loss. In this case, the RPO indicates that the maximum data loss that can be tolerated is 1 hour.

If your system takes 30 minutes to restore to the backup and bring up the system, it defines your RTO as half an hour. This means the maximum downtime that can be tolerated is 30 minutes. The RTO is the time it takes to restore the entire system after a failure that causes downtime, which is 30 minutes in this case.

An organization typically decides on an acceptable RPO and RTO based on the user experience and financial impact on the business in the event of system unavailability. Organizations consider various factors when determining the RTO/RPO, including the loss of business revenue and damage to their reputation due to downtime. IT organizations plan solutions to provide effective system recovery as per the defined RTO and RPO. You can see now how data is the key to system recovery, so let's learn some methods to minimize data loss.

Replicating data

Data replication and snapshots are the key to disaster recovery and making your system reliable. Replication creates a copy of the primary data site on the secondary site. In the event of primary system failure, the system can fail over to the secondary system and keep working reliably. This data could be your file data stored in a **NAS drive**, **database snapshot**, or **machine image snapshot**. Sites could be two geo-separated on-premises systems, two separate devices on the same premises, or a physically separated public cloud.

Data replication is not only helpful for disaster recovery, but it can speed up an organization's agility by quickly creating a new environment for testing and development. Data replication can be synchronous or asynchronous.

Synchronous versus asynchronous replication

Synchronous replication creates a data copy in real time. Real-time data replication helps to reduce the RPO and increase reliability in the event of a disaster. However, it is expensive as it requires additional resources in the primary system for continuous data replication.

Asynchronous replication creates copies of data with some lag or as per the defined schedule. However, asynchronous replication is less expensive as it uses fewer resources compared to synchronous replication. You may choose asynchronous replication if your system can work with a longer RPO.

In terms of database technology such as Amazon RDS, synchronous replication is applied if we create an RDS with multiple Availability Zone failover. For read replicas, there is asynchronous replication, and you can use that to serve report and read requests.

As illustrated in the following architecture diagram, in synchronous replication, there is no lag of data replication between the master and standby instance of the database, while, in the case of asynchronous replication, there could be some lag while replicating the data between the master and replication instance:

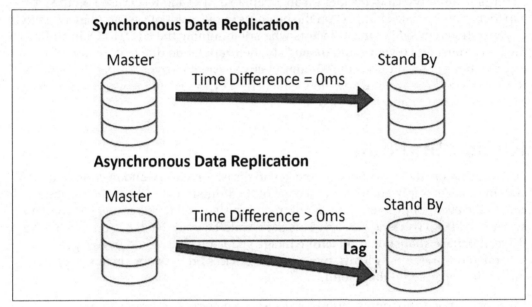

Figure 9.2: Synchronous and asynchronous data replication

Let's explore some methods of data replication for the synchronous and asynchronous approaches.

Replication methods

The replication method is an approach to extract data from the source system and create a copy for data recovery purposes. Different replication methods are available to store a copy of data as per the storage type for business process continuation. Replications can be implemented in the following ways:

- **Array-based replication**: In this, built-in software automatically replicates data. However, both the source and destination storage arrays should be compatible and homogeneous to replicate data. A storage array contains multiple storage disks in a rack.

Large enterprises use array-based replication due to the ease of deployment and the reduction in the compute power host system. You can choose array-based replication products such as HP Storage, EMC SAN Copy, and NetApp SnapMirror.

- **Network-based replication**: This can copy data between a different kind of heterogeneous storage array. It uses an additional switch or appliance between incompatible storage arrays to replicate data. In network-based replication, the cost of replication could be higher as multiple players come into the picture. You can choose from networked-based replication products such as NetApp Replication X and EMC RecoverPoint.

- **Host-based replication**: In this, you install a software agent on your host that can replicate data to any storage system such as NAS, SAN, or DAS. You can use a host-based software vendor, for example, Symantec, Commvault, CA, or Vision Solution. It's highly popular in **Small and Medium-Sized Businesses (SMBs)** due to lower upfront costs and heterogeneous device compatibility. However, it consumes more compute power as the agent needs to be installed on the host operating system.

- **Hypervisor-based replication**: This is VM-aware, which means copying the entire virtual machine from one host to another. As organizations mostly use virtual machines, it provides a very efficient disaster recovery approach to reduce the RTO. Hypervisor-based replication is highly scalable and consumes fewer resources than host-based replication. It can be carried out by native systems built into VMware and Microsoft Windows. You can choose a product such as Zerto to perform hypervisor-based replication or another product from various vendors.

Previously, in *Chapter 3, Attributes of the Solution Architecture*, you learned about scalability and fault tolerance. In *Chapter 6, Solution Architecture Design Patterns*, you learned about various design patterns to make your architecture highly available. Now, you will discover multiple ways to recover your system from failure and make it highly reliable.

Planning disaster recovery

Disaster recovery (DR) is about maintaining business continuation in the event of system failure. It's about preparing the organization for any possible system downtime and the ability to recover from it. DR planning covers multiple dimensions, including hardware and software failure. While planning for DR, always ensure you consider other operational losses, including power outages, network outages, heating and cooling system failures, physical security breaches, and other incidents, such as fires, floods, or human error.

Organizations invest effort and money in DR planning as per system criticality and impact. A revenue-generating application needs to be up all of the time as it significantly impacts company image and profitability. Such an organization invests lots of effort in creating their infrastructure and training their employees for a DR situation. DR is like an insurance policy that you have to invest in and maintain even when you don't utilize it, as in the case of unforeseen events, a DR plan will be a lifesaver for your business.

Bases of business criticality, such as software applications, can be placed on a *spectrum of complexity*. There are four DR scenarios, sorted from highest to lowest RTO/RPO as follows:

- Backup and restore
- Pilot light
- Warm standby
- Multi-site

As shown in the following diagram, in DR planning, as you progress with each option, your RTO and RPO will reduce while the cost of implementation increases. You need to make the right trade-off between RTO/RPO requirements and cost per your application reliability requirements:

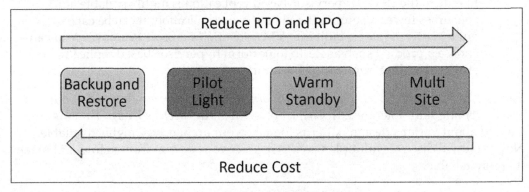

Figure 9.3: The spectrum of DR options

Let's explore each of the options mentioned above in detail with the technology choices involved. Note that public clouds such as AWS enable you to operate each of the preceding DR strategies cost-effectively and efficiently.

Business continuity is about ensuring critical business functions continue to operate or function quickly in the event of disasters. As organizations opt to use the cloud for DR plans, let's learn about the various DR strategies between on-premises environments and the cloud.

Backup and restore

Backup and restore is the lowest cost option but it results in a higher RPO and RTO. This method is simple to get started and highly cost-effective as you only need backup storage space. This backup storage could be a tape drive, hard disk drive, or network access drive. As your storage needs increase, adding and maintaining more hardware across regions could be a daunting task. One of the most cost-effective and straightforward options is to use the cloud as backup storage. Amazon S3 provides unlimited storage capacity at a low cost and with a pay-as-you-go model.

The following diagram shows a basic DR system. In this diagram, the data is in a traditional data center, with backups stored in AWS. AWS Import/Export or Snowball are used to get the data into AWS, and the information is later stored in Amazon S3:

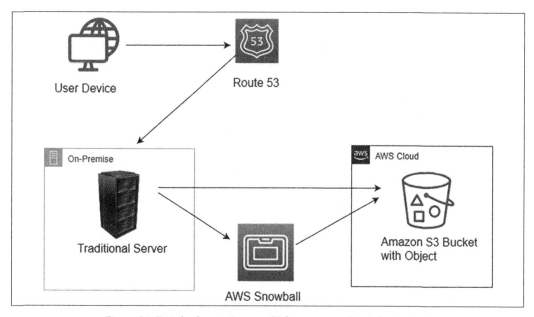

Figure 9.4: Data backup to Amazon S3 from on-premises infrastructure

You can use other third-party solutions available for backup and recovery. Some of the most popular choices are NetApp, VMware, Tivoli, Commvault, and CloudEndure. You need to take backups of the current system and store them in Amazon S3 using a backup software solution. Make sure to list the procedure to restore the system from a backup on the cloud, which includes the following:

1. Understand which **Amazon Machine Image (AMI)** to use or build your own machine image as required with pre-installed software and security patches.

2. Document the steps to restore your system from a backup.

3. Document the steps to route traffic from the primary site to the new site in the cloud.

4. Create a run book for deployment configuration and possible issues with their resolutions.

If the primary site located on-premises goes down, you will need to start the recovery process. As shown in the following diagram, in the preparation phase, create a custom **Amazon Machine Image (AMI)**, which is pre-configured with the operating system and the required software, and store it as a backup in Amazon S3. Store any other data such as database snapshots, storage volume snapshots, and files in Amazon S3:

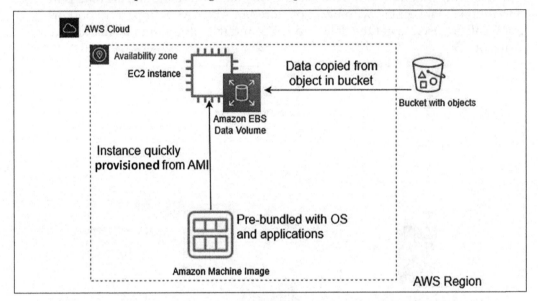

Figure 9.5: Restoring systems from Amazon S3 backups in the cloud

If the primary site goes down, you need to perform the following recovery steps:

1. Bring up the required infrastructure by spinning up Amazon EC2 server instances using machine images with all security patches and required software and put them behind a load balancer with an auto-scaling configuration as required.

2. Once your servers are up and running, you need to restore data from the backup stored in Amazon S3.

3. The last task is to switch over traffic to the new system by adjusting the DNS records to point to AWS.

It would be a better approach to automate elements of your infrastructure, such as networking, server, and database deployment, and bring it up by running the **AWS CloudFormation template**.

This DR pattern is easy to set up and relatively inexpensive. However, in this scenario, both the RPO and RTO will be high; the RTO will be the downtime until the system gets restored from the backup and starts functioning, while the RPO that is lost depends upon the system's backup frequency. Let's explore the next approach, pilot light, which provides improvements to your RTOs and RPOs.

Pilot light

The pilot light is the next lowest-cost DR method after backup and restore. As the name suggests, you need to keep the minimum number of core services up and running in different regions. You can spin up additional resources quickly in the event of a disaster.

You would probably actively replicate the database tier, then spin up instances from a VM image or build out infrastructure using infrastructure as code such as **CloudFormation**. Just like the pilot light in your gas heater, a tiny flame that is always on can quickly light the entire furnace to heat the house.

The following diagram shows a pilot light DR pattern. In this case, the database is replicated into AWS, with Amazon EC2 instances of the web servers and application servers ready to go, but not currently running:

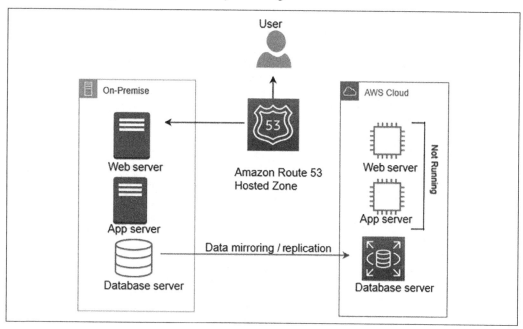

Figure 9.6: The pilot light data replication to DR site scenario

A pilot light scenario is pretty much similar to backup and restore, where you take a backup of most of the components and store them passively. However, you maintain active instances with a lower capacity for critical components such as a database or authentication server, which can take a significant time to come up. You need to automatically start all required resources, including network settings, load balancers, and virtual machine images as needed. As the core pieces are already running, recovery time is faster than the backup and restore method.

The pilot light is very cost effective as you are not running all of the resources at full capacity. You need to enable the replication of all critical data to the DR site—in this case, the AWS cloud. You can use the **AWS Data Migration Service** to replicate data between on-premises and cloud databases. For file-based data, you can use **Amazon File Gateway**. Many third-party-managed tools provide data replication solutions efficiently, such as Attunity, Quest, Syncsort, Alooma, and JumpMind.

If the primary system fails, as shown in the following diagram, you start up the Amazon EC2 instances with the latest copy of the data. Then, you redirect Amazon Route 53 to point to the new web server:

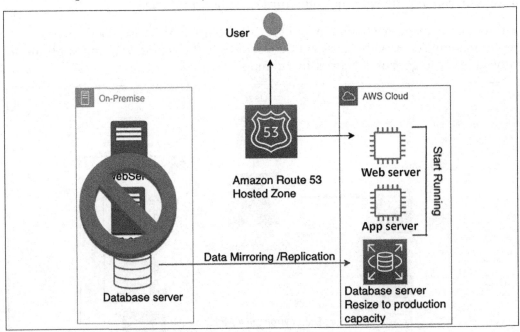

Figure 9.7: Recovery in the pilot light method

For the pilot light method, in the case of a disaster environment, you need to perform the following steps:

1. Start the application and web servers that were in standby mode. Further, scale-out application servers with horizontal scaling using a load balancer.

2. Vertically scale up the database instance that was running in low capacity.

3. Finally, update the DNS record in your router to point to the new site.

In pilot light, you bring up the resources around the replicated core dataset automatically and scale the system as required to handle the current traffic. A pilot light DR pattern is relatively easy to set up and inexpensive. However, in this scenario, the RTO takes longer to automatically bring up a replacement system, while the RPO largely depends on the replication type. Let's explore the next approach, warm standby, which further improves your RTOs and RPOs.

Warm standby

Warm standby, also known as **fully working low-capacity standby**, is like the enhanced version of the pilot light. It is the option where you use the agility of the cloud to provide low-cost DR. It saves the server cost and allows data to recover more quickly by having a small subset of services already running.

You can decide whether your DR environment should be enough to accommodate 30% or 50% of production traffic. Alternatively, you can also use this for non-production testing.

As shown in the following diagram, two systems are running in the warm standby method—the central system and a low-capacity system—on a cloud such as AWS.

You can use a router such as Amazon Route 53 to distribute requests between the central system and the cloud system:

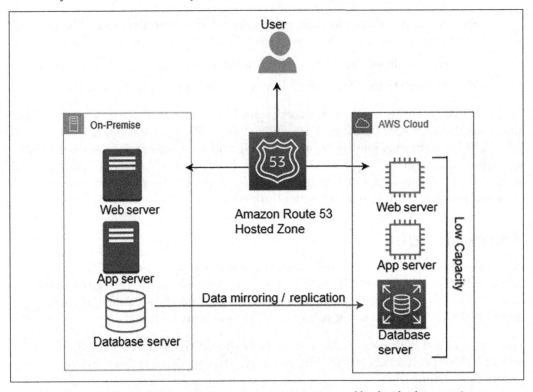

Figure 9.8: Warm standby scenario running an active-active workload with a low capacity

When it comes to databases, warm standby takes a similar approach to the pilot light, where data is continuously replicating from the main site to the DR site. However, in warm standby, you are running all necessary components 24/7; but they do not scale up for production traffic.

Often, the organization chooses a warm standby strategy for more critical workloads, so you need to make sure there are no issues in the DR site using continuous testing. The best approach to take is A/B testing, where the leading site will handle significant traffic. A small amount of traffic, approximately 1% to 5%, is routed to the DR site. This will make sure that the DR site is able to serve traffic when the primary site is down. Also, make sure to patch and update the software on the DR site regularly.

As shown in the following diagram, during the unavailability of the primary environment, your router switches over to the secondary system, which is designed to automatically scale its capacity up in the event of a failover from the primary system:

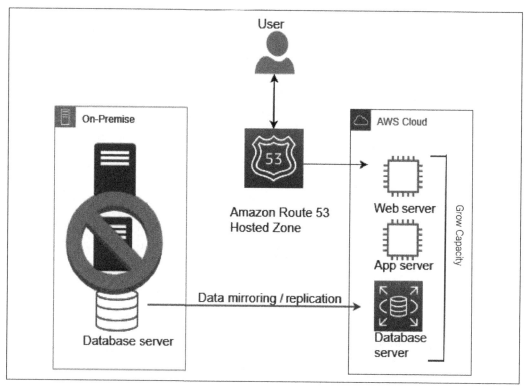

Figure 9.9: Recovery phase in the warm standby scenario

Suppose a failure occurs in the primary site. In that case, you can take the following approach:

1. Perform an immediate transfer of the critical production workload traffic to the DR site. Increase traffic routing from 5% to 100% in the secondary site. For example, in an e-commerce business, you first need to bring up your customer-facing website to keep it functioning.

2. Scale up the environment that was running on low capacity. You can apply vertical scaling for databases and horizontal scaling for servers.

3. As you scale up the environment, other non-critical workloads working in the background can now be transferred, such as warehouse management and shipping.

Your DR process becomes more efficient if your application is an all-in cloud, where entire infrastructures and applications are hosted in the public cloud, such as AWS.

The AWS cloud allows you to use cloud native tools efficiently; for example, you can enable a multi-AZ failover feature in the Amazon RDS database to create a standby instance in another Availability Zone with continuous replication.

In the case of the primary database, when an instance goes down, an in-built automatic failover takes care of switching the application to the standby database without any application configuration changes. Similarly, you can use automatic backup and replication options for all kinds of data protection.

A warm standby DR pattern is relatively complex to set up and expensive. The RTO is much quicker than the pilot light for the critical workload. However, for non-critical workloads, it depends upon how quickly you can scale up the system, while the RPO largely depends upon the replication type. Let's explore the next approach, multi-site, which provides near-zero RTOs and RPOs.

Multi-site

Lastly, the multi-site strategy, also known as a hot standby, helps you achieve near-zero RTO and RPO. Your DR site is a replica of the primary site with continuous data replication and traffic flow between sites. It is known as multi-site architecture due to the automated load balancing of traffic across regions or between on-premise and the cloud.

As shown in the following diagram, multi-site is the next level of DR, having a fully functional system running in the cloud at the same time as on-premises systems:

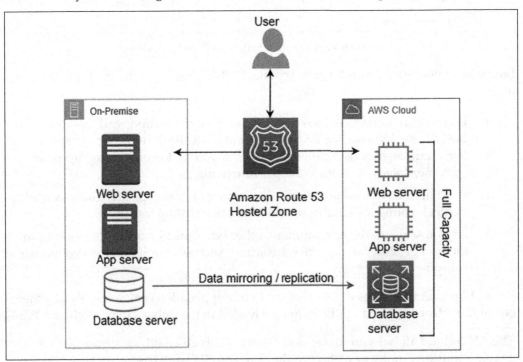

Figure 9.10: Multi-site scenario running an active-active workload with full capacity

The advantage of the multi-site approach is that it is ready to take a full production load at any moment. It's similar to warm standby but runs at full capacity on the DR site. If the primary site goes down, all traffic can be immediately failed over to the DR site, which is an improvement over the loss in performance and time when switching over and scaling up the DR site in the case of a warm standby.

A multi-site DR pattern is most expensive as it requires redundancy to be built for all components. However, the RTO is much quicker for all workloads in this scenario, while the RPO largely depends upon the replication type. Let's explore some best practices around DR to make sure your system is running reliably.

Applying best practices for DR

As you start thinking about DR, here are some important considerations:

- **Start small and build as needed**: Make sure you first bring up the critical workloads that have the most business impact and build upon this to bring up less critical loads. Streamline the first step of taking a backup, as often organizations lose data as they didn't have an efficient backup strategy. Take backups of everything, whether it is your file server, machine image, or databases.

- **Apply the data backup life cycle**: Keeping lots of active backups could increase costs, so make sure to apply a life cycle policy to archive and delete data as per your business needs. For example, you can choose to keep a 90-day active backup and, after that period, store it in low-cost archive storage such as a tape drive or Amazon Glacier. After 1 or 2 years, you may want to set a life cycle policy to delete the data. Compliance with standards such as PCI-DSS may require users to store data for 7 years, and in that case, you must opt for archival data storage to reduce costs.

- **Check your software licenses**: Managing software licenses can be a daunting task, especially in the current microservice architecture environment, where you have several services running independently on their virtual machines and databases. Software licenses could be associated with several installations, a number of CPUs, and several users. It becomes tricky when you go for scaling. You need to have enough licenses to support your scaling needs.

- **For horizontal scaling, you need to add more instances with software installed, and in vertical scaling, you need to add more CPU or memory**: You need to understand your software licensing agreement and ensure you have the appropriate license to fulfill system scaling. Also, make sure you don't buy excessive licenses, which you may not utilize and will cost you more money. Overall, make sure to manage your license inventory like your infrastructure or software.

- **Test your solutions often**: DR sites are created for rare DR events and are often overlooked. You need to make sure your DR solution is working as expected to achieve high reliability in case of an incident. Compromising a defined SLA can violate contractual obligations and result in the loss of money and customer trust.

- **Play gameday**: One way to test your solution often is by playing *gameday*. To play gameday, you choose a day when the production workload is small and gather all of the team responsible for maintaining the production environment. You can simulate a disaster event by bringing down a portion of the production environment and let the team handle the situation to keep the environment up and running. These events make sure you have working backups, snapshots, and machine images to handle disaster events.

- **Always monitor resources**: Put a monitoring system to make sure automated failover to the DR site occurs if an event occurs. Monitoring helps you to take a proactive approach and improves system reliability by applying automation. Monitoring capacity saves you from resource saturation issues, which can impact your application's reliability.

Creating a DR plan and performing regular recovery validation helps to achieve the desired application reliability. Let's learn more about improving reliability through the use of the public cloud.

Improving reliability with the cloud

In previous sections, you have seen examples of a cloud workload for the DR site. Many organizations have started to choose the cloud for DR sites to improve application reliability, as the cloud provides various building blocks. Also, cloud providers such as AWS have a marketplace where you can purchase multiple ready-to-use solutions from providers.

The cloud provides data centers that are available across geographic locations at your fingertips. You can choose to create a reliability site on another continent without any hassle. With the cloud, you can easily create and track the availability of your infrastructure, such as backups and machine images.

In the cloud, easy monitoring and tracking help make sure your application is highly available as per the business-defined SLA. The cloud enables you to have fine control over IT resources, cost, and handling trade-offs for RPO/RTO requirements. Data recovery is critical for application reliability. Data resources and locations must align with RTOs and RPOs.

The cloud provides easy and effective testing of your DR plan. You inherit features available in the cloud, such as the logs and metrics for various cloud services. Built-in metrics are a powerful tool for gaining insight into the health of your system.

With all available monitoring capabilities, you can notify the team of any threshold breach or trigger automation for system self-healing. For example, AWS provides CloudWatch, which collects logs and generates metrics while monitoring different applications and infrastructure components. It can trigger various automations to scale your application.

The cloud provides a built-in change management mechanism that helps to track provisioned resources. Cloud providers extend out-of-the-box capabilities to ensure applications and operating environments are running known software and can be patched or replaced in a controlled manner. For example, AWS provides AWS System Manager, which has the capability of patching and updating cloud servers in bulk. The cloud has tools to back up data, applications, and operating environments to meet requirements for RTOs and RPOs. Customers can leverage cloud support or a cloud partner for their workload handling needs.

With the cloud, you can design a scalable system, which can provide flexibility to add and remove resources automatically to match the current demand. Data is one of the essential aspects of any application's reliability. The cloud offers out-of-the-box data backup and replication tools, including machine images, databases, and files. In a disaster, all of your data is backed up and appropriately saved in the cloud, which helps the system recover quickly.

Regular interaction across the application development and operation team will help address and prevent known issues and design gaps, thereby reducing the risk of failures and outages. Continually architect your applications to achieve resiliency and distribute them to handle any outages. Distribution should span different physical locations to achieve high levels of availability.

Summary

In this chapter, you learned about various principles to make your system reliable. These principles include making your system self-healing by applying automation rules and reducing the impact in the event of failure by designing a distributed system where the workload spans multiple resources.

Overall system reliability heavily depends on your system's availability and its ability to recover from disaster events. You learned about synchronous and asynchronous data replication types and how they affect your system reliability. You learned about various data replication methods, including array-based, network-based, host-based, and hypervisor-based methods. Each replication method has its pros and cons. There are multiple vendors' products available to achieve the desired data replication.

You learned about various disaster planning methods depending on the organization's needs and the RTO and RPO. You learned about the backup and restore method, which has high RTO and RPO, and it is easy to implement. The pilot light method improves your RTO/RPO by keeping critical resources such as databases active in the DR site. The warm standby and multi-site methods maintain an active copy of a DR site's workload and help achieve a better RTO/RPO as you increase application reliability by lowering the system's RTO/RTO, the system's complexity, and costs. You learned about utilizing the cloud's built-in capability to ensure application reliability.

Solution design and launch may not happen too often, but operational maintenance is an everyday task. In the next chapter, you will learn about the alerting and monitoring aspects of solution architecture. You will learn about various design principles and technology choices to make your application operationally efficient and apply operational excellence.

Join our book's Discord space

Join the book's Discord workspace for a monthly *Ask me Anything* session with the authors: https://packt.link/SAHandbook

10
Operational Excellence Considerations

Application maintainability is one of the main aspects that a solution architect should consider during architectural design. Every new project starts with lots of planning and resources at the beginning. Teams spend the initial months creating and launching your application. After the production launch, the application needs several things to be taken care of to keep operating. You need to continually monitor your application to find and resolve any issues on a day-to-day basis.

The operations team needs to handle application infrastructure, security, and any software issues to make sure your application is running reliably without any problems or issues. Often, an enterprise application is complex in nature, with a defined **Service-Level Agreement (SLA)** regarding application availability. Your operations team needs to understand business requirements and prepare themselves accordingly to respond to any event.

Operation excellence should be implemented across various components and layers of architecture. In modern microservice applications, there are so many moving parts involved that make system operations and maintenance a complicated task. Your operations team needs to put proper monitoring and alert mechanisms in place to tackle any issues that can hamper the business flow. Operational issues involve coordination from several teams for *preparation* and *resolution*. Operation expenditures are one of the significant costs that an organization puts aside to run a business.

In this chapter, you will learn various design principles applicable to achieving operational excellence for your solution.

The operational aspect needs to consider every component of the architecture. You will get an understanding of the right selection of technologies to ensure operational maintainability at every layer of software application. You will learn the following best practices of operational excellence in this chapter:

- Designing principles for operational excellence
- Selecting technologies for operational excellence
- Achieving operational excellence in the public cloud

By the end of this chapter, you will know various processes and methods to achieve operational excellence. You will learn about best practices that you can apply throughout application design, implementation, and post-production to improve application operability.

Designing principles for operational excellence

Operational excellence is about running your application with the minimal possible interruption to gain maximum business value. It is about applying continuous improvements to make the system efficient.

The following sections talk about the standard design principles that can help you strengthen your system's maintainability. You will find that all operational excellence design principles are closely related to and complement each other.

Automating manual tasks

Technology has been moving fast in recent times, and so IT operations need to keep up with that, where hardware and software inventories are procured from multiple vendors. Enterprises are building hybrid cloud and multi-cloud systems, so you need to handle both on-premises and cloud operations. All modern systems have a decidedly more extensive user base, with various microservices working together and millions of devices connected in a network. There are many moving parts in an IT operation, so this makes it difficult to run things manually.

Organizations maintain agility, and operations have to be fast to make use of the required infrastructure for new service development and deployment. The operations team has a more significant responsibility to keep services up and running and recover quickly in case of an event. Now, it is required to take a proactive approach in IT operations, rather than waiting for an incident to happen and then reacting.

Your operations team can work very efficiently by applying automation. Manual jobs need to be automated so that the team can focus on more strategic initiatives rather than getting overworked with tactical work. Spinning up a new server or starting and stopping services should be automated by taking an **Infrastructure as Code (IaC)** approach. Automating active discovery and response for any security threat is most important, to free up the operations team. Automation allows the team to devote more time to innovation.

For your web-facing application, you can detect anomalies in advance before they impact your system, using machine learning prediction. You can raise an automated security ticket if someone exposes your server to the world with HTTP port 80. You can pretty much automate the entire infrastructure and redeploy it multiple times as a *one-click solution*. Automation also helps to prevent human error, which can occur even if a person is doing the same job repetitively. Automation is now a must-have for IT operations.

Making incremental and reversible changes

Operational optimization is an ongoing process, whereby continuous effort is required to identify the gap and improve upon it. Achieving operational excellence is a journey. There are always changes required in all parts of your workload to maintain it—for example, often, operating systems of your server need to be updated with a security patch provided by your vendor. Various software that your application is using need a version upgrade. You need to make changes in the system to adhere to new compliance requirements.

You should design your workload in such a way that it allows all system components to get updated regularly, so the system will benefit from the latest and most significant updates available. Automate your flow so that you can apply small changes to avoid any significant impact. Any changes should be reversible, to restore system working conditions in the case of any issues. Incremental changes help to do thorough testing and improve overall system reliability. Automate any change management to avoid human error and achieve efficiency.

Predicting failures and responding

Preventing failures is vital to achieving operational excellence. Failures are bound to happen, and it's critical to identify them as far in advance as possible. During architecture design, anticipate failure to make sure you design for failure so that nothing will fail. Assume that everything will fail all the time and have a backup plan ready. Perform regular exercises to identify any potential source of failure. Try to remove or mitigate any resource that could cause a failure during system operation.

Create a test scenario based on your SLA that potentially includes a system **Recovery Time Objective (RTO)** and **Recovery Point Objective (RPO)**. Test your scenario, and make sure you understand their impact. Make your team ready to respond to any incident by simulating in a production-like scenario. Test your response procedure to make sure it is resolving issues effectively and create a confident team that is familiar with response execution.

Learning from mistakes and refining

As operational failures occur in your system, you should learn from the mistake and identify the gap. Make sure those same events do not occur again, and you should have a solution ready in case a failure gets repeated. One way to improve is by running **root cause analysis**, also called **RCA**.

During RCA, you need to gather the team and ask five *whys*. With each *why*, you peel off one layer of the problem, and, after asking the last *why*, you get to the bottom of the issue. After identifying the actual cause, you can prepare a solution by removing or mitigating the resources and update the operational runbook with the ready-to-use solution.

As your workload evolves with time, you need to make sure the operation procedure gets updated accordingly. Make sure to validate and test all methods regularly, and that the team is familiar with the latest updates in order to execute them.

Keeping the operational runbook updated

Often, a team overlooks documentation, which results in an outdated runbook. A runbook provides a guide to executing a set of actions in order to resolve issues arising due to external or internal events. A lack of documentation can make your operation people-dependent, which can be risky due to team attrition. Always establish processes to keep your system operations people-independent, and document all the aspects.

In the runbook, you want to keep track of all previous events and actions taken by team members to resolve them, so that any new team members can provide a quick resolution of similar incidents during operation support. Automate your runbook through the script so that it can get updated automatically as new changes roll out to the system.

Your runbook should include the defined SLA in relation to RTO/RPO, latency, scalability performance, and so on. The system admin should maintain a runbook with steps to start, stop, patch, and update the system. The operations team should include the system testing and validation result, along with the procedure to respond to the event.

Automate processes to annotate documents as a team applies changes to the system, and also after every build. You can use annotation to automate your operation, and it is easily readable by code. Business priorities and customer needs continue to change, and it's essential to design operations to support evolution over time.

Selecting technologies for operational excellence

The operations team needs to create procedures and steps to handle any operational incidents and validate the effectiveness of their actions. They need to understand the business need to provide efficient support. The operations team needs to collect systems and business metrics to measure the achievement of business outcomes.

The operational procedure can be categorized into three phases—planning, functioning, and improving. Let's explore technologies that can help in each phase.

Planning for operational excellence

The first step in the operational excellence process is to define operational priorities to focus on the high business impact areas. Those areas could be applying automation, streamlining monitoring, developing team skills as the workload evolves, and focusing on improving overall workload performance. There are tools and services available that crawl through your system by scanning logs and system activity. These tools provide a core set of checks that recommend optimizations for the system environment and help to shape priorities.

After understanding the priorities, you need to design the operation, which includes the workloads to design and building the procedures to support them. The design of a workload should consist of how it will be implemented, deployed, updated, and operated. An entire workload can be viewed as various application components, infrastructure components, security, data governance, and operations automation.

While designing for an operation, consider the following best practices:

- Automate your runbook with scripting to reduce human error, which creates an operating workload.

- Use resource identification mechanisms to execute operations based on defined criteria such as environment, various versions, application owner, and roles.

- Make incident responses automated so that, in the case of an event, the system should start self-healing without much human intervention.

- Use various tools and capabilities to automate the management of server instances and overall systems.

- Create script procedures on your instances to automate the installation of required software and security patches when the server gets started. These scripts are also known as bootstrap scripts.

After the operation design, create a checklist for operational readiness. These checklists should be comprehensive to make sure the system is ready for operation support when going live in production. This includes logging and monitoring, a communication plan, an alert mechanism, a team skillset, a team support charter, a vendor support mechanism, and so on. For operational excellence planning, the following are the areas where you need appropriate tools for preparation:

- IT asset management
- Configuration management

Let's explore each area in more detail, to understand the available tools and processes.

IT asset management

Operational excellence planning requires a list of IT inventories and tracks their use. These inventories include infrastructure hardware such as physical servers, network devices, storage, end-user devices, and so on. You also need to keep track of software licenses, operational data, legal contracts, compliance, and so on. IT assets include any system, hardware, or information that a company is using to perform a business activity.

Keeping track of IT assets helps an organization to make strategic and tactical decisions regarding operational support and planning. However, managing IT assets in a large organization could be a very daunting task. Various **IT Asset Management (ITAM)** tools are available for the operations team to help in the asset management process. Some of the most popular ITAM tools are **SolarWinds**, **Freshservice**, **ServiceDesk Plus**, **Asset Panda**, **PagerDuty**, **Jira Service Desk**, and so on.

IT management is more than tracking IT assets. It also involves monitoring and collecting asset data continuously, to optimize usage and operation costs. ITAM makes the organization more agile by providing end-to-end visibility and the ability to apply patches and upgrades quickly. The following diagram illustrates **ITAM**:

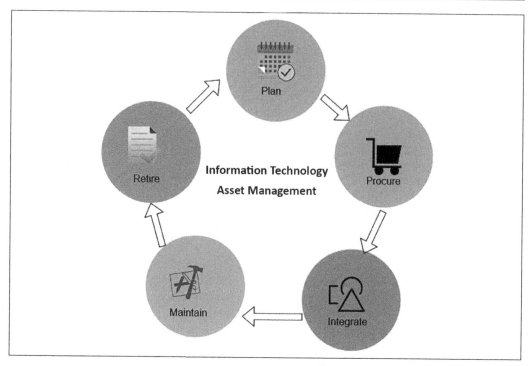

Figure 10.1: ITAM process

As shown in the preceding diagram, the ITAM process includes the following phases:

- **Plan**: An asset life cycle starts with planning, which is a more strategic focus to determine the need for overall IT assets and procurement methods. It includes cost-benefit analysis and total cost of ownership.

- **Procure**: In the procurement phase, organizations acquire the asset based on the outcome of planning. They may also decide to develop some holdings as required — for example, in-house software for logging and monitoring.

- **Integrate**: In this phase, an asset is installed in the IT ecosystem. It includes operation and support of the asset, and defines user access — for example, installing a log agent to collect logs from all the servers in a centralized dashboard, and restricting monitoring dashboard metrics to the IT operations team.

- **Maintain**: In the maintenance phase, the IT operations team keeps track of assets, and acts to upgrade or migrate based on the asset life cycle — for example, applying a security patch provided by the software vendor. The other example is keeping track of the end of life for licensed software, such as a plan to migrate from Windows Server 2008 to Windows 2022, as the old operating system is getting to the end of its life.

- **Retire**: In the retirement phase, the operations team disposes of the end-of-life asset. For example, if an old database server is getting to the end of its life, then the team takes action to upgrade it and migrates the required users and support to the new server.

ITAM helps organizations adhere to **ISO 19770** compliance requirements. It includes software procurement, deployment, upgrade, and support. ITAM provides better data security and helps to improve software compliance. It provides better communication between business units such as operation, finance, marketing teams, and frontline staff. Configuration management is another aspect that helps to maintain IT inventory data along with details such as owner and their current state. Let's learn more about it.

Configuration management

Configuration management maintains **Configuration Items** (**CIs**) to manage and deliver an IT service. CIs are tracked in the **Configuration Management Database** (**CMDB**). The CMDB stores and manages system component records with their attributes such as their type, owner, version, and dependency with other components. The CMDB keeps track of whether the server is physical or virtual, the operating system and its version (that is, Windows 2022 or **Red Hat Enterprise Linux** (**RHEL**) 8.0), the owner of the server (that is, support, marketing, or HR), and whether it has a dependency on other servers such as order management, and so on.

Configuration management is different from asset management. Asset management handles the entire life cycle of an asset, from planning to retirement, while CMDB is a component of asset management that stores configuration records of an individual asset. As shown in the following diagram, configuration management implements the integration and maintenance part of asset management:

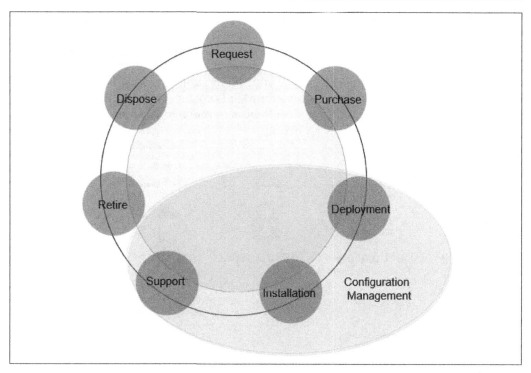

Figure 10.2: IT asset life cycle versus configuration management

Configuration management, as shown in the preceding diagram, implements the deployment, installation, and support part of asset management. The configuration management tool can help the operations team to reduce downtime by providing readily available information on asset configuration.

Implementing effective change management helps us to understand the impact of any changes in the environment. The most popular configuration management tools are Chef, Puppet, Ansible, and Bamboo. You will learn more details about them in *Chapter 12, DevOps and Solution Architecture Framework.*

IT management becomes easier if your workload is in a public cloud such as **Amazon Web Services (AWS)**, Microsoft Azure, or **Google Cloud Platform (GCP)**. Cloud vendors provide inbuilt tools to track and manage IT inventories and configuration in one place. For example, AWS provides services such as AWS Config, which tracks all IT inventories that spin up as a part of your AWS cloud workload, and services such as **AWS Trusted Advisor**, which recommends cost, performance, and security improvements, which you can use to decide how to manage your workload. You can see an example in the following screenshot:

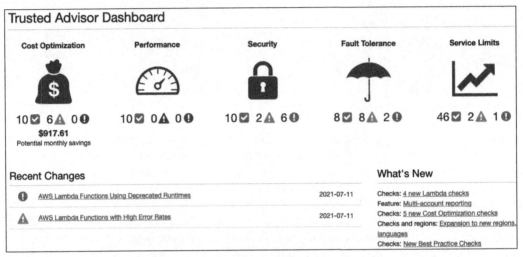

Figure 10.3: AWS Trusted Advisor dashboard

As shown in the preceding screenshot, the AWS **Trusted Advisor Dashboard** is showing 6 security issues that you can further explore to find out more details.

Configuration management helps to continuously monitor and record your IT resource configurations and allows you to automate the evaluation of recorded configurations against desired configurations. Configuration management offers the following benefits:

- **Continuous monitoring**: Continuously monitor and record configuration changes of your IT resources.

- **Change management**: Track the relationships among resources and review resource dependencies prior to making changes.

- **Continuous assessment**: Continuously audit and assess the overall compliance of your IT resource configurations with your organization's policies and guidelines.

- **Enterprise-wide compliance monitoring**: View the compliance status across your enterprise and identify non-compliant accounts. You can dive deeper to view the status for a specific region account.

- **Manage third-party resources**: Publish the configuration of third-party resources such as GitHub repositories, Microsoft Active Directory resources, or any on-premises and on-cloud server.

- **Operational troubleshooting**: Capture a comprehensive history of your AWS resource configuration changes to simplify troubleshooting of your operational issues.

Configuration management helps you to perform security analysis, continuously monitor the configurations of your resources, and evaluate their configurations for potential security weaknesses. It helps you to assess compliance with your internal policies and regulatory standards by providing you visibility into the configuration of your IT resources as well as third-party resources, and evaluating resource configuration changes against your desired configurations on a continuous basis.

The enterprise creates a framework such as an **Information Technology Infrastructure Library (ITIL)**, which implements an **Information Technology Service Management (ITSM)** best practice. An ITIL provides a view on how to implement ITSM.

In this section, you learned about asset management and configuration management, which is part of the ITIL framework and more relevant to operational excellence. ITSM helps organizations to run their IT operations daily. You can learn more about ITIL from its governing body AXELOS by visiting their website (`https://www.axelos.com/best-practice-solutions/itil`). AXELOS offers ITIL certification to develop skills in the IT service management process. As you have learned about planning, let's explore the functioning of IT operations in the next section.

The functioning of operational excellence

Operational excellence is determined by proactive monitoring and quickly responding to recover in the case of an event. By understanding the operational health of a workload, it is possible to identify when events and responses impact it. Use tools that help understand the operational health of the system using **metrics** and **dashboards**. You should send log data to centralized storage and define metrics to establish a benchmark.

By defining and knowing what a workload is, it is possible to respond quickly and accurately to operational issues. Use tools to automate responses to operational events supporting various aspects of your workload. These tools allow you to automate responses for operational events and initiate their execution in response to alerts.

Make your workload components replaceable, so that rather than fixing the issue you can improve recovery time by replacing failed components with known good versions. Then, analyze the failed resources without impacting a production environment. For the functioning of operational excellence, the following are the areas where appropriate tools are needed:

- Monitoring system health
- Handling alerts and incident response

Let's understand each area in more detail with information on the available tools and processes.

Monitoring system health

Keeping track of system health is essential to understanding *workload behavior*. The operations team uses system health monitoring to record any anomalies in the system component, and acts accordingly. Traditionally, monitoring is limited to the infrastructure layer keeping track of the server's CPU and memory utilization. However, monitoring needs to be applied to every layer of the architecture. The following are the significant components where monitoring is applied.

Infrastructure monitoring

Infrastructure monitoring is essential and is the most popular form of monitoring. Infrastructure includes components required for hosting applications. These are the core services such as storage, servers, network traffic, load balancer, and so on. Infrastructure monitoring may consist of metrics, such as the following:

- **CPU usage**: Percentage of CPU utilized by the server in a given period
- **Memory usage**: Percentage of **Random-Access Memory (RAM)** utilized by the server in a given period
- **Network utilization**: Network packets *in and out* over the given period
- **Disk utilization**: Disk read/write throughput and **Input/Output Operations per Second (IOPS)**
- **Load balancer**: Number of request counts in a given period

There are many more metrics available, and organizations need to customize those monitoring metrics as per their application monitoring requirement. The following screenshot shows a sample monitoring dashboard for network traffic:

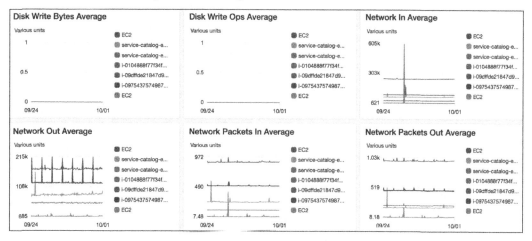

Figure 10.4: Infrastructure monitoring dashboard

You can see the preceding system dashboard showing a spike in one day in the **Network In Average** pane, with color-coding applied for different servers. The operations team can dive deep into each graph and resources to get a more granular view to determine overall infrastructure health.

Application monitoring

Sometimes, your infrastructure is all healthy except applications having an issue due to some bug in your code or any third-party software issues. You may have applied some vendor-provided operating system security patch that messed up your application. Application monitoring may include metrics, such as the following:

- **Endpoint invocation**: Number of requests in a given period
- **Response time**: Average response time to fulfill the request
- **Throttle**: Number of valid requests spilled out as the system runs out of capacity to handle the additional requests
- **Error**: Application throws an error while responding to a request

The following screenshot shows a sample application endpoint-monitoring dashboard:

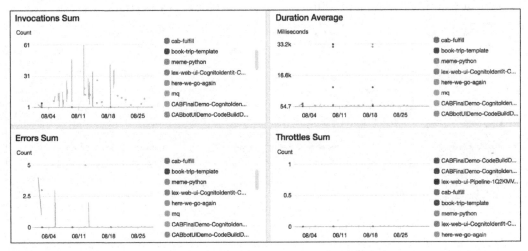

Figure 10.5: Application monitoring dashboard

There could be many more metrics based on application and technology — for example, a memory garbage collection amount for a Java application, a number of HTTP POST and GET requests for a RESTful service, a count of 4XX client errors, a count of 5XX server errors for a web application, and what they might be looking for that would indicate poor application health.

Platform monitoring

Your application may be utilizing several third-party platforms and tools that need to be monitored. These may include the following:

- **Memory caching**: Redis and Memcached
- **Relational database**: Oracle Database, Microsoft SQL Server, Amazon **Relational Database Service (RDS)**, PostgreSQL
- **NoSQL database**: Amazon DynamoDB, Apache Cassandra, MongoDB
- **Big data platform**: Apache Hadoop, Apache Spark, Apache Hive, Apache Impala, Amazon **Elastic MapReduce (EMR)**
- **Containers**: Docker, Kubernetes, OpenShift
- **Business intelligence tool**: Tableau, MicroStrategy, Kibana, Amazon QuickSight
- **Messaging system**: MQSeries, **Java Message Service (JMS)**, RabbitMQ, **Simple Queue Service (SQS)**

- **Search**: Elasticsearch, Solr search-based application

Each of the aforementioned tools has its own set of metrics that you need to monitor to make sure your application is healthy as a whole. The following screenshot shows the monitoring dashboard of a relational database platform:

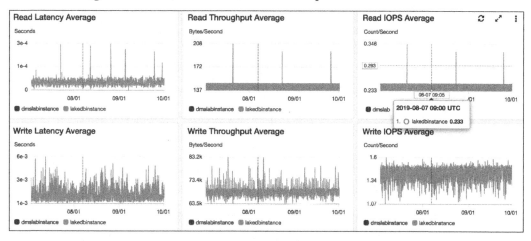

Figure 10.6: Platform monitoring dashboard for a Relational Database Management System (RDBMS)

In the preceding dashboard, you can see the database has lots of write activity, which is showing that the application is continuously writing data. On the other hand, read events are relatively consistent except for some spikes.

Log monitoring

Traditionally, log monitoring was a manual process, and organizations took a reactive approach to analyze logs when issues were encountered. However, with more competition and increasing expectations from users, it has become essential to take quick action before the user notices the issue. For a proactive approach, you should have the ability to stream logs in a centralized place and run queries to monitor and identify the issue.

For example, if some product page is throwing an error, you need to know the error immediately and fix the problem before the user complains, else you will suffer a revenue loss. In the case of any network attack, you need to analyze your network log and block suspicious IP addresses. Those IPs may be sending an erroneous number of data packets to bring down your application. Monitoring systems such as AWS CloudWatch, Logstash, Splunk, Google Stackdriver, and so on provide an agent to install in your application server. The agent will stream logs to a centralized storage location. You can directly query to central log storage and set up alerts for any anomalies.

The following screenshot shows a sample network log collected in a centralized place:

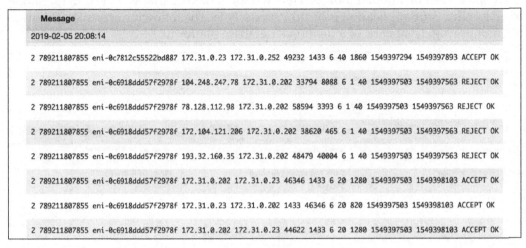

Figure 10.7: Raw network log streamed in a centralized datastore

You can run a query in these logs and find out the top 10 source IP addresses with the highest number of reject requests, as shown in the following screenshot:

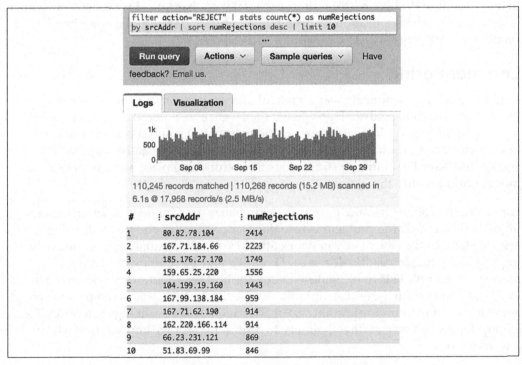

Figure 10.8: Insight from raw network log by running query

As shown in the preceding query editor, you can create a graph and put an alarm in for if the number of rejections detected crosses a certain threshold, such as more than 5,000.

Security monitoring

Security is a critical aspect of any application. Security monitoring should be considered during solution design. As you learned when we looked at security in the various architectural components in *Chapter 8, Security Considerations*, security needs to be applied at all layers. You need to implement security monitoring to act and respond to any event. The following significant components show where monitoring needs to be applied:

- **Network security**: Monitor any unauthorized port opening, suspicious IP address, and activity

- **User access**: Monitor any unauthorized user access and suspicious user activity

- **Application security**: Monitor any malware or virus attack

- **Web security**: Monitor a **Distributed Denial of Service (DDoS)** attack, SQL injection, or **Cross-Site Scripting (XSS)**

- **Server security**: Monitor any gap in security patches

- **Compliance**: Monitor any compliance lapses such as violations of **Payment Card Industry (PCI)** compliance checks for payment applications or the **Health Insurance Portability and Accountability Act (HIPAA)** for healthcare applications

- **Data security**: Monitor unauthorized data access, data masking, and data encryption at rest and in transit

For monitoring, you can use various third-party tools such as Imperva, McAfee, Qualys, Palo Alto Networks, Sophos, Splunk, Sumo Logic, Symantec, Turbot, and so on.

One example of security monitoring using **Amazon Detective** for the AWS cloud is shown below:

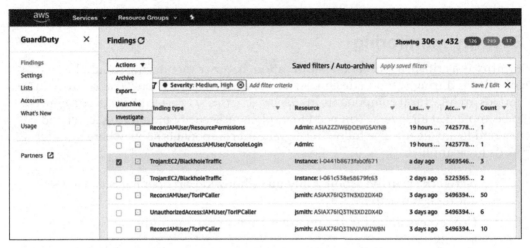

Figure 10.9: Security monitoring using Amazon GuardDuty

While you are putting application monitoring tools in place to monitor all components of your system, it is essential to monitor the monitoring system. Make sure to monitor the host of your monitoring system. For example, if you're hosting your monitoring tool in Amazon **Elastic Compute Cloud (EC2)**, then AWS CloudWatch can monitor the health of EC2.

Handling alerts and incident response

Monitoring is one part of operational excellence functioning; the other part involves handing alerts and acting upon them. Using alerts, you can define the system threshold and when you want to work. For example, if the server CPU utilization reaches 70% for 5 minutes, then the monitoring tool records high server utilization and sends an alert to the operations team to take action to bring down CPU utilization before a system crash. Responding to this incident, the operations team can add the server manually. When automation is in place, autoscaling triggers the alert to add more servers as per demand. It also sends a notification to the operations team, which can be addressed later.

Often, you need to define the alert category, and the operations team prepares for the response as per the alert severity.

The following levels of severity provide an example of how to categorize alert priority:

- **Severity 1**: Sev1 is a critical priority issue. A Sev1 issue should only be raised when there is a significant customer impact, for which immediate human intervention is needed. A Sev1 alert could be that the entire application is down. The typical team needs to respond to these kinds of alerts within 15 minutes and requires 24/7 support to fix the issue.

- **Severity 2**: Sev2 is a high-priority alert that should be addressed in business hours. For example, the application is up, but the rating and review system is not working for a specific product category. The typical team needs to respond to these kinds of alerts within 24 hours and requires regular office hours' support to fix the issue.

- **Severity 3**: Sev3 is a medium-priority alert that can be addressed during business hours over days—for example, the server disk is going to fill up in 2 days. The typical team needs to respond to these kinds of alerts within 72 hours and requires regular office hours' support to fix the issue.

- **Severity 4**: Sev4 is a low-priority alert that can be addressed during business hours over the week—for example, **Secure Sockets Layer** (**SSL**) certification is going to expire in 2 weeks. The typical team needs to respond to these kinds of alerts within the week and requires regular office hours' support to fix the issue.

- **Severity 5**: Sev5 falls into the notification category, where no escalation is needed, and it can be simple information—for example, sending a notification that deployment is complete. Here, no response is required in return since it is only for information purposes.

Each organization can have different alert severity levels as per their application needs. Some organizations may want to set four levels for severity, and others may go for six. Also, alert response times may differ. Maybe some organization wants to address Sev2 alerts within 6 hours on a 24/7 basis, rather than waiting for them to be addressed during office hours.

While setting up an alert, make sure the title and summary are *descriptive* and *concise*. Often, an alert is sent to a mobile (as an SMS) or a pager (as a message) and needs to be short and informative enough to take immediate action. Make sure to include proper metrics data in the message body.

In the message body, include information such as *The disk is 90% full in production-web-1 server* rather than just saying *The disk is full*. The following screenshot shows an example alarm dashboard:

Figure 10.10: Alarm dashboard

As shown in the preceding alarm dashboard, there is one alarm in progress when a NoSQL Amazon DynamoDB database table called **testretail** is using a low write capacity unit and causing unnecessary additional cost. The bottom and top two alarms have an **OK** status as data is collected during monitoring that is well within the threshold. There may be other alarms showing **Insufficient data**, which means there are not enough data points to determine the state of resources you are monitoring. You should only consider this alarm valid if it can collect data and move into the **OK** state.

Testing of incident response in the case of critical alerts is important to make sure you are ready to respond as per the defined SLA. Make sure your threshold is set up correctly so that you have enough room to address the issue, and, also, don't send too many alerts. Make sure that as soon as the issue is resolved, your alert gets reset to the original setting and is ready to capture event data again.

An incident is any unplanned disruption that impacts the system and customer negatively. The first response during an incident is to recover the system and restore the customer experience. Fixing the issue can be addressed later as the system gets restored and starts functioning. The automated alert helps to discover the incident actively and minimizes user impact. This can act as a failover to a disaster recovery site if the entire system is down, and the primary system can be fixed and restored later.

For example, Netflix uses the **Simian Army** (https://netflixtechblog.com/the-netflix-simian-army-16e57fbab116), which has **Chaos Monkey** to test system reliability. Chaos Monkey orchestrates the random termination of a production server to test if the system can respond to disaster events without any impact on end users. Similarly, Netflix has other monkeys to test various dimensions of system architecture, such as **Security Monkey**, **Latency Monkey**, and even **Chaos Gorilla**, which can simulate outage of the entire availability zone.

Monitoring and alerts are critical components to achieving operational excellence. All monitoring systems typically have an alert feature integrated with them. A fully automated alert and monitoring system improves the operations team's ability to maintain the health of the system, provide expertise to take quick action, and excel in the user experience.

As you monitor your application environment, it's important to apply continuous improvement and achieve excellence. Let's learn in more detail about improving operational excellence.

Improving operational excellence

Continuous improvement is required for any process, product, or application to excel. Operational excellence needs continuous improvement to attain maturity over time. You should keep implementing small incremental changes as you perform **RCA (Root Cause Analysis)** and learn lessons from various operations' activities.

Learning from failure will help you to anticipate any operational event that may be planned (such as deployments) or unplanned (such as utilization surge). You should record all lessons learned and update remedies in your operation runbook. For operational improvement, the following are the areas where you need appropriate tools:

- IT operation analytics
- Root cause analysis
- Auditing and reporting

IT operations analytics

IT Operations Analytics (ITOA) is the practice of gathering data from various resources to make a decision and predict any potential issue that you may encounter. It's essential to analyze all events and operational activities in order to improve. Analyzing failures will help to predict any future event and keep the team ready to provide the appropriate response.

Implement a mechanism to collect the logs of operations events, various activities across workloads, and infrastructure changes. You should create a detailed activity trail and maintain an activity history for audit purposes.

A large organization could have hundreds of systems generating a massive amount of data. You need a mechanism to ingest and store all logs and event data for a length of time, such as 90 or 180 days, to get insight. ITOA uses big data architecture to store and analyze multiple terabytes of data from all over the place. ITOA helps to discover any issue that you could not find by looking at individual tools and helps to determine dependencies between various systems, providing a holistic view.

As shown in the following diagram, each system has its own monitoring tool that helps to get insights and maintains individual system components. For operation analytics, you need to ingest this data in a centralized place. All operation data collection in one place gives a single source of truth, where you can query required data and run analytics to get a meaningful insight:

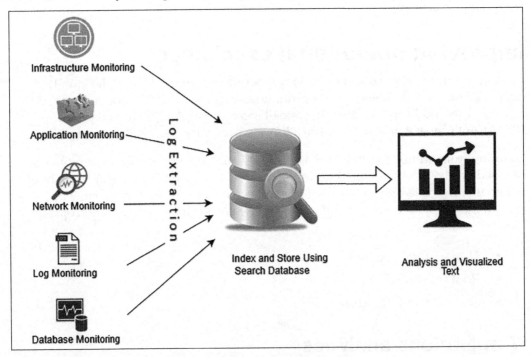

Figure 10.11: Big data approach for ITOA

To create an operation analytics system, you can use scalable big data storage such as Amazon **Simple Storage Service (S3)**. You can also store data in an on-premises Hadoop cluster. For data extraction, the agent can be installed in each server, which can send all monitoring data to a centralized storage system. You can use the Amazon CloudWatch agent to collect data from each server and store it in S3.

Third-party tools such as **ExtraHop** and **Splunk** can help to extract data from various systems.

Once data is collected in centralized storage, you can perform a transformation to make data ready for search and analysis. Data transformation and cleaning can be achieved using a big data application such as Spark, MapReduce, AWS Glue, and so on. To visualize the data, you can use any business intelligence tool such as Tableau, MicroStrategy, Amazon QuickSight, and so on. Here, we are talking about building an **Extract, Transform, and Load** (ETL) pipeline. You will learn more details in *Chapter 13, Data Engineering for Solution Architecture*. You can further perform machine learning to do predictive analysis on a future event.

You will learn more about machine learning in *Chapter 14, Machine Learning Architecture*.

Root cause analysis

For continuous improvement, it is essential to prevent any errors from happening again. If you can identify problems correctly, then an efficient solution can be developed and applied. It's important to get to the root cause of the problem to fix the problem. **Five whys** is a simple, yet most effective, technique to identify the root cause of a problem.

In the *five whys technique*, you gather the team for a retrospective look at an event and ask five consecutive questions to identify actual issues. Take an example where data is not showing up in your application monitoring dashboard. You will ask five whys to get to the root cause.

Problem: The application dashboard is not showing any data.

1. Why: Because the application is unable to connect with the database
2. Why: Because the application is getting a database connectivity error
3. Why: Because the network firewall is not configured to the database port
4. Why: Because the configuring port is a manual check and the infrastructure team missed it
5. Why: Because the team doesn't have the tools for automation

Root Cause: Manual configuration error during infrastructure creation.

Solution: Implement a tool for automated infrastructure creation.

In the preceding example, at first glance the issue looks like it is related to the application. After the *five whys* analysis, it turns out to be a bigger problem and there is a need to introduce automation to prevent similar incidents.

RCA helps the team to document lessons learned and continuously build upon it for operational excellence. Make sure to update and maintain your runbook-like code and share best practices across the team.

Auditing and reporting

Auditing is one of the essential activities to create recommendations and identify any malicious activity in the system by internal or external interference. An audit becomes especially important if your application needs to be compliant as per regulatory body requirements—for example, PCI, HIPAA, **Federal Risk and Authorization Management Program (FedRAMP)**, **International Organization for Standardization (ISO)**, and so on. Most of the compliant regulatory bodies need to conduct regular audits and verify each activity going on in the system to prepare a compliance report and grant a certificate.

An audit is essential to prevent and detect security events. A hacker may silently get into your system and systematically steal information without anyone noticing. Regular security audits can uncover a hidden threat. You may want to conduct a regular audit for cost optimization to identify if resources are running idle when not required. Also, determine resource demand and available capacity so that you can plan.

In addition to alert and monitoring, the operations team is also responsible for saving the system from any threat by enabling and conducting the audit. An IT audit makes sure you safeguard IT assets and license protection and that you ensure data integrity and operations adequately to achieve your organizational goal. The following screenshot shows a data audit stored in an Amazon S3 bucket using Amazon Macie, which is a data security and data privacy service that uses machine learning and pattern matching to discover and protect your sensitive data in AWS.

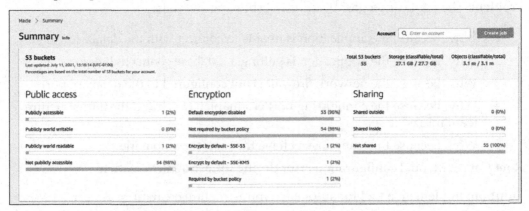

Figure 10.12: Data audit report summary from Amazon Macie

The data audit report in the preceding screenshot shows data accessibility, encryption, and data sharing reports along with data storage and size details.

Auditing steps include planning, preparing, evaluation, and reporting. Any risk item needs to be highlighted in the report, and follow-ups will be conducted to address open issues.

For operational excellence, the team can perform internal audit checks to make sure all systems are healthy and that proper alerts are in place to detect any incidents.

Achieving operational excellence in the public cloud

A public cloud provider such as AWS, GCP, or Azure provides many inbuilt capabilities and guidance to achieve operational excellence in the cloud. Cloud providers advocate automation, which is one of the most essential factors for operational excellence. Taking the example of the AWS cloud, the following services can help to achieve operational excellence:

- **Planning**: Operational excellence planning includes the identification of gaps and recommendations, automating via scripting, and managing your fleet of servers for patching and updates. The following AWS services help you in the planning phase:
    - **AWS Trusted Advisor**: AWS Trusted Advisor checks your workload based on prebuilt best practices and provides recommendations to implement them
    - **AWS CloudFormation**: With AWS CloudFormation, the entire workload can be viewed as code, including applications, infrastructure, policy, governance, and operations
    - **AWS Systems Manager**: AWS Systems Manager provides the ability to manage cloud servers in bulk for patching, updates, and overall maintenance

- **Functioning**: Once you have created operational excellence best practices and applied automation, you need continuous monitoring of your system to be able to respond to an event. The following AWS services help you in system monitoring, alerts, and automated responses:
    - **Amazon CloudWatch**: CloudWatch provides hundreds of inbuilt metrics to monitor workload operation and trigger alerts as per the defined threshold. It provides a central log management system and triggers an automated incident response.
    - **AWS Lambda**: The AWS service used to automate responses to operational events is AWS Lambda.

- **Improving**: As incidents come into your system, you need to identify their pattern and root cause for continuous improvement. You should apply the best practice to maintain the version of your scripts. The following AWS services will help you to identify and apply system improvements:

  - **Amazon OpenSearch**: OpenSearch helps to learn from experience. Use OpenSearch to analyze log data to gain insight and use analytics to learn from experience.
  - **AWS CodeCommit**: Share learning with libraries, scripts, and documentation by maintaining them in the central repository as code.

AWS provides various capabilities to run your workload and operations as code. These capabilities help you to automate operations and incident response. With AWS, you can easily replace failed components with a good version and analyze the failed resources without impacting the production environment.

On AWS, aggregate the logs of all system operation and workload activities, and infrastructure, to create an activity history, such as with AWS CloudTrail. You can use AWS tools to query and analyze operations over time and identify a gap for improvement. In the cloud, resource discovery is easy, as all assets are located under the API- and web-based interfaces within the same hierarchy. You can also monitor your on-premises workload from the cloud. For security auditing in the AWS cloud Amazon GuardDuty and Amazon Detective provide great insight and details across multiple accounts.

Operational excellence is a continuous effort. Every operational failure should be analyzed to improve the operations of your application. By understanding the needs of your application's load, documenting regular activities as a runbook, following steps to guide issue handling, using automation, and creating awareness, your operations will be ready to deal with any failure event.

Summary

Operational excellence can be achieved by working on continuous improvement as per operational needs, and lessons learned from past events using RCA. You can achieve business success by increasing the excellence of your operations. Build and operate applications that increase efficiency while building highly responsive deployments. Use best practices to make your workloads operationally excellent.

In this chapter, you learned about the design principles to achieve operational excellence. These principles advocate operation automation, continuous improvement, taking an incremental approach, predicting failure, and being ready to respond.

You learned about various phases of operational excellence and the corresponding technology choices. In the planning phase, you learned about ITAM to track the inventory of IT resources and identify dependencies between them using configuration management.

You learned about alerts and monitoring in the functioning phase of operational excellence. You considered various kinds of monitoring, with examples such as infrastructure, application, log, security, and platform monitoring. You learned about the importance of alerts, and how to define alert severity and respond to it.

During the improvement phase of operational excellence, you learned about analytics in IT operations by building a big data pipeline, methods to perform RCA using the *five whys*, and the importance of auditing to save the system from any malicious behaviors and unnoticed threats. You learned about operational excellence in the cloud and different inbuilt tools that can be utilized for operational excellence in the AWS cloud.

As of now, you have learned best practices in the areas of performance, security, reliability, and operational excellence. In the next chapter, you will learn about best practices for cost optimization. You will also learn about various tools and techniques to optimize overall system costs and how to leverage multiple tools in the cloud to manage IT expenditure.

Join our book's Discord space

Join the book's Discord workspace for a monthly *Ask me Anything* session with the authors: https://packt.link/SAHandbook

11
Cost Considerations

One of the primary goals of any business is to increase profitability while serving its customers. Cost is the key parameter of discussion when a project is initiated. Having an application upgrade and adding new product features heavily depends upon the amount of funding available. The product's cost is everyone's responsibility and needs to be considered in every phase of the product life cycle (from planning to post-production). This chapter will help you understand the best practices for optimizing costs for your IT solutions and operations.

Cost optimization is a continuous process and needs to be managed carefully without sacrificing customer experience. Cost optimization *doesn't mean* cost reduction but reduces the business risk by maximizing **return on investment (ROI)**. You will need to understand your customer needs before planning any cost optimization and act accordingly. Often, if customers are looking for quality, they are ready to pay a higher price.

In this chapter, you will learn various design principles for the cost optimization of your solution. The cost aspect needs to be considered for every phase and component of the architecture. You will get an understanding of the right selection of technology to ensure cost optimization at every layer. You will learn the following best practices of cost optimization in this chapter:

- Design principles for cost optimization
- Techniques for cost optimization
- Cost optimization in the public cloud

By the end of the chapter, you will have learned about various techniques to optimize cost without risking business agility and outcome. You will have learned different methods to monitor the cost and apply governance for cost control.

Design principles for cost optimization

Cost optimization includes increasing business value and minimizing risk while reducing the cost of running a business. You need to plan by estimating the budget and forecasting expenditure. To realize cost gain, you need to implement a cost-saving plan and closely monitor your expenditure.

You can follow several principles that help you achieve cost optimization. The following sections talk about the common design principles that allow you to optimize cost. You will find that all cost optimization design principles are closely related and complement each other.

Calculating the total cost of ownership

Often, organizations tend to overlook the **total cost of ownership** (TCO) and decide based on the upfront cost to acquire software and services, known as **capital expenditure (CapEx)**. While the upfront cost determination is essential, in the long run, the TCO matters the most. The TCO includes both CapEx and **operational expenditure (OpEx)**, covering all the dimensions of the application life cycle. The CapEx cost consists of the price organizations pay upfront to acquire services and software, while OpEx includes the cost of operation, maintenance, training, and retirement of software applications. It would be best to consider all associated costs to help make more strategic decisions while calculating your ROI in the long run.

For example, when you buy a refrigerator, which will run 24/7, you look for an energy-saving rating to keep your electricity bill low. You are ready to pay a higher price up front as you know the total cost over time will be lower due to the saving in the energy bill.

Now let's take an example of a data center. There is an upfront hardware acquisition cost involved, the CapEx. However, the data center setup requires additional ongoing costs, the OpEx, which includes heating, cooling, rack maintenance, infrastructure administration, security, and so on.

For a typical use case, when you are purchasing and implementing software, consider the following costs to calculate the TCO:

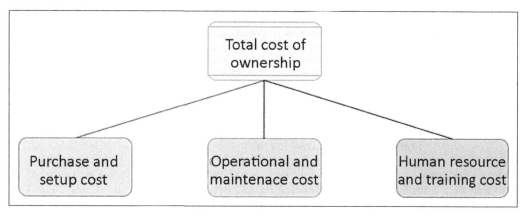

Figure 11.1: TCO for software

Let's look at this at a more granular level. Each TCO component has the following common costs involved for *off-the-shelf* software such as Oracle or an MS SQL database:

- **Purchase and setup costs**: These are the upfront cost to acquire the software and the services to deploy software. This includes the following:
    - Software price includes software with user licenses
    - Hardware cost includes purchasing a server and storage to deploy software
    - Implementation cost consists of the time and effort to get it ready for production
    - Migration cost includes moving data to the new system

- **Operational and maintenance costs**: This continues the cost of service to keep the software running for the business use case. This cost includes the following:
    - Software maintenance and support
    - Patching and updates
    - Enhancement
    - Data center cost to maintain hardware server
    - Security

- **Human resources and training costs**: This is the overhead cost to train staff to use the software to address business activities. This cost includes the following:

  - Application admin staff
  - IT support staff
  - Functional and technical consultant
  - Training cost and training tools

When looking for a solution, you will have multiple choices (such as taking out a subscription for a **Software as a Service (SaaS)** product such as **Salesforce CRM**). The SaaS model is mostly subscription based, so you need to determine whether you are getting the desired ROI for a more significant number of uses. You can take a hybrid approach and use the cloud to handle your hardware by choosing the **Infrastructure as a Service (IaaS)** option and installing off-the-shelf software. Overall, if the available software doesn't meet your requirements, you can choose to build it yourself. In any scenario, you should calculate the TCO to decide where you can make the maximum ROI. Let's look at budget and forecast planning, which can help to control TCO and achieve ROI.

Planning the budget and forecast

Every business needs to plan its expenditure and calculate ROI. Planning the budget gives guidance to organizations and teams on cost control. Organizations plan a long-term budget for 1-5 years, which helps them to run the business based on the funding required. These budgets then come down to the individual project and application levels. During solution design and development, the team needs to consider the available budget and plan accordingly. The budget helps to quantify what the business wants to achieve. The forecast provides an estimate of what the company is making.

You can consider budget as important strategic planning in the long run, and the forecast provides an estimate at a more tactical level to decide the business direction. In application development and operation, you can quickly lose track of the budget and overrun expected costs in the absence of a budget and a forecast. These two terms may be confusing, so let's understand the clear difference between a budget and a forecast:

Budget	Forecast
Represents future results and cash flow for business objectives that you want to achieve	Represents revenue and the current situation of the business

Plans for the long term, for example, 1-5 years	Plans month to month or quarterly
Is adjusted infrequently, maybe once a year, based on business drivers	Is updated regularly based on actual business progress
Helps to decide business directions such as organization restructuring based on actual cost versus budgeted cost	Helps to adjust short-term operational costs such as additional staffing
Helps to determine performance by comparing planned cost versus actual cost	Isn't used for performance variation but for streamlining progress

Forecast information helps you take immediate action, while the budget may become unachievable due to changes in the market. As shown in the following diagram, while you are working on day-to-day solutions, developments based on historic expenditure forecasts can prompt you to adjust the next month's cost:

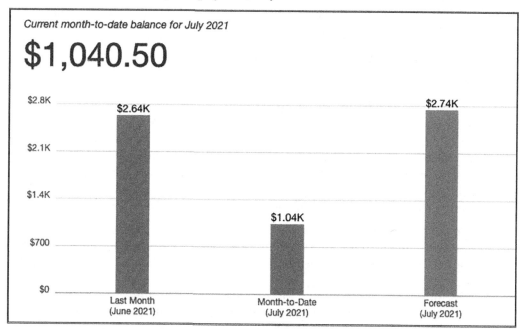

Figure 11.2: Billing and forecast report

In the preceding billing and forecast report, your monthly budget is $2,000, and the forecast shows that you will overrun your budget by the end of the month. Here, the forecast helps you act and control costs to stay within budget. Let's look at the mechanism to improve cost efficiency by managing demand and services in the next section.

Managing demand and service catalogs

Almost every organization has a centralized IT team, which works with internal business partners such as the application development team and the support teams of various business units. The IT team manages the demand for IT infrastructure, including the cost of all software and hardware, as well as support to manage application hosting. Often, business partners lack understanding of the cost drivers for the IT services that they use. For example, application development teams tend to overprovision their development or test environment, causing an additional cost.

Other factors that get the right sizing and demand forecasting from various organization units can help to match supply and demand. By consolidating all requirements in one place, an organization can benefit from economies of scale. You may achieve a lower variable cost because a large contract can achieve higher economies of scale. The right demand from all organization units is aggregated, which translates into lower prices.

Organizations can take one of the following two approaches to manage demand and services:

- **Demand management**: To save costs in your existing IT environments (where you may observe overspending may be prevalent), you can take the *demand-led approach*. It helps to improve cost efficiency in the short term, as you are not introducing many new services. You can analyze historical data to understand factors that are driving demand and capture cases of overprovisioning. You should establish a process between the IT team and business partners to streamline operational costs for IT services.

- **Service catalog management**: If there is a demand for new services and you don't have much historical data, you can take the *service-led approach*. In this approach, you need to understand the demand for the most frequently used services and create a catalog. For example, suppose the development team asks for a Linux server with a MySQL database to create a dev environment. In that case, the IT team can create a service catalog that helps the dev team acquire a small Linux and a database server. Similarly, the IT team can identify the most common set of services and attach a granular cost.

Each approach can have a significant cost saving in the short and long term. However, these transformations present substantial challenges as you need to change the project planning and approval process. The business and finance team need to align and understand the clear relationship between business growth and increased IT capacity. The cost model needs to be built around the most efficient approach by combining offerings from the cloud, on-premises, and off-the-shelf.

Keeping track of expenditure

You can find individual system costs by tracking expenditure and linking it to the system or business owner. Transparent expenditure data helps identify ROI and reward owners, optimizing resources and reducing cost. It can help you to determine what it costs every month for a department or project.

Saving cost is a shared responsibility, and you need to have a mechanism to hold everyone accountable for cost-saving. Often, organizations introduce a **show-back** or **charge-back** mechanism to share cost responsibility between organizational units.

The centralized billing account informs each organization unit regarding their expenditure in the show-back approach but doesn't charge the actual amount. Each business unit within an organization manages its budget under a master payee account in the charge-back mechanism. The master account charges back the amount to the business units as per their IT resource consumption every month.

When starting cost control for your organization, it is better to start with show-back as a stepping stone and move to charge-back as the organizational model matures. For each business unit, you should create expenditure awareness by configuring notifications so that teams get an alert as they approach the forecasted or budgeted amount of consumption. You should create a mechanism to monitor and control your cost by appropriately assigning them to the right business initiative. Provide visibility to create accountability for cost expenditures for each team. Cost tracking will help you to understand team operations.

Each workload is different; you should use the pricing model that suits your workload to minimize cost. Establish mechanisms that ensure business objectives are achieved by applying cost optimization best practices. You can avoid overspending by defining a tagging strategy to link business units with specific expenditure and using the **check-and-balance** approach.

Continuous cost optimization

If you follow cost optimization best practices, you should have a good cost comparison with existing activity. It's always possible to reduce the cost of your applications that are migrated and matured over time. Cost optimizations should never end until the cost of identifying money-saving opportunities is more than the amount of money you will save. Until that point is reached, you should continually monitor your expenditure and look for new ways to save on cost. You should keep finding an area to save costs by removing idle resources.

For an architecture that is balanced in terms of its cost and performance, ensure that the cost paid for resources is well utilized and avoids any significantly underutilized IT resources such as server instances.

A biased utilization metric showing exceptionally high or low cost will harm your organization's business.

Application-level metrics for cost optimization need to be considered carefully. For example, introduce archival policies to control data storage capacity. To optimize the database, you should check for appropriate database deployment needs, such as if multi-location deployments for the database are essential or whether provisioned **Input/Output Operations Per Second (IOPS)** are applicable as per your database utilization needs. To reduce your administrative and operational overhead, you can use the SaaS model to help your employees focus on applications and business activities.

To identify a gap and apply necessary changes for cost-saving, you should implement resource management and change control processes during the project life cycle. Your goal is to help your organization design the architecture as optimally and cost-effectively as possible. Keep looking for new services and features that might directly reduce your costs.

Let's learn some techniques that can help you to optimize the cost and increase ROI.

Techniques for cost optimization

To gain a competitive edge and keep up with rapid growth, enterprises are investing more in technology. With economic instability, cost optimization becomes an essential but challenging task. These companies spend a lot of time and research on reducing costs in the procurement process, operation, and vendors. Many companies even share data centers, call centers, and workspaces as a cost-saving method. Sometimes organizations delay upgrades to avoid buying new expensive hardware.

The organization can save more if it takes a broader look into the overall information technology architecture across its business units. Improving existing architecture can open doors to bring more opportunities and business to the company, even if it requires a bit more adjustment in the budget. Let's identify the focus area where companies can save money and gain more revenue with techniques such as moving to the cloud, simplified architecture, virtualization, and shared resources.

Reducing architectural complexity

Organizations often lack a centralized IT architecture, resulting in each business unit trying to build its own set of tools. Lack of overall control causes a lot of duplicate systems and data inconsistency. IT initiatives in individual business units are driven by a short-term goal.

In such cases, business units are not well aligned with long-term organizational vision, such as the digital transformation of the entire organization. Further, it adds complexity to maintain and upgrade those systems. Taking a simple step to define set standards and avoid duplication can help to save costs.

In the following diagram, you can see a complex architecture on the left-hand side, where business units are working in their own application without any standardization, causing duplicate applications with a lot of dependencies. This kind of architecture results in high costs and risks. Any new experiment takes a long time to market, which results in losing the competitive edge. A standard process can provide a holistic view and high flexibility to create an agile environment by applying automation, which helps to reduce the overall cost and results in a more significant ROI:

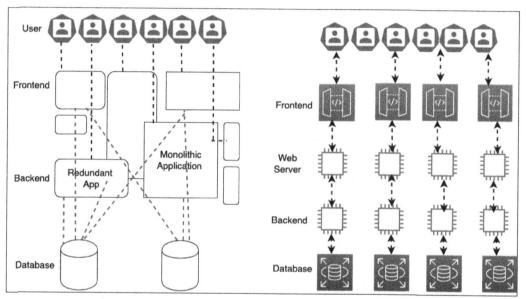

Figure 11.3: Architectural standardization

The first thing is to eliminate duplication and identify the function reuse across the business unit to reduce the architectural complexity. During *gap analysis* of existing architecture, you will find there is so much code, so many existing components, and a project that can be reused across the organization to support your business requirement. To reduce the complexity of IT architecture, think of an out-of-the-box solution that fits your business needs and provides an ROI. Customization should be your last approach if no other option is available.

Any new application needs to have an accessible integration mechanism to interact with the existing system using **service-oriented architecture (SOA)**. Harmonizing the user interface design across the application provides a set of standard UI packages, which can be reused for any new application.

Similarly, other modules can be reutilized with service-oriented design. You learned about SOA patterns in *Chapter 6, Solution Architecture Design Patterns*, which help you keep all the different pieces of software working separately and still communicating with each other to build an entire system.

In the modular approach, each team is responsible for developing a service, which every team across the organization can use to avoid duplication. As an architect, you should help the team create a service-oriented design, where each team handles individual architecture components as a service that can be developed independently. With the help of microservices architecture, you can deploy an entire application in a modular way. If one component is not working, you can rework it without impacting the whole application. For example, a payment service developed to collect payment from a customer visiting an e-commerce website can also be utilized to make payments to vendors in the vendor management system.

Once you set up a centralized IT architecture, taking a modular approach helps you keep the cost down. Empowering your IT architecture team can help to align organizational units with the company's vision and support other parallel projects to follow the overall strategy. It also helps to provide consistency in other critical services that are often overlooked, such as legal, accounting, and human resources.

With the help of the IT architecture team, you can get excellent feedback and make sure that projects are aligned with business needs and requirements. By overseeing the overall architecture across teams, an architect can advise whether there is any duplicate effort, project, process, or system that is not aligned with the business need. The centralized architecture will reduce complexity and tech debt, bring more stability, and increase quality. The overall idea of centralized architecture is to increase IT efficiency, so let's learn more about that.

Increasing IT efficiency

Nowadays, every company uses and consumes IT resources. A lot of funding is consumed by too many servers, laptops, storage capacity, and software licenses. The license is one of the resources that is sometimes underused, undiscovered, idle, or installed incorrectly and consumes a lot of funding. A centralized IT team can lead the effort for license optimization by keeping track of used software licenses and retiring additional licenses. They can save costs by negotiating a bulk discount with the vendor.

To increase IT efficiency, you may want to cancel non-compliant projects that take additional funding and resources. Also, you should help teams to revisit the strategy to support or terminate any unused and non-aligned projects continuously. The following methods can be considered for cost optimization:

- Re-evaluate projects with high costs, as they may not be well aligned with the business vision. Reshape projects that have high value but no direct impact on the IT strategy.

- De-prioritize projects that have little to no business value even though they are aligned with the IT strategy.

- Cancel non-compliant projects with low business value.

- Decommission or retire unused applications.

- Replace old legacy systems by modernizing them to reduce maintenance costs.

- Avoid duplicate projects by reutilizing existing applications.

- Wherever possible, consolidate data and develop an integrated data model. You will learn about maintaining a centralized data lake in *Chapter 13, Data Engineering for Solution Architecture*.

- Consolidate vendor procurement across the organization to save costs on IT support and maintenance expenditure.

- Consolidate any system that does the same thing as payment and access management.

- Eliminate costly, wasteful, overprovisioned projects and expenditure.

Moving to the cloud can be an excellent consideration to increase IT resources efficiently and reduce costs. The public cloud providers, such as **Amazon Web Services (AWS)**, offer a *pay-as-you-go* model that means you only pay for what you are using. For example, the developer desktop can shut down during non-working hours and weekends, reducing workspace costs by up to *70%*. The batch processing system needs to be brought up only to process jobs and can be shut down immediately afterward. It works just like any electrical appliance that you switch off when not required to save electricity costs.

Applying automation is a great mechanism to increase overall IT efficiency. Automation helps eliminate costly human labor and reduces the time spent performing daily routine jobs without error. Automate things wherever possible to provision servers, run monitoring jobs, and process data.

Make sure to do the right trade-off to improve results while deciding to optimize costs. Let's take an example. If you are going to a theme park where you want to go on lots of good rides, you are willing to pay a higher price to see the value of the money you are spending. To attract more customers, if the vendor decided to reduce the price and make adjustments by lowering the number of enjoyable rides, there is a chance that you will go to another theme park as you are looking for a good time. Here, competitors will gain an edge and attract existing customers, while the current vendor will lose business. In this case, cost reduction is adding business risk, which is not the right cost-optimization approach.

Your goal should be measurable, and these measures should focus on both business output and the cost of your system. The quantitative measure helps you understand the impact of increasing output and reducing the cost. The organizational and team-level goals must align with the end users of the application. At the organizational level, the goals will be across organizational business units. At the team level, they will be more aligned with individual systems. You can set up a goal at the business unit level, for example, to reduce the cost per transaction by 10% every quarter or 15% every six months. Defining the goal ensures that systems improve over their lifetime.

Applying standardization and governance

Organizations need a strategy to analyze misalignment and overconsumption, reduce complexity, and define guidelines to use appropriate and efficient systems and implement a process wherever it is required. Creating and implementing these guidelines will help companies develop a standard infrastructure and reduce duplicate projects and complexity.

To implement governance, you need to set up resource limits across the organization. Putting the service catalog in place with **Infrastructure as Code (IaC)** helps ensure that teams are not overprovisioned with resources beyond their allocated capacity. You should have a mechanism to understand and take action on business requirements quickly. Take both resource creation and decommissioning into account when applying resource limits and defining the process to change them.

Businesses operate multiple applications by various teams. These teams can belong to different business units within their revenue stream. Determining resource costs to the application and business unit or team drives efficient usage behavior and helps reduce cost. You can define resource capacity based on cost attribution and the group's, organization unit's, or department's requirements. To organize the cost structure, you can use resource tagging along with account structuring.

As shown in the following screenshot, you can organize your accounts in different organization units such as HR and Finance, and each department under the organization unit can have its own accounts. For example, here, **HR** has separate accounts for **Payroll** and **Marketing**, while **Finance** has individual accounts for **Sales** and **Marketing**:

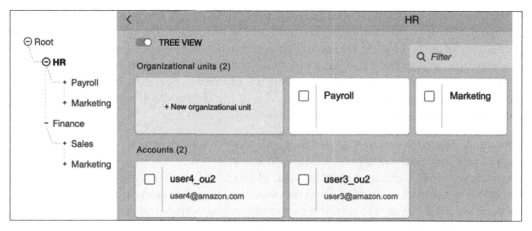

Figure 11.4: Enterprise account structure for organization units (OUs)

In the preceding account structuring strategy, you can control costs at each business unit and department level. Adopting a charge-back mechanism for each department increases accountability for cost at a more granular level, which helps to optimize cost. Account structuring helps you to apply high security and compliance standards across the organization. As each account is linked to a parent account, you can significantly deal with the mass utilization of resources from vendors by consolidating expenditure across the organization.

Resource cost tagging

As shown in the following screenshot, to get complete cost visibility and consolidation across resources, you can tag each resource provisioned at the team level, which provides more granular control:

Key (128 characters maximum)	Value (256 characters maximum)
Type	AppServer
Environment	Dev
Department	Marketing
Business Unit	Finance

Add another tag (Up to 50 tags maximum)

Figure 11.5: Resource tagging for cost visibility

In the preceding diagram, you can see the tagging strategy, which indicates that the given server is for application deployment and is utilized by the development team. This server is owned by the marketing department of the Finance business unit. In this way, the organization can get a granular level of cost expenditure visibility, and the team will be more frugal in their spending. However, you may want to adopt the show-back mechanism at the team level and the charge-back mechanism at the department and business unit level.

You can define your mechanism for tagging, where you can attach a name and value, such as resource name and owner name, to any resource. Almost every public cloud provider provides tagging capabilities out of the box. For on-premises, you can embed server metadata such as DNS name or hostname. Tagging not only helps you to organize costs but also to define a capacity limit, security, and compliance. It can be an excellent tool for inventory management and keeping an eye on the growing need for resources at every level of the organization. The following screenshot shows the cost sorted by the **aws:createdBy** tag, which helps to determine the cost of each resource that is auto-created by AWS:

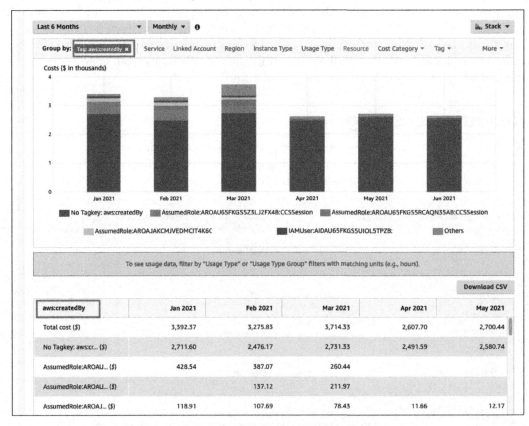

Figure 11.6: Resources amount expenditures dashboard for a cost tag

Business leaders should evaluate the overall requirement to create efficient IT architectures. Collaboration is required to develop a robust IT architecture and define governance across functional teams to set up accountability. Also, set up a standard to review the architecture, create the baseline for any new project initiative, and explain the process that will ensure that the system complies with the correct architecture and identify the route to improvement.

Engage all impacted stakeholders within your business in usage and cost discussions. The CFO and application owners must understand resource consumption and purchasing options. Department owners must understand the overall business model and the monthly billing process. This will help to set the direction for the business units and the whole company.

Make sure third-party vendors are aligned to your financial goals and can adjust their engagement models. Vendors should provide a cost analysis of any application they own and develop. Each team within the organization should be able to translate business, cost, or usage factors from management into system adjustments, which help the application implement and achieve the company's desired goals.

Monitoring cost usage and report

Accurate cost factors help you to determine the profitability of business units and products. Cost tracking helps you to allocate resources at the right place to increase ROI. Understanding cost drivers helps you to control your business expenditure.

To optimize costs, you must know your expenditure pattern across the organization. You need to have visibility of IT expenditure over a period of time to determine cost-saving opportunities. You can take the required steps for cost optimization and understand the impact by creating a visualization of cost trends, which shows historical costs and forecasts by resources and departments across the organization. Your team needs to gather data by logging all data points, analyzing them with monitoring, and creating a visualization report.

To identify cost-saving opportunities, you need a detailed insight into your workload resource utilization. Cost optimization depends on your ability to forecast future spending and put methods in place to align cost and usage as per your forecast. The following are the primary areas where you should have data visualizations for cost-saving:

- Determine the most significant investments in resources
- Analyze and understand your expenditure and usage data
- Budget and forecast
- Receive an alert when you exceed your budgeted or forecasted thresholds

The following report is showing resource expenditure over six months in AWS. Looking at the visualization, you can see that the graph database service **Amazon Neptune**, represented by the second bar in each month, is consuming the highest costs with an increase in the trend starting in March 2021. As the business unit can visualize the high cost in May and June, it prompts the system admin to take an in-depth look at cost optimizations and find overprovisioned resources. The admin performs cleanup by stopping additional servers, which will bring down the cost:

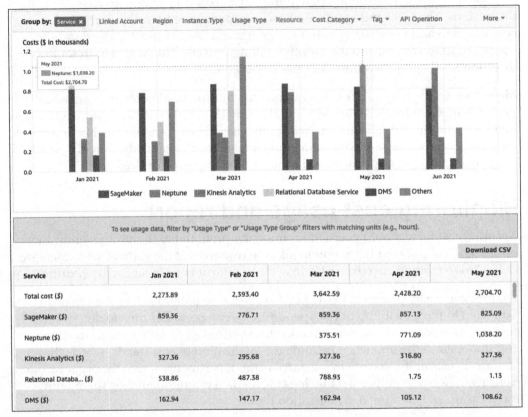

Figure 11.7: Resource cost and usage report

The preceding report helps business owners to understand cost patterns and take a reactive approach to cost control. The reactive approach caused hidden costs, which went undetected for a specified period. With the proactive approach, the forecast can help business owners to make a decision ahead of time.

The following report shows daily cost expenditure in the filled bars and forecast spending in the empty bars with estimated ranges. Looking at the report, you can see that it is likely that cost may increase in the next couple of months, and you can take action to understand cost attributes and control costs:

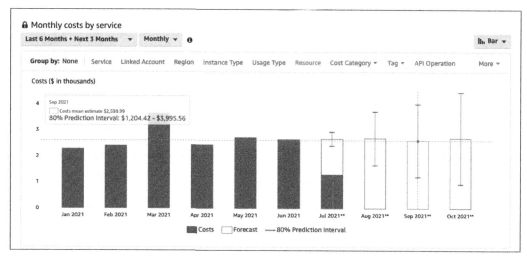

Figure 11.8: Cost trend and cost forecast report

Monitoring your costs against the budget can give you another proactive measure to control costs. Setting up an alert when expenditure reaches a certain proportion of the budget (for example, 50% or 80%) helps you review and adjust your ongoing costs.

In the following report, you can visually determine the current cost against the budgeted cost, which was very high a year ago with an actual cost of $7,397 compared to the budgeted $2,500. Based on the following report, IT admins were able to take action to optimize the cost and bring it down to within the monthly budget.

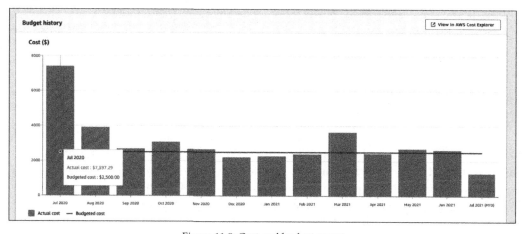

Figure 11.9: Cost and budget report

Cost and budget reports help you to control costs by taking proactive action. Combining your actual running costs with budgets and forecasts provides a great deal of cost control daily.

You can also set up an alert when your actual cost reaches a certain threshold in the budget or forecast. It alerts you proactively via email or mobile message and tells you to take proactive action to control costs.

In the following screenshot, you can see an alert has been set up for when the actual cost reaches 80% of the budget. You can set up multiple alerts to get information when the cost reaches, for example, 50% and 80% of the budget or forecast:

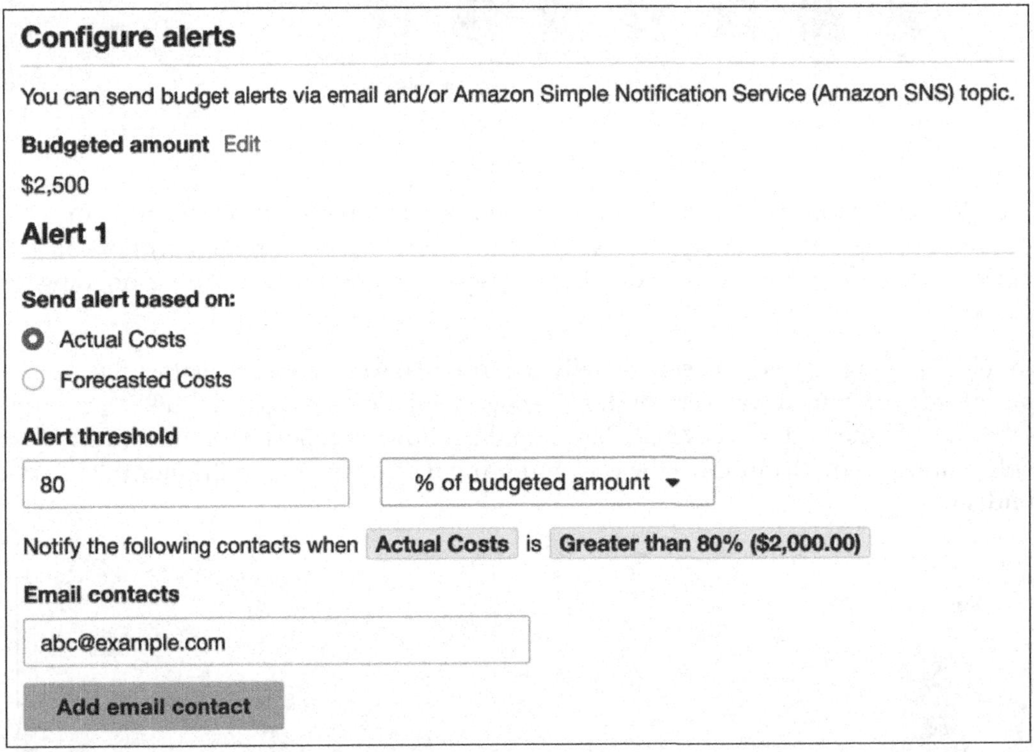

Configure alerts

You can send budget alerts via email and/or Amazon Simple Notification Service (Amazon SNS) topic.

Budgeted amount Edit

$2,500

Alert 1

Send alert based on:

◉ Actual Costs

○ Forecasted Costs

Alert threshold

| 80 | % of budgeted amount ▾ |

Notify the following contacts when **Actual Costs** is **Greater than 80% ($2,000.00)**

Email contacts

abc@example.com

Add email contact

Figure 11.10: Alert based on actual cost

One way to do cost control is by right-sizing your environment with resource monitoring and trigger alarms for over or underutilization. Analysis of resources can be performed using monitoring tools such as **Splunk** or **CloudWatch** and custom logs, where customized metrics such as application memory utilization of your system can be monitored to perform right-sizing. Low utilization of a resource could be a criterion for identifying opportunities for cost optimization. For example, CPU utilization, RAM utilization, network bandwidth, and the number of connections to the application can be analyzed and monitored.

You need to be careful when resizing your environment to ensure you are not impacting the customer experience. The following are best practices to apply when you perform right-sizing:

- Make sure monitoring reflects the end user experience. Select the correct period. For example, performance metrics should cover 99% of the user's request-response time rather than taking an average response time.

- Select the correct monitoring cycle, such as every hour, day, or week. For example, if you are conducting daily analyses, you might miss a weekly or monthly cycle of high utilization and under provision your system.

- Assess the cost of change against the cost-saving. For example, you may have to perform additional testing or engage resources to perform resizing. This cost-benefit analysis will help you to assign resources.

Identify application utilization against your business requirement, for example look at how many user requests are expected to come by the end of the month or during peak season. Identifying and optimizing the utilization gap allows you to save costs. To do this, use the right tool that covers all dimensions from cost-saving to system utilization and the impact on customer experience due to changes, and then utilize reports to understand the business ROI impact due to cost changes. The public cloud follows a different cost model, and it's often an on-demand pay-as-you-go cost structure.

You have to be very diligent when using cloud resources as every second counts toward your cost, and it can be costly if you overlook cost optimization and monitoring. Let's learn more details about cost optimization in the public cloud.

Cost optimization in the public cloud

Public clouds, such as **AWS**, **Microsoft Azure**, and **Google Cloud Platform (GCP)**, provide a great deal of cost optimization with the *pay-as-you-go* model. The public cloud cost model allows customers to trade CapEx for variable expenses, paying for IT resources as they consume them. OpEx is usually lower due to economies of scale. It could be cost-effective to be in the cloud and benefit from continued price reductions that occur over time. The other advantage is that you get additional tools and functionality out of the box with a cloud provider such as AWS, which helps you achieve better agility.

You need a different mindset when defining the cloud cost structure model as it is pretty different from traditional cost models, which most enterprises have been following for decades. You have all the infrastructure available at your fingertips in the cloud, which requires greater control and regulation.

Clouds provide several tools for cost governance and regularization. For example, in AWS, you can set up service limits for each account, so the dev team cannot utilize more than ten servers, and production can have the required number of servers and databases with a buffer.

All resources are associated with accounts in the cloud, so it's easy to keep track of IT resource inventories in a single place and monitor their utilization. In addition to that, you get tools to collect data across various IT resources and provide suggestions. As shown in the following screenshot, **AWS Trusted Advisor** crawls through all resources in the account and offers cost-saving recommendations based on resource utilization:

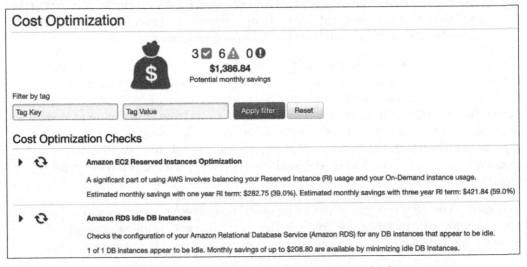

Figure 11.11: Cost-saving suggestions from AWS Trusted Advisor

In the preceding screenshot, AWS Trusted Advisor has detected continuous utilization of the application server (**Elastic Compute Cloud, EC2**) and advises buying a reserve instance by paying one year up front with a 40% cost saving. Further checks have identified an underutilized database (Amazon RDS) and suggest shutting it down to make a potential saving.

The cloud can provide an excellent value proposition for cost-saving. To begin with, you can create a hybrid cloud, where you establish connectivity between your on-premises data center and the cloud. You can move development and test servers to the cloud to determine cost structure and potential savings. Once you have set up cost governance in the cloud, move more workload as per the cost-benefit analysis. However, you need to assess your workload and whether it can be moved to the cloud and define a strategy. You learned about cloud migration in *Chapter 5, Cloud Migration and Hybrid Cloud Architecture Design*.

Increasingly, public cloud providers are offering managed services, which eliminates any infrastructure maintenance cost and overheads for alert and monitoring configurations. A managed service reduces the total cost of ownership by reducing cost as service adoption increases.

Summary

Cost optimization is a continuous effort from application inception (from proof-of-concept to implementation and post-production). You need to review architectures and cost-saving efforts continuously.

In this chapter, you learned about design principles to optimize costs. Before making any purchase decision, you should consider the total cost of ownership for the entire life cycle of software or hardware. Planning a budget and keeping track of forecasts help you to stay on the cost optimization path. Always keep track of your expenditures and look for possible opportunities for cost optimization without affecting user experience or business value.

You learned about the various techniques for cost optimization, which include reducing architectural complexity by simplifying enterprise architecture and setting a standard that everyone can follow. It's recommended to avoid duplication by identifying and consolidating idle and repeated resources to negotiate the bulk purchase cost. Apply standardization across the organization to limit resource provision and develop a standard architecture. Tracking data for your actual costs against budgets and forecasts can help you to take proactive action. You learned about various reports and alerts that can help to control costs. You also learned about cost optimization in the cloud, which can help you further to optimize value.

Automation and agility are major factors that increase resource efficiency, and DevOps can provide a great deal of automation. In the next chapter, you will learn about various DevOps components and DevOps strategies to deploy your workload in the most automated way efficiently.

Join our book's Discord space

Join the book's Discord workspace for a monthly *Ask me Anything* session with the authors: https://packt.link/SAHandbook

12

DevOps and Solution Architecture Framework

In traditional environments, the development team and the IT operations team work in silos. The development team gathers requirements from business owners and develops the applications. System administrators are solely responsible for operations and for meeting uptime requirements. These teams generally do not have any direct communication during the development life cycle, and each team rarely understands the processes and needs of the other team.

Each team has its own set of tools, processes, and redundant approaches, which sometimes results in conflict. For example, the development and **quality assurance (QA)** teams could be testing the build on a specific patch of the **operating system (OS)**. However, the operations team deploys the same build on a different OS version in the production environment, causing issues and delays in the delivery.

DevOps is a methodology that promotes collaboration and coordination between developers and operational teams to deliver products or services continuously. This approach is constructive in organizations where the teams rely on multiple applications, tools, technologies, platforms, databases, devices, and so on in the process of developing or delivering a product or service.

Although there are different approaches to the DevOps culture, all are about achieving a common goal. DevOps is about delivering a product or service in the shortest amount of time by increasing operational efficiency through shared responsibilities. DevOps helps to deliver without compromising on quality, reliability, stability, resilience, or security.

In this chapter, you will learn about the following DevOps topics:

- Introducing DevOps
- Understanding the benefits of DevOps
- Understanding the components of DevOps
- Introducing DevOps in security
- Combining DevSecOps and CI/CD
- Implementing a CD strategy
- Implementing continuous testing in the CI/CD pipeline
- Using DevOps tools for CI/CD
- Implementing DevOps best practices
- Building DevOps and DevSecOps in the cloud

By the end of this chapter, you will have learned about the importance of DevOps in application deployment, testing, and security. You will also learn DevOps best practices and different tools and techniques to implement them.

Introducing DevOps

In a **DevOps** (short for **development and operations**) approach, the development team and the operations team work collaboratively during the build and deployment phases of the software development life cycle, sharing responsibilities, and providing continuous feedback. The software builds are tested frequently throughout the build phase on production-like environments, allowing early detection of defects.

Sometimes, you will find a software application development and its operations are handled by a single team, where engineers work across the entire application life cycle, from development and deployment to operations. Such a team needs to develop a range of skills that are not limited to a single function. Application testing and security teams may also work more closely with the operations and development teams, from the inception to the production launch of an application.

Speed enables organizations to stay ahead in the competition and address customer requirements quickly. Good DevOps practices encourage software development engineers and operations professionals to work better together. This results in closer collaboration and communication, leading to a shorter **time to market**, reliable release, improved code quality, and better maintenance.

Developers benefit from feedback provided by the operations teams and create strategies for testing and deployment.

System administrators don't have to implement defective or untested software in production environments because they participate in the *build phase*. As all stakeholders in the software development and delivery life cycle collaborate, they can also evaluate the tools they intend to use at each step of the process, verify compatibility between the devices, and determine whether any tools can be shared across the teams.

DevOps is a combination of culture and practices. It requires organizations to change their culture by breaking down the barriers between all teams in the product development and delivery life cycle. DevOps is not just about development and operations; instead, it involves the entire organization, including management, business/application owners, developers, QA engineers, release managers, the operations team, and system administrators.

DevOps is gaining popularity as the preferred operating culture, especially for organizations that deal with cloud or distributed computing. Let's learn about some of the various benefits of DevOps and why it is important for your application workload.

Understanding the benefits of DevOps

The goal of DevOps is a **CI/CD (continuous integration and continuous deployment)** model that is repeatable, reliable, stable, resilient, and secure. These properties improve operational efficiency. To achieve this goal, teams must collaborate and get involved in the development and delivery process. All technical team members should have experience with the processes and tools involved in the development pipeline. A mature DevOps process provides benefits, as shown in the following diagram:

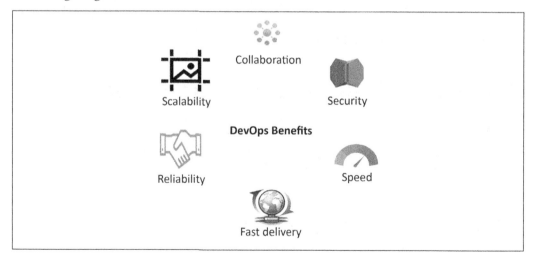

Figure 12.1: Benefits of DevOps

These benefits of DevOps are detailed further here:

- **Speed**: Releasing product features quickly helps to accommodate changing business needs of your customers and expand your market. A DevOps model enables an organization to achieve results faster.

- **Fast delivery**: DevOps processes facilitate more efficiency by automating end-to-end pipelines, from code build to code deploy and production launch. Rapid delivery helps you to innovate faster. The faster release of bug fixes and features allows you to gain a competitive edge.

- **Reliability**: DevOps processes provide all checks to ensure delivery quality and safe application updates rapidly. DevOps practices such as CI and CD embed automation testing and security checks for a positive end-user experience.

- **Scalability**: DevOps helps to scale your infrastructure and application on an on-demand basis by including automation everywhere.

- **Collaboration**: The DevOps model builds a culture of ownership whereby the teams consider their actions. The operations and dev teams work together in a shared responsibility model. Collaboration simplifies the process and increases efficiency.

- **Security**: In an agile environment, making frequent changes requires stringent security checks. The DevOps model automates security and compliance best practices, monitors them, and takes corrective action in an automated way.

The DevOps model optimizes the productivity of the development team and the reliability of system operations. As teams closely collaborate, this helps to increase efficiency and improve quality. Teams take full ownership of the services they deliver, often beyond the traditional scope of their roles, and develop thinking from a customer point of view to solve any issue.

Understanding the components of DevOps

DevOps tools and automation bring together development and system operations. The following are critical components of a DevOps practice:

- CI/CD
- Continuous monitoring and improvement
- Infrastructure as code
- Configuration management

A best practice across all the elements is **automation**. Automating processes allows you to efficiently perform these operations in a fast, reliable, and repeatable fashion. Automation can involve scripts, templates, and other tools. In a thriving DevOps environment, infrastructure is managed as code. Automation enables DevOps teams to set up and tune test and production environments rapidly. Let's explore more details about each component.

Continuous integration/cotinuous deployment

In **CI** (**Continuous Integration**), developers commit code frequently to a code repository. The code is built frequently. Each build is tested using automated unit tests and integration tests. In **CI** (**Continuous Integration**), you go a step further and deploy your code frequently in production. Builds are deployed to test environments and are tested using automated and possibly manual tests. Successful builds pass tests and are deployed to staging or production environments. The following diagram illustrates the impact of CI versus CD in the software development life cycle:

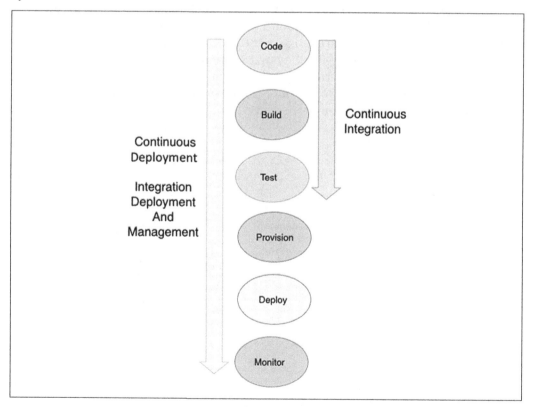

Figure 12.2: CI/CD

As shown in the preceding diagram, CI refers to the building and unit testing stages of the software development life cycle. Every update that is committed in the code repository creates an automated build and test. CD is an essential aspect of CI that extends the CI process further to deploy the build in production. In CI/CD practices, several people work on the code. They all must use the latest working build for their efforts. Code repositories maintain different versions of the code and also make the code accessible to the team. You check out the code from the repository, make your changes or write new code in your local copy, compile and test your code, and frequently commit your code back to the main repository.

CI automates most of the software release process. It creates an automated flow that builds, tests, and then stages the update. However, a developer must trigger the final deployment to a live production environment that is *not automated*. It expands upon CD by deploying all code changes to a testing environment and/or a production environment after the build stage. If CD is implemented correctly, developers will always have a tested and deployment-ready build.

The concepts in the following diagram illustrate everything related to the automation of an application, from code commits into a code repo to the deployment pipeline. It shows an end-to-end flow from the build to the production environment, where the developer checks in the code change in the code repository, which is pulled by the CI server. The CI server triggers the build to create a deployment package with new application binaries and corresponding dependencies. These new binaries are deployed in a targeted development or testing environment. Also, binaries get checked into the artifact repository for safe version-controlled storage:

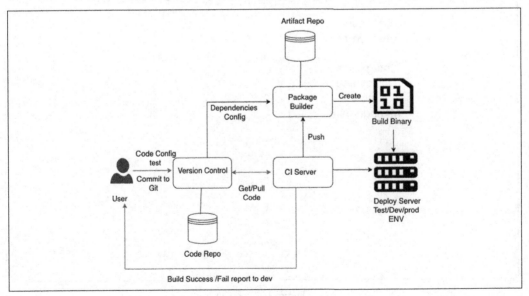

Figure 12.3: CI/CD for DevOps

In CI/CD, software development life cycle phases such as code, build, deploy, and test are automated using the DevOps pipeline. The deploy and provision phase needs to be automated using **Infrastructure as Code (IaC)** scripts. Monitoring can be automated with various monitoring tools.

A robust CD pipeline also automates the provisioning of infrastructure for testing and production environments and enables monitoring and management of test and production environments. CI/CD provides multiple benefits to the team, such as improving developer productivity by saving time on building, testing, and deploying code. It helps the dev team to detect and fix bugs quickly and launch feature updates faster in the production environment.

CD does not mean that every change committed by the developer goes into production. Instead, it means that every change is *ready* to go into production. When the changes are staged and tested in the stage environment, a manual approval process initiates and gives a green signal to deploy to production. Thus, in CD, deploying to production becomes a business decision and is still automated with tools.

Continuous monitoring and improvement

Continuous monitoring helps us to understand application and infrastructure performance impacts on the customer. By analyzing data and logs, you can learn how code changes impact users. Active monitoring is essential in the era of 24/7 services and constant updates to both applications and infrastructure. You can be more proactive about monitoring services by creating alerts and performing real-time analysis.

You can track various metrics to monitor and improve your DevOps practice. Examples of DevOps-related metrics are as follows:

- **Change volume**: This is the number of user stories developed, the number of lines of new code, and the number of bugs fixed.

- **Deployment frequency**: This indicates how often a team is deploying an application. This metric should generally remain stable or show an upward trend.

- **Lead time from development to deployment**: The time between the beginning of a development cycle to the end of deployment can be used to identify inefficiencies in the intermediate steps of the release cycle.

- **Percentage of failed deployments**: The percentage of failed deployments, including the number of deployments that resulted in outages, should be low.

This metric should be reviewed in conjunction with the change volume. Analyze potential points of failure if the change volume is low but the number of failed deployments is high.

- **Availability**: Track how many releases caused failures that possibly resulted in violations of **Service-Level Agreements (SLAs)**. What is the average downtime for the application?

- **Customer complaint volume**: The number of complaint tickets filed by customers indicates the quality of your application.

- **Percentage change in user volume**: The number of new users signing up to use your application and the resulting increase in traffic can help you scale your infrastructure to match the workload.

After you deploy builds to the production environment, it is essential to monitor your application's performance continuously. As we discussed automating environments, let's explore more details on IaC (**Infrastructure as Code**).

Infrastructure as Code

Provisioning, managing, and even deprecating infrastructure is a costly activity in terms of human effort. Furthermore, repeated attempts to build and modify environments manually can be fraught with errors. Whether working from prior experience or a well-documented runbook, the tendency for a human to make a mistake is a statistical probability.

We can automate the task of creating a complete environment. Task automation can help to complete repetitive tasks and provide significant value effortlessly. With IaC, we can define our infrastructure in the form of **templates**. A single template may consist of a part or the entirety of an environment. More importantly, this template can be used repeatedly to create the same environment again.

In IaC, infrastructure is spun up and managed using code and CI. An IaC model helps you interact with infrastructure programmatically at scale and avoid human errors by automating resource configuration. That way, you can work with infrastructure the same way you would with code by using code-based tools. As the infrastructure is managed through code, the application can be deployed using a standardized method, and any patches and versions can be updated repeatedly without any errors. Some of the most popular IaC scripting tools are Ansible, Terraform, Azure Resource Manager, Google Cloud Deployment Manager, Chef, Puppet, and AWS CloudFormation.

The following is a code sample from AWS CloudFormation, which provides infrastructure as code capability to automated infrastructures on the AWS cloud platform.

```
{
"AWSTemplateFormatVersion" : "2010-09-09",
"Description" : "Create a S3 Storage with parameter to choose own
bucket name",
"Parameters": {
    "S3NameParam" : {
        "Type": "String",
        "Default" : "architect-book-storage",
        "Description" : "Enter the S3 Bucket Name",
        "MinLength" : "5",
        "MaxLength" : "30"
            }
        },

"Resources" : {
    "Bucket" : {
        "Type" : "AWS::S3::Bucket",
        "DeletionPolicy" : "Retain",
            "Properties" : {
                "AccessControl" : "PublicRead",
                "BucketName" : {"Ref" : "S3NameParam" },
                "Tags" : [ {"Key" : "Name" , "Value" : "MyBucket"} ]
                        }
                }
        },

"Outputs" : {
    "BucketName" : {
        "Description" : "BucketName" ,
        "Value" : { "Ref" : "S3NameParam"}
                }
            }
        }

}
```

The preceding code creates Amazon S3 object storage with the option for the user to provide their choice of storage name as shown below:

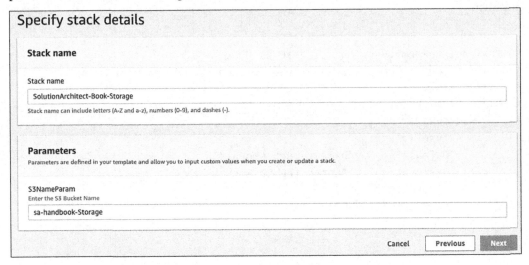

Figure 12.4: Infrastructure as code using AWS CloudFormation

After execution of the code, Amazon S3 object storage gets created as you can see in **Outputs**:

Figure 12.5: Automated AWS S3 object storage creation using AWS CloudFormation

The provided code can be used by multiple teams to create any amount of Amazon S3 storage. As data is so important, the admin chose to add bucket `"DeletionPolicy": "Retain"`, which makes sure storage doesn't get deleted when infrastructure comes down and data is safe. You can see how you can implement standardization, consistency, and compliance across organizations using IaC. Configuration management is another important aspect of the DevOps process. Let's learn more about it.

Configuration management

Configuration management (CM) is the process of using automation to standardize resource configurations across your entire infrastructure and applications. CM tools such as Chef, Puppet, and Ansible can help you manage IaC and automate most system administration tasks, including provisioning, configuring, and managing IT resources. By automating and standardizing resource configurations across the development, build, test, and deployment phases, you can ensure consistency and eliminate failures caused by misconfiguration.

CM can also increase the productivity of your operations by allowing you to automatically deploy the same configuration to hundreds of nodes at the push of a button. CM can also be leveraged to deploy changes to configurations.

Although you can use registry settings or databases to store system configuration settings, a configuration management application allows you to maintain version control as well, in addition to storage. CM is also a way to track and audit configuration changes. If necessary, you can even maintain multiple versions of configuration settings for various versions of your software.

CM tools include a controller machine that manages server nodes. For example, Chef requires a client agent application installed on each server to manage, and a master Chef application installs on the controller machine. Puppet also works the same way with a centralized server. However, Ansible has a decentralized approach and doesn't require installing agent software on the server nodes. The following table shows a high-level comparison between the popular configuration management tools:

	Ansible	**Puppet**	**Chef**
Mechanism	Controller machine applies changes to servers using **Secure Shell (SSH)**	Master synchronizes changes to Puppet node	Chef workstation looks for changes in Chef servers and pushes them to the Chef node
Architecture	Any server can be the controller	Centralized control by Puppet master	Centralized control by Chef server
Script Language	YAML	Domain-specific on Ruby	Ruby
Scripting Terminology	Playbook and roles	Manifests and modules	Recipes and cookbooks
Test Execution	Sequential order	Non-sequential order	Sequential order

CM tools provide a domain-specific language and set of features for automation. Some of these tools have a steep learning curve whereby the team has to learn the tool. AWS provides a managed platform called OpsWorks to manage Chef and Puppet in the cloud. It provides various attributes to manage IT infrastructure through automation as shown below:

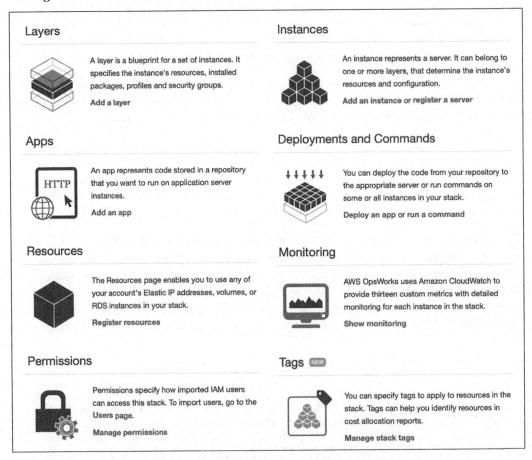

Figure 12.6: AWS OpsWorks service capabilities for managed Chef and Puppet

Security has become a priority for any organization, so complete automation security is the need of the hour. Organizations are moving to tight security implementations and monitoring to avoid human error, using the DevOps process popularly known as **DevSecOps**. Let's explore **DevSecOps** (short for **development, security, and operations**) in the next section.

Introducing DevSecOps

We are now more focused on security than ever. In many situations, security is the only way to win customer trust. DevSecOps is about the automation of security and the implementation of security at scale. The development team is constantly making changes, and the DevOps team is publishing them in production (changes are often customer-facing). DevSecOps is required to ensure application security in the overall process.

DevSecOps is not there to audit code or CI/CD artifacts. Organizations should implement DevSecOps to enable speed and agility, but not at the expense of validating security. The power of automation is to increase product feature launch agility while remaining secure by implementing the required security measures. A DevSecOps approach results in built-in security and is not applied as an afterthought. DevOps is about adding efficiency to speed up the product launch life cycle, while DevSecOps validates all building blocks without slowing the life cycle.

To institute a DevSecOps approach in your organization, start with a solid DevOps foundation across the development environment, as security is everyone's responsibility. To create collaboration between development and security teams, you should embed security in the architecture design from inception. To avoid any security gaps, automate continuous security testing and build it into the CI/CD pipeline. To keep track of any security breach, apply to extend monitoring to include security and compliance by monitoring for drift from the design state in real time. Monitoring should enable alerting, automated remediation, and removing non-compliant resources.

Codifying everything is a basic requirement that opens up infinite possibilities. The goal of DevSecOps is to keep the pace of innovation, which should meet the pace of security automation. A scalable infrastructure needs scalable security, requiring automatic incident response remediation to implement continuous compliance and validation.

Combining DevSecOps and CI/CD

A DevSecOps practice needs to be embedded with every step of the CI/CD pipeline. DevSecOps ensures the security of the CI/CD pipeline by managing the right access and roles assigned to each server and making sure the build servers such as Jenkins are hardened to be protected from any security glitch. In addition to that, we need to make sure that all artifacts are validated and code analysis is in place. It's better to be ready for incident response by automating continuous compliance validation and incident response remediation.

The following diagram provides us with multiple stages to test security boundaries and catch security issues and compliance with policies as early as possible:

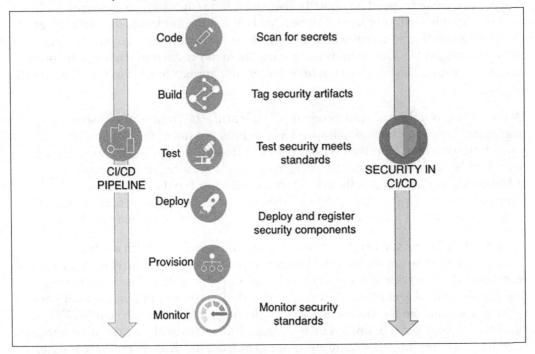

Figure 12.7: DevSecOps and CI/CD

At each integration point, you can identify different issues, as illustrated in the preceding diagram:

- In the coding phase, scan all code to ensure no secret key or access key is hardcoded in between code lines.

- During the build, include all security artifacts such as the encryption key and access token management, and tag them for easy identification.

- During the test, scan the configuration to make sure all security standards are met by test security.

- In the deploy and provision phase, make sure all security components are registered. Perform a checksum to make sure there are no changes in the build files. A checksum is a technique used to determine the authenticity of received files. Operating systems provide a checksum command to validate the file and make sure no changes are made during file transfer.

- Monitor all security standards during the monitoring phase. Perform continuous audit and validation in an automated way.

To identify security vulnerabilities at various stages, you can integrate multiple tools into DevSecOps pipelines and aggregate the vulnerability findings. **Application security testing (AST)** using tools that automate the testing, analysis, and reporting of security vulnerabilities is essential for application development. AST can be broken down into the following four categories to scan security vulnerabilities in software applications:

- **Software composite analysis (SCA)**: SCA evaluates the open-source software's security, license compliance, and code quality in a codebase. SCA attempts to detect publicly disclosed vulnerabilities contained within a project's dependencies. Popular SCA tools are OWASP Dependency-Check, Synopsys' Black Duck, WhiteSource, Synk, and GitLab.

- **Static application security testing (SAST)**: SAST scans an application before the code is compiled. SAST tools give developers real-time feedback as they code, helping them fix issues before passing the code build phase. It is a white-box testing methodology that analyzes source code to find security vulnerabilities that make your applications susceptible to attack. The best thing about SAST is that it can be introduced very early on in the DevOps cycle, during coding, as it does not require a working application and can take place without code being executed. Popular SAST tools are SonarQube, PHPStan, Coverity, Synk, Appknox, Klocwork, CodeScan, and Checkmarx.

- **Dynamic application security testing (DAST)**: DAST looks for security vulnerabilities by simulating external attacks on an application while the application is running. It attempts to penetrate an application from the outside by checking its exposed interfaces for vulnerabilities and flaws—this type of black-box security testing is also known as a web application vulnerability scanner. Popular DAST tools are OWASP ZAP, Netsparker, Detectify Deep Scan, StackHawk, Appknox, HCL AppScan, GitLab, and Checkmarx.

- **Interactive application security testing (IAST)**: IAST analyzes code for security vulnerabilities while the app is run by an automated test or activity validating application functionality. IAST tools report vulnerabilities in real time and do not add extra time to your CI/CD pipeline. IAST tools are deployed in a QA environment to implement automated functional tests. Popular IAST tools are GitLab, Veracode, CxSAST, Burp Suite, Acunetix, Netsparker, InsightAppSec, and HCL AppScan.

You will learn about integrating some of the above tools in the DevOps pipeline later in the chapter, under the *Building DevOps and DevSecOps in the cloud* section. DevSecOps CI/CD gives us confidence that the code is validated against the corporate security policy.

It helps to avoid any infrastructure and application failure in later deployment due to different security configurations. DevSecOps maintains agility and ensures security at scale without affecting DevOps' pace of innovation. Let's learn about the CD strategy in the DevOps pipeline.

Implementing a CD strategy

CD provides seamless migration of the existing version to the new version of the application. Some of the most popular techniques to implement through CD are as follows:

- **In-place deployment**: Update application in a current server
- **Rolling deployment**: Gradually roll out the new version in the existing fleet of servers
- **Blue-green deployment**: Gradually replace the existing server with the new server
- **Red-black deployment**: Instant cutover to the new server from the existing server
- **Immutable deployment**: Stand up a new set of servers altogether

Let's explore each option in more detail.

In-place deployment

In-place deployment is a method of rolling out a new application version on an existing fleet of servers. The update is done in one deployment action, thereby requiring some degree of downtime. On the other side, there are hardly any infrastructure changes needed for this update. There is also no need to update existing **Domain Name System (DNS)** records. The deployment process itself is relatively quick. If the deployment fails, redeployment is the only option for restoration.

As a simple explanation, you are replacing the existing application version (v1) on the application infrastructure with the new version (v2). In-place updates are low-cost and fast to deploy.

Rolling deployment

With a rolling deployment, the server fleet is divided into groups, so it doesn't need to be updated simultaneously. The deployment process runs both old and new software versions on the same server fleet but with different subgroups. A rolling deployment approach helps to achieve zero downtime. If a new version deployment fails, then only a subset of servers is impacted from the entire fleet, and the risk is minimal because half of the fleet will still be up and running. A rolling deployment helps to achieve zero downtime; however, deployment time is little more than in-place deployment.

Blue-green deployment

The idea behind blue-green deployment is that your blue environment is your existing production environment carrying live traffic. In parallel, you provision a green environment, which is identical to the blue environment other than the new version of your code. When it's time to deploy, you route production traffic from the blue environment to the green environment. If you encounter any issues with the green environment, you can roll it back by reverting traffic to the original blue environment. DNS cutover and swapping auto-scaling groups are the two most common methods to re-route traffic in blue-green deployment.

Using auto-scaling policies, you can gradually replace existing instances with instances hosting the new version of your application as your application scales out. This option is best used for minor releases and small code changes. Another option is to leverage DNS routing to perform sophisticated load balancing between different versions of our application.

As illustrated in the following diagram, after creating a production environment that hosts the new version of our application, you can use the DNS route to shift a small portion of traffic to the new environment:

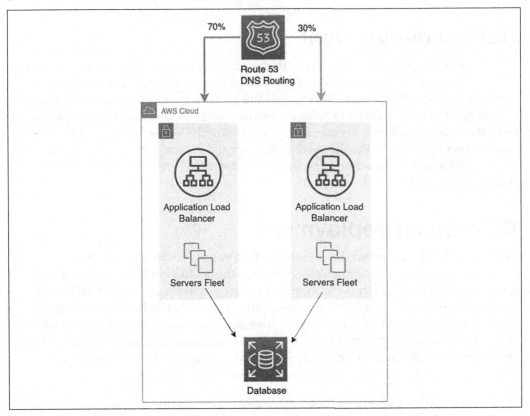

Figure 12.8: Blue-green deployment DNS gradual cutover

Test the green environment with a fraction of production traffic; this is called **canary analysis**. If the environment has functional issues, you'll be able to tell right away and switch traffic back before impacting your users significantly. Continue to gradually shift traffic, testing the ability of the green environment to handle the load. Monitor the green environment to detect issues, providing an opportunity to change traffic back, thus limiting the blast radius. Finally, when all the metrics are right, decommission the blue environment and release the resources.

Blue-green deployment helps to achieve zero downtime and provides easy rollback. You can customize the time to deploy as per your needs.

Red-black deployment

In red-black deployment, before standing up a new version of a system, first, perform canary testing. The canary replaces around 1% of its existing production system with the latest version of the application and monitors the newest version for errors. If the canary clears this initial test, the system is deemed ready for deployment.

In preparation for the switchover, a new version of the system stands up side by side with the old version of the system. The initial capacity of the new system is set manually by examining how many instances are currently running in production and setting this number as the desired capacity for the new auto-scaling group. Once the new system is up and running, both systems are red. The current version is the only version accepting traffic.

The system is then cut over from the existing version to the new version using the DNS service. At this point, the old version is regarded as black; it is still running but is not receiving any traffic. If any issues are detected with the new version, reverting becomes as simple as pointing the DNS server back to the old version's load balancer.

Red-black deployment is also known as **dark launch** and is slightly different from blue-green deployment. In red-black deployment, you do sudden DNS cutover from the old version to the new version, while in blue-green deployment, the DNS gradually increases traffic to the new version. Blue-green deployments and dark launches can be combined to deploy both versions of software side by side. Two separate code paths are used, but only one is activated. A feature flag activates the other code path. This deployment can be used as a beta test where you can explicitly enable the new features.

Immutable deployment

An immutable or disposable upgrade is an easier option if your application has unknown dependencies. An older application infrastructure that has been patched and re-patched over time becomes more and more difficult to upgrade. This type of upgrade technique is more common in an immutable infrastructure.

During the new release, a new set of server instances are rolled out by terminating older instances. For disposable upgrades, you can set up a cloned environment with deployment services such as Chef, Puppet, Ansible, and Terraform or use them combined with an auto-scaling configuration to manage the updates.

In addition to downtime, you need to consider the cost while designing your deployment strategy. Consider the number of instances you need to replace and your deployment frequency to determine the cost. Use the approach that best fits, taking your budget and downtime into consideration.

In this section, you learned about various CD strategies that help you to make your application release more efficient and hassle-free. You need to perform application testing at every step for high-quality delivery, which often requires significant effort. A DevOps pipeline can help you automate the testing process and increase the quality and frequency of feature releases. Let's learn more about continuous testing in the CI/CD pipeline.

Implementing continuous testing in the CI/CD pipeline

DevOps is key for the continually changing business scenarios based on customer feedback, demand for new features, or shifts in market trends. A robust CI/CD pipeline ensures further features/feedback are incorporated in less time, and customers get to use the new features faster.

With frequent code check-ins, having a good testing strategy baked into your CI/CD pipeline ensures you close that feedback loop with quality. Continuous testing is essential in balancing the CI/CD pipeline. While adding software features rapidly is good, ensuring that the features adhere to good quality is achieved by continuous testing.

Unit tests form the most significant amount of your testing strategy. They typically run on the developer's machine and are the fastest and cheapest. A general rule of thumb is to incorporate 70% of your testing efforts in unit testing. Bugs caught at this stage can be fixed relatively quickly, with fewer complexities.

The developer often performs unit tests, and once the code is ready, it is deployed for integration and system testing. These tests require their environments and sometimes separate testing teams, which makes the testing process costlier. Once the team ensures that all intended features are working as expected, the operations team needs to run performance and compliance tests. These tests need production-like environments and are costly. Also, **user acceptance testing (UAT)** needs a replica of production-like environments, causing more expense.

As illustrated in the following diagram, developers perform unit tests to test code changes/new features in the development phase. Testing is usually done on a developer's machine after coding is complete.

It is also recommended to run static code analysis on the code changes and do code coverage, adherence to coding guidelines, and so on. Smaller unit tests with no dependencies run faster. Therefore, the developer can find out quickly if the test has failed:

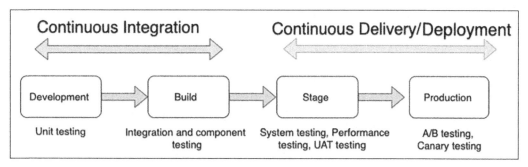

Figure 12.9: Continuous testing in CI/CD

The **build phase** is the first phase to test for integration between different components and individual components themselves. The build phase is also an excellent time to test if the code committed by a developer breaks any existing feature and to perform regression testing.

A **staging environment** is a mirror of the production environment. An end-to-end system test is performed at this stage (the UI, backend logic, and API are tested extensively). Performance testing tests the application performance under a particular workload. Performance tests include load tests and stress tests. UAT is also performed at this stage in readiness for production deployment. Compliance testing is done to test for industry-specific regulatory compliance.

A strategy such as A/B testing or canary analysis is used to test the new application version in the production phase. In A/B testing, the new application version is deployed to a small percentage of production servers and tested for user feedback. Gradually, depending on how well the users receive the new application, the deployment is increased to span all production servers.

A/B testing

Often, in software development, it isn't clear which implementation of a feature will be most successful in the real world. An entire computer science discipline — **human/computer interaction (HCI)** — is devoted to answering this question. While UI experts have several guidelines to help them design suitable interfaces, the best choice of design often can only be determined by giving it to users and seeing whether they can use the design to complete a given task.

As shown in the following diagram, A/B testing is a testing methodology in which two or more different versions of features are given to different sets of users. Detailed metrics on the usage of each implementation are gathered, and UI engineers examine this data to determine which implementation should be adopted going forward:

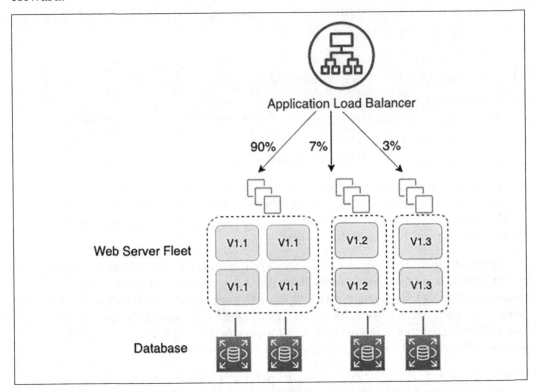

Figure 12.10: Split users by feature experiment using A/B testing

It's easy to launch several different versions of your application, each containing different implementations of a new feature. DNS routing can be used to send the majority of traffic to the current system while also sending a fraction of the existing traffic to the versions of the system running the new features. DNS round-robin resolution is supported by most DNS resolvers and is an effective way to spread incoming traffic.

Load and performance testing are other important factors. For Java-based applications, you can use JMeter to load-test a relational database by issuing **Java Database Connectivity (JDBC)** commands. MongoDB can use Mongo-Perf, which can generate a reproducible load on the database and record the response time. You can then hit the components and services that use the database and also simultaneously test the database.

One common way to measure the load on instances is through what is called **micro-benchmarking**. In micro-benchmarking, you measure the performance of a small sub-component of your system (or even a snippet of code) and then attempt to extrapolate general performance data from this test result. In the case of testing a server, you may test a slice of the system on a new instance type and compare that measurement to the same slice measured on your currently running system, which is now using another server type and configuration.

Using DevOps tools for CI/CD

To build a CI/CD pipeline, a developer requires various tools. These include a code editor, a source repository, a build server, a deployment tool, and orchestrating an overall CI pipeline. Let's explore some popular technology choices of developer tools for DevOps, both in the cloud and on-premises.

Code editor

DevOps is a hands-on coding role, where you often need to write a script to automate the environment. You can use the **ACE editor** or the **cloud-based AWS Cloud9 integrated development environment (IDE)**. You can use a web-based code editor on your local computer or install a code editor in your local server that connects to the application environments—such as dev, test, and prod—to interact. An environment is where you store your project's files and run the tools to develop your apps. You can save these files locally on the instance or server or clone a remote code repository into your environment. The AWS Cloud9 IDE is the cloud-native IDE provided as a managed service.

The Ace editor lets you write code quickly and easily. It's a web-based code editor but provides performance similar to popular desktop-based code editors such as Eclipse, Vim, and **Visual Studio Code (VS Code)**, and so on. It has standard IDE features such as live syntax and matching parentheses highlighting, auto-indentation and completion, toggling between tabs, integration with version control tools, and multiple cursor selections. It works with large files, having hundreds of thousands of lines without typing lag. It has built-in support for all popular coding languages and debugging tools, and you can also install your tools. For a desktop-based IDE, VS Code and Eclipse are other popular code editor options that DevOps engineers can choose.

Source code management

There are multiple choices available for your source code repository. You can set up, run, and manage your Git server, where you will be responsible for everything.

You can choose to use a hosting service such as GitHub or Bitbucket. If you are looking for a cloud solution, then **AWS CodeCommit** offers a secure, highly scalable, and managed source control system where you can host private Git repositories.

You need to set up authentication and authorization for your code repository to provide access to authorize team members for code to read or write. You can apply data encryption in transit and at rest. When you push into the code repository (git push), it encrypts the data and then stores it. When you pull from the code repository (git pull), it decrypts the data and then sends it back to the caller. The user must be an authenticated user with the proper access level to the code repository. Data can be encrypted in transit by transmitting through encrypted network connections using HTTPS or SSH protocols.

Continuous integration server

A CI server is also known as a **build server**. With teams working on multiple branches, it gets complicated to merge back into the main branch. CI, in this scenario, plays a key role. CI server hooks provide a way to trigger the build based on the event when code is committed to the repository. Hooks, which are incorporated in almost every version control system, refer to custom scripts triggered by specified necessary actions in a repository. Hooks can run either on the client side or on the server side.

Pull requests are common for developers to notify and review each other's work before it is merged into common code branches. A CI server provides a web interface to review changes before adding them to the final project. If there are any problems with the proposed changes, the source code can be sent back to the developer to tweak as per the organization's coding requirements.

As shown in the following diagram, server-side hooks in combination with the CI server are used to increase the velocity of integration:

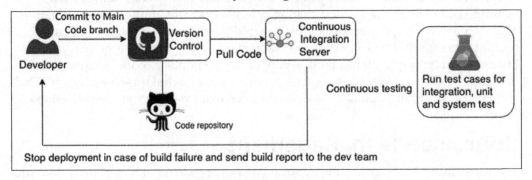

Figure 12.11: Automation of CI

As illustrated in the preceding diagram, using post-receive, you can direct new branches to trigger tests on a CI server to verify that the new build integrates correctly and that all units function correctly. The developer is notified of test failures and then knows to merge their branch with the mainline only after fixing the problems. The developer can build from their branch, test the changes there, and get feedback on how well their changes work before deciding whether to merge their branch into the mainline.

Running integration and unit tests significantly reduces resistance when that branch is merged into the mainline. Hooks can also be customized to test merges into the mainline and block any merges that don't pass. Integration is all accomplished best with a CI server.

Jenkins is the most popular choice to build the CI server. However, you have to maintain security and patching of the server by yourself. For native cloud options and managed services, you can use managed code-build services such as AWS CodeBuild, eliminating the need for server administration and significantly reducing costs with a **pay-as-you-go** model. The service scales as per your demand. Your team is empowered to focus on pushing code and lets a service build all the artifacts.

As illustrated in the following diagram, you can host the Jenkins cluster in the AWS **Elastic Compute Cloud (EC2)** server's fleet and auto-scale as per build load:

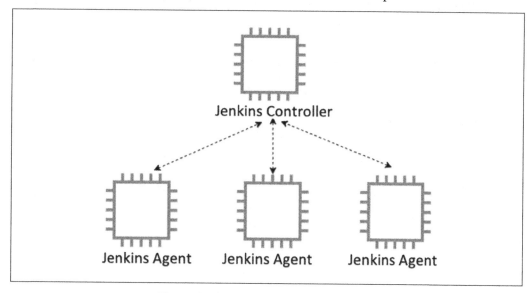

Figure 12.12: Auto-scaling of Jenkins CI servers

The **Jenkins Controller** offload builds to the agent node instance in the case of overload. When the load goes down, the **Jenkins Controller** automatically terminates agent instances.

While a CI server helps you build the correct version of code from a source code repository by collaborating across team members of the development team, code deployment helps the team get code ready for testing and release for end-user consumption. Let's learn about code deployment in more detail.

Code deployment

Once your build is ready, you can use the Jenkins server for deployment or choose AWS CodeDeploy as a cloud-native managed service. You can use other popular tools such as Chef or Puppet to create a deployment script. The options for specifying a deployment configuration are as follows:

- **OneAtATime**: Only a single instance in a deployment group at a time installs a new deployment. Suppose a deployment on a given instance fails. In that case, the deployment script will halt the deployment and return an error response detailing the number of successful versus the number of failed installations.

- **HalfAtATime**: Half of the instances in the deployment group install a new deployment. The deployment succeeds if half of the instances successfully install the revision. HalfAtATime can again be a good option for production/ test environments where half of the instances are updated to a new revision, and the other half remain available in production at an older revision.

- **AllAtOnce**: Each instance installs the latest revision available whenever it next polls the deployment service. This option is best used for development and test deployments as it has the potential to install a non-functioning deployment on every instance in a deployment group.

- **Custom**: You can use this command to create a custom deployment configuration specifying a fixed number of healthy hosts that must exist in a deployment group at any given time. This option is a more flexible implementation of the OneAtATime option. It allows for the possibility that a deployment may fail on one or two instances that have become corrupt or are improperly configured.

The following diagram illustrates life cycle events during deployment:

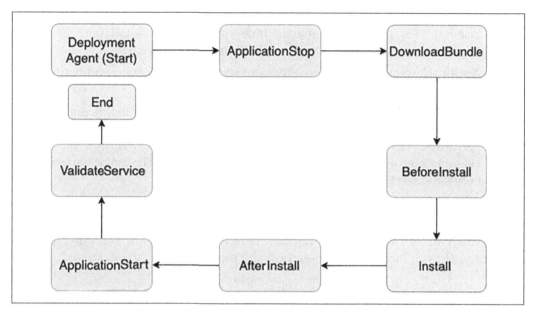

Figure 12.13: Deployment life cycle event

The deployment agent runs through a series of steps to execute a deployment. These steps are called life cycle events. In the preceding diagram, steps highlighted in light boxes can be controlled by human intervention; however, steps highlighted in darker boxes are automated and controlled by a deployment agent. Here are more details about each step:

- **ApplicationStop**: To trigger a deployment, the first requirement is to stop the application server so that traffic stops serving while files are copied. Examples of software application servers are Tomcat, JBoss, or WebSphere servers.

- **DownloadBundle:** After stopping the application server, the deployment agent starts downloading a pre-built deployment bundle from an artifactory such as JFrog Artifactory. The artifactory stores the application binary, which can be deployed and tested for application before the new version launch.

- **BeforeInstall**: The deployment agent triggers pre-install steps such as creating a backup of the current version and any required configuration update via a script.

- **Install**: In this step, deployment agents start the installation—for example, running an Ant or Maven script to install a Java application.

- **AfterInstall**: The deployment agent triggers this step after your application installation is completed. It may include updating post-installation configuration, such as local memory setting and log parameters.

- **ApplicationStart**: In this step, the agent starts the application and notifies the success or failure operations team.

- **ValidateService**: The validation step fires after everything else is done and gives you a chance to do a sanity check on the app. It includes steps such as performing automated sanity tests and integration tests to verify if the new version of the application has been installed properly. The agent also sends a notification to the team when testing is successful.

You have learned about various code deployment strategies and steps as independent components. However, to set up an automated CI/CD pipeline, you need to stitch all the DevOps steps together. Let's learn more about the code pipeline, which can help you build an end-to-end CI/CD pipeline.

Code pipeline

The code pipeline is about orchestrating everything together to achieve CD. The entire software release process is fully automated in CD, including build and deployment to the production release. Over some time, with experiments, you can set up a mature CI/CD pipeline. The path to the production launch is automated, thus enabling the rapid deployment of features and immediate customer feedback. You can use cloud-native managed services such as AWS CodePipeline to orchestrate the overall code pipeline or use the Jenkins server.

The code pipeline enables you to add actions to stages in your CI/CD pipeline. Each action can be associated with a provider that executes the action. The code pipeline action's categories and examples of providers are as follows:

- **Source**: Your application code needs to be stored in a central repository with version control called **source code repositories**. Some of the popular code repositories are AWS CodeCommit, Bitbucket, GitHub, **Concurrent Versions System (CVS)**, **Subversion (SVN)**, and so on.

- **Build**: The build tool pulls code from the source code repository and creates an application binary package. Some of the popular build tools are AWS CodeBuild, Jenkins, Solano CI, and so on. Once the build is completed, you can store binaries in an artifactory such as JFrog.

- **Deploy**: The deployment tool helps you to deploy application binaries on the server. Some popular deployment tools are AWS Elastic Beanstalk, AWS CodeDeploy, Chef, Puppet, Jenkins, and so on.

- **Test**: Automated testing tools help you to complete and perform post-deployment validation. Some popular test validating tools are Jenkins, BlazeMeter, Ghost Inspector, and so on.

- **Invoke**: You can use an events-based script to invoke activities such as backup and alert. Any scripting language such as a shell script, PowerShell, and Python can be used to invoke various customized activities.

- **Approval**: Approval is an essential step in CD. You can either ask for manual approval by an automated email trigger or approval can be automated from tools.

In this section, you learned about various DevOps tools to manage the **Software Development Life Cycle (SDLC)**, such as a code editor, a repository, and build, test, and deployment tools. The other tools you need to integrate into DevOps pipelines are continuous logging, continuous monitoring, and operation handling, which you learned in *Chapter 10, Operational Excellence Considerations*. As of now, you have learned about various DevOps techniques for each SDLC phase. Let's learn more about best practices and anti-patterns.

Implementing DevOps best practices

While building a CI/CD pipeline, consider your need to create a project and add team members to it. The project dashboard provides visibility to the code flow through the deployment pipeline, monitoring the build, triggering alerts, and tracking application activities. The following diagram illustrates a well-defined DevOps pipeline:

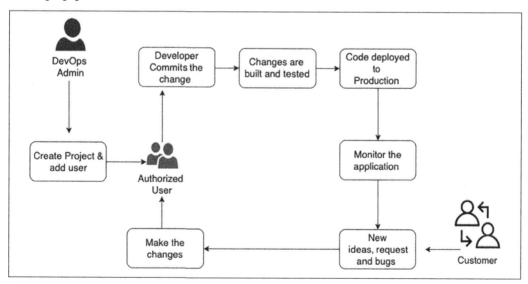

Figure 12.14: CI/CD workflow best practice

Consider the following points while designing the pipeline:

- **The number of stages**: Stages could be development, integration, system, user acceptance, and production. Some organizations also include dev, alpha, beta, and release stages.

- **Types of tests in each stage**: Each stage can have multiple types of tests such as unit tests, integration tests, system tests, UATs, smoke tests, load tests, and A/B tests at the production stage.

- **The sequence of a test**: Test cases can be run in parallel or need to be in sequence.

- **Monitoring and reporting**: Monitor system defects and failures and send notifications as failures occur.

- **Infrastructure provisioning**: Methods to provision infrastructure for each stage.

- **Rollback**: Define the rollback strategy to fall back to the previous version if required.

Having a system that requires manual intervention where it's avoidable slows down your process. So, automating your process using CD will accelerate your process.

Another common anti-pattern is keeping configuration values for a build inside the code itself or even having developers use different tools in their build processes, leading to inconsistent builds between developers. It takes lots of time and effort to troubleshoot why particular builds work in one environment and not in others. To overcome this, it is better to store build configurations outside of code. Externalizing these configurations to tools that keep them consistent between builds enables better automation and allows your process to scale much more quickly. Not using a CD process can lead to last-minute, middle-of-the-night rushes to get a build to work. Design your CD process to *fail fast* to reduce the likelihood of any last-minute surprises.

To apply architecture best practice at each step of application development, the twelve-factor methodology can be used, as recommended by The Twelve-Factor App (`https://12factor.net/`), which is adopted by enterprises for end-to-end development and delivery of web applications. This applies to all coding platforms regardless of programming languages. Nowadays, most applications are built as web apps and utilize a cloud platform. Let's learn about how to build end-to-end DevOps along with security automation in the cloud.

Building DevOps and DevSecOps in the cloud

As you have learned in previous sections, building a CI/CD pipeline requires multiple tools, and adding security automation on top of that increases the complexity. Integrating various tools and aggregating the vulnerability findings can be a challenge to do from scratch. A public cloud provider such as AWS provides the flexibility to build DevSecOps pipelines with easy integrations of cloud-native and third-party tools and aggregate security findings.

The following DevSecOps pipeline architecture covers CI/CD practices, including SCA, SAST, and DAST tools to visualize the concepts of security automation in the pipeline:

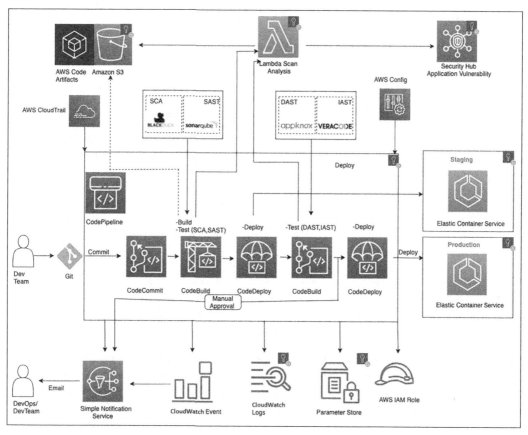

Figure 12.15: DevSecOps CI/CD pipeline architecture in the AWS cloud

As shown in the preceding diagram, the CI/CD pipeline gets triggered when a developer commits the code in GitHub. An event gets generated to start the AWS CodePipeline using AWS CloudWatch. AWS CodePipeline orchestrates the CI/CD pipeline including code commit, build, and deploy. AWS CodeBuild packages the build and uploads the artifacts to AWS CodeArtifact. AWS CodeBuild retrieves the authentication information such as scanning tool tokens from AWS Parameter Store to initiate the scanning.

You need to integrate AST tools in your pipeline to implement DevSecOps. CodeBuild scans the code with an SCA tool such as Synopsys' Black Duck or WhiteSource, and an SAST tool such as SonarQube or Coverity. SCA or SAST devices may detect vulnerabilities that need to post into AWS Security Hub. AWS CodeBuild invokes the Lambda function to consolidate all security findings in one place under AWS Security Hub. You can also add IAST such as Veracode or CxSAST while the app goes through an automated test to validate application functionality. CodeDeploy deploys the code to the staging AWS **Elastic Container Service (ECS)** environment if there are no vulnerabilities.

After the deployment succeeds, CodeBuild triggers the DAST scanning with the OWASP ZAP or Appknox tool. Again, if there are any vulnerabilities, CodeBuild invokes the Lambda function, which posts security findings into AWS Security Hub. Suppose DAST finds no security issues. In that case, the build can advance for approval, and the pipeline notifies the approver for action to push the build into the production AWS ECS environment. During the CI/CD pipeline run, AWS CloudWatch monitors all the changes and sends email notifications to DevOps and the dev team through SNS notifications.

AWS CloudTrail tracks any critical changes such as pipeline update, deletion, and creation, and sends notifications to the DevOps team for audit purposes. Further, AWS Config tracks all the configuration changes.

For DevSecOps, CI/CD pipeline security is implemented using AWS IAM roles to restrict access to required resources only. Any pipeline data at rest and in transit is protected using encryption and SSL. You can use AWS Parameter Store to store sensitive information such as API tokens and passwords.

Aggregation of security findings in one place in Security Hub provides opportunities to automate the remediation. Based on the security finding, you can trigger a Lambda function to take the needed remediation action. For example, if someone accidentally opens an SSH port to everyone, it can automatically block the servers from internet traffic. Automation takes away the burden from the DevOps and security teams as they can now address the vulnerabilities from one tool instead of logging into multiple dashboards.

For any team, identifying the security threat during the early stages of application development can drastically reduce the overall cost of application changes. Doing it in an automated fashion can accelerate the delivery of these changes. A DevSecOps pipeline is critical to building a thriving application development environment.

DevOps combines culture, practices, and tools that combine application development with its operations. DevOps practice enables organizations to deliver new application features at speed. DevSecOps takes it a step further by integrating security into DevOps. With DevSecOps, you can provide secure and compliant application changes rapidly while running operations consistently with automation.

Summary

In this chapter, you have learned about the key components of a strong DevOps practice: CI, CD, and continuous monitoring and improvement. The agility of CI/CD can be achieved only by applying automation everywhere. To automate, you learned about IaC and configuration management. You also looked at various automation tools such as Chef, Puppet, and Ansible to automate configuration management.

As security is the priority, you learned about DevSecOps, which is DevOps in security. CD is one of the key aspects of DevOps. You learned about various deployment strategies, including rolling, blue-green, and red-black deployment. Testing is another aspect of ensuring the quality of your product. You learned about the concept of continuous testing in DevOps and how A/B testing can help improve the product by taking direct feedback from a customer in the live environment.

You have learned about the stages in a CI/CD pipeline. You have learned about the tools and services that you can use and best practices that you can follow for a robust CI/CD pipeline. You have learned how individual services work and discussed how to integrate services to build a sophisticated solution.

Until this point, you have learned about various aspects of solution architecture. As every organization has lots of data, they put great effort into getting insight into their data. In the next chapter, you will learn about collecting, processing, and consuming data to get a more in-depth insight.

Join our book's Discord space

Join the book's Discord workspace for a monthly *Ask me Anything* session with the authors: https://packt.link/SAHandbook

13

Data Engineering for Solution Architecture

In the internet and digitization era, data is being generated everywhere with high velocity and volume. Getting insight from these huge amounts of data at a fast pace is challenging. We need to innovate continuously to ingest, store, and process this data to derive business outcomes.

With the convergence of cloud, mobile, and social technologies, advancements in many fields such as genomics and life sciences are growing at an ever-increasing rate. Tremendous value is found in mining this data for more insight. Modern stream processing systems need to produce continual results based on data with high input rates at low latency.

The concept of *big data* refers to more than just the collection and analysis of data. The actual value for organizations in their data can be used to gain insight and create competitive advantages. Not all big data solutions must end in visualization. Many solutions such as **Machine Learning** (**ML**) and other predictive analytics feed these answers programmatically into other software or applications, extracting the information and responding as designed.

As with most things, getting faster results costs more, and big data is no exception. Some answers might not be needed immediately, so the solution's latency and throughput can be flexible enough to take hours to be completed. Other responses, such as in predictive analytics, may be needed as soon as the data is available.

In this chapter, you will learn about the following topics to handle and manage your big data needs:

- What is big data architecture?
- Designing for a big data processing pipeline
- Data ingestion, storage, processing, and analytics
- Data visualization
- Designing big data architecture
- Big data architecture best practices

By the end of this chapter, you will know how to design big data and analytics architecture. You will learn about the big data pipeline steps, including data ingestion, storage, processing, and visualization, along with various architecture patterns.

What is big data architecture?

The sheer volume of collected data can cause problems. With the accumulation of more and more data, managing and moving data along with its underlying big data infrastructure becomes increasingly difficult. The rise of cloud providers has facilitated the ability to move applications to the cloud. Multiple sources of data result in increased volumes, velocity, and variety. The following are some common computer-generated data sources:

- **Application server logs**: Application logs and games
- **Clickstream logs**: From website clicks and browsing
- **Sensor data**: Weather, water, wind energy, and smart grids
- **Images and videos**: Traffic and security cameras

Computer-generated data can vary from semi-structured logs to unstructured binaries. Computer-generated data sources can produce pattern-matching or correlations in data that generate recommendations for social networking and online gaming. You can also use computer-generated data to track applications or service behavior such as blogs, reviews, emails, pictures, and brand perceptions.

Human-generated data includes email searches, natural language processing, sentiment analysis on products or companies, and product recommendations. Social graph analysis can produce product recommendations based on your circle of friends, jobs you may find interesting, or even reminders based on your circle of friends' birthdays, anniversaries, and so on.

Typical barriers you hear from analytics teams that prevent them from delivering the most value to their organization are:

- **Limited insight into customer experiences and operations**: To create new customer experiences, organizations need better visibility into their business. Complex and costly data collection and processing systems and added scale costs require organizations to limit the types and amounts of data they collect and analyze.

- **Need to make quicker decisions**: This is a two-part problem:
  1. Traditional data systems are being overwhelmed, resulting in existing workloads taking a long time to complete.
  2. More decisions need to be made in seconds or minutes, requiring systems to collect and process data in real time.

- **Enabling innovation with machine learning**: Organizations are adding and growing their data science teams to help optimize and grow their business. These users need easier access to data with their choice of tools without the traditional red tape and process that will slow them down.

- **Technical staff and cost to scale self-managed infrastructures**: Customers who manage infrastructure on-premises face difficulties in quickly scaling to meet business demand. Managing infrastructure, high availability, scaling, and operational monitoring is difficult to get right, especially at scale. AWS Managed Services allows customers to focus on building their data applications, not on managing the tools.

In **big data architecture**, the general flow of a significant data pipeline starts with data and ends with insight. How you get from start to finish depends on a lot of factors. The following diagram illustrates a data workflow pipeline that will help you design your data architecture:

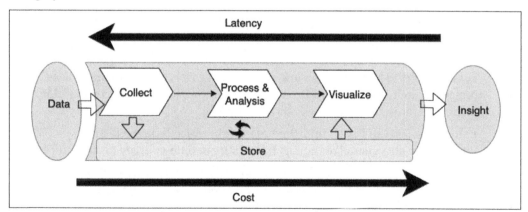

Figure 13.1: Big data pipeline for data architecture design

As shown in the preceding diagram, the standard workflow of the big data pipeline includes the following steps:

1. Data is collected (ingested) by an appropriate tool.

2. The data is stored persistently.

3. The data is processed or analyzed. The data processing/analysis solution takes the data from storage, performs operations, and then stores the processed data again.

4. The data is then used by other processing/analysis tools or by the same tool again to get further answers from the data.

5. To make answers useful to business users, they are visualized using a **business intelligence** (**BI**) tool or fed into an ML algorithm to make future predictions. Once the appropriate answers have been presented to the user, this gives them insight into the data they can then use to make further business decisions.

The tools you deploy in your pipeline determine your *time-to-answer* which is the latency between when your data was created and when you can get insight from it. The best way to architect data solutions while considering latency is to determine how to balance throughput with cost because a higher performance and subsequently reduced latency usually results in a higher price.

Designing big data processing pipelines

One of the critical mistakes many big data architectures make is handling multiple stages of the data pipeline with one tool. A fleet of servers managing the end-to-end data pipeline, from data storage and transformation to visualization, may be the most straightforward architecture, but it is also the most vulnerable to breakdowns in the pipeline. Such tightly coupled big data architecture typically does not provide the best possible balance of throughput and cost for your needs. When you are designing a data architecture, use FLAIR data principles as explained below:

*   **F**: Findability. The ability to view which data assets are available, access metadata including ownership and data classification, and other mandatory attributes for data governance and compliance

*   **L**: Lineage. The ability to find the data origin, trace data back, and understand and visualize data as it flows from data sources to consumption

*   **A**: Accessibility. The ability to request a security credential granting entitlement to access the data asset. It also requires a networking infrastructure to facilitate efficient access

- **I**: Interoperability. Data is stored in a format that will be accessible to most, if not all, internal processing systems
- **R**: Reusability. Data is registered with a known schema, and attribution of the data source is clear. May encompass **MDM (Master Data Management)** concepts

Big data architects recommend decoupling the pipeline between ingestion, storage, processing, and getting insight. There are several advantages to decoupling storage and processing in multiple stages, including increased *fault tolerance*. For example, if something goes wrong in the second round of processing and the hardware dedicated to that task fails, you won't have to start again from the beginning of the pipeline; your system can resume from the second storage stage. Decoupling your storage from various processing tiers gives you the ability to read and write to multiple data stores.

The following diagram illustrates various tools and processes to consider when designing a big data architecture pipeline:

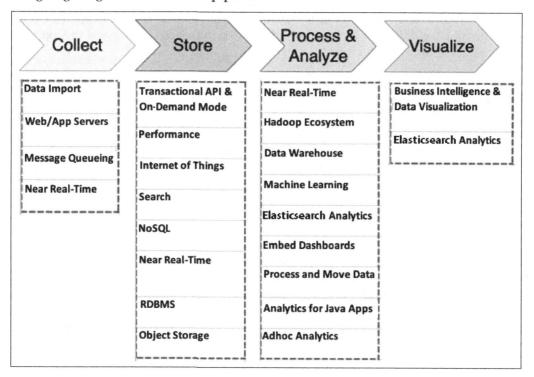

Figure 13.2: Tools and processes for big data architecture design

The things you should consider when determining the right tools for your big data architectures include the following:

- The structures of your data
- The maximum acceptable latency
- The minimum acceptable throughput
- The typical access patterns of your system's end-users

Your data structure impacts both the tools you use to process it and where you store it. The ordering of your data and the size of each object you're storing and retrieving are also essential considerations. The time-to-answer is determined by how your solution weighs latency/throughput and cost.

User access patterns are another essential component to consider. Some jobs require the regular joining of many related tables, and others require daily or less-frequent storage data. Some jobs require a comparison of data from a wide range of data sources, and other jobs pull data from only one unstructured table. Knowing how your end-users will most often use the data will help you determine the breadth and depth of your big data architecture. Let's dive deep into each process and the tools involved in big data architecture.

Data ingestion

Data ingestion is the act of collecting data for transfer and storage. There are lots of places that data can be onboarded. Predominantly, data ingestion falls into one of the categories from databases, streams, logs, and files. Among these, databases are the most popular. These typically consist of your main upstream transactional systems that are the primary data storage for your applications. They take on both relational and non-relational flavors, and there are several techniques for extracting data out of them.

Streams are open-ended sequences of time-series data such as clickstream data from websites or IoT devices, usually published into an API we host. Logs get generated by applications, services, and operating systems. A data lake is a great place to store all of the data for centralized analysis. Data lakes provide a single source of truth to store all data in one place and break data silos across various business units in the organization. In a later section of this chapter, *Designing big data architectures*, you will learn more about data lakes. Files come from self-hosted filesystems or via third-party data feeds via FTP or APIs. As shown in the following diagram, use the type of data your environment collects and how it is collected to determine what kind of ingestion solution is ideal for your needs:

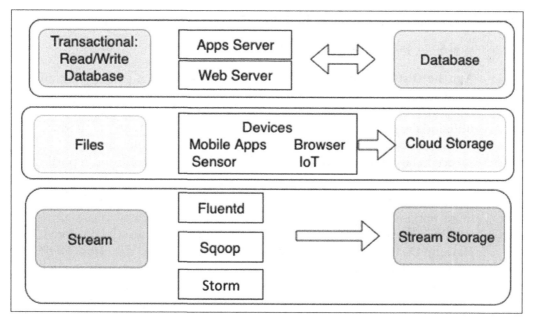

Figure 13.3: Type of data ingestion

As shown, transactional data storage must be able to store and retrieve data quickly. End-users need quick and straightforward access to the data, which makes app and web servers the ideal ingestion methods. For the same reasons, NoSQL and **Relational Database Management System (RDBMS)** databases are usually the best solutions for these kinds of processes.

Data transmitted through individual files is typically ingested from connected devices. A large amount of file data does not require fast storage and retrieval compared to transactional data. For file data, often a transfer is one-way, where data is produced by multiple resources and ingested into a single object or file storage for later use.

Stream data such as clickstream logs should be ingested through an appropriate solution such as **Apache Kafka** or **Fluentd**. Initially, these logs are stored in stream storage solutions such as Kafka, so they're available for real-time processing and analysis. Long-term storage of these logs is best in a low-cost solution such as object storage.

Streaming storage decouples your collection system (producers) from the processing system (consumers). It provides a persistent buffer for your incoming data. The data can be processed, and you can pump the data at a rate dependent on your needs. Let's learn about some popular data ingestion technologies.

Technology choices for data ingestion

Let's look at some popular open source tools for data ingestion and transfer:

- **Apache DistCp**: DistCp stands for *distributed copy* and is part of the Hadoop ecosystem. The DistCp tool is used to copy large data within a cluster or between clusters. DistCp achieves the efficient and fast copying of data by utilizing the parallel processing distribution capability with MapReduce. It distributes directories and files into map tasks to copy file partitions from source to target. DistCp also does error handling, recovery, and reporting across clusters.

- **Apache Sqoop**: Sqoop is also part of the Hadoop ecosystem project and helps to transfer data between Hadoop and relational data stores such as RDBMS. Sqoop allows you to import data from a structured data store into **Hadoop Distributed File System (HDFS)** and to export data from HDFS into a structured data store. Sqoop uses plugin connectors to connect to relational databases. You can use the Sqoop extension API to build a new connector or use one of the included connectors that support data exchange between Hadoop and common relational database systems.

- **Apache Flume**: Flume is open-source software and is mainly used to ingest a large amount of log data. Apache Flume collects and aggregates data to Hadoop reliably and in a distributed manner. Flume facilitates streaming data ingestion and allows analytics.

More open-source projects are available for streaming, such as Apache Storm and Apache Samza, to provide a means of reliably processing unbounded data streams.

Ingesting data to the cloud

Public cloud providers such as AWS provide an array of big data services to store and process data on a large scale. The following are some options to move your data to the AWS cloud and utilize the scalability offered by the cloud provider:

- **AWS Direct Connect**: AWS Direct Connect provides up to 100 Gbps of private connectivity between the AWS cloud and your data center. A dedicated network connection reduces network latency and increases bandwidth throughput. It provides a more reliable network speed compared to internet connections where data has to hop through multiple routers. Direct Connect creates a cross-connect between the router managed either by you or a Direct Connect partner, depending on whether you are co-located in one of the AWS Direct Connect locations and the router in that location that AWS owns. The circuit itself provides both a public and a private **Virtual Interface (VIF)**.

You can use the private VIF to directly access the resources running within your **Virtual Private Cloud (VPC)** on AWS and the public VIF to access the public endpoints for AWS services such as **Amazon Simple Storage Service (S3)**.

- **AWS Snowball**: If you want to transfer a large amount of data, such as hundreds of **terabytes (TB)** or **petabytes (PB)**, to the cloud, it could take years over the internet. AWS Snowball provides a tamper-proof 80 TB storage appliance that can transfer a large amount of data. It works like a large hard disk that you can plug into your on-premises data storage server, load all data, and ship it to AWS. AWS will place your data in a designated location in the cloud storage. AWS Snowball has other flavors, such as Snowball Edge, which comes with compute power along with 100 TB of storage and fulfills the use case of handling data in a remote location, such as on a cruise ship or an oil rig. It is like a small data center where you can load data and perform some analytics using the built-in compute functionality. Data can be loaded to the cloud as soon as the appliance comes online. If you have PBs of data, you can use Snowmobile, a physical 45-foot shipping container with which you can transfer 100 PB of data in one go from your data center to the AWS cloud.

- **AWS Data Migration Service (DMS)**: AWS DMS makes it easy to securely migrate or replicate your databases and data warehouses to AWS. In DMS, you can create a data migration task, which will be connected to on-premises data via a source endpoint and uses AWS-provided storage such as RDS and Amazon S3 as the target endpoint. DMS supports full data dumps and ongoing **change data capture (CDC)**. DMS also supports homogeneous (MySQL-to-MySQL) and heterogeneous (MySQL-to-Amazon Aurora) database migrations.

AWS provides more tools, such as **AWS DataSync** for continuous file transfer to AWS from on-premises and **AWS Transfer for SFTP** to securely ingest data from the SFTP server. As you ingest the data, it needs to be put in suitable storage to fulfill the business needs. Similarly, other public cloud providers such as Azure and GCP provide various options to ingest data in their cloud. Streaming data is also becoming very important to ingest and analyze. You will learn more about streaming data in the *Streaming data store* section. Let's learn more about techniques to choose the right storage and the available storage choices.

Storing data

One of the most common mistakes when setting up storage for a big data environment is using one solution, frequently an RDBMS, to handle all of your data storage requirements.

You will have many tools available, but none of them are optimized for the task they need to complete. One solution is not necessarily the best for all of your needs; the best solution for your environment might be a combination of storage solutions that carefully balance latency with cost. An ideal storage solution uses the right tool for the right job. The following diagram combines multiple factors related to your data and the storage choice associated with it:

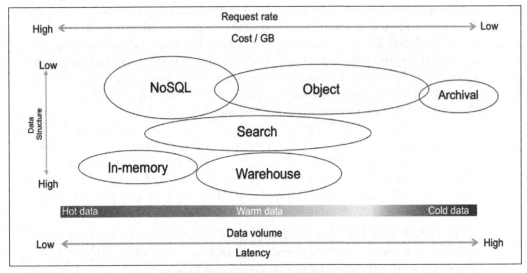

Figure 13.4: Understanding data storage

As shown in the proceeding diagram, choosing a data store depends upon the following factors:

- **How structured is your data?** Does it adhere to a specific, well-formed schema, as with Apache weblogs (logs are generally not well structured and are unsuitable for relational databases), standardized data protocols, and contractual interfaces? Is it completely arbitrary binary data, as in images, audio, video, and PDF documents? Or, is it semi-structured with a general structure but with potentially high variability across the records, as in JSON or CSV?

- **How quickly does new data need to be available for querying?** Is it a real-time scenario where decisions are made as new records stream in, such as campaign managers making adjustments based on conversion rates or a website making product recommendations based on user behavior similarity? Is it a daily, weekly, or monthly batch scenario, such as model training, financial statement preparation, or product performance reporting? Or is it somewhere in between, such as with user engagement emails, where it doesn't require real-time action, but you can have a buffer of a few minutes or even a few hours between the user action and the touchpoint?

- **What is the size of the data ingest?** Is the data ingested record by record as data comes in, such as with JSON payloads from REST APIs that measure at just a few KBs at best? Is it a large batch of records arriving all at once, such as system integrations and third-party data feeds? Or is it somewhere in between, such as with a few micro-batches of clickstream data aggregated together for more efficient processing?

- **What is the total volume of data and its growth rate?** Are you in the realm of GBs and TBs, or do you intend to store PBs or even **exabytes (EBs)**? How much of this data is required for your specific analytics use cases? Do the majority of your queries only require a specific rolling window of time? Or, do you need a mechanism to query the entirety of your historical dataset?

- **What the cost will be to store and query the data in any particular location**: When it comes to any computing environment, we generally see a *triangle of constraints* between performance, resilience, and low cost. The better the performance and the higher the resilience you want your storage to have, the more expensive it will be. You may wish to have quick queries over petabytes of data but decide to settle on querying TBs of data in a compressed format to meet your cost requirements.

Finally, what type of analytic queries will run against the data? Will it be powering a dashboard with a fixed set of metrics and drill-down? Will it participate in large numerical aggregations rolled up by various business dimensions? Or, will it be used for diagnostics, leveraging string tokenization for full-text searching and pattern analysis?

When you determine all characteristics of your data and understand the data structure, you can then assess which solution you need to use for your data storage. Let's learn about the various solutions for storing data.

Technology choices for data storage

As we discussed, a single tool can't do everything. You need to use the right tool for the right job, and a data lake enables you to build a highly configurable big data architecture to meet your specific needs. Business problems are far too broad, deep, and complex for one tool to solve everything, especially big data and analytics.

For example, hot data will need to be stored and processed in memory, so caches or in-memory databases like Redis or SAP Hana are appropriate. AWS offers the ElastiCache service, providing a managed Redis or Memcached environment. NoSQL databases are ideal when facing high velocity but small-sized records, for example, user-session information or IoT data. NoSQL databases are also useful for content management to store data catalogs. Let's learn about the most popular and commonly used storage for structured data.

Structured data stores

Structured data stores have been around for decades and are the most familiar technology choice for storing data. Most transactional databases such as Oracle, MySQL, SQL Server, and PostgreSQL are row-based due to dealing with frequent data writes from software applications. Organizations often repurpose transactional databases for reporting purposes, requiring frequent data reads but much fewer data writes. Looking at high data-read requirements, more innovation is coming into querying on structured data stores, such as the columnar file format, which helps to enhance data read performance for analytics requirements.

Row-based formats store the data in rows in a file. Row-based writing is the fastest way to write the data to the disk, but it is not necessarily the quickest read option because you need to skip over a lot of irrelevant data. Column-based formats store all the column values together in the file. This leads to better compression because the same data types are now grouped. It also typically provides better read performance because you can skip columns that are not required.

Let's look at common choices for the structured data store. Take an example where you need to query the total number of sales in a given month from the order table, which has fifty columns. In a row-based architecture, the query will scan the entire table with all fifty columns, but in columnar architecture, the query will just scan the order sales column, thus improving data query performance. Let's look into more details about relational databases, focusing on transaction data and data warehousing to handle data analytics needs.

Relational databases

RDBMS is more suitable for **Online Transaction Processing (OLTP)** applications. Some popular relational databases are Oracle, MSSQL, MariaDB, PostgreSQL, and so on. Some of these traditional databases have been around for decades. Many applications, including e-commerce, banking, and hotel booking, are backed by relational databases. Relational databases are very good at handling transaction data where complex joint queries between tables are required. Looking at transaction data needs, the relational database should adhere to the **Atomicity, Consistency, Isolation, Durability (ACID)** principles, as follows:

- **Atomicity**: Atomicity means the transaction will be executed fully from end to end, and, in the case of any error, the entire transaction will roll back.

- **Consistency**: Consistency means that when transactions are completed, all data should be committed to the database.

- **Isolation**: Isolation requires that multiple transactions can run concurrently in isolation without interfering with each other.

- **Durability**: In case of any interruption, such as a network or power failure, the transaction should be able to resume to the last known state.

Often, data from relational databases is offloaded to data warehousing solutions for reporting and aggregation purposes. Let's learn more about data warehousing.

Data warehousing

Data warehouse databases are more suitable for **Online Analytical Processing (OLAP)** applications. Data warehouses provide fast aggregation capabilities over vast volumes of structured data. While these technologies, such as Amazon Redshift, Netezza, and Teradata, are designed to execute complex aggregate queries quickly, they are not optimized for high volumes of concurrent writes. So, data needs to be loaded in batches, preventing warehouses from serving real-time insights over hot data.

Modern data warehouses use a columnar base to enhance query performance. Examples of this include Amazon Redshift, Snowflake, and Google BigQuery. These data warehouses provide very fast query performance due to columnar storage and improved I/O efficiency. In addition to that, data warehouse systems such as Amazon Redshift increase query performance by parallelizing queries across multiple nodes and taking advantage of **massively parallel processing (MPP)**.

Data warehouses are central repositories that store accumulations of data from one or multiple sources. They store current and historical data used to help create analytical reports for business data analytics. However, data warehouses store data centrally from various systems, but they cannot be treated as a data lake. Data warehouses handle only structured relational data, while data lakes work with structured and unstructured data such as JSON logs, and CSV data.

Data warehouse solutions such as Amazon Redshift can process petabytes of data and provide decoupled compute and storage capabilities to save costs. In addition to columnar storage, Redshift uses data encoding, distribution, and zone maps to increase query performance. More traditional row-based data warehousing solutions include Netezza, Teradata, and Greenplum.

However, data warehouses cause various applications' data to be placed in separate physical locations. Data architects then have to build entirely new infrastructure around the data warehouse. The limitations of data warehouses became evident with the increasing variety of enterprise data such as text, IoT, images, audio, and videos. In addition, the rise of ML and AI introduced iterative algorithms that required direct data access and were not based on SQL. You will learn more about overcoming these challenges in a later section of this chapter, *Designing big data architectures*.

NoSQL databases

NoSQL databases such as DynamoDB, Cassandra, and MongoDB address the scaling and performance challenges you often experience with a relational database. As the name suggests, NoSQL means a non-relational database. NoSQL databases store data without an explicit and structured mechanism to link data from different tables (no joins, foreign keys, and normalization enforced).

NoSQL utilizes several data models, including columnar, key-value, search, document, and graph. NoSQL databases provide scalable performance, high availability, and resilience. NoSQL typically does not enforce a strict schema, and every item can have an arbitrary number of columns (attributes), which means one row can have four columns, while another row can have ten columns in the same table. The partition key is used to retrieve values or documents containing related attributes. NoSQL databases are highly distributed and can be replicated. They are durable and don't experience performance issues when highly available.

SQL versus NoSQL databases

SQL databases have been around for decades, and most of us are probably already very familiar with relational databases. Let's learn some significant differences between SQL and NoSQL databases:

Properties	SQL Databases	NoSQL Databases
Data model	In SQL databases, the relational model normalizes data into tables containing rows and columns. A schema includes tables, columns, relationships between tables, indexes, and other database elements.	NoSQL databases do not enforce a schema. A partition key is commonly used to retrieve values from column sets. It stores semi-structured data such as JSON, XML, or other documents such as data catalogs and file indexes.
Transaction	SQL-based traditional RDBMSes support and are compliant with the transactional data properties of ACID.	To achieve horizontal scaling and data model flexibility, NoSQL databases may trade some ACID properties of traditional RDBMSes.
Performance	SQL-based RDBMSes were used to optimize storage when storage was expensive and minimize the disk footprint. For traditional RDBMSes, performance has mostly relied on the disk. To achieve performance query optimizations, index creation and modifications to the table structure are required.	For NoSQL, performance depends upon the underlying hardware cluster size, network latency, and how the application is calling the database.

Scale	SQL-based RDBMS databases are easiest to scale vertically with high configuration hardware. The additional effort requires relational tables to span across distributed systems, such as performing data sharding.	NoSQL databases are designed to scale horizontally using distributed clusters of low-cost hardware to increase throughput without impacting latency.

Depending on your data, various categories of NoSQL data stores exist to solve a specific problem. Let's understand the types of NoSQL databases.

Types of NoSQL data store

The following are the major NoSQL database types:

- **Columnar databases**: Apache Cassandra and Apache HBase are the popular columnar databases. The columnar data store helps you scan a particular column when querying the data rather than scanning the entire row. Suppose an item table has ten columns with one million rows, and you want to query the number of a given item available in inventory. In that case, the columnar database will apply the query to the item quantity column rather than scanning the entire table.

- **Document databases**: Some of the most popular document databases are MongoDB, Couchbase, MarkLogic, DynamoDB, DocumentDB, and Cassandra. You can use a document database to store semi-structured data in JSON and XML formats.

- **Graph databases**: Popular graph database choices include Amazon Neptune, JanusGraph, TinkerPop, Neo4j, OrientDB, GraphDB, and GraphX on Spark. A graph database stores vertices and links between vertices called **edges**. Graphs can be built on both relational and non-relational databases.

- **In-memory key-value stores**: Some of the most popular in-memory key-value stores are Redis and Memcached. They store data in memory for read-heavy applications. Any query from an application first goes to an in-memory database and, if the data is available in the cache, it doesn't hit the master database. The in-memory database is suitable for storing user-session information, which results in complex queries and frequently requests data such as user profiles.

NoSQL has many use cases, but you need to index all your data to build a data search. Let's learn more about search data stores.

Search data stores

The Elasticsearch service is one of the most popular search engines for big data use cases like clickstream and log analysis. Search engines work well for warm data that can be queried ad hoc across any number of attributes, including string tokens.

Amazon OpenSearch Service provides data search capabilities and the support of open source Elasticsearch clusters and includes API access. It also provides Kibana as a visualization mechanism to search for indexed data stores. AWS manages capacity, scaling, and patching of clusters, removing any operational overhead. Log search and analysis is a popular big data use case where OpenSearch helps you analyze log data from websites, server fleets, IoT sensors, and so on. OpenSearch and Elasticsearch are utilized by various applications in industries such as banking, gaming, marketing, application monitoring, advertisement technology, fraud detection, recommendations, and IoT. Now ML-based search services, such as Amazon Kendra, are also available, which provide more advanced search capabilities using natural language processing.

Unstructured data stores

When you look at the requirements for an unstructured data store, it seems that Hadoop is a perfect choice because it is scalable, extensible, and very flexible. It can run on consumer hardware, has a vast ecosystem of tools, and appears to be cost-effective to run. Hadoop uses a *master-and-child-node* model, where data is distributed between multiple child nodes, and the master node coordinates jobs for running queries on data. The Hadoop system is based on MPP, making it fast to perform queries on all types of data, whether structured or unstructured.

When a Hadoop cluster is created, each child node created from the server comes with a block of the attached disk storage called a local HDFS disk store. You can run the query against stored data using common processing frameworks like Hive, Pig, and Spark. However, data on the local disk persists only for the life of the associated instance.

If you use Hadoop's storage layer (HDFS) to store your data, you are coupling storage with compute. Increasing storage space means having to add more machines, which increases compute capacity as well. For maximum flexibility and cost-effectiveness, you need to separate compute and storage and scale them both independently. Overall, object storage is more suited to data lakes to store all kinds of data in a cost-effective and performant manner. Cloud-based data lakes backed by object storage provide flexibility to decouple compute and storage. Let's learn more about object storage.

Object storage

Object storage refers to data stored and accessed with units often referred to as objects stored in buckets. In object storage, files or objects are not split into data blocks, but data and metadata are kept together. There is no limit on the number of objects stored in a bucket, and they are accessed using API calls (usually through HTTP GET and PUT) to read and write from and to buckets. Typically, object storage is not filesystem mounted on operating systems because the latency of API-based file requests and lack of file-level locking provide poor performance as a filesystem. Object storage offers scale and has a flat namespace reducing management overhead and metadata management. Object storage has become more popular with the public cloud and go-to storage to build a scalable data lake in the cloud. The most popular object storage is Amazon S3, Azure Blob storage, and Google storage in GCP.

Blockchain data store

With the rise in cryptocurrencies, you must have heard about blockchain a lot. Blockchain technology enables the building of decentralized applications that can be verified by multiple parties rather than depending upon a single authority. Blockchain achieves decentralized verification by facilitating a blockchain network (peer-to-peer network) where participants have access to a shared database to record transactions. These transactions are immutable and independently verifiable by design.

Blockchain is not just about crypto; blockchain technologies help to solve two types of customer needs. In the first case, multiple parties work with a centralized authority to maintain verifiable transaction records. For example, manufacturers can store data from multiple systems in a centralized ledger. In the event of issues, manufacturers can quickly trace the root cause of defects and take preventive actions. Similarly, government vital record offices can implement a centralized ledger that maintains a trusted and complete record of the digital history of their citizens in a single place for vital records such as birth certificates and marriage certificates.

In other use cases, multiple parties work together in a decentralized setting where a centralized trusted authority is not required. For example, financial consortiums can reduce the time and complexity of cross-boundary payments and asset transfers by directly working with multiple parties such as insurance, trading vendors, and banks in a decentralized way. Similarly, retailers can partner with third-party loyalty programs to build seamless rewards programs for their customers without needing a central bank or vendor to process rewards.

To maintain record sanity, customers need a centralized ledger that records all application data changes and maintains an immutable record of these changes to a ledger database.

This database should be highly performant, immutable, and cryptographically verifiable, eliminating the need to build complex audit tables or set up blockchain networks. One such ledger database is Amazon **Quantum Ledger Database (QLDB)**, which maintains a complete and verifiable history of data changes in an application that they own and manage in a centralized way.

Customers need the immutable and verifiable capability provided by a ledger and want to allow multiple parties to transact without a trusted central authority. In that case, they can use a scalable blockchain service. If you are looking for managed blockchain, some of the most popular blockchain networks include **Amazon Managed Blockchain (AMB)**, **R3 Corda**, **Ethereum**, and **Hyperledger**.

Streaming data processing used to be a niche technology, but now it's becoming common as every organization wants to get fast insight from real-time data processing. Let's learn more about streaming data stores.

Streaming data stores

Streaming data has a continuous data flow with no start and end. Now lots of data coming from various real-time resources needs to be stored and processed quickly, such as stock trading, autonomous cars, smart spaces, social media, e-commerce, gaming, and ride apps, and so on. Netflix provides real-time recommendations based on the content you are watching, and Lyft rideshare uses streaming to connect passengers to a driver in real time.

Storing and processing streaming data is a challenging task as there is a continuous stream of data coming, and you cannot predict the storage capacity. Along with high volume, streaming data comes with very high velocity, which requires a scalable storage system that can store the data and provide the ability to replay it. Data streams can become very expensive to maintain and complex to manage over time. Popular streaming data storage is Apache Kafka, Apache Flink, Apache Spark Streaming, Apache Samza, and Amazon Kinesis. Now, AWS also provides managed Kafka, known as Amazon Managed Streaming for Kafka. Let's learn more details about streaming data ingestion and storage technology:

- **Amazon Kinesis**: Amazon Kinesis offers three capabilities. The first, **Kinesis Data Streams (KDS)**, is a place to store a raw data stream to perform any downstream processing of the desired records. The second is **Amazon Kinesis Data Firehose (KDF)** to facilitate transferring these records into common analytic environments like Amazon S3, Elasticsearch, Redshift, and Splunk. Firehose will automatically buffer up all the records in the stream and flush out to the target as a single file or set of records based on either a time or data-size threshold that you can configure or whichever is reached first.

The third is **Kinesis Data Analytics (KDA)** to perform analytics on the records of the stream by performing SQL operations. The output can subsequently flow into further streams you create to build an entire serverless streaming pipeline.

- **Amazon Managed Streaming for Kafka (MSK)**: MSK is a fully managed, highly available, and secure service. Amazon MSK runs applications on Apache Kafka in the AWS cloud without needing Apache Kafka infrastructure management expertise. Amazon MSK provides a managed Apache Kafka cluster with a ZooKeeper cluster to maintain configuration and build a producer/consumer for data ingestion and processing.

- **Apache Flink**: Flink is another open-source platform for streaming data and batch data processing. Flink consists of a streaming dataflow engine that can process bounded and unbounded data streams. A bounded data stream has a defined start and end, while an unbounded data stream has a start but no end. Flink can perform batch processing as well on its streaming engine and supports batch optimizations.

- **Apache Spark Streaming**: Spark Streaming helps ingest live data streams with high throughput and a fault-tolerant, scalable manner. Spark Streaming divides the incoming data streams into batches before sending them to the Spark engine for processing. Spark Streaming uses DStreams, which are sequences of **resilient distributed datasets (RDDs)**.

- **Apache Kafka**: Kafka is one of the most popular open-source streaming platforms that helps you publish and subscribe to a data stream. A Kafka cluster stores a recorded stream in a Kafka topic. A producer can publish data in a Kafka topic, and consumers can take the output data stream by subscribing to the Kafka topic.

Streaming storage needs to persist a continuous stream of data and provide the ability to maintain the order if required. You will learn more about streaming architecture in the upcoming section, *Streaming data architecture*. Once you ingest and store data, it's important to process the data in the desired structure to visualize and analyze for business insights. Let's learn more details about data processing and transformation.

Processing data and performing analytics

Data analytics is the process of ingesting, transforming, and visualizing data to discover valuable insights for business decision-making. Over the previous decade, more data has been collected, and customers are looking for greater insights into their data.

These customers also want these insights in the least amount of time, sometimes even in real time. They want more ad hoc queries to answer more business questions. To answer these questions, customers need more powerful and efficient systems.

Batch processing typically involves querying large amounts of cold data. In batch processing, it may take hours to get answers to business questions. For example, you may use batch processing to generate a billing report at the end of the month. Stream processing in real time typically involves querying small amounts of hot data, and it takes only a short amount of time to get answers. MapReduce-based systems such as Hadoop are examples of platforms that support the batch jobs category. Data warehouses are examples of platforms that support the query engine category.

Streaming data processing activities ingest a sequence of data and incrementally update functions in response to each data record. Typically, they ingest continuously produced streams of data records, such as metering data, monitoring data, audit logs, debugging logs, website clickstreams, and location-tracking events for devices, people, and physical goods.

The following diagram illustrates a data lake pipeline for processing, transforming, and visualizing data using the AWS cloud tech stack:

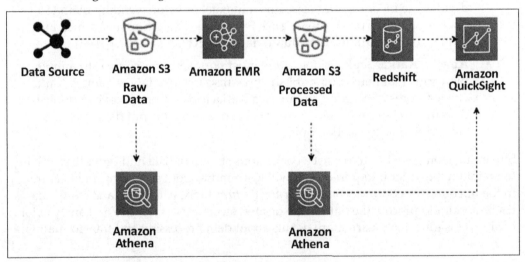

Figure 13.5: Data lake ETL pipeline for big data processing

Here, the **Extract, Transform, Load (ETL)** pipeline uses Amazon Athena for ad hoc querying of data stored in Amazon S3. The data ingested from various data sources (for example, web application servers) generates log files that persist into S3. These files are then transformed and cleansed into a set form required for meaningful insights using Amazon **Elastic MapReduce (EMR)** and loaded into Amazon S3. Amazon EMR provides a managed Hadoop server in the cloud to perform data processing using various open source technologies such as Hive, Pig, Spark, and so on.

These transformed files are loaded into Amazon Redshift using the `COPY` command and visualized using Amazon QuickSight. Using Amazon Athena, you can query the data directly from Amazon S3 when the data is stored and after transformation (with aggregated datasets). You can visualize the data from Athena in Amazon QuickSight. You can easily query these files without changing your existing data flow.

Let's look at some popular tools for data processing.

Technology choices for data processing and analysis

The following are some of the most popular data processing technologies that help you to perform transformation and processing for a large amount of data:

- **Apache Hadoop** uses a distributed processing architecture in which a task is mapped to a cluster of commodity servers for processing. Each piece of work distributed to the cluster servers can be run or re-run on any server. The cluster servers frequently use HDFS to store data locally for processing. The Hadoop framework takes a big job, splits it into discrete tasks, and processes them in parallel. It allows for massive scalability across an enormous number of Hadoop clusters. It's also designed for fault tolerance, where each of the worker nodes periodically reports its status to a master node, and the master node can redistribute work from a cluster that doesn't respond positively. Some of the most popular frameworks used with Hadoop are Hive, Presto, Pig, and Spark.

- **Apache Spark** is an in-memory processing framework. Apache Spark is a massively parallel processing system with different executors that can take apart a Spark job and run tasks in parallel. To increase the parallelism of a job, add nodes to the cluster. Spark supports batch, interactive, and streaming data sources. Spark uses **directed acyclic graphs** (DAGs) for all the stages during the execution of a job. The DAGs can keep track of your data or lineage transformations during the jobs and efficiently minimize the I/O by storing the DataFrames in memory. Spark is also partition-aware to avoid network-intensive shuffles.

- **Hadoop User Experience** (HUE) enables you to run queries and scripts on your cluster through a browser-based user interface instead of the command line. HUE provides the most common Hadoop components in a user interface. It enables browser-based viewing and tracking of Hadoop operations. Multiple users can access the cluster via HUE's login portal, and administrators can manage access manually or with LDAP, PAM, SPNEGO, OpenID, OAuth, and SAML2 authentication. HUE allows you to view logs in real time and provides a metastore manager to manipulate Hive metastore contents.

- **Pig** is typically used to process large amounts of raw data before storing it in a structured format (SQL tables). Pig is well suited to ETL operations such as data validation, data loading, data transformation, and combining data from multiple sources in multiple formats. In addition to ETL, Pig also supports relational operations such as nested data, joins, and grouping. Pig scripts can use unstructured and semi-structured data (such as web server logs or clickstream logs) as input. In contrast, Hive consistently enforces a schema on input data. Pig Latin scripts contain instructions on filtering, group, and joining data, but Pig is not intended to be a query language. Hive is better suited to querying data. The Pig script compiles and runs to transform the data based on the instructions in the Pig Latin script.

- **Hive** is an open-source data warehouse and query package that runs on top of a Hadoop cluster. SQL is a widespread skill to have that helps the team make an easy transition into the big data world. Hive uses a SQL-like language called **Hive Query Language (HQL)**, making it easy to query and process data in a Hadoop system. Hive abstracts the complexity of writing programs in a coding language such as Java to perform analytics jobs.

- **Presto** is a Hive-like query engine, but it is much faster. It supports the ANSI SQL standard, which is easy to learn and the most popular skill set. Presto supports complex queries, joins, and aggregation functions. Unlike Hive or MapReduce, Presto executes queries in memory, which reduces latency and improves query performance. You need to be careful while selecting the server capacity for Presto, as it needs to have high memory. A Presto job will restart in the event of memory spillover.

- **HBase** is a NoSQL database developed as a part of the open-source Hadoop project. HBase runs on HDFS to provide non-relational database capabilities for the Hadoop ecosystem. HBase helps to store large quantities of data in columnar format with compression. Also, it provides a fast lookup because large portions of the data cache are kept in memory while cluster instance storage is still used.

- **Apache Zeppelin** is a web-based editor for data analytics built on top of the Hadoop system, also known as a Zeppelin notebook. It uses the concept of an interpreter for its backend language and allows any language to be plugged into Zeppelin. Apache Zeppelin includes some basic charts and pivot charts. It's very flexible in terms of any output from any language backend that can be recognized and visualized.

- **Ganglia** is a Hadoop cluster monitoring tool. However, you need to install Ganglia on the cluster during launch. The Ganglia UI runs on the master node, which you can see using an SSH tunnel. Ganglia is an open-source project designed to monitor clusters without impact on their performance. Ganglia can help to inspect the performance of the individual servers in your cluster and the performance of clusters as a whole.

- **JupyterHub** is a multi-user Jupyter notebook. Jupyter Notebook is one of the most popular tools among data scientists to perform data engineering and ML. The JupyterHub notebook server provides each user with a Jupyter notebook web-based IDE. Multiple users can use their Jupyter notebooks simultaneously to write and execute code for exploratory data analytics.

- **Amazon Athena** is an interactive query service for running queries on Amazon S3 object storage using standard ANSI SQL syntaxes. Amazon Athena is built on top of Presto and extends ad hoc query capabilities as a managed service. The Amazon Athena metadata store works like the Hive metadata store to use the same DDL statements from the Hive metadata store in Amazon Athena. Athena is a serverless and managed service, which means all infrastructure and software handling and maintenance is taken care of by AWS, and you can directly start running your query in the Athena web-based editor.

- **Amazon Elastic MapReduce** (**EMR**) is essentially Hadoop in the cloud. You can utilize the Hadoop framework with the power of the AWS cloud using EMR. EMR supports all the most popular open-source frameworks, including Apache Spark, Hive, Pig, Presto, Impala, HBase, and so on. EMR provides decoupled compute and storage, which means you don't always have to keep running a large Hadoop cluster; you can perform data transformation and load results into persistent Amazon S3 storage and shut down the server. EMR provides autoscaling and saves you from the administrative overhead of installing and updating servers with various software.

- **AWS Glue** is a managed ETL service, which helps in data processing, data cataloging, and ML transformations to find duplicate records. AWS Glue Data Catalog is compatible with the Hive data catalog and provides a centralized metadata repository across various data sources, including relational databases, NoSQL, and files. AWS Glue is built on top of a warm Spark cluster and provides ETL as a managed service. AWS Glue generates code in PySpark and Scala for common use cases so that you are not starting from scratch to write ETL code. Glue job authoring functionality handles any errors in the job and provides logs to understand underlying permission or data formatting issues. Glue provides workflows that help you build an automated data pipeline with simple drag-and-drop functionality.

Data analysis and processing are huge topics that warrant a book on their own. This section gave a very high-level overview of popular and common tools used for data processing. There are many more proprietary and open-source tools available. As a solution architect, you need to be aware of various tools available on the market to make the right choice for your organization's use case.

Business analysts need to create reports and dashboards and perform ad hoc queries and analyses to identify data insights. Let's learn about data visualization in the next section.

Visualizing data

Data insights are used to answer important business questions such as revenue by customer, profit by region, or advertising referrals by site, among many others. In the big data pipeline, enormous amounts of data are collected from a variety of sources. However, it is difficult for companies to find information about inventory per region, profitability, and increases in fraudulent account expenses. Some of the data you continuously collect for compliance purposes can also be leveraged for generating business.

The two significant challenges of BI tools are the cost of implementation and the time it takes to implement a solution. Let's look at some technology choices for data visualization.

Technology choices for data visualization

The following are some of the most popular data visualization platforms, which help you to prepare reports with data visualization as per your business requirements:

- **Amazon QuickSight** is a cloud-based BI tool for enterprise-grade data visualizations. It comes with a variety of visualization graph presets such as a line graph, pie charts, treemaps, heat maps, histograms, and so on. Amazon QuickSight has a data-caching engine known as **Super-fast, Parallel, In-memory Calculation Engine (SPICE)**, which helps render visualizations quickly. You can also perform data preparation tasks such as renaming and removing fields, changing data types, and creating new calculated fields. QuickSight also provides ML-based visualization insights and other ML-based features such as auto forecast predictions.

- **Kibana** is an open-source data visualization tool used for stream data visualization and log exploration. Kibana offers close integration with Elasticsearch and uses it as a default option to search for data on top of the Elasticsearch service. Like other BI tools, Kibana also provides popular visualization charts such as histograms, pie charts, and heat maps and offers built-in geospatial support.

- **Tableau** is one of the most popular BI tools for data visualization. It uses a visual query engine, which is a purpose-built engine used to analyze big data faster than traditional queries. Tableau offers a drag-and-drop interface and the ability to blend data from multiple resources.

- **Spotfire** uses in-memory processing for faster response times, enabling extensive datasets from various resources. It provides the ability to plot your data on a geographical map and share it on Twitter. With Spotfire recommendations, it inspects your data automatically and makes suggestions about how to best visualize it.

- **Jaspersoft** enables self-service reporting and analysis. It also offers drag-and-drop designer capability.

- **Power BI** is a popular BI tool provided by Microsoft. It provides self-service analytics with a variety of visualization choices.

Data visualization is an essential and massive topic for solution architects. As a solution architect, you need to be aware of the available tools and make the right choice as per your business requirements for data visualization.

Now you have learned about various data pipeline components, from ingestion, storage, and processing to visualization. Let's put them together and learn how to orchestrate a big data architecture in the next section.

Designing big data architectures

Big data solutions are comprised of data ingestion, storage transformation, and visualization in a repeated manner to run daily business operations. You can build these workflows using the open source or cloud technologies you learned about in previous sections.

First, you need to learn which architecture style is right for you by working backward from the business use case. You need to understand the end-user of your big data architecture and create a user persona to understand the requirement better. To identify key personas you are targeting with big data architecture, you need to understand some of the following points:

- Which teams, units, or departments inside your organization are they a part of?

- What is their level of data analysis and data engineering proficiency?

- What tools do they typically use?

- Do you need to cater to employees, customers, or partners of the organization?

For your reference, taking an example of a retail store chain analysis, you may identify the following personas:

- **Product manager** persona who owns a product line/code but only sees turnover for their product.

- **Store manager** persona who wants to know the sales turnover and product mix for a single store (only able to see their store).
- **Admin** persona to have access to all data.
- **Data analyst** to access all data with PII data redacted.
- **Customer retention managers** want to understand repeated customer traffic.
- **Data scientists** need access to raw and processed data to build recommendations and forecast.

Once you understand your user persona, next identify business use cases that these personas are looking to solve, for example:

- How many customers are spending more over time? Less over time? Describe these customers.
- Of those customers who are spending more over time, which categories are growing at a faster rate?
- Of those customers who are spending less over time, in which categories are they becoming less engaged?
- Which demographic factors (e.g. household size, presence of children, income) appear to affect customer spending? Which demographic factors appear to affect engagement with certain categories?
- Is there evidence to suggest that direct marketing improves overall engagement?
- Does direct marketing for one category improve engagement in other categories?

While you get details on the use case, the essential aspect of building your data architecture is to understand access patterns and data retention, which can be analyzed by using the following queries:

- How often do key users and personas run their reports, queries, or models?
- What is their expectation for data freshness?
- What is their expectation of data granularity?
- What portion of data is most frequently accessed for analysis?
- How long do you intend to retain data for analysis?
- At what point can data age out of the data lake environment?

There is always some kind of sensitivity attached when you deal with data. Each country and area has its local regulatory compliance requirements, which solutions architects need to understand, such as:

- What compliance requirements does your business have?

- Are you subject to data locality, data privacy, or data redaction requirements?

- Who is authorized to see which records and which attributes in the dataset?

- How will you enforce the deletion of records on request?

- Where can you store data, for example, local to geolocation, county, or global?

As a data architect, you also need to consider the return on investment and how it will help overall business decisions. To understand, you may want to go through the following points:

- What primary business processes and decisions does your data lake support?

- What level of granularity is required for these decisions?

- What is the impact of data latency on business decisions?

- How do you plan to measure success?

- What is the expected return on the time and material invested?

Ultimately, you want to build a data architecture where you can provide flexibility to make technology choices. For example, use the best of cloud-based managed services and open-source technologies to capitalize on existing skills and investments. You want to build big data solutions to take advantage of parallelism to achieve high performance and scalability. It would be best if you make sure any components of your big data pipeline can scale in or scale out independently so that you can adjust it according to different business workloads.

To utilize the full potential of your solution, you want to provide interoperability with existing applications so that components of the big data architecture are also used for machine learning processing and enterprise BI solutions. It will enable you to create an integrated solution across data workloads. Let's learn about some big data architecture patterns.

Data lake architecture

A data lake is a centralized repository for both structured and unstructured data. The data lake is a combination of the different kinds of data found in the corporation. It has become the place where you can offload all enterprise data to a low-cost storage system such as Amazon S3. You have access to data using a generic API and open file formats, such as Apache Parquet and ORC. The lake stores data as is, using open-source file formats to enable direct analytics and machine learning uses.

The data lake is becoming a popular way to store and analyze large volumes of data in a centralized repository. Data can be stored as is in its current format, and you don't need to convert data into a predefined schema, which increases the data ingestion speed. As illustrated in the following diagram, the data lake is a single source of truth for all data in your organization:

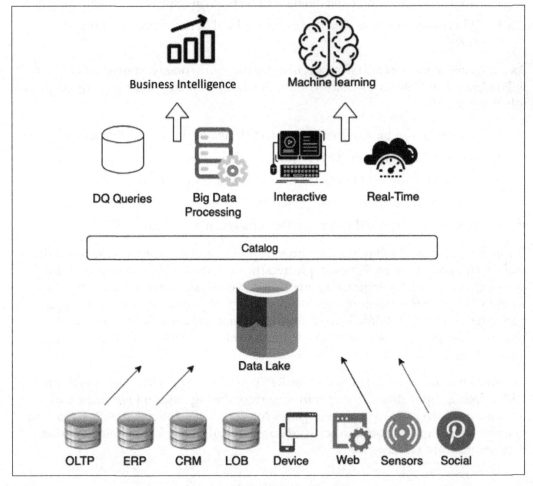

Figure 13.6: Object store for data lake

The following are the benefits of a data lake:

- **Data ingestion from various sources**: Data lakes let you store and analyze data from multiple sources such as relational and non-relational databases and streams in one centralized location for a single source of truth. This answers questions such as *why is the data distributed in many* places? And *where is the single source of truth?*

- **Collecting and efficiently storing data**: A data lake can ingest any kind of data structure, including semi-structured and unstructured data, without the need for any schema. This answers questions such as *how can I ingest data quickly from various sources and in multiple formats and store it efficiently at scale?*

- **Scale up with the volume of generated data**: Data lakes allow you to separate the storage and compute layers to scale each component separately. This answers questions such as *how can I scale up with the volume of data generated?*

- **Applying analytics to data from different sources**: With a data lake, you can determine the schema on reading and create a centralized data catalog on data collected from various resources. This enables you to perform quick ad hoc analysis. This answers questions such as *can I apply multiple analytics and processing frameworks to the same data?*

You need an unlimited scalable data storage solution for your data lake. Decoupling your processing and storage provides a significant number of benefits, including the ability to process and analyze the same data with a variety of tools. Although this may require an additional step to load your data into the right tool, Amazon S3 as your central data store provides even more benefits than traditional storage options. The following diagram provides a view of the data lake using AWS services:

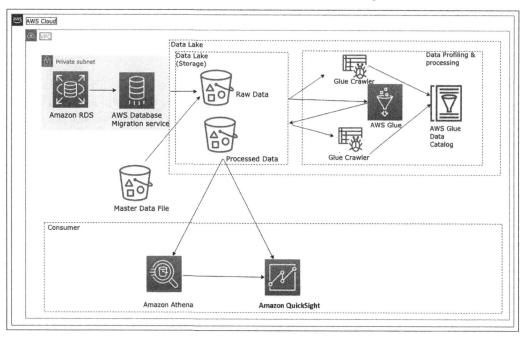

Figure 13.7: Data lake architecture in AWS platform

The preceding diagram depicts a data lake using Amazon S3 storage. Data is ingested to centralized storage from various resources such as relational databases and master data files. All of the data is stored in the raw layer of the data lake in its original format. This data is cataloged and transformed using the AWS Glue service. AWS Glue is a serverless data cataloging and ETL service based on the Spark framework in the AWS cloud platform. Transformed data is stored in the data lake's process layer, which can be consumed for different purposes. Data engineers can run ad hoc queries using Amazon Athena, a serverless query service built on top of managed Presto instances, and use SQL to query the data directly from Amazon S3. Business analysts can use Amazon QuickSight, Tableau, or Power BI to build visualizations for business users or load selective data in Amazon Redshift to create a data warehouse mart. Finally, data scientists can consume this data using Amazon SageMaker to perform machine learning.

The beauty of the data lake is that you are future-proofing your architecture. Twelve months from now, there may be new technology you want to use. With your data in the data lake, you can insert this new technology into your workflow with minimal overhead. By building modular systems in your big data processing pipeline, with shared object storage such as Amazon S3 as the backbone, you can replace specific modules when they become obsolete or when a better tool becomes available.

One tool cannot do everything. You need to use the right tool for the right job, and data lakes enable you to build a highly configurable big data architecture to meet your specific needs. Business problems are far too broad, deep, and complex for one tool to solve everything, especially big data and analytics.

However, with time organizations realized that data lakes have their limitations. As data lakes use cheap storage, organizations store as much of their data as they can in data lakes, providing the flexibility of open, direct access to files. Quickly data lakes started becoming **data swamps** due to issues of data quality and granular data security. However, to address the data lake's performance and quality issues, the organization processes a small subset of data in the data lake to a downstream data warehouse to use in BI applications for important decisions.

The dual system architecture between a data lake and data warehouse requires continuous data engineering to maintain and process data between these two systems. Each data processing step risks incurring failures that reduce data quality, while keeping the data lake and warehouse consistent is difficult and costly. Apart from paying for continuous data-processing costs, users pay double the storage cost for data copied to a warehouse. To address the dual-system problem, a new type of architecture is emerging called the data lakehouse. Let's learn more details about lakehouse architecture.

Lakehouse architecture

A new architecture paradigm has emerged called **lakehouse architecture** to address the limitations of data lakes and data warehouses. Lakehouse architecture aims to leverage the benefits of both, leveraging the scale of a data lake to ingest and store an ever-increasing amount of data in open formats that customers want to analyze, and enabling the user-friendliness of SQL queries and guarantees of a data warehouse. The main aspects of lakehouse architecture are:

- Data storage in open-data formats
- Decoupled storage and compute
- Transactional guarantees
- Support diverse consumption needs
- Secure and governed

Let's look at what the stages in a data lakehouse pattern are.

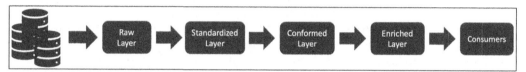

Figure 13.8: Lakehouse architecture layers

These layers can be described as follows:

- **Raw Layer**: This layer acts as the landing zone for all the source data in the format delivered by the source. The data here can be stored for a more extended period and archived for audit and reproducibility purposes.

- **Standardized Layer**: As the data that arrives in the raw layer can be in specific formats as delivered by the source, the standardized layer is used to store the data in a standard format (typically Parquet) after performing schema validations, schema evolution control, data quality rules, tokenization rules, and cleansing rules for the data. A typical example of a cleansing rule is standardizing the DateTime format to a standard format (e.g. ISO 8601). The data stored here is also optimized for analytical queries as it is partitioned and stored in columnar format. This data is typically also cataloged in a central data catalog for discovery. This layer acts as the consumption layer for standardized raw data in the organization.

- **Conformed Layer**: Typically, in any organization, some common entities/ subject areas are well defined and commonly understood and used across the organization. Such entities can be treated as confirmed entities and end up in the conformed layer.

The definition of these common entities needs to be governed centrally as they are usually formed based on the master data of an organization. All these entities are also logged in the central data catalog with clear ownership and metadata for PII/PCI, retention, purpose, and so on. One of the benefits of managing the conformed entities centrally is clear enterprise ownership. As several parties use this data within the organization, if the ownership is distributed, the definitions can become ambiguous, and maintenance and retention of history, governance, and data management of these conformed entities can become a challenge.

- **Enriched Layer**: This is more of a logical layer, as it is aimed at data engineering teams, who would create their data products combining conformed entities and standardized raw data. Primarily, these business domain-focused teams would have many end products useful for a particular business domain; however, in some cases, these could also be products useful for other business domains. These could be called "golden datasets" with a proper business definition and can be offloaded to the data lake for sharing. All the end product datasets of this layer should also be added to the central data catalog with proper labels, metadata, and the purpose of the datasets.

The following diagram shows a sample lakehouse architecture using Redshift Spectrum for data sharing. Amazon Redshift Spectrum provides the ability to query data from the data lake without storing data in the data warehouse. Suppose you were already using Amazon Redshift for data warehousing. In that case, you don't need to load the entire data into the Amazon Redshift cluster. Still, you can simply use the spectrum to query data directly from the Amazon S3 data lake and combine it with data warehouse data.

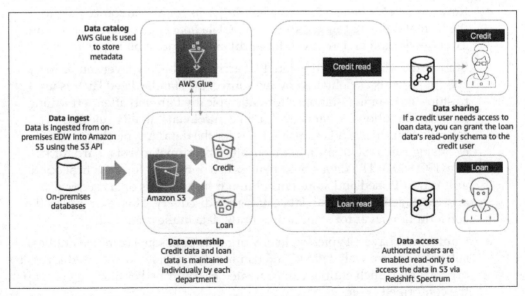

Figure 13.9: Lakehouse architecture in AWS cloud platform using Redshift Spectrum

Data is ingested from an on-prem **enterprise data warehouse (EDW)** into S3 using the S3 API in the preceding diagram. AWS Glue is used to store the metadata and the credit and loan data individually. Data analysts in the loan department would be granted read-only access to the loan data for data access. Similarly, credit analysts would be granted read-only access to the credit data. For data sharing, if a credit analyst needs access to the loan data, the credit analyst can be given the loan data's read-only schema.

There are benefits of lakehouse architecture; however, it doesn't solve the problem for large organizations having a complex application landscape driven by geographically separated business units. These business units have built data lakes and data warehouses as their analytical sources. Each business unit may merge multiple internal application data lakes to support their business. Centralized enterprise data lakes or data lakehouses are difficult to achieve as the pace of change is generally low and it's difficult to meet all requirements across different business units. To handle this problem, you need domain-oriented decentralized data ownership and architecture. That's where data mesh comes into the picture. Let's learn more about data mesh architecture.

Data mesh architecture

The major difference between data mesh and data lake architecture is that rather than trying to combine multiple domains into a centrally managed data lake, data is intentionally left distributed. Data mesh provides a pattern that allows a large organization to connect multiple data lakes/lakehouses within large enterprises, and to facilitate sharing with partners, academia, and even competitors. Data mesh marks a welcome architectural and organizational paradigm shift in how we manage large analytical datasets. The paradigm is founded on four principles:

1. Domain-oriented decentralization of ownership and architecture
2. Data served as a product
3. Federated data governance with centralized audit controls
4. Common access that makes data consumable

Data mesh is an organizational architecture that addresses these dimensions: domain-oriented decentralized data ownership and architecture, data as a product, self-serve data infrastructure as a platform, and federated computational governance. It encourages data-driven agility and supports domain-local governance through a lightweight centralized policy. Data mesh provides better ownership by isolating data resources with clear accountability. The core concept of data mesh is to feature data domains as nodes, which exist in data lake accounts.

A data producer contributes one or more data products to a central catalog in a data mesh account where federated data governance is applied to how data products are shared, delivering discoverable metadata and audibility. A data consumer searches for a catalog and gains access to a data product by accepting a resource share via the data mesh pattern. Below is a data mesh architecture in the AWS cloud:

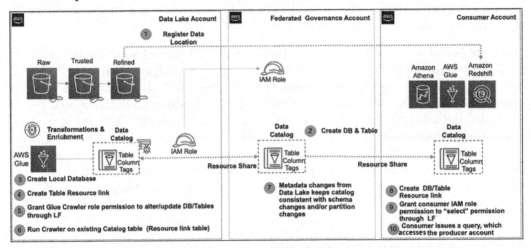

Figure 13.10: Data mesh architecture in AWS cloud platform

The following are the components implemented to build a data mesh as shown in the preceding diagram:

- Central AWS account where data products are registered, which is comprised of databases, tables, columns, and rows.

- Access control tags and tag access policies managed centrally.

- Stored data permissions that implement sharing with a consumer. Permissions can be direct or based on tags.

- Applies security and governance policies to producer and consumer accounts and the data products they publish.

With a data mesh architecture, you can aim to accelerate the independent delivery of the business domain lakehouses. Data mesh increases data security and compliance within domains and enables self-service data product creation, discovery, and subscription, allowing consumers to access data products transparently. There is a growing need to provide fast insight and act quickly based on customer needs, which makes streaming data analytics an essential aspect of any business. Let's learn more details about streaming data analytics architecture.

Streaming data architecture

Streaming data is one of the fastest-growing data segments. You need to ingest real-time data from various resources such as video, audio, application logs, website clickstreams, and IoT telemetry data and quickly process to provide fast business insights. Streaming data use cases follow a similar pattern: data flows from data producers through streaming storage and data consumers to storage destinations. Sources continuously generate data delivered via the ingest stage to the stream storage layer, where it's durably captured and made available for streaming processing. The stream processing layer processes the data in the storage layer and sends the processed information to a specified destination.

Streaming data architecture is different as it needs to process a continuous stream of massive data with very high velocity. Often this data is semi-structured and needs a good amount of processing to get actionable insights. While designing streaming data architecture, you need to easily scale data storage while getting real-time pattern identification from time-series data.

You need to think about the producer who generated a stream of data, such as IoT sensors, how to store the data and process it using a real-time data processing tool, and finally, how to query the data in real time. The following diagram shows a streaming data analytics pipeline using a managed service in the AWS platform:

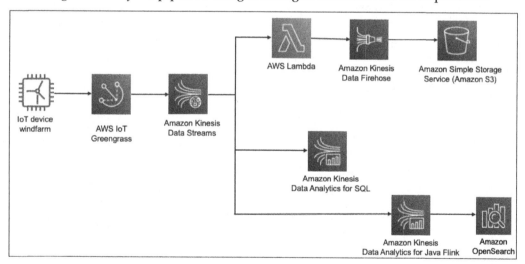

Figure 13.11: Streaming data analytics for IoT data

In the preceding diagram, data is ingested from the windfarm to understand wind turbine health and speed. It's important to control wind turbines in real time to avoid costly repairs in the case of high wind speeds beyond the limit that the wind turbine can handle.

The wind turbine data is ingested to Kinesis Data Streams using AWS IoT. Kinesis Data Streams can retain the streaming data for up to a year and provide replay capability. These are subjected to the fan-out technique to deliver the data to multiple resources, where you can massage data using Lambda and store it to Amazon S3 for further analytics using Amazon Kinesis Firehose.

You can perform real-time queries on streaming data using simple SQL queries with Kinesis Data Analytics for SQL. You can automate a data pipeline to transform streaming data in real time using Kinesis Data Analytics for Java Flink and store the processed data in Amazon OpenSearch to get data insights. You can add Kibana on top of OpenSearch to visualize the wind turbine data in real time.

The challenge with these use cases is the set-up time and effort that developers require to create the resources and establish the best practices needed by the streaming data services (such as access control, logging capabilities, and data integrations). The above solution is data agnostic and easily customizable, enabling customers to quickly modify pre-configured defaults and start writing code to include their specific business logic.

Big data architecture best practices

In previous sections, you learned about various big data technology and architecture patterns. Let's look at the following reference architecture diagram with different layers of a data lake architecture to learn best practices.

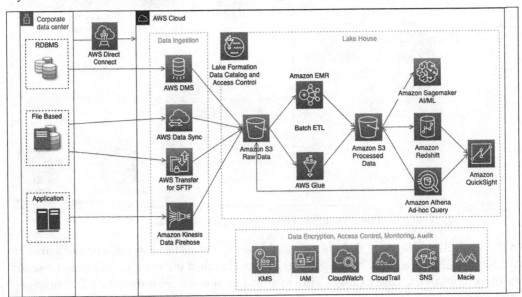

Figure 13.12: Data lake reference architecture

The preceding diagram depicts an end-to-end data pipeline in a data lake architecture using the AWS cloud platform with the following components:

- AWS Direct Connect to set up a high-speed network connection between the on-premises data center and AWS to migrate data. If you have large volumes of archive data, it's better to use the AWS Snow family to move it offline.

- A data ingestion layer with various components to ingest streaming data using Amazon Kinesis, relational data using AWS **Data Migration Service (DMS)**, secure file transfer using AWS Transfer for SFTP, and AWS DataSync to update data files between cloud and on-prem systems.

- A centralized data storage for all data using Amazon S3, where data storage has multiple layers to store raw data, processed data, and archive data.

- A cloud native data warehouse solution, Amazon Redshift, with Redshift Spectrum to support lakehouse architecture.

- An ad hoc query functionality using Amazon Athena.

- A quick ETL pipeline based on Spark using AWS Glue.

- Amazon EMR to re-utilize existing Hadoop scripts and other Apache Hadoop frameworks.

- Amazon Lake Formation to build comprehensive data cataloging and granular access control at the data lake level.

- The AI/ML extension with Amazon SageMaker.

Other components include Amazon **KMS (Key Management Service)** for data encryption, Amazon **IAM (Identity and Access Management)** for access control, Amazon Macie for PII data detection to adhere to data compliance such as PCI-DSS, CloudWatch to monitor the operation, and CloudTrail to audit the data lake activities.

You need to validate your big data architecture using the following criteria:

- Security
  - Classify data and define corresponding data protection policies using resource-based access control.
  - Implement a strong identity foundation using user permission and **Single Sign-On (SSO)**.
  - Enable environment and data traceability for audit purposes.
  - Apply security at all layers and protect data in transit and at rest using SSL and encryption at rest at all layers.
  - Keep people away from data such as locking down write access to production datasets.

- Reliability
    - Enforce data hygiene using automated data profiling using data cataloging.
    - Manage the lifecycle of data assets, transitioning, and expiration using data tiering between the data warehouse and data lake.
    - Preserve data lineage by maintaining the history of data movement through the data catalog.
    - Design resiliency for analytics pipelines and monitor system SLAs with automated recovery of ETL job failures.

- Performance efficiency
    - Use data profiling to improve performance with data validation and to build a sanitization layer.
    - Continuously optimize data storage, such as using data compression with Parquet format, data partition, file size optimization, and so on.

- Cost optimization
    - Adopt a consumption model and determine if you need an ad hoc or fast query pattern.
    - Delete out-of-use data. Define data retention rules and delete or archive data that is out of the retention period.
    - Decouple compute and storage with a data lake-based solution.
    - Implement migration efficiency using different migration strategies for various data sources and volumes.
    - Use managed and application-level services to reduce the cost of ownership.

- Operational excellence
    - Perform operations as code using tools such as CloudFormation, Terraform, and Ansible.
    - Automate operations such as building an orchestration layer with Step Functions or Apache Airflow.
    - Anticipate failure in advance by continuously monitoring and automating the recovery of ETL job failures.
    - Measure the health of your workload.

You can use the above checklist as a guide to validate your big data architecture. Data engineering is a very vast topic that warrants multiple books to cover each topic in depth.

In this chapter, you learned about various components of data engineering with a popular architecture pattern, which will help you get started and explore the topic in more depth.

Summary

In this chapter, you learned about the big data architecture and components for a big data pipeline design. You learned about data ingestion and various technology choices available to collect batch and stream data for processing. As the cloud is central to storing the vast amounts of data being produced today, you learned about the various services available to ingest data in the AWS cloud ecosystem.

Data storage is one of the central points when it comes to handling big data. You learned about various kinds of data stores, including structured and unstructured data, NoSQL, and data warehousing, with the appropriate technology choices associated with each. You learned about data lake architecture and its benefits.

Once you collect and store data, you need to transform it to get insights into that data and visualize your business requirements. You learned about data processing architecture and technology choices to choose open source and cloud-based data processing tools as per your data requirements. These tools help you to get data insights and visualizations as per the nature of your data and organizational needs.

You learned about various big data architecture patterns, including data lake, lakehouse, data mesh, and streaming data architecture, along with reference architecture. Finally, you learned big data architecture best practices by putting all your learning together in the reference architecture.

As you collect more data, it's always beneficial to get future insights, which can be exceptionally beneficial for business. To predict future outcomes based on historical data, you often need machine learning. Let's learn more about machine learning and how to make your data architecture future-proof in the next chapter.

Join our book's Discord space

Join the book's Discord workspace for a monthly *Ask me Anything* session with the authors: https://packt.link/SAHandbook

14

Machine Learning
Architecture

In the previous chapter, you learned about ingesting and processing big data and getting insights to understand your business. In the traditional way of running a business, the organization's decision-maker looks at past data and uses their experience to plot the future course of company direction. It's not just about setting up the business vision but also improving the end-user experience by predicting their needs and delighting them or automating day-to-day decision-making activities such as loan approval.

However, with the sheer amount of data availability, now, it's become difficult for the human brain to process all data and predict the future. That's where **machine learning (ML)** helps us predict future courses of action by looking at a large amount of historical data. Most enterprises are either investing in ML today or planning to do so. It is fast becoming the technology that helps companies differentiate themselves—by creating new products, services, and business models to innovate and gain a competitive advantage.

ML is great for solving business problems because of the countless use cases possible in different lines of business across a company and the high degree of impact these use cases can make. Commercial and government industries can benefit from deploying ML tools that help them achieve better outcomes in less time. AI/ML is a great way to solve problems across different lines of business, for example, build a new level of customer service with call center intelligence, or help marketing teams deliver on their personalization objectives by using a ML-based personalized marketing campaign.

In this chapter, you will learn about the following topics to handle and manage your ML needs:

- What is machine learning?
- Data science and machine learning
- ML model overfitting versus underfitting
- Supervised and unsupervised ML model
- Machine learning architecture
- MLOps
- Deep learning
- Natural language processing
- Design principles for ML architecture

By the end of this chapter, you will know how to design ML architecture. You will learn about the various ML models and ML workflow. You will understand the process of creating an ML model pipeline through feature engineering, model training, inference, and model evaluation.

What is machine learning?

ML drives better customer experiences, more efficient business operations, and faster, more accurate decision making. With the rise in compute power and the proliferation of data, ML has moved from the periphery to be a core differentiator for businesses and organizations across industries. ML use cases can apply to most businesses, like personalized product and content recommendations, contact center intelligence, virtual identity verification, and intelligent document processing. And there are customized use cases built for a specific industry—like clinical trials in pharma or assembly line quality control in manufacturing.

Let's say your company wants to send marketing offers to potential customers for a new toy launch, and you have been tasked to develop a system to identify who to target for the marketing campaign. Your customer base could be millions of users to which you need to apply predictive analytics, and ML can help you solve such a complex problem.

ML uses technology to discover trends and patterns and compute mathematical predictive models based on past factual data. ML can help to solve complex problems such as the following:

- When you may not know how to create complex code rules to make a decision; for example, if you want to recognize people's emotions in image and speech, there are no easy ways to code the logic to achieve that.

- When you need to analyze a large amount of data for decision making, the volume of data is too large for a human to do it efficiently. For example, while a human can do it with spam detection, the amount of data makes it impractical to do this quickly.

- When relevant information may only become available dynamically when you need to adapt and personalize user behavior based on individual data; examples are individualized product recommendations or website personalization.

- When there are many tasks with a lot of data available, you cannot track the information fast enough to make a rule-based decision—for example, fraud detection and natural language processing.

Humans handle data prediction based on the results of their analyses and their experience. Using ML, you can train a computer to provide expertise based on available data and get a prediction based on new data. Some of the industry ML use cases are listed below:

- **Predictive maintenance**: Predict if a component will fail before failure based on sensor data. Example applications include predicting failure and **remaining useful life (RUL)** of automotive fleets, manufacturing equipment, and IoT sensors. The key value is increased vehicle and equipment up-time and cost savings. This use case is widely used in the automotive and manufacturing industries.

- **Demand forecasting**: Use historical data to forecast key demand metrics faster and make more accurate business decisions around production, pricing, inventory management, and purchasing/re-stocking. The key value is meeting customer demand, reducing inventory carrying costs by reducing surplus inventory, and reducing waste. This use case is used mainly in financial services, manufacturing, retail, and **consumer packaged goods (CPG)** industries.

- **Fraud detection**: Automate the detection of potentially fraudulent activity and flag it for review. The key value is reducing costs associated with fraud and maintaining customer trust. This use case is used mainly in financial services and online retail industries.

- **Credit risk prediction**: Explain individual predictions from a credit application to predict whether the credit will be paid back or not (often called a *credit default*). The key value is identifying bias and satisfying regulatory requirements. This use case is used mainly in financial services and online retail industries.

- **Extract & analyze data from documents**: Understand text in written and digital documents and forms, extract information, and use it to classify items and make decisions. This use case is commonly used in the healthcare, financial services, legal, mechanical and electrical, and education industries.

- **Personalized recommendations**: Make customized recommendations based on historical trends. Common in the mechanical and electrical, retail, and education (most likely recommending classes) industries.

- **Churn prediction**: Predict customer likelihood to churn; often used in retail, education, and **software as a service (SaaS)**.

The main idea behind ML is to make available a training dataset to an ML algorithm and have it predict something from a new dataset, for example, feeding some historical stock market trend data to an ML model and having it predict how the market will fluctuate in the next 6 months to 1 year.

While developing ML solutions, data and code must come together carefully and should evolve in a controlled way, toward the common goal of a robust and scalable ML system; data for training, testing, and inference will change over time, across different sources, and needs to be met with changing code. Without a systematic approach, there can be divergence in how code and data evolve that causes problems in production, gets in the way of smooth deployment, and leads to results that are hard to trace or reproduce. Let's learn how data science goes hand in hand with ML in the next section.

Working with data science and ML

ML is all about working with data. The quality of the training data and labels is crucial to the success of an ML model. High-quality data leads to a more accurate ML model and the right prediction. Often in the real world, your data has multiple issues such as missing values, noise, bias, outliers, and so on. Part of data science is the cleaning and preparing of your data to get it ready for ML.

The first thing about data preparation is to understand business problems. Data scientists are often eager to jump into the data directly, start coding, and produce insights. However, without a clear understanding of the business problem, any insights you develop have a high chance of becoming a solution that cannot address the problem at hand. It makes much more sense to start with a straightforward user story and business objectives before getting lost in the data. After building a solid understanding of the business problem, you can begin to narrow down the ML problem categories and determine whether ML will be suitable to solve your particular business problem.

Data science includes data collection, analysis, preprocessing, and feature engineering. Exploring the data provides us with necessary information such as data quality and cleanliness, interesting patterns in the data, and likely paths forward once you start modeling.

Data prep is the first step of building an ML model. It is time-consuming and constitutes up to 80% of the time spent in ML development. Data preparation has always been considered tedious and resource-intensive due to the inherent nature of data being "dirty" and not ready for ML in its raw form. "Dirty" data could include missing or erroneous values, outliers, and so on. Feature engineering is often needed to transform the inputs to deliver more accurate and efficient ML models.

Data preparation often needs multiple steps. While most "standalone data preparation tools" provide data transformation and feature engineering and visualization, few tools offer built-in model validation. And all of these data preparation steps are considered separate from ML. What's needed is a framework that provides all these capabilities in one place and is tightly integrated with the rest of the ML pipeline. Therefore, data preparation modules need curation and integration before they are deployed in production.

As shown in the following diagram, data preprocessing and learning to create an ML model are interconnected—your data preparation will heavily influence your model, while the model you choose heavily influences the type of data preparation you will do. Finding the correct balance is highly iterative and is very much an art (or trial and error):

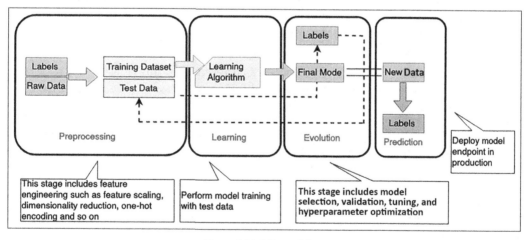

Figure 14.1: ML workflow

As shown in the preceding diagram, the ML workflow includes the following phases:

- **Preprocessing**: In this phase, the data scientist preprocesses the data and divides it into training, validation, and testing datasets. Your ML model gets trained with the training dataset to fit the model and is evaluated using the validation dataset. Once the model is ready, you can test it using a testing dataset. Considering the amount of data and your business case, you need to divide the data into training, testing, and validation sets, perhaps keeping 70% of the data for training, 10% for validation, and 20% for testing. Features are independent attributes of your dataset that may or may not influence the outcome. Feature engineering involves finding the right feature, which can help to achieve model accuracy. The label is your target outcome, which is dependent on feature selection. You can apply dimensionality reduction to choose the right feature, which filters and extracts the most compelling feature for your data.

- **Learning**: You select the appropriate ML algorithm as per the business use case and data in the learning phase. The learning phase is the core of the ML workflow, where you train your ML model on your training dataset. To achieve model accuracy, you need to experiment with various hyperparameters and perform model selection.

- **Evaluation**: Once your ML model gets trained in the learning phase, you want to evaluate the accuracy with a known dataset. You use the validation dataset kept aside during the preprocessing step to assess your model. Required model tuning needs to be performed as per the evaluation result if your model prediction accuracy is not up to the exceptions as determined by validation data.

- **Prediction**: Prediction is also known as inference. In this phase, you deployed your model and started making a prediction. These predictions can be made in real time or in batches.

As per your data input, the ML model often has overfitting or underfitting issues, which you must consider to get the right outcome.

Evaluating ML models – overfitting versus underfitting

In overfitting, your model fails to generalize. You will determine an overfitting model that performs well on the training set but poorly on the test set.

This typically indicates that the model is too flexible for the amount of training data, and this flexibility allows it to *memorize* the data, including noise. Overfitting corresponds to high variance, where small changes in the training data result in significant changes to the results.

In underfitting, your model fails to capture essential patterns in the training dataset. Typically, underfitting indicates the model is too simple or has too few explanatory variables. An underfitting model is not flexible enough to model real patterns and corresponds to high bias, indicating that the results show a systematic lack of fit in a certain region.

The following graph illustrates the clear difference between overfitting and underfitting as they correspond to a model with a good fit:

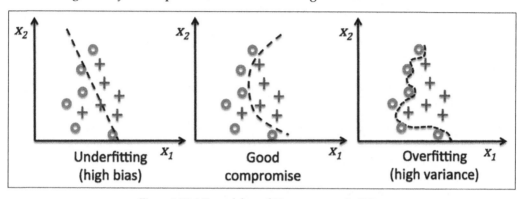

Figure 14.2: ML model overfitting versus underfitting

The ML model categorizes two data point categories illustrated by the preceding graphs' red points and green crosses. The ML model tries to determine whether a customer will buy a given product or not. The chart shows predictions from three different ML models. You can see an overfitted model (on the right) traversing through all red data points in training and failing to generalize the algorithm for real-world data outside of the training dataset. On the other hand, the underfitted model (on the left) leaves out several data points and produces an inaccurate result. A good model (shown in the middle) provides clear data point predictions in most cases. Creating a good ML model is like creating art, and you can find the right fit with model tuning.

The ML algorithm is categorized into supervised and unsupervised learning at the heart of the overall ML workflow.

Supervised and unsupervised machine learning algorithms

In supervised learning, the algorithm is given a set of training examples where the data and target are known. It can then predict the target value for new datasets containing the same attributes. For supervised algorithms, human intervention and validation are required, such as photo classification and tagging.

In unsupervised learning, the algorithm is provided with massive amounts of data, and it must find patterns and relationships between the data. It can then draw inferences from datasets.

Human intervention is not required in unsupervised learning, for example, auto-classification of documents based on context. It addresses the problem where correct output is not available for training examples, and the algorithm must find patterns in data using clustering.

Reinforcement learning is another category where you don't tell the algorithm what action is correct but give it a reward or penalty after each action in a sequence.

The following are the popular ML algorithm types used for ML:

- **Linear regression**: Let's use the price of houses as a simple example to explain linear regression. Say we have collected many data points representing the prices of homes and their sizes on the market, and we plot them on a two-dimensional graph. Now we try to find a line that best fits these data points and use it to predict the price of a house of a new size.

- **Logistic regression**: Estimates the probability of the input belonging to two classes, positive and negative.

- **Neural networks**: The ML model acts like the human brain, where layers of nodes are connected in a neural network. Each node is one multivariate linear function with a univariate nonlinear transformation. The neural network can represent any nonlinear function and address problems generally hard to interpret, such as image recognition. Neural networks are expensive to train but fast to predict.

- **K-nearest neighbors**: It chooses the number of k neighbors. It finds the k-nearest neighbors of the new observation that you want to classify and assigns the class label by majority vote. For example, you want to categorize your data into five clusters, so your k value will be five.

- **Support Vector Machines (SVMs)**: Support vectors are a popular approach in research, but not so much in the industry. SVMs maximize the margin, the distance between the decision boundary (hyperplane) and the support vectors (the training examples closest to the boundary).

SVMs are not memory efficient because they store the support vectors, which grow with the size of the training data.

- **Decision trees**: In a decision tree, nodes are split based on features to have the most significant **Information Gain** (**IG**) between the parent node and its split nodes. The decision tree is easy to interpret and flexible; not many feature transformations are required.

- **Random forests and ensemble methods**: A random forest is an ensemble method in which multiple models are trained, and their results are combined, usually via majority vote or averaging. A random forest is a set of decision trees. Each tree learns from a different randomly sampled subset. Randomly selected features are applied to each tree from the original feature sets. Random forests increase diversity by randomly selecting the training dataset and a subset of features for each tree, reducing variance through averaging.

- **K-means clustering**: It uses unsupervised learning to find data patterns. K-means iteratively separates data into *k* clusters by minimizing the sum of distances to the center of the closest cluster. It first assigns each instance to the nearest center and then re-computes each center from assigned instances. Users must determine or provide the *k* number of clusters.

Zeppelin, RStudio, and Jupyter notebooks are the most common environments for data engineers doing data discovery, cleansing, enrichment, labeling, and preparation for ML model training. Spark provides the Spark ML library, which implements many standard high-level estimator algorithms such as regressions, page rank, k-means, and more.

For algorithms that leverage neural networks, data scientists use frameworks such as TensorFlow and MXNet, or higher-level abstractions such as Keras, Gluon, or PyTorch. Those frameworks and common algorithms can be found in the Amazon SageMaker service, which provides a full ML model development, training, and hosting environment. As the cloud is becoming a go-to platform for ML model training, let's learn about some available ML cloud platforms.

Machine learning in the cloud

ML development is a complex and costly process. There are barriers to adoption at each step of the ML workflow, from collecting and preparing data, which is time-consuming and undifferentiated, to choosing the right ML algorithm, which is often done by trial and error, to lengthy training times, which leads to higher costs. Then there is model tuning, which can be a very long cycle and requires adjusting thousands of different combinations. Once you've deployed a model, you must monitor it and then scale and manage its production.

To solve these challenges, all major public cloud vendors provide an ML platform that facilitates ease of training, tuning, and deploying ML models anywhere at a low cost. For example, Amazon SageMaker is one of the most popular platforms that provides end-to-end ML services. SageMaker provides users with an integrated workbench of tools brought together in one place through SageMaker Studio. Users can launch Jupyter Notebook and JupyterLab environments instantly through SageMaker Studio. SageMaker also provides complete experiment management, data preparation, and pipeline automation and orchestration to help make data scientists more productive. SageMaker also provides a fully managed RStudio platform, which is one of the most popular IDEs among R developers for ML and data science projects.

SageMaker provides fully managed servers in the cloud to make this easy for data scientists and developers. But even beyond notebooks, SageMaker provides other managed infrastructure capabilities as well. From distributed training jobs, data processing jobs, and even model hosting, SageMaker takes care of all of the scaling, patching, high availability, and so on associated with building, training, and hosting models. Similarly, GCP provides the Google Cloud AI platform with different services to perform ML experiments, and Microsoft Azure offers Azure Machine Learning Studio.

In addition to the managed ML platform, cloud vendors also provide ready-to-use **artificial intelligence (AI)** services. AI services allow developers to add intelligence to any application without needing ML skills easily. The pre-trained models provide ready-made intelligence for your applications and workflows to help you do things like personalizing the customer experience, forecasting business metrics, translating conversations, extracting meaning from documents, and more. For example, AWS provides the Amazon Comprehend AI service, which has pre-trained models that support entity detection, key phrase detection, and sentiment analysis natively in multiple languages.

Data scientists leverage the managed cloud environment to do data preparation and set up a model training cluster to start their training job. When complete, they can one-click-deploy the model and begin serving inferences over HTTP as you learn about algorithms and ML workflow to build a ML pipeline. Let's learn more about some of the important things to consider when you are designing ML architecture.

Building machine learning architecture

Creating an ML pipeline consists of multiple phases and requires iterative improvement. Building a robust and scalable workflow from a loose collection of code is a complex and time-consuming process, and many data scientists don't have experience building workflows. An ML workflow can be defined as an orchestrated sequence that involves multiple steps. Data scientists and ML developers first need to package numerous code recipes and then specify the order they should execute, keeping track of code, data, and model parameter dependencies between each step.

Added complexity to ML workflows warrants monitoring changes in data used for training and predictions because changes in the data could introduce bias, leading to inaccurate predictions. In addition to monitoring the data, data scientists and ML developers also need to monitor model predictions to ensure they are accurate and don't become skewed toward particular results over time. As a result, it can take several months of custom coding to get the individual code recipes to execute in the correct sequence and as expected.

ML architectures need to protect model artifacts and require self-service capabilities for model development and training. Your ML architecture needs to be an automated end-to-end evidence capture of the entire model development lifecycle across development, training, and deployment. ML application should use a **continuous integration and continuous deployment** (**CI/CD**) pipeline integrated with change control systems for model management and deployment. The environments require pre-defined security configurations. The following are the ML architecture components with examples from the **Amazon Web Services** (**AWS**) ML platform to understand it better.

Prepare and label

To make data ready for ML, you need to run your data processing workloads, such as feature engineering, data validation, model evaluation, and model interpretation. The feature also preprocesses datasets to convert the input datasets into a format expected by the ML algorithm you're using. You can use the various tools and techniques mentioned in the previous section, on processing data and performing analytics, to wrangle data as per your ML needs. A managed ML platform like **Amazon SageMaker** also provides a data wrangler and feature store capability to make the data processing job easier for you. Amazon SageMaker is a fully managed service that offers the ability to build, train, and deploy ML models quickly. Other ML platforms are Azure ML Studio, H2O.ai, SAS, Databricks, and the Google AI platform.

During data processing, you often need to label your data, and it becomes laborious in the case of image processing. Data labeling helps you build and manage highly accurate training datasets quickly. You can use third-party vendors who help you to label the image, such as Labelbox, CrowdAI, Docugami, and Scale. You can also automate the labeling process using AI services such as **SageMaker Ground Truth**, which continuously learns from labels provided by humans to improve annotation quality. Automatic annotations significantly lower labeling costs; once your data is ready, the next step is to select the suitable algorithm and build the model.

Select and build

While creating a ML model, you first want to understand business problems clearly, which will help you select the right algorithm. As explained in the previous section, you can choose from a list of algorithms and ML frameworks, both *supervised and unsupervised machine learning algorithms*. Once you select the suitable algorithm for your use case to build an ML model, you need a platform to train and develop your model.

Jupyter notebooks and RStudio are the most popular platforms among data scientists to build ML models. You can use cloud platforms such as Amazon SageMaker to spin up Jupyter notebooks or RStudio Workbench. AWS provides SageMaker Studio and RStudio a web-based visual interface where you can perform all ML development steps.

To select your model, you can choose several built-in ML algorithms that you can use for various problem types or get hundreds of algorithms and pre-trained models available in the cloud marketplace, making it easy to get started quickly. The next step is to train and tune the model. Let's learn more about it.

Train and tune

It would be best to get a distributed compute cluster, perform the training, and output the result that applications can consume for training. Model tuning is also known as hyperparameter tuning, which is a critical aspect of achieving result accuracy. You need to find the best model version by running multiple training jobs on the dataset using the algorithm and ranges of hyperparameters. Then it would be best if you chose the correct hyperparameter values that result in a model that performs the best, as measured by a metric that you prefer.

While you are tuning the model, you need to have the ability to debug the model, which helps to capture real-time metrics during training, such as training and validation, confusion matrices, and learning gradients, to help improve model accuracy. You need to capture the input parameters, configurations, and results and store them as experiments so that you can search for previous experiments by their characteristics, review previous experiments with their results, and compare experiment results visually. Most managed ML platforms, such as Amazon SageMaker, provide all these features like model autotuning, experiment, and debugger.

Amazon SageMaker also provides Autopilot, which automatically looks at raw data and applies feature processors. It picks the best set of algorithms, trains, tunes multiple models, tracks their performance, and ranks the models based on performance. Once your model is ready, you need to deploy it and manage it in production to get helpful insights.

Deploy and manage

You need to deploy your trained model into production to start generating predictions for real-time or batch data. You need to apply auto-scaling for ML instances across multiple locations for high redundancy and set up the restful HTTPS endpoint for your application. Your application needs to have an API call to an ML endpoint to achieve low latency and high throughput. This type of architecture allows you to integrate your new models into your application quickly because model changes no longer require application code changes.

Data can change quickly based on seasonality or unpredicted events, making it essential to monitor your model for accuracy and business relevance and remediate concept drift. Today, one of the significant factors that can affect the accuracy of deployed models is if the data that is used to generate predictions differs from the data used to train the model. For example, changing economic conditions could drive new interest rates affecting home purchasing predictions. This is called concept drift, whereby the patterns the model uses to make predictions no longer apply. You need to automatically detect concept drift in deployed models and provide detailed alerts that help identify the source of the problem.

In most deep learning applications, making predictions using a trained model—a process called inference—can be a significant factor in the compute costs of the application. A whole GPU instance may be oversized for model inference. In addition, it can be challenging to optimize the GPU, CPU, and memory needs of your deep learning application. You need to solve these problems by adding the right GPU-powered inference acceleration to production instances with no code changes.

Model compatibility is another crucial factor during deployment. Once a model has been built and trained using MXNet, TensorFlow, PyTorch, or XGBoost, you can choose your target hardware platform from Intel, NVIDIA, or ARM. You need to compile your trained ML models to run optimally and efficiently deploy compiled models to Edge devices and provide high performance and low-cost inference. You should have the ability to run large-scale ML inference applications like image recognition, speech recognition, natural language processing, personalization, and fraud detection as you learn various stages of building and deploying ML models. Let's look at a reference architecture to connect all components.

Machine learning reference architecture

The following architecture depicts a bank loan approval workflow based on customer data built on the AWS cloud platform.

Here, customer data ingested into the cloud and ML framework decides on the customer loan application.

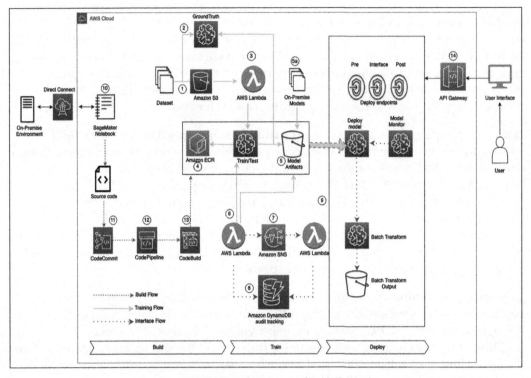

Figure 14.3: ML architecture in the AWS cloud

In designing the above architecture, some fundamental design principles to consider as a guide are:

- Training workflow:
    1. Datasets enter the process flow using S3. This data may be raw input data or preprocessed from on-premises datasets.
    2. Ground Truth is used to build a high-quality training labeled dataset for ML models. If required, the data can use the Ground Truth service to label the data.
    3. AWS Lambda can be used for data integration, preparation, and cleaning before datasets are passed to SageMaker.
    4. Data scientists will interface with SageMaker to train and test their models. The Docker images used by SageMaker are stored in ECR and can be custom images with custom toolsets that have been created through the build flow steps below or use one of the pre-built Amazon images.

5. Model artifacts to be used as part of the deployment phase are output to S3. The output from the SageMaker model can also be used to label data using Ground Truth. Models that have been pre-built and trained on-premises or other platforms can be deposited into the model artifacts S3 bucket and deployed using SageMaker.

6. AWS Lambda can trigger an approval workflow based on a new model artifact being deposited into the S3 bucket.

7. Amazon Simple Notification Service can be used to provide an automatic or manual approval workflow based on human intervention to deploy the final model. The supporting Lambda function takes the output from SNS to deploy the model.

8. DynamoDB is used to store all model metadata, actions, and other associated data for audit tracking.

9. To host the final model, we deploy the endpoint with associated configuration as part of the final step in the workflow.

- Build flow:

    1. SageMaker notebook instances are used to prepare and process data and to train and deploy ML models. These notebooks can be accessed via a VPC endpoint for the SageMaker service.

    2. CodeCommit provides the repository for the source code to trigger the build jobs required for any custom Docker images used by SageMaker.

    3. The CodePipeline service manages the end-to-end build pipeline for the custom Docker images and uses the CodeBuild service for the build/test phase.

    4. CodeBuild will build and perform unit testing of the custom Docker image and push it to Amazon ECR (this process can be managed centrally or by business functions requiring the tools).

- Inference flow:

    1. As SageMaker endpoints are private, Amazon API Gateway exposes the model endpoint to end-users for inference.

    2. Batch transform jobs are typically used to get inferences for an entire dataset. Using a trained model and dataset, the output from the batch job is stored in S3.

    3. SageMaker Model Monitor is used to monitor production models to alert them to any quality issues.

This section taught you how to build a ML architecture with a CI/CD pipeline following ML architecture design principles. Earlier in this book, you learned about DevOps to automate and operationalize your development workload. As ML is becoming mainstream, MLOps become important to learn ML at scale in production. Let's explore more details on operationalizing the ML workload with MLOps.

Machine learning operations

An ML workflow is a set of operations developed and executed to produce a mathematical model, which eventually is designed to solve a real-world problem. But there is no value of these models until they are deployed in production, other than proofs of concept. ML models almost always require deployment to a production environment to provide business value.

At the core, **Machine Learning Operations** (**MLOps**) takes an experimental ML model into a production system. MLOps is an emerging practice different from traditional DevOps because the ML development lifecycle and ML artifacts are different. The ML lifecycle involves using patterns from training data, making the MLOps workflow sensitive to data changes, volumes, and quality. Additionally, matured MLOps should support monitoring both ML lifecycle activities and production model monitoring.

MLOps framework implementation makes it simple for organizations to feel confident in building a mature MLOps framework, eliminating extensive coding. Like any other workload, you want to develop MLOps by applying best practices such as security, reliability, high availability, performance, and cost for the deployment phase of the ML lifecycle. Let's look at some MLOps principles.

MLOps principles

Any changed code, data, or model should trigger the build process in the ML development pipeline. An ML pipeline should follow the below MLOps principles while developing ML systems:

1. **Automation**: Deployment of ML models in production should be automated. The MLOps team should automate the end-to-end ML workflow from data engineering to model interference in production without any manual intervention. The MLOps pipeline can trigger model training and deployment based on events such as calendar scheduling, messaging, monitoring, data changes, model training code changes, and application code changes.

2. **Versioning**: Versioning is an essential aspect of MLOps, the same as DevOps. Every ML model and related scripts version should be maintained in a version control system such as GitHub to make the models reproducible and auditable.

3. **Testing**: ML systems require extensive testing and monitoring. Each ML system should have at least the following three scopes for testing:

   - Features and data tests include validating data quality and selecting the right features for your ML model

   - Model development tests include business metric tests, model staleness tests, and model performance validation tests

   - ML infrastructure tests include ML API usage tests, full ML pipeline integration tests, and training and production server availability tests

4. **Reproducibility**: Every phase of a ML workflow should be reproducible, which means that data processing, ML model training, and ML model deployment should produce identical results given the same input. It will ensure a robust ML system.

5. **Deployment**: MLOps is an ML engineering culture that includes CI/CD and **Continuous Training/Continuous Monitoring (CT/CM)**. Automated deployment/testing helps discover problems quickly and in the early stages. This enables the fast fixing of errors and learning from mistakes.

6. **Monitoring**: Model performance may degrade in production for reasons such as data drift. This means new models must be shipped into production constantly to address performance decline or improve model fairness. Once the ML model has been deployed, it needs to be monitored to ensure that the ML model performs as expected.

Having learned about MLOps design principles in this section, let's consider some best practices to apply MLOps in your machine leaning workload.

MLOps best practices

Due to many moving parts (data, model, or code) and challenges in solving business problems using ML, MLOps can be a challenging task.

Based on the principles outlined in the previous section, as follows are the best practices that ML engineers/full-stack data scientists should practice while deploying the ML solutions in production, which will help reduce the "technical debts" and "maintenance overhead" in ML projects and drive most business value out of it:

1. **Design considerations**: To develop a maintainable ML system, the architecture/system design should be modular and, as much as possible, loosely coupled.

   Having a loosely coupled architecture allows the teams to work independently, without relying on other teams for support and services, enabling them to work quickly and deliver value to the organization.

2. **Data validation**: Data validation is very crucial for a successful ML system. In production, data may create a variety of issues. If the statistical properties of data are different from training data properties, the training data or the sampling process were faulty. **Data drift** might cause statistical properties to change for successive batches of data. Data drift may cause model performance to degrade over time as input data properties change in comparison to the data used during ML model training.

3. **Model validation**: Reusing models is different from reusing software. You need to tune models to fit each new scenario. Validating models before promoting them into production is very important. To establish the adequate performance of the model on live data, you should perform online and offline data validation.

4. **Model experiment tracking**: Always keep track of ML model experiments. Experimenting may involve trying out different code combinations (preprocessing, training, and evaluation methods), data, and hyperparameters. Each unique combination produces metrics that you need to compare to your other experiments.

5. **Code quality check**: Every ML model specification (ML training code that creates an ML model) should go through a code review phase. It's good practice to include this code quality check as the first step of a pipeline triggered by a pull request.

6. **Naming conventions**: Following a standard naming convention (like *PEP8* for Python programming) in your ML code helps mitigate the challenge of the **Changing Anything Changes Everything (CACE)** principle. It also helps team members establish familiarity with your project quickly.

7. **Model predictive service performance monitoring**: Other than project metrics (such as RMSE and AUC-ROC) that evaluate a model's performance in relation to business objectives, operational metrics such as latency, scalability, and service update are also crucial to monitor to avoid business losses.

8. **Continuous Training (CT)** and **Continuous Monitoring (CM) process**: Model performance may degrade in production for reasons such as data drift. It means new models must be deployed into production constantly to improve model fairness. This calls for CT/CM.

9. **Resource utilization**: Understanding the requirements of your system during the training and deployment phases helps your team optimize the cost of your experiments.

MLOps plays a crucial role in the industrialization of AI. MLOps combines ML, DevOps, and data engineering with the goal of reliably and efficiently building, deploying, and maintaining ML systems in production. Deep learning is now the go-to mechanism to solve complex ML problems. Let's learn some more details about deep learning.

Deep learning

ML is not just about forecasting numbers but also solving complex problems using neural language processing. These use cases include complex scenarios processed by the human brain, such as building an automated chatbot impersonating humans, reading handwritten text, image recognition, transcribing videos/audios, and converting text to audio and vice versa. **Deep learning** has the ability to solve such use cases by mimicking the human brain.

While ML needs a pre-defined set of labeled data using supervised learning, deep learning uses a neural network for unsupervised learning to simulate human brain behaviors by using a large amount of data to develop learning capabilities for machines. Deep learning is a neural network of multiple layers where you don't need to do data labeling upfront. However, you can use both labeled data and unlabeled data with deep learning, depending upon your use case. The following diagram shows a simple deep learning model:

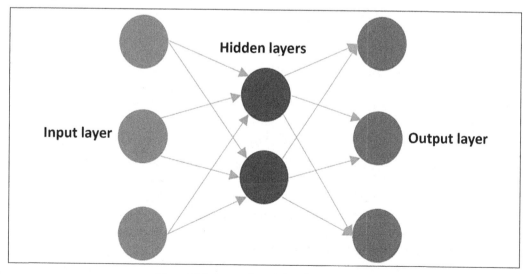

Figure 14.4: A overview of deep learning layers

In the preceding diagram, a deep learning model has interconnected nodes where input layers provide data input through various nodes. This data goes through multiple hidden layers to calculate the output and deliver final model inference through the output node layer. The input and output layers are visible layers, and learning happens in the middle layer through weights and bias, as shown in the diagram below:

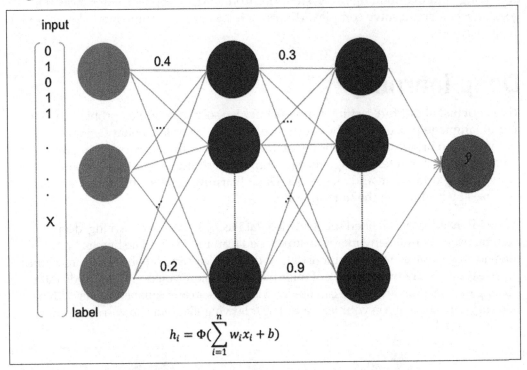

$$h_i = \Phi(\sum_{i=1}^{n} w_i x_i + b)$$

Figure 14.5: Deep learning neural network model

As shown in the preceding diagram, you can see a series of hidden layers in between where each layer applies some weight functions to these interconnected nodes to learn the pattern the same as the human brain, to provide the desired outcome. You can see **label** data is coming as input and going through neural network nodes with their weight (**0.2, 0.4, 0.3, and 0.9**) indicated between vertices.

Weight is a neural network parameter that transforms input data within the hidden layers. Weight decides how much influence the input will have on the output. It represents the strength of the connection between nodes. If the weight from node A to node B has a greater degree, it means that neuron A has greater influence over neuron B. Weights near zero means changing this input will not have any effect on the output. If weights are negative, this means increasing the input will decrease the output and vice versa.

The above learning method is called **forward propagation**, where data flows from the input to the output layer. Another technique called **back propagation** uses algorithms to calculate errors in predictions and then adjust the weights and biases of the function by moving backward through the layers to train the model. With the help of forwarding and backward propagation, you can build a neural network to make predictions and correct errors and gradually become more accurate with the training algorithm.

Deep learning has different types of neural networks. The two most common are **Convolution Neural Networks (CNNs)**, used on computer vision and image classifications, and **Recurrent Neural Networks (RNNs)**, used for natural language processing and speech recognition. Some of the most popular frameworks to build neural network models are:

- **TensorFlow**: It is an open-source software library for ML. TensorFlow's main API is written in Python and has experimental support for other languages. It has built-in support for many neural network architectures.

- **MXNet**: MXNet is also an open-source software library for deep learning natively implemented in C++ and has built-in support for many network architectures. Its API is available in multiple languages such as Python, Scala, Clojure, R, Julia, Perl, and Java (inference only).

In addition to the above, other popular deep learning frameworks are PyTorch, Chainer, Caffe2, ONNX, Keras, Gluon, and so on. The idea of this section is to provide you with a high-level view of deep learning. It is a complex topic and requires an entire book to cover the basics. You will find multiple books available on each of the frameworks. Deep learning model training requires a large amount of processing power and could be very costly. However, public cloud providers such as AWS, GCP, and Azure make it easy to make available high-powered GPU-based instances to train these models with the pay-as-you-go method.

Now, ML is applicable everywhere, which includes solving customer problems such as predictive maintenance, providing accurate forecasting for businesses, or building personalized recommendations for end-users. ML use cases are not only limited to customer problems, but also help you to handle your IT applications by optimizing your workload with predictive scaling, identifying log patterns, fixing errors before they cause issues in production, or budget forecasting for IT infrastructure. So, it's important for solution architects to be aware of ML use cases and associated technology.

Overall, ML and AI are very vast topics and warrant multiple books to understand them in more detail. In this chapter, you just learned an overview of ML models, types, and the ML workflow.

Summary

In this chapter, you learned about ML architecture and components for a ML workflow. You learned about how data and ML go hand in hand. It is essential to get high-quality data with feature engineering to build the right ML model.

You learned about ML model validation by recognizing model overfit versus underfit situations. You also learned about various supervised and unsupervised ML algorithms. As the cloud is becoming a go-to platform for ML model training and deployment, you learned about ML platforms in popular public cloud providers.

Further, you learned about the ML workflow, including data preprocessing, modeling, evaluation, and prediction. Also, you learned about building ML architecture with a detailed reference architecture built in AWS cloud platforms. MLOps is essential for putting ML models in production. You learned about MLOps principles and best practices. Further, you got an overview of deep learning, which helps solve complex problems by mimicking the human brain.

There are millions of small devices connected to the internet, referred to collectively as the IoT. You need to understand the various components available in the cloud to collect, process, and analyze IoT data to produce meaningful insights. In the next chapter, you will learn more details about IoT use cases and solve them. You will learn about challenges with IoT systems and the techniques used to scale them.

Join our book's Discord space

Join the book's Discord workspace for a monthly *Ask me Anything* session with the authors: https://packt.link/SAHandbook

15

The Internet of Things Architecture

As internet connectivity is increasing, there is an increasing number of small devices everywhere with small memory and compute capacities. These sensors connect various physical entities, such as your home alarm, thermal sensors, and car, and the data from millions of these connected devices needs to be collected and analyzed. For example, weather data collected from multiple sensors can be utilized to forecast weather for wind energy and farming. There are billions of connected devices in homes, factories, oil wells, hospitals, cars, and thousands of other places that are fueling digital transformation, generating huge volumes of data and growing exponentially.

The **Internet of Things (IoT)** is much more than just a collection of data from sensors and devices. Comprehensive IoT solutions include devices, local data collection and analysis, and cloud services to collect, store, and analyze data. You need integration with devices to operate even without internet connectivity, and when connections are possible, they can connect to report data and status.

IoT solutions require device connectivity and messaging services, fleet management, and device update services. They need to ensure device and fleet security, including audit and anomaly detection; on top of that, you should perform analytics functionality for noisy and intermittent IoT data. To get full business value in real time, you should build machine learning models and then deploy them back to devices to optimize processes and outcomes.

In this chapter, you will learn about the following topics to handle and manage your connected IoT devices:

- What is the Internet of Things?
- Components of IoT architecture
- Managing IoT devices
- Connecting and controlling IoT devices
- Performing analytics on IoT data
- IoT in the cloud
- Building an industrial IoT solution
- Implementing a digital twin

By the end of this chapter, you will know how to design IoT solution architecture. You will learn about the various component of IoT solutions, including device management, device connectivity, device security, and getting insights from IoT data through analytics and machine learning.

What is the Internet of Things?

Imagine if you knew the state of everything and could reason on top of that data; what problems would you solve? IoT is all about telling the state of everything, everywhere. IoT refers to a network ecosystem of physical devices with an IP address and connected to the internet. While IoT devices are multiplying in number, the complexity of leveraging your IoT devices currently is growing with them.

You need to ingest data from IoT sensors, store it for analysis via streaming, and provide results quickly. There are large numbers of devices in homes, healthcare facilities, factories, cars, and many other places. You increasingly need solutions to connect with these devices and to collect, store, and analyze device data to improve operational efficiency.

IoT solutions provide you with the ability to collect data from all those deceives and acquire insights. IoT is a critical enabler for emerging technologies like AI/ML, robotics, video analytics, mobile, and voice. IoT is at the heart of these emerging technologies as access to device data is crucial to train machine learning models, deliver intelligence, and drive business efficiency. There are multiple industrial use cases that enterprises are solving using IoT, such as:

- **Optimize manufacturing**: By capturing machine performance data, you can improve the performance and productivity of industrial processes. You can gain insight into machine performance and replace parts before they become broken with predictive maintenance.

- **Healthcare**: With IoT, you can bring healthcare to patients anytime and everywhere. Doctors can remotely monitor patient health and take action in case of any health alert. Now everyone is using wellness applications embedded in wearable devices such as the Apple Watch and Fitbit to be better aware of their health and share health data directly with their primary care.

- **Inventory tracking**: IoT helps to maintain just-in-time inventory and optimize warehouse operation costs. You can track inventory levels and auto-place replenishment orders. With IoT sensors, you can pretty much automate entire warehouse operations from receiving to replenishment, packing, and shipping.

- **Connected homes**: Using IoT-enabled devices such as smart switches, smart thermostats, and smart cameras, you can enhance user experiences in homes, buildings, and cities. You can operate the entire facility and optimize capacity using intelligent devices or equip homes with smart security devices to help you monitor your home from anywhere, anytime.

- **Agriculture**: This is an important area for human survival, and IoT sensors for humidity, weather, and temperature are helping to grow healthier crops with greater efficiency. You can determine when to water the crop by combining data from humidity sensors and weather forecasts.

- **Energy efficiency**: You can manage energy resources more efficiently with IoT, such as monitoring wind farm and solar farm energy production in real time, and plan maintenance.

- **Transforming transportation**: IoT is helping shape the future of transportation with connected and autonomous vehicles. The most popular use case you can see is Tesla cars, equipped with IoT sensors and powering full self-drive features by collecting thousands of data points in real time.

- **Enhancing safety**: IoT devices help improve safety in the home, the office, and the factory floor by continuously monitoring and providing alerts ahead of any equipment malfunction or security incident to take immediate action.

IoT strategies empower the enterprise with the intelligence needed to build new services and improve products and services over time, enjoying better relationships with their customers. Data-driven discipline results in making faster, more intelligent decisions that lead to revenue growth and greater operational efficiency. With IoT, organizations either become more efficient and lower costs or build entirely new services and products, driving new business. These are some of the most critical challenges to any IoT device architecture. You need to ensure the security and management of devices in addition to data collection and performing insights on top of it. Let's learn more about the various attributes of IoT architecture.

Components of IoT architecture

In the use cases mentioned in the previous section, organizations have many devices across multiple product lines. They needed an architecture to ingest various telemetry measures and attributes to support real-time consumption by users and service applications. At a high level, IoT architecture consists of three components, as shown in the following diagram:

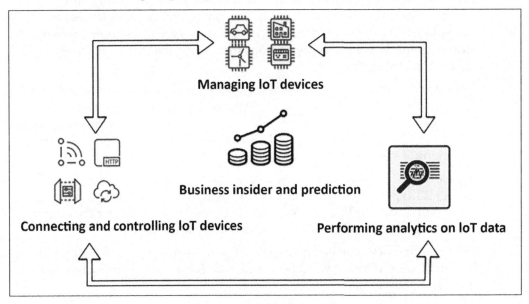

Figure 15.1: IoT architecture cycle

As shown in the preceding diagram, the IoT architecture cycle has three elements:

1. **Managing IoT device software**: To build IoT solutions, you need to deploy a large number of devices, ranging from thousands to millions. These devices should have the ability to generate the data required for the use case and perform an operation at the edge as required. The first thing you need to figure out is, *how can I build devices that operate at the edge?*

2. **Handling IoT device connectivity and control**: Managing millions of devices and securing them is a tedious task. On top of that, you want them to be updated with the latest software/firmware or they may need to be maintained in different versions. You also need to group for ease of management and make sure they are securely connected. The second thing you need to understand is how to control, manage, and secure your devices at scale.

3. **Performing IoT analytics services**: Once your devices are deployed and connected, you need to collect a large volume of data arriving at high velocity and gain insights to derive business value.

In the final action, you need to design how to make sense of your IoT data and take the appropriate actions.

So now, to build an IoT architecture, you have three questions to answer from the architecture layers mentioned above. While deep diving into the architecture, you want to embed examples from available technology choices in each of the preceding elements. Let's explore the first element of IoT architecture in more detail to learn IoT device software management in greater depth.

Managing IoT devices

When it comes to IoT devices, you want to understand how to build and operate intelligent device software at the edge. With the increased availability of the internet, you can find almost every device equipped with support for either a microcontroller or microprocessor. **A microcontroller unit (MCU)** is a single chip containing a simple processor with memory; it is used in devices such as industrial sensors, thermostats, smart switches, and lightbulbs. Microcontrollers make up more than 80% of all connected and connectable devices. A **microprocessor unit (MPU)** extends compute and processing power on edge devices. It has memory and I/O components connected externally; these are more powerful devices, such as your laptop, computer, cameras, and routers. Let's now learn about microcontroller device management and connectivity.

Microcontroller device management

When it comes to microcontroller-based devices, FreeRTOS is one of the most popular **real-time operating systems (RTOSes)**. FreeRTOS includes a kernel and set of IoT libraries suitable for use across all industry sectors that make it easy to securely connect your small, low-power devices to more powerful edge devices and gateways. FreeRTOS help to easily program connected microcontroller-based devices and collect data to send for analysis and scale IoT applications across millions of devices. It helps to keep edge devices secure with security credentials and key management, and it also keeps your data secure with transport layer encryption.

MCU devices can connect to AWS IoT Core using MQTT Pub/Sub messaging or HTTPS-based file downloads from cloud or uploads to cloud storage for cloud connectivity to ingest and analyze data. MQTT is an OASIS standard messaging protocol for IoT. It is a lightweight publish/subscribe messaging transport ideal for connecting remote devices with a small code footprint and minimal bandwidth. FreeRTOS extends cellular LTE and the Wi-Fi abstraction layer, which helps to continue communication, collecting data, and taking actions without a cloud connection.

FreeRTOS provides an AWS IoT Device Defender library for device security, making it easy to report device-side metrics to detect anomalies when these metrics deviate from expected behavior. Device Defender also continuously audits the IoT configurations associated with your FreeRTOS devices to ensure that they comply with security best practices, such as auditing and monitoring devices, reporting TCP connections, and detecting anomalies.

FreeRTOS is fully supported and integrated with the AWS cloud. AWS supports a fully integrated firmware update service for FreeRTOS with integrated code signing using AWS IoT Device Management and supports **over-the-air (OTA)** software updates. OTA is a critical piece of the IoT value proposition and a vital part of the end-to-end security solution.

As MCU devices are more powerful and provide the ability to extend data analytics capabilities to the edge, AWS provides IoT Greengrass to connect these devices to the AWS cloud. Also, FreeRTOS provides convenient APIs that make it easy to connect to AWS Greengrass devices. Suppose the Greengrass Core device loses connection to the cloud. In that case, FreeRTOS devices in the Greengrass group can continue to communicate with each other over the local network, so your applications continue to run even with intermittent connectivity. Let's learn about MPU device management and building data collection capability near the data source.

Microprocessor device management

It's not always applicable to collect IoT data in a central place and perform analytics to gain some insights. You need to collect data at the edge and perform analytics locally in scenarios where internet connectivity is impossible, such as airplanes, cruise ships, or remote areas. It is also applicable when you cannot store data in other locations due to compliance or need ultra-fast latency, such as managing the robot fleet on the factory floor. In such cases, your devices need to reduce latency, reduce costs, and improve regulatory compliance at the edge location. Often, MPU devices are preferred for such use cases as they are much more powerful than MCU devices. They can also work as a gateway and manage multiple MCU devices at the edge.

AWS provides IoT Greengrass, which helps extend AWS services onto your devices to act locally on the data they generate to get immediate data insight and take action. With Greengrass, devices don't need to send your data to a distant cloud; data is stored locally, saving time when milliseconds matter. Also, it provides a choice of sending only the data you need to the cloud, which lowers costs. Greengrass-enabled devices continue to route local messages when data needs to stay local for data sovereignty laws, ensuring that data is secure and kept local.

AWS IoT Greengrass consists of two parts—an IoT edge runtime and cloud service. Using the Greengrass edge runtime on a device helps customers add device intelligence through local processing, data management, and ML inference and seamlessly connect it to AWS cloud services.

The Greengrass cloud service allows customers to deploy and manage IoT applications across their device fleets remotely. The following is a high-level overview of the pre-integrated analytics and ML services with IoT Greengrass in the AWS cloud:

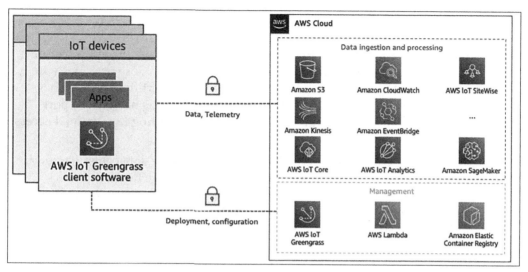

Figure 15.2: AWS IoT Greengrass pre-integrated AWS cloud services

Sometimes, IoT devices are not directly connected to the cloud. They communicate with hubs or gateways locally, which then connect to the cloud. For such use cases, the Greengrass edge runtime can be installed on hubs or gateways and helps device developers to build, deploy, and manage IoT edge applications on their gateways. Furthermore, the gateway enables the provision of intelligence for all devices connected locally to the gateway.

AWS Greengrass embeds local lambda compute, local messaging, local device shadows for data and state synchronization, and communication security in connected devices. OTA makes installing updated versions of Greengrass Core easier to access new features, bug fixes, and security enhancements using AWS IoT Device Management.

Finally, you want to make sure your device is connected and working with cloud IoT services. AWS provides IoT Device Tester, a test automation application that lets you test FreeRTOS or AWS IoT Greengrass on your choice of devices. You can test whether FreeRTOS cloud connectivity, OTA, and security libraries function correctly on top of microcontroller board device drivers for MCU devices. For MPU devices, you can test if the combination of the device's CPU architecture, Linux kernel configuration, and drivers works with AWS Greengrass.

Now, let's learn more about the second component of architecture device connectivity and control to connect, manage, and secure your device.

Connecting and controlling IoT devices

Nowadays, you have millions of devices generating gigabytes and terabytes of data every second. So the next question is, *how I can connect my data securely and handle the data they generate at scale?* This is not only about data ingestion. You need to consider other factors, such as the following:

- **Identity service**: You need to identify services to manage the authorization of devices and provision unique identities at scale. IoT Core provides you with the capability to bring your root CA and client certificates or let the IoT platform generate certificates for you. IoT platforms need to support SigV4, X.509, and custom authentication, while providing fine-grained access control with IoT policies down to the MQTT topic level.

- **Device gateway:** This securely connects devices to the data center or cloud. The data gateway should automatically provision large fleets of devices with unique identities on their first connection using fleet provisioning and facilitate automatic device registration with just-in-time registration. The data gateway should securely connect devices to the cloud or data center and other devices at scale. For connection reliability, the data gateway needs to establish long-lived connections for bi-directional communication over MQTT, WebSocket, or HTTP, and secure communications over TLS 1.2 mutual authentication.

- **Message broker**: This processes and routes data messages to the data center or cloud. The message broker needs to route data from IoT devices with scalable, low-latency, and reliable message routing. It needs to provide publish/subscribe for decoupled devices and applications and facilitate two-way message streaming. The IoT message broker helps to understand and control the status of your device at any time and retain messages for offline devices and extends support for **Quality of Service (QoS)** messaging for MQTT:

  - QoS level 0 means, at most, one-time delivery of messages. It is also called **fire and forget**, where there is no guarantee of delivery as the recipient does not acknowledge receipt.

  - QoS level 1 guarantees that a message is delivered at least once to the receiver, but the message can also get duplicated due to the re-delivery of the same message.

  - QoS level 2 is the highest level of service in MQTT. It guarantees that each message is received only once; however, it is the slowest method and needs a four-part handshake between the sender and the receiver.

- **Rules engine** — This triggers actions on your devices as per business needs. A rules engine ingests large amounts of data, pre-processes it, and makes it available to other analytics, reporting, and visualization services. Rules engines need to have built-in functions for math, string manipulation, dates, and so on for data transformation and provide the capability to filter data before routing to other services for ML and analytics.

- **Device Shadow** — This enables applications to interact with devices even when they are offline and help to understand and control the status of your device at any time. Device Shadow should represent the device state by maintaining the last known state for offline devices, such as *the last known color of the light bulb is red*. Device Shadow should make real-time state changes based on action from the application and control devices via changes of state, for example, changing the light bulb's color to blue. Once a device's connectivity gets established, it automatically synchronizes.

- **Device registry** — This enables automatic device registration and helps to manage them. A device registry defines and catalogs devices for easy use by performing simple searches such as *which devices were made in 2016?*, or by defining thing types; for example, BMW and Audi are of the *Car* thing type to enable standardization of attributes and policies across devices. To simplify further, you can define groups such as sensors in a wind turbine to enable simpler management for running jobs and setting policies. It is better to use a managed IoT platform such as AWS IoT Core, which provides all of the above services. AWS IoT Core allows the secure connection of any number of devices to the cloud and other devices without requiring you to provision servers. You can route, process, and act upon data from connected devices and enable your applications to interact with devices even when they are offline. IoT Core provides AWS services to reason on top of the data through analytics, AI, and ML as part of cloud ecosystems.

- **AWS IoT Device Management (DM)** helps to register, organize, monitor, and remotely manage a growing fleet of connected devices. It registers many devices using bulk registration, organizes devices into groups, performs OTA firmware updates, and facilitates end-to-end management of all IoT devices with a fully managed web application.

- **AWS IoT Device Defender (DD)** is a fully managed IoT security service that facilitates the securing of a fleet of connected devices on an ongoing basis. It monitors IoT resources associated with appliances and the entire device fleet for abnormal behavior that might indicate a potential security issue. Device Defender sends alerts if something doesn't look right, such as traffic from devices to an unauthorized IP address or spikes in outbound traffic that might indicate that a device is participating in a DDoS attack. Finally, through its integration with IoT Device Management, IoT Device Defender lets you take corrective action to secure your devices.

AWS provides IoT Core, Device Managment , and Device Defender, collectively known as IoT connectivity and control services, which provide the ability to connect, manage, and secure devices. As you are collecting data from millions of IoT devices, getting insights from your data becomes very important. Let's learn more details about techniques for performing analytics on IoT data.

Performing analytics on IoT data

IoT data is challenging to analyze because it isn't the highly structured data usually processed by analytics tools designed for business intelligence and web analytics. Instead, IoT data comes from sensors attached to moving machinery with intermittent connections, controllers with poor Wi-Fi or wireless coverage, or lots of other places where signals get lost or weakened. The data from these devices can frequently have significant gaps and false readings. Also, IoT data is often only meaningful in the context of other data from external sources. For example, farmers need to enrich humidity sensor data with expected rainfall on the field to determine when to water their crops.

The incoming real-world IoT data needs to be enriched by combining it with other data such as time, location, and additional information, which creates challenges for businesses. To make their applications perform well, they frequently need to design custom logic to clean false readings, fill in gaps in the data, and enrich it with contextual information. They also need to store the process data appropriately before even crunching the data for their application. This requires custom code that takes time to build, test, and maintain and adds processing costs to IoT applications.

You can see that there are a lot of common data management and analytics tasks across IoT applications, including processing and enriching data, provisioning and partitioning databases, and writing complex queries. All data processing needs to be constantly developed as devices evolve, fleet sizes change, and new analytics requirements emerge. A company like C3 IoT provides sophisticated analytics, and cloud vendors such as AWS have created services such as **AWS IoT Analytics** to perform IoT data analysis at scale.

AWS IoT Analytics is a managed service that collects, pre-processes, enriches, stores, analyzes, and visualizes IoT device data at scale. It allows you to gather only the data you want to store and convert raw data to meaningful information.

Most of the IoT data is timestamp bound, so AWS IoT Analytics stores device data in a time series data store for analysis to get a deeper insight into the health and performance of assets and visualize your IoT datasets.

Overall, to design your IoT architecture, you should choose the right device software for your IoT project based on your hardware choice, software environment, and use case. If you employ highly constrained devices, typically, microcontrollers recommend using FreeRTOS and the IoT Device SDK. You can use AWS IoT Greengrass if you have microprocessor-powered IoT devices. Greengrass accelerates your device applications' development using pre-built processing and connectivity capabilities and remotely deploys and manages device software at the edge.

Once you are ready with your device, you can use AWS IoT Core, Device Management, and Device Defender to connect and control your device and perform data insights on top of collected data using AWS IoT data analytics. As the cloud is becoming a go-to place for data collection and analytics on a large scale, we will take examples from IoT services offered by one of the leading cloud providers, Amazon Web Services. Now, let's learn more about IoT in the cloud.

IoT in the cloud

Because IoT solutions can be complex and multidimensional, you need to remove the complexity of implementing IoT in the business and securely help customers connect any number of devices to the central server. When it comes to IoT, cloud providers have managed service offerings to achieve scalability to millions of devices. Some of the most popular cloud IoT platforms are Google Cloud IoT, AWS IoT Core, Azure IoT Hub, IBM Watson IoT, and Oracle IoT. Let's look into AWS IoT offerings to understand the workings of IoT systems, and the other cloud providers such as GCP and Azure, who have IoT offerings along the same lines.

The AWS cloud helps in processing and acting upon device data and reading and setting device states at any time. AWS provides the infrastructure to scale as needed, so organizations can gain insights into their IoT data, build IoT applications and services that better serve their customers, and help move their businesses toward full IoT exploitation.

The following diagram illustrates the components of AWS IoT:

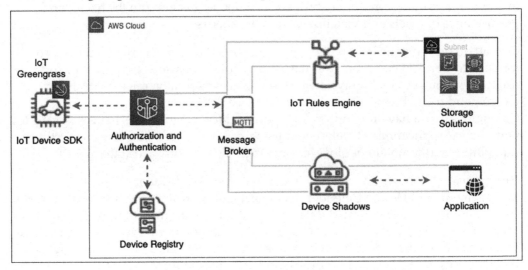

Figure 15.3: IoT architecture on an AWS platform

The following are the details of each IoT component and how they are connected in the preceding diagram:

- **IoT Greengrass**: AWS IoT Greengrass is installed on edge devices and helps to send IoT messages to the AWS cloud.

- **The IoT Device SDK**: The AWS IoT Device SDK helps to connect IoT devices to your application. The IoT Device SDK provides an API to connect and authenticate devices to the application. It helps to exchange messages between devices and AWS IoT cloud services using the MQTT or HTTP protocols. The IoT Device SDK supports C, Arduino, and JavaScript.

- **Authentication and authorization**: AWS IoT facilitates mutual authentication and encryption to exchange data with only authorized devices. AWS IoT uses authentication mechanisms such as SigV4 and X.509 certificates. You can attach authentication to all connected devices by attaching a certificate and handling authorization remotely.

- **IoT message broker**: The message broker supports the MQTT and HTTP protocols and establishes secure communication between IoT devices and cloud services such as the AWS IoT rules engine, Device Shadow, and other AWS services.

- **The IoT rules engine**: The IoT rules engine helps to manage data pipelines for IoT data processing and analytics. The rules engine looks at IoT data to perform streaming analytics and connect to other AWS storage services such as Amazon S3, DynamoDB, and Elasticsearch.

- **Device Shadow service**: The Device Shadow service helps you maintain a device's status when it is offline due to the loss of network connectivity in a remote area. As soon as the device comes online, it can resume its state from Device Shadow. Any application connected to the device can continue working by reading data from the shadow using a RESTful API.

- **Device registry**: The device registry helps identify IoT devices and helps to manage millions of devices at scale. The registry stores device metadata such as the version, manufacturer, and reading method (Fahrenheit versus Celsius, for example).

As of now, you are familiar with IoT service offerings in the cloud. As IoT is becoming very common in the manufacturing industry for handling machine data and optimizing production, it developed the concept of **Industrial IoT (IIoT)**. Let's learn more about this now.

Building an industrial IoT solution

Industrial customers seek to gain insights into their industrial data and achieve outcomes such as lower energy costs, detecting and fixing equipment issues, spotting inefficiencies in manufacturing lines, improving product quality, and improving production output. These customers are looking for visibility into **operational technology (OT)** data from machines and **product life cycles (PLCs)** systems for performing **Root Cause Analysis (RCA)** when a production line or a machine goes down. Furthermore, IoT improves production throughput without compromising product quality by understanding micro-stoppages of machinery in real time.

Data collection and organization across multiple sources, sites, or factories are challenging to build and maintain. Organizations need a consistent representation of all their assets that can be easily shared with users and used to build applications, at a plant, across plants, and at a company level. Data collected and organized using on-premises servers is isolated to one plant. Most data collected on-premises is never analyzed and thrown away due to a lack of open and accessible data.

The best practice is to extract data from databases commonly found in industrial facilities, transfer it to the centralized storage in the data center or cloud, and structure it to be easily searchable by users and applications. On top of that data, you can derive common industrial performance metrics such as **Overall Equipment Efficiency (OEE)**, monitor operations across multiple industrial facilities, and build applications to analyze industrial equipment data, prevent costly equipment issues, and reduce gaps in production. To design industrial IoT architecture, you need to perform the following steps:

- Ingest data from industrial equipment, data servers, and historian databases

- Collect, organize, and analyze industrial data at scale
- Read data from onsite equipment using industrial protocols and standards such as OPC-UA, Modbus, and Ethernet/IP
- Create visual representations of physical assets, process equipment data streams, and compute industrial performance metrics
- Access local dashboards to view real-time and historical equipment data, even when temporarily disconnected from the internet
- Consume asset data to create local or cloud applications that optimize factory output quality, maximize asset utilization, and identify equipment maintenance issues

To address the growing need for IIOT, a leading cloud provider such as AWS provides a managed service, **AWS IoT SiteWise**, which collects data from the plant floor with a local gateway, structures and labels that data, and generates real-time KPIs and metrics to make better data-driven decisions.

Data is collected from equipment across all sites during ingestion and sent to AWS IoT SiteWise from AWS IoT Core. Then it creates model assets that are virtual representations of physical assets. SiteWise helps to digitize, contextualize, and model entire production environments without customers having to maintain their infrastructure. Customers can represent complex equipment hierarchies using rich information modeling.

Event management is critical for detecting changes across complex industrial systems. There is a need to continuously monitor data from your equipment to identify their state, detect changes, and trigger the appropriate responses when changes occur. AWS provides AWS IoT Events, which builds simple logic to evaluate incoming telemetry data to detect stateful changes in equipment or a process. It detects events from data across thousands of sensors and triggers responses to optimize operations. Instead of relying on the manual inspection of parts, machines, or products, it can notify maintenance teams of issues more quickly or instruct a device to shut down. For example, you could alert a technical support rep when equipment runs abnormally or apply the fix.

Because you configure AWS IoT Events using logical expressions rather than complex code, adjusting to changes such as the addition of new equipment is easy. You can scale across thousands of devices in your fleet. AWS IoT Events integrates with other AWS services that handle and analyze IoT data, such as AWS IoT Core and AWS IoT Analytics. Customers can identify and ingest the data they need to evaluate right from the AWS IoT Events console. IoT Events can trigger actions in AWS Lambda, SQS, SNS, Kinesis Firehose, IoT Core, and so on. Let's look at an IIoT reference architecture to bring all pieces together.

Connected Factory IoT architecture

The **Connected Factory (CF)** solution is designed to bring together capabilities to transform manufacturing operations. CF makes it easy for customers to unblock data from their legacy systems, visualize the data in near real time, perform deeper analytics to optimize operations, and improve productivity and asset availability. The key focus for the CF offering is to commoditize industrial data collection and develop repeatability. Let's look at the following diagram, which demonstrates IoT architecture for implementing connected factory solutions on the AWS cloud platform.

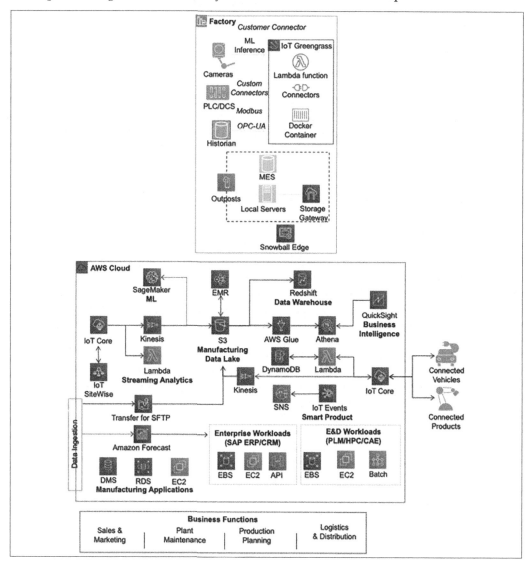

Figure 15.4: Connected Factory architecture in the AWS cloud

As shown in the preceding diagram, AWS IoT Greengrass is deployed at the edge of the factory floor to collect equipment data and other data ingested from servers at the facility. Data lands in the AWS cloud through IoT Core, and IoT SiteWide helps to build a model of physical devices. Data from various facilities is stored in Amazon S3 to build a manufacturing data lake that can be further loaded in Redshift for data warehousing and processed through the ETL pipeline using AWS Glue and ad hoc queries performed using Amazon Athena. Finally, you can use QuickSight to visualize data for business users.

Streaming data is transformed and processed through Amazon Kinesis and provides input back to product equipment or shipment information to the vehicle. You can also see ML components perform production forecasting and post that data in ERP and PLM systems to optimize production efficiency. Amazon SageMaker performs ML at the edge to understand and alert on equipment health to reduce downtime.

When it comes to training staff on equipment and creating a simulation, adding a visualization layer makes sense. This is now possible with the availability of **AR/ VR (Augmented Reality/Virtual Reality)**. That's where digital twins come into the picture. Let's learn more details about digital twins.

Implementing a digital twin

A digital twin is a digital replica of a physical machine. In a digital twin, you build a virtual representation of the machine using AR/VR to visualize a real-time data overlay. It helps to see real-time operational and health data, combined with machine learning; you can draw insights from real-world behavior such as performing a proactive maintenance model. A digital twin can be handy for simulating what-if scenarios to determine the optimum KPI for the machine, and building immersive education and training to handle the equipment.

A digital twin continuously collects real-time data using IoT and can control the machine's operation from a digital replica. It provides an immersive experience of the living model of a machine and helps with early warning, prediction, and optimization. A digital twin performs the following tasks, as shown in the following diagram:

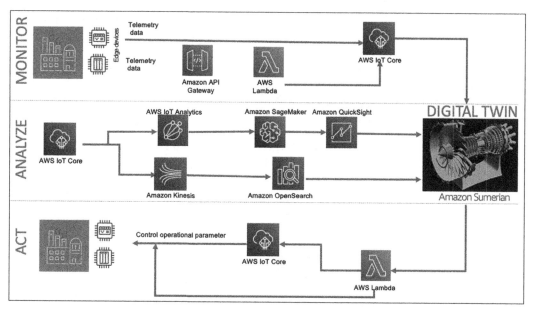

Figure 15.5: Modeling the mind of the machine with a digital twin

As shown in the preceding diagram, a digital twin manages a machine by:

- **Monitoring**: The digital twin collects and analyzes the data by replicating a digital copy in the virtual world. Machine telemetry data can come from sensors ingested by the cloud, such as AWS, using AWS IoT Core. The factory floor data can be ingested by building an API wrapper around the on-premises applications.

- **Analyzing**: To build a digital replica, you can use popular AR/VR technology such as Microsoft HoloLens, Amazon Sumerian, or Oculus. You can create a data overlay on top of the digital replica to show how data flows from various sensors. Further analytics can be performed using AWS IoT Analytics. To build data visualization and search capabilities, you can use Amazon OpenSearch and QuickSight. The digital twin can be controlled over voice using AI-powered services such as Amazon Alexa. ML capability can be implemented using Amazon SageMaker to train, tune, and deploy the ML model.

- **Acting**: As you get data insights and predictions, you can take the required action by sending messages back to the operations team. You can use AWS IoT Events and AWS Lambda to notify operational applications by creating automated maintenance tickets for staff on the ground. AWS IoT Core can take your message and apply direct operations to the machine. If a cooling fan is running abnormally or getting hotter than expected, you can stop the machine directly from the digital twin.

Let's take a reference architecture of a digital twin for an aircraft jet engine, as shown in the following diagram. Here, you collect engine temperature and speed data in real time using IoT sensors and show data overlays in a digital engine replica to gain insights and take action.

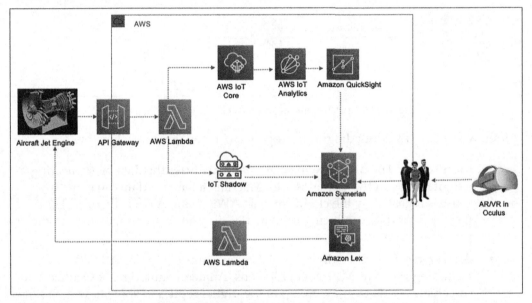

Figure 15.6: Digital twin architecture for an aircraft jet engine

As shown in the preceding diagram, temperature and engine speed data were sent from a jet engine to the AWS cloud through IoT Core. AWS IoT Analytics performed data processing to collect insights into the sensor data collected and visualized information in the Amazon QuickSight dashboard. The jet engine's current state is maintained using Device Shadow, so if sensors go offline, you can still perform simulations. Here, a jet engine digital replica was created using the Amazon Sumerian virtual reality platform and deployed in Oculus. Using the Amazon Lex AI service, you can start/stop the actual engine with your voice or a message.

IoT is a very vast topic that warrants an entire book. In this chapter, you learned about the various components of IoT architecture that have industrial uses.

Summary

There are millions of small devices connected to the internet, referred to collectively as the IoT. In this chapter, you learned about IoT and the components of IoT architecture. IoT is all about processing unstructured telemetry data from sensors and machines in high volumes and at speed. To handle such data, you need to have a scalable system, and you learned about IoT in the cloud with examples from AWS IoT services.

Devices are one of the central points when it comes to building IoT solutions. You learned about two major types of device software, including an MCU and an MPU, and methods to ingest these devices' data. You learned about the various techniques for controlling IoT devices, including device authentication, a device registry, and device management at scale, as well as the AWS IoT Device Management service. Security is the most pressing job, and it applies to IoT devices as well; you learned about various mechanisms for managing and securing IoT devices with AWS IoT Device Defender.

Once you collect and store data, you need to transform data to get insights into that data and visualize your business requirements. You learned about the various components available in the cloud to collect, process, and analyze IoT data to produce meaningful insights. Industrial IoT is becoming very popular for optimizing production and reducing operational downtime. You learned about IIoT and how AWS IoT SiteWide helps to address IIoT operations at scale. You also learned about Connect Factory IoT architecture and its functioning in detail.

Combining AR/VR technology with IoT provides an immersive experience. You learned about the digital twin concept, where a virtual replica of a physical machine gets created with real-time data overlay. You learned about a jet engine digital twin architecture with different components to monitor, analyze, and act using the digital twin model.

Until now, we have relied on supercomputers with significant numbers of GPUs and CPUs to solve the majority of problems. But with the increased use of technology, supercomputers are becoming slow in cases where millions and billions of combinations are required to solve a problem in complex use cases such as molecular analysis and building a financial risk model. For such kinds of use cases, quantum computing may be the ideal technology. We are still in the early stages of the quantum evolution, but organizations have started experimenting with it. In the next chapter you will learn about quantum computing, its use cases, and the options available.

Join our book's Discord space

Join the book's Discord workspace for a monthly *Ask me Anything* session with the authors: `https://packt.link/SAHandbook`

16

Quantum Computing

Quantum technologies are a rapidly growing and interdisciplinary field of science and engineering. Until now, we've depended upon supercomputers to solve most problems, but **quantum computing** (**QC**) accelerates complex calculations exponentially, resulting in a very powerful supercomputer. As per quantum physics, a *quantum* is the smallest unit of any physical property and refers to the properties of atomic particles, such as electrons, neutrinos, and photons. QC can solve computational problems beyond classical computers' reach by utilizing the laws of quantum mechanics to process information in new ways.

QC is a new paradigm in computing that speeds up solutions to complex problems, giving not 10x performance improvement but 10^x. This approach to computing could transform chemical engineering, material science, drug discovery, financial portfolio optimization, and machine learning.

QC is still in the research stage, and it may take some years before it gets commercialized. Quantum technology is complex but, in this chapter, you will learn QC concepts in a simplified way by exploring the following topics:

- The building blocks of quantum computers
- The working mechanism of quantum computers
- Quantum gates
- Quantum circuits
- Types of quantum computers
- Quantum computing in the cloud

By the end of this chapter, you will understand the foundations of QC. You will know about the workings of quantum computers, including their building blocks, types, and various use cases. You will also learn about the logic behind quantum algorithms, such as quantum gates and circuits, and how quantum computers work behind the scenes.

The building blocks of quantum computers

The basic building block of a quantum computer is the **qubit**. Qubits in QC are similar to bits in classical computing, but they behave very differently. Let's learn more about qubits.

Qubits

Classical bits can hold only a position of 0 or 1, but qubits can hold positions between 0 and 1, and multiple positions at once. Qubits are quantum systems that scientists and engineers can control. Some examples of qubits are atoms, molecules, and photons.

Quantum states are represented by the little flags ")", called **Dirac notation**. A single classical bit is denoted by 0 or 1, while a single quantum bit (qubit) is denoted by complex linear combinations of $|0\rangle$ and $|1\rangle$. Qubits are two-dimensional vectors with complex coefficients, as shown below:

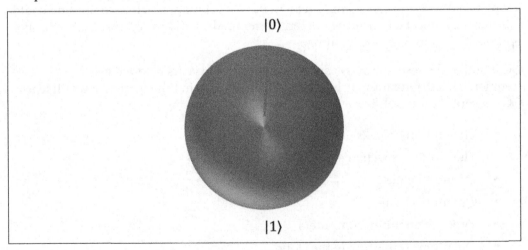

Figure 16.1: Bloch sphere – abstract representation of a qubit

In the preceding diagram, a qubit is represented using a **Bloch sphere**. A Bloch sphere is a representation of the pure state space of a qubit, named after the physicist Felix Bloch. The blue arrow indicates the state of the qubit at any given time. You can see two states represented in the diagram with $|0\rangle$ and $|1\rangle$. When represented as two-dimensional vectors, the values of $|0\rangle$ and $|1\rangle$ are:

$$|0\rangle = \begin{pmatrix} 1 \\ 0 \end{pmatrix} \qquad |1\rangle = \begin{pmatrix} 0 \\ 1 \end{pmatrix}$$

The possible states of two qubits can be basis vectors $|00\rangle, |01\rangle, |10\rangle, |11\rangle$, in addition to superpositions, as opposed to the possible states of two classical bits, which are 00 or 01 or 10 or 11.

Quantum computers utilize the unique behavior of quantum physics, such as superposition and entanglement. Let's understand these concepts.

Superposition

To simplify, let's take an example of classical fair coin-tossing to understand the various concepts of QC. Tossing a coin gives you a head or a tail with a 50-50 chance, as with a classical computer. 1 bit has two possible values—we can assume heads being 1 and tails being 0. Quantum computers use qubits to process information, and 1 qubit represents one quantum state, which could be any state while a coin is being tossed. Imagine if you were able to look at a coin and see both heads and tails simultaneously, as well as every state in between: the coin would be in superposition.

A qubit itself isn't very useful. However, we can create vast computational spaces by creating many spaces and connecting them in a state called superposition. In superposition, quantum particles represent a combination of all possible states. They fluctuate until they're observed and measured. In this case, if you flip 50 coins simultaneously, a qubit can be in a superposition of heads and tails, and 50 qubits can be in any superposition of 2^{50} states. Now you can see that a small quantum computer with just 50 qubits can store one million billion complex numbers derived from $2^{50} \sim 1,000,000,000,000,000$.

Now that you have learned about qubits, let's see how two qubits work together through quantum entanglement.

Entanglement

Entanglement is the ability of quantum particles to correlate with each other. Quantum computers can calculate exponentially more information and solve more complicated problems by entangling more qubits in a system. Entangled qubits form a single system and, by relating to each other, draw a correlation and get an outcome. You can use the measurements from one qubit to draw conclusions about the others.

Quantum entanglement allows qubits, which behave randomly, to be perfectly correlated with each other. Let's understand entangling from a programming point of view in the table below by comparing the properties of classical bits to qubits.

	Classical Computer: Copying X Bit to Y Bit	**Quantum Computer: Entangling X Qubit and Y Qubit**
Correlation	X bit and Y bit are uncorrelated after copying	X qubit and Y qubit correlate; measuring X affects Y instantaneously
Referencing	May assign by reference on same data so X bit and Y bit may point to the same data	Entangled qubits exist individually, but they correlate
Reversibility	It's irreversible—the reverse of an operation like copying back X to Y would destroy Y	It's reversible—the entangled qubits X and Y can be unentangled
Correction	For error correction, bits can be restored from a previous copy	Quantum error correction uses many entangled qubits

As you can see in the above table, entangling is not copying. Using quantum algorithms and quantum entanglement, specific complex problems can be solved more efficiently than with classical computers as you can relate multiple qubits to draw a conclusion and utilize them to store large values. An array of qubits can use superposition to represent 2^64 possible values at a time, which allows a quantum computer to solve complex problems that are impossible for standard computers.

Now you understand the building blocks of QC. Let's explore more of their working mechanism and what makes them so fast.

The working mechanism of quantum computers

You learned about qubits in the previous section. Now, to build quantum computers, physical qubits are built in a lab, and the quantum computer has an area that houses the qubits.

The unit that houses the qubits is kept at a temperature just above absolute zero to maximize the qubits' coherence and reduce interference. The low temperature helps to stabilize and control the qubits. A vacuum chamber can also be used to help minimize vibrations and stabilize the qubits. Signals can be sent to the qubits by using various methods, including microwaves, lasers, and voltage.

You must be wondering how quantum computers run so fast. A quantum computer runs so fast because it tries all answers to a problem in parallel. Is that true? Well, not really, not in the sense that multiple calculations are all happening in parallel universes. That said, qubits can hold 0 and 1 values at the same time using superposition, and let them influence each other with entanglement. This opens up new possibilities for building clever quantum algorithms to speed up computation.

To make quantum computers faster, one promising quantum algorithm that's used is called Grover's search. Suppose you need to find one item from a list of N items. On a classical computer, you'd have to check N/2 items on average, and in the worst case, you would need to check all N items. Using Grover's search on a quantum computer, you can find the item after checking roughly √N of them. This represents a remarkable increase in processing efficiency and time saved. For example, if you wanted to find one item in a list of 1 trillion, and each item took 1 microsecond to check, on a classical supercomputer the search might take over a week, but a quantum computer accomplishes the same task in a matter of seconds.

Let's use the analogy of making music. When musicians play beautiful music, they make it by styling the sound of a musical chord, the same way quantum computers work by manipulating the amplitudes of the state vector. To write a song, you figure out what notes you need and put them together into a musical arrangement; in the same way, to program a quantum computer, you arrange qubits into a quantum circuit and run the circuit. Finally, when you produce music, your band comes together and plays the musical instruments in a way that sounds good; in the same way, you set quantum circuits so that the answer given is the most probable one.

Compared to classical computers, quantum computers can create vast multidimensional spaces to represent very large problems. Quantum algorithms then find solutions in this space and translate them back into forms we can use and understand. Due to superposition, quantum interference in the intrinsic behavior of a qubit can influence the probability of it collapsing. Quantum computers are designed and built to reduce noise as much as possible and ensure the most accurate results. Quantum logic is built by various types of logical gates. Let's learn more details about building quantum logic.

Quantum gates

Whether classical or quantum, a logic gate is any physical structure or system that takes a set of binary inputs (1s and 0s or spin-up/spin-down electrons) and gives a single binary output: a 1 (that is, a spin-up electron), or one of two states of superposition. What governs the outcome is a *Boolean function*. You can think of a Boolean function as a rule for responding to Yes/No questions. The gates are combined into circuits and the circuits are combined into CPUs or other computational components.

To understand gates better, let's look at the Bloch sphere in 3D space, which represents the direction of a quantum particle, such as an electron's spin, along a corresponding axis. You learned about the Bloch sphere in the previous topic, *The building blocks of quantum computers*.

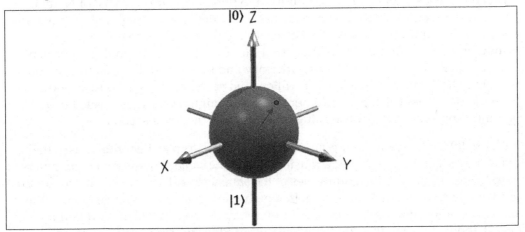

Figure 16.2: 3D representation of an electron's spin along with its axes

The preceding diagram represents a qubit in 3D space; qubits can be placed in a spin-up state along the X, Y, and Z axis using quantum gates. Quantum gates operate on qubits, as opposed to classical gates operating on 0 or 1 bits, which makes it possible for quantum gates to use *superposition* (other states between 0 and 1) and *entanglement (relating two qubits to drive an outcome)*.

Many types of gates are utilized to build a quantum circuit, and the simplest one is the single-qubit Pauli gate. Let's learn more about the Pauli gate.

Pauli gates

The Pauli gate is named after Wolfgang Pauli, and is based on the better-known Pauli matrices.

Pauli gates are very useful for calculating changes to the spin of a single electron. Today's quantum gates use electron spin as the favored property for a qubit. Pauli gates act on only one qubit at a time. This translates to simple 2 x 2 matrices with only 4 elements apiece. Pauli gates come in three types: Pauli-X, Pauli-Y, and Pauli-Z.

Pauli-X Gate: A Pauli-X gate can be related to a classical NOT gate and is often called *the quantum NOT* gate. The following denotes it:

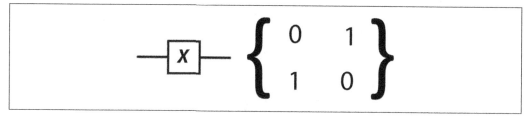

Figure 16.3: Pauli-X gate

Now, If you take a linear state of a single qubit vector and pass it through a Pauli-X gate, it will flip to another side, for instance, from $|0\rangle$ to $|1\rangle$ and vice versa.

Pauli-Y Gate: This looks a lot like the X-gate, but with i (square root of -1) in place of the lower-left 1 and negative i in the upper-right corner. The following denotes it:

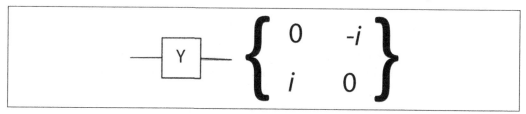

Figure 16.4: Pauli-Y gate

When a qubit in the form of an electron passes through a Y-gate, it spins to the Y axis in 3D space.

Pauli-Z Gate: This looks kind of like a mirror image of the X-gate, but with a negative sign in the lower right. The following denotes it:

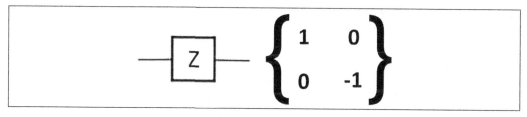

Figure 16.5: Pauli-Z gate

When a qubit in the form of an electron passes through a Z-gate, it flips to the Z axis in 3D space.

The Y-gate and the Z-gate also change the spin of a qubit electron. But let's look at another very important gate, Hadamard, which you will see in any quantum circuit.

The Hadamard gate

Hadamard is also known as the H-gate, and it shows up everywhere in QC. The Hadamard gate has the *quantum* capacity to transform a definite quantum state of a qubit, such as a superposition of *both* spin-up and spin-down simultaneously. The following denotes it:

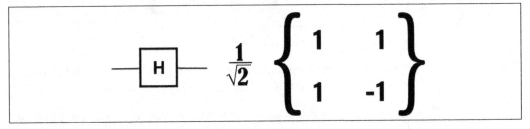

Figure 16.6: Hadamard gate

Once you send an electron through an H-gate, it will become like a coin in mid-air; with 50/50 odds, it will end up heads or tails when it lands. The H-gate is very useful for performing the initial computation in a quantum program as it transforms *initialized* qubits back into their natural fluid state to leverage their full quantum powers. An H-gate maps X→Z and Z→X as it operates between two states simultaneously, so an H-gate is required to make superpositions.

There are several more quantum gates. Let's explore some popular gates.

Other quantum gates

There are many other quantum gates you're bound to use. While some gates operate on single qubits, others operate on several qubits at a time. Let's look at some more gates that operate on a single qubit, which can be visualized as transformations around a Bloch sphere:

- **X-Gate**: Also referred to as a flip-bit, this performs π rotation around the X axis, changing Z→-Z and back again if done twice.

- **Z-Gate**: Also referred to as a phase-flip, this performs π rotation around the Z-axis, changing X→-X and back again if done twice.

- **S-Gate**: This performs $\pi/2$ rotation around the Z-axis and maps X→Y. This gate further extends the H-gate to make complex superpositions.

- **S'-Gate**: This is the inverse of the S-gate and maps X→-Y. It performs $-\pi/2$ rotation around the Z-axis.

- **T-Gate**: This performs $\pi/4$ rotation around the Z-axis.

- **T'-Gate**: This is the inverse of the T-gate and performs $-\pi/4$ rotation around the Z-axis.

Some of the other popular gates are the Toffoli gate, the Fredkin gate, the NOT-gate square root, the Deutsch gate, the swap gate (and the swap-gate square root), the Controlled-NOT gate (C-NOT), and other controlled gates. But we are not going to explore all the gates; we've covered the main ones above. You've learned about all the basic gates, so let's see how to put them together and build a quantum circuit.

Quantum circuits

Now you've learned about some of the fundamental quantum gates, so the next question is how to perform quantum logic. To build a quantum algorithm, you need to use well-controlled qubits for computing. Those qubits can interact and change states as desired. An algorithm is built by manipulating quantum states (vectors) using quantum gates (matrices). Let's look at the Boolean circuit in a classical computer built with three inputs.

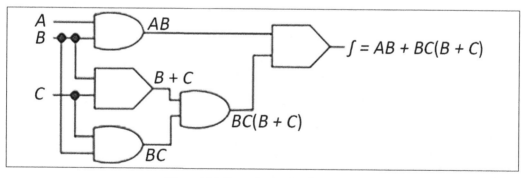

Figure 16.7: Operation in a Boolean circuit

In the preceding diagram, you have a combination of multiple Boolean gates where an AND gate is multiplying two inputs, resulting in A & B→AB and B & C→BC. Further, an OR gate is adding two inputs, resulting in B & C→B + C. You can see that by roping these gates in a circuit, an algorithm has been built.

That is the way classic computers work. Now, let's take a look at the quantum circuit in the following diagram, which you can compare with the above Boolean circuit:

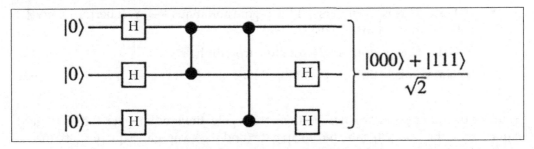

Diagram 16.8: Operation in a quantum circuit

In the preceding diagram, you pass three qubits with zero vector state. They pass through the H-gate and change the state to create a superposition over the course of some further steps (we're avoiding the details here, as it's beyond the scope of this chapter to explain the full complexities of quantum algorithms), resulting in one of two equally likely final measurement outcomes, [000] and [111], each over the square root of 2, as shown in *Figure 16.6*.

Basic quantum circuits consist of three basic modules:

1. **Initialize**: Prepare the initial state
2. **Execute**: Execute unitary gates on the qubits
3. **Measure**: Measure the qubits on some reference basis

Here, in the quantum circuit, the digital Boolean circuit problem is broken down into a sequence of a few basic building blocks: a set of universal gates mentioned in the previous section and an error correction process to achieve fault tolerance. There are growing numbers of quantum algorithms, such as:

- **Number theory**: Factoring, discrete log, subset-sum, and cryptanalysis
- **Optimization**: Constraint satisfaction, solving linear systems, solving ODEs, PDEs
- **Oracular**: Search, hidden subgroup, hidden shift, order finding
- **Simulation/approximation**: Knot invariants, QAOA, SDPs, direct simulation

We are not going to go into the details of algorithms as this is a very vast topic. These algorithms are generally use case-agnostic, and QC can be used in any application with one of many problems at its core. These algorithms will be helpful when we have a universal fault-tolerant quantum computer. In this section, we explained the basic building blocks of quantum computers to understand the future trends in the coming decade.

Quantum computers are at a very early stage and there is a lot to explore. You will only want to use such computers if your organization's problems require high-level calculations and the storage of large values beyond the limits of classical computers, such as calculating trillions of numbers at once.

You've looked at gate-based QC; another type of QC is available called quantum annealing. In **quantum annealing**, quantum operations are analog rather than gate-based digital operations. These are more complex and special-purpose optimization machines. Quantum annealing is used to encode a solution to an optimization problem by finding the ground state of a problem, or the zero-point energy of the system.

Let's get into the real world and see the types of quantum computer hardware that are available.

Types of quantum computers

As you learned in the previous section, there are two QC paradigms. The first is gate-based using quantum computers, with fewer, higher-quality qubits for general-purpose devices. Most quantum computers are gate-based, such as **Rigetti and IonQ**.

The second QC paradigm involves quantum annealers with many qubits built for special purposes. **D-Wave**-built quantum computers are based on quantum annealing. D-Wave provides quantum computers of up to 2,000 qubits. Let's look at some quantum computers based on the different types of particles used:

- **Trapped Ions**: The first quantum logic gate was demonstrated in 1995 using trapped atomic ions. It uses two internal states of ions, whose positions are controlled with electric fields in "ion traps" as their fundamental quantum element. The state of each ion can be changed using controlled microwave radiation. These pulses can be arranged to couple the states of two or more ions to create entanglement between the ions.

- **Rydberg Atoms**: This is similar to trapped-ions QC, but neutral atoms are used instead of charged ions for the qubits. Laser tweezers are used to keep the particles in place instead of electric fields. As with trapped-ions qubits, optical and microwave pulses are used for qubit manipulation. What makes this different compared to trapped ions is its potential for building multidimensional arrays.

- **Superconducting Qubits**: This is considered the forefront of qubit modalities for digital quantum computation and quantum annealing. Microwave radiation is used to manipulate the state.

Adjacent quantum particles can be electronically coupled together to create entangled states. They exhibit quantized energy levels due to quantized states of electronic charge or magnetic flux, for example.

As QC gains more traction, public cloud providers such as AWS, Google, Microsoft Azure, and IBM have started providing easy access to quantum computers through their cloud platforms. Let's learn about some real-life use cases where QC will be useful.

Quantum computing in real life

Quantum computers are collections of specialized quantum systems that can be systematically controlled over a period of time to perform a desired task. QC is not a replacement for current computers and may not solve problems where you don't need complex calculations. As an analogy, you can see light bulbs versus candlelight as equivalent to QC versus current computers. It doesn't matter how much advancement you put into candles; you cannot convert candles into light bulbs — they are entirely different technologies.

Let's take an example of choosing the seating arrangements for 15 people. At first glance, it may look straightforward, but if you calculate, there are more than 1.3 trillion (factorial of 15) possible ways to seat just 15 people. Imagine if you needed to solve this problem for 100 people: you would run out of memory and compute. Classical supercomputers don't have the working memory to hold the countless combinations of real-world problems. The way they are designed means they would take a long time, analyzing each combination one after another.

In the same vein, think about other real-world problems, like if Amazon wants to optimize drivers' routes across 100 cities to find the optimal route for quick deliveries. Another use case would be if a pharma company wants to build a drug repurposing platform by simulating molecules to understand drug interactions better. These problems are hard to solve using classical computer technology, due to the high number of calculations required.

Some other real-time use cases that can be solved by QC include:

- **Optimization**: Optimization can be a very complex process, involving finding the right solution among millions and billions of combinations. You can optimize your product quality, cost, and efficiency. Solving complex optimization through quantum algorithms helps us better manage complex problems, such as airplane gate assignment, package deliveries, traffic control, and energy storage.

- **Machine learning**: Machine learning is already helping business and science even with classical computers. However, training machine learning models has a relatively high cost, which has hindered the field's scope and capacity for development. Quantum computers can help speed up progress in this area with faster training and larger amounts of data.

- **Internet searches**: Internet searching is another area where you need to optimize and index trillions of pieces of information. QC can help to make searching faster for high or even unlimited amounts of data.

- **Simulation**: Quantum computers work exceptionally well for modeling other systems in their computation. They can handle the complex systems that would overwhelm classical computers. Examples of quantum systems that we can model include drug simulation, photosynthesis, superconductivity, and complex molecular formations.

- **Cryptography**: Classical cryptography using RSA depends upon the intractability of integer factorization or discrete logarithms. Encryption and decryption problems can be solved more efficiently using quantum computers.

QC works very differently to classical computers. As you now understand some QC use cases, let's learn more details about the building blocks of quantum computers.

Quantum computing in the cloud

Like any other technology, public cloud providers facilitate easy access to QC. Procuring quantum computers is very costly, and it's still at the very initial stage where you may not see a return on your investment in the near term. But you don't want to miss the bus; you want to get your foot in the door with this upcoming technology that has the potential to change the world as we see it today. The public cloud is the perfect place to access quantum computers and try out your use case.

Amazon Web Services provides a QC service called Amazon Braket. AWS doesn't have quantum computers, but they provide access to other gate-based and annealing-based quantum computers through their platform. AWS provides access to D-Wave's Advantage and 2,000 qubit computers, IonQ, and Rigetti quantum computers through their Braket platform. Amazon Braket provides a hardware-agnostic quantum platform with scalable circuit simulators in the AWS Cloud and end-to-end integration with AWS Cloud services. Similarly, Azure Quantum also operates through a partner network.

Google Quantum AI provides access to superconductor-based quantum computers based on the Sycamore processor with 54 qubits. It has a single qubit and double qubit-based circuit. Google provides a Python framework called Cirq to build and optimize quantum circuits. Their Weber quantum computer is 53 qubits.

IBM's quantum computer is based on superconductors. IBM uses superfluids to chill their superconductors to about a hundredth of a degree Celsius above absolute zero. After electrons are put through the superconductors, they pair up into something called Cooper pairs, which quantum tunnel through something called a Josephson junction. These are superconducting qubits. By firing photons at a qubit, we can control its behavior and get it to hold, change, and read out information. IBM creates vast computational spaces using programmable gates by creating many qubits and connecting them in a superposition state. Finally, quantum entanglement allows qubits, which behave randomly, to be perfectly correlated with each other. Using quantum algorithms that exploit quantum entanglement, specific complex problems can be solved more efficiently than on classical computers.

QC is a very complex and vast topic. We are still scratching the surface right now, and there are many more things to come in the future. It may take another decade to realize the full potential of quantum computers and build robust, fault-tolerant quantum computers. However, this chapter should have given you an idea of this potential next technological revolution and the possibilities of solving complex future problems that looked impossible until now, like space travel and human genome decoding.

Summary

QC has a lot of potential to solve complex problems that even the most powerful supercomputers cannot solve. Now the world has started to build quantum computers and algorithms, yet we are just scratching the surface, and it may take another 5 to 10 years before we start realizing the commercial value.

In this chapter, you learned about QC and some real-life use cases where QC can be advantageous. QC is not the answer to every problem, and it is only applicable to complex calculations where classical computers won't work.

You learned about the key building block of the quantum computer, the qubit, and how multiple qubits work together in a state of superposition and entanglement to solve a complex problem. You learned about the working mechanism of the quantum computer and understood why they are faster than classical computers.

To perform operations on qubits, you learned about QC gates, such as Pauli and Hadamard gates, which apply to single qubits, and other gates. You also learned about quantum annealing, which is a different paradigm based on analog rather than digital gates. Further more, you put together these gates and understood how QC circuits work compared to classical Boolean circuits.

Finally, you learned about various types of quantum computers and the technology behind them.

You also learned about quantum computer providers such as D-Wave, Rigetti, and IonQ. You learned about the Amazon Braket platform, which provides easy access to multiple quantum computers in a pay-as-you-go model. You learned about working on IBM quantum computers and Google quantum processors.

While, in this chapter, we looked far into the future, many legacy workload enterprises are working to modernize. With time, organizations tend to accumulate technology debt, and many legacy applications are sitting in the data center, creating costs and consuming resources. In the next chapter, you will learn about legacy application transformation and modernization. You will learn about the challenges with legacy systems and the techniques used to modernize them.

Join our book's Discord space

Join the book's Discord workspace for a monthly *Ask me Anything* session with the authors: `https://packt.link/SAHandbook`

17

Rearchitecting Legacy Systems

Today's organizations are operating in a challenging environment. The pace of change is unprecedented. Regulators and institutions are imposing new reporting and security requirements, new technologies are disrupting consumers' expectations and perceptions, and the ecosystem is constantly evolving as new players enter the market. As a result, organizations are redefining their business models to provide the customer focus, agility, and technology they need to attract talent, be competitive, and grow.

Application modernization has become a critical component of these new business models to rapidly stand-up dev/test environments, experiment with new ideas, and then develop new products and services. In addition to eliminating the need to invest in expensive and cumbersome infrastructure, the new system enables innovation through the broad set of technologies it makes available.

Legacy systems are the applications that have been deployed in your data center for decades without undergoing many changes. In a fast-changing technology environment, these systems get outdated and are challenging to maintain. Legacy systems are defined by their age and their inability to meet growing business needs due to the underlying architecture and technology.

Often, large enterprises deal with legacy applications to run crucial day-to-day business tasks. These legacy systems are spread across industries such as healthcare, finance, transportation, manufacturing, and supply chain industries. Companies have to spend heavily on the maintenance and support of these systems, which warrants the need to architect legacy systems.

Rearchitecting and modernizing legacy applications helps organizations be more agile and innovative and optimizes cost and performance.

In this chapter, you will learn about challenges and issues with legacy applications and techniques to rearchitect them. Rewriting complex legacy applications may pose an additional risk of business disruption, so you will learn about refactoring applications or considering the option to migrate into a more flexible infrastructure. The following topics will be covered in this chapter:

- Learning the challenges of legacy systems
- Defining a strategy for system modernization
- Looking at legacy system modernization techniques
- Defining a cloud migration strategy for legacy systems
- Mainframe migration with the public cloud

By the end of the chapter, you will have learned about various challenges and modernization drivers for legacy systems. You will learn various strategies and techniques for the modernization of legacy systems. As the public cloud is becoming a go-to strategy for many organizations, you will also learn about the cloud migration of legacy systems.

Learning the challenges of legacy systems

A legacy application presents significant challenges for an organization. On the one hand, there are critical applications that an organization has been using for decades. On the other hand, legacy applications are holding back the organization's pace of innovation.

In a hugely competitive environment, end users are looking for the most modern, technologically advanced applications. All new features usually come with the latest software, and legacy applications limit your ability to add those features and benefit end users. The following diagram shows some significant challenges that organizations are facing with legacy systems:

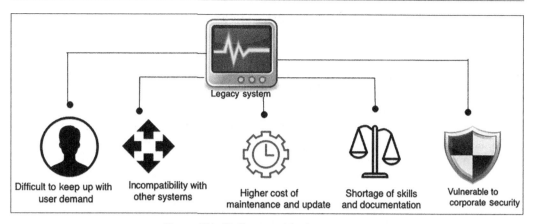

Figure 17.1: Challenges with a legacy system

At the top level, the CIO owns an application portfolio that represents the business processes of the organization. The portfolio of applications can be from hundreds to thousands depending upon the organizations' size. There are four discernable decision patterns in a large enterprise:

- **Chief Information Officer (CIO)**: The CIO owns the business applications decisions. Here, the decision is developed in-house to modernize an old app or prioritize the use of SaaS. Common priorities are consumer experience/ user experience and supply chain.

- **Chief Security Officer (CSO)**: As the CIO makes application-priority decisions, the transformation or modernization of those apps drives the modernization of the security model. This means a complete revisit of old on-premises approaches to security, a move away from hardware appliances, a move to the cloud, and working with third-party software vendors who have approaches for security for a cloud world.

- **VP of Big Data**: They receive data streams like never before. The possibilities are so much more flexible and scalable that many companies make big data their second driver for the use of the public cloud, after developer productivity.

- **VP of Infrastructure and Operations**: They have to go through substantial process and people skill changes, as this team has to adopt new tools, abandon old tools, and move to a mixed world of ITSM and DevSecOps for new modernized apps using new tools across serverless, containers, and SaaS. This team is modernizing their software tooling at a prolific pace but is also under pressure to reduce costs while being more agile.

Before we dive into the solution, it's important to understand the issues clearly. Let's explore the challenges of legacy systems in more depth to understand them better.

Difficulty in keeping up with user demand

Customer focus is the key to business success and being unable to keep up with the latest technology trends can harm a business significantly. You can take the example of Nokia, which used to lead the global mobile phone market. As smartphones came into play nearly a decade ago, Nokia still stuck with a legacy system, resulting in near bankruptcy. It was a similar story with Kodak—one of the largest businesses in the camera industry. Kodak was unable to move with digital innovation and adopt it into its systems, which resulted in Kodak becoming bankrupt in 2012. There are many such examples of large enterprises being unable to survive due to a lack of legacy modernization and innovation.

In the current climate of fast-changing technology and fierce competition, users are very demanding. Now, organizations have to change as per the user's terms, as they have multiple choices. As technology moves, the user moves with it and starts using the most recent and popular applications. Your competitors can jump ahead if they are providing new features that the user needs.

A legacy system also poses challenges for enterprise applications with an internal user base. An old system built on mainframes primarily uses the command line, which is not user-friendly in the digital age. In contrast, new-generation workers demand a more user-friendly approach to perform their routine tasks. However, you may face significant resistance from management, who may have been working with legacy systems for decades and are used to them.

The technology at the core of large enterprises is often outdated and comprises systems dating back decades. Organizations running their core systems on legacy, on-premises technology face severe challenges when it comes to enabling modern experiences for their customers. Many systems are the product of multiple mergers and acquisitions, resulting in fractured data siloes, excessive infrastructure costs, and slow development time. This creates inefficient processing and decision making, a lack of business agility, poor customer responsiveness, and high maintenance costs. Under these conditions, it's challenging for IT to meet the modern needs of internal stakeholders and customers.

Higher cost of maintenance and update

As legacy systems have been all set up and working for decades, they may look less expensive. But over time, the total cost of ownership turns out to be higher, as support and updates for old systems are usually more costly.

Often, those updates are not available out of the box, and lots of manual workarounds are required to maintain the system. Most legacy systems are not very automation-friendly, resulting in more human effort.

Legacy systems mostly have a large chunk of proprietary software, which results in significantly higher license fees. In addition to that, old software no longer receives support from providers, and buying additional support out of the life cycle could be very costly. On the other hand, modern systems mainly adopt open source technologies that drive the cost down. The operational outage from a legacy system can take more time and drive up operating expenses. People with the skill set to maintain legacy systems (such as DB2, COBOL, Fortran, Delphi, and Perl) are hard to find, increasing hiring costs and system risk significantly.

Legacy systems are pretty significant in the aspect of code. Unused code adds another layer of unnecessary maintenance and complexity to a system. Legacy applications have been in operation for decades and, over time, many changes will have been accommodated without code being cleaned, which amounts to lots of technical debt. Any initiative to reduce technical debt could be risky due to unknown impacts and dependencies. As a result, organizations are forced to invest in unnecessary code and system maintenance for fear of breaking the system by making any significant changes.

However, modernizing legacy systems may be costly due to unknown dependencies and outages. A careful **cost-benefit analysis** (CBA) needs to be considered and the **return on investment** (ROI) needs to be determined when deciding to proceed with modernization. As stakeholders don't see the immediate benefit of modernization, procuring finances for legacy modernization can be challenging.

Shortage of skills and documentation

Legacy technologies (such as mainframes) have multiple complex components that depend on each other. They are extensive proprietary and costly servers that are not readily available if someone wants to develop skills on their own. It is challenging to retain application development resources and even more challenging to hire people with hands-on experience with old technology and operating systems.

Often, legacy systems are two or more decades old, and most of the workforce with the relevant skills to manage them has retired. Also, these systems may not have the documentation to keep a record of the years of work that went into them. There are chances of significant knowledge loss as an old workforce rotates with a new workforce. A lack of knowledge makes it risky to change the system due to unknown dependencies. Any small feature requests are challenging to accommodate due to system complexity and skills shortages.

New cutting-edge technologies such as big data, machine learning, and the **Internet of Things (IoT)** are built on new technology platforms. As new technologies are not well integrated with legacy systems, an organization may lose out to a competitor if it cannot use the full capabilities of emerging technologies. A modern system helps build an organization's brand as an innovative company where most of the new generation of the workforce wants to work. Development and training are an even more significant source of expense for legacy technologies.

Often, automation helps to reduce costs by reducing human effort. Many tools are available in modern systems to build automation—such as DevOps pipelines, code review, and automation testing—that a legacy system may not utilize, resulting in additional cost.

Vulnerable to corporate security issues

Security is the top priority for any organization and system. A legacy application that runs on an old operating system (such as Windows XP or Windows 2008) is vulnerable to security issues due to a lack of vendor support. Software vendors continuously determine new security threats and release patches to accommodate them in the latest software version to secure them. Any legacy software announced as **End of Life (EOL)** from a vendor doesn't get a new security patch, which leaves your application running in the old software version, exposed to several security threats.

System health checks are often ignored for legacy applications, which makes them more vulnerable to security attacks. The skills gap makes it difficult to provide continuous support and help, which means systems are run in an insecure manner. A single vulnerability can pose a high risk of exposing your application, database, and critical information to attackers.

In addition to a security vulnerability, legacy applications are hard to maintain due to compliance. As compliances keep changing over time to enforce more tight security around data handling and usage, legacy systems require changes to adhere to local governance and compliance needs.

For example, the European Union's new **General Data Protection Regulation (GDPR)** compliance requires each system to enable users to request to delete their data. While modern systems can provide these features out of the box in an automated and self-service manner, this may need to be performed manually and becomes more complex in legacy systems.

Adhering to compliance needs can lead to more operation costs and time-consuming maintenance.

Incompatibility with other systems

In addition to end users, every system needs to integrate with other IT systems. Those systems may be associated with different departments, clients, partners, or suppliers. The various systems need to exchange data in a standard format that evolves. Almost every few years, files and data format standards are changed to increase data exchange efficiency, and most systems need to change to adopt them. Hard-to-change legacy systems that stick to using an old format could result in system incompatibility and a system that your suppliers and partners may not want to use. An inability to accommodate standard needs adds significant risk to businesses due to complex workarounds and lost productivity.

Adding a workaround for simple business needs may make a system more complex. Modern systems are built on a service-oriented architecture, making it easier to accommodate any new requirement by adding a new service independently. Old systems are often built with a monolithic architecture, and adding any new feature means you need to rebuild and test the entire system.

Modern architectures are API-oriented and can be easily integrated with other systems to offload heavy lifting. For example, a taxi-booking app uses Google Maps for **Global Positioning System (GPS)** navigation or Facebook and Twitter for user authentication. A lack of APIs makes these integrations harder in a legacy system, resulting in complex custom code.

As load increases from another dependent upstream system, a legacy application can face a *scalability issue*. Often, legacy applications are built with a monolithic architecture and are hardware-dependent. Scalability is a big challenge with a monolithic system, as it cannot scale horizontally due to hardware dependency and vertical scaling being limited to the maximum system capacity. Breaking monolithic applications into microservices can help with scaling challenges and help keep up with the load.

In addition to software maintenance, legacy applications are also costly for hardware infrastructure as they run on a particular version. They spread across multiple databases with duplicate data and similar functionality. Due to their monolithic nature, it's hard to consolidate and use the flexibility of cloud-based infrastructures to save costs. Let's look at some critical advantages of system modernization.

Benefits of system modernization

Creating a future digital strategy by addressing the growing need for legacy system modernization can have many advantages, as shown in the following diagram:

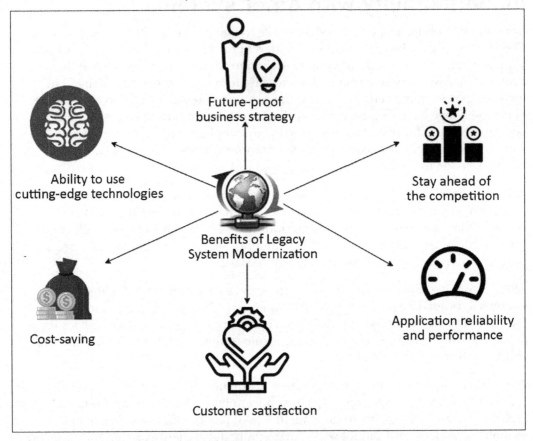

Figure 17.2: Benefits of legacy system modernization

The following are the significant benefits of application modernization:

- **Customer satisfaction**: Using the latest technology gives a better **user interface (UI)**, **user experience (UX)**, and an omnichannel experience. Consumers have grown accustomed to real-time access to information from any device, any location, at any time through their personal experiences. You don't need to build different variations of the UI; it can be built once and deployed across devices such as laptops, tablets, and smartphones. A fast and slick UI leads to better customer experience and business growth.

- **Future-proof business strategy**: Modernizing your application allows you to be more agile and innovative. The team can accommodate the changing needs of the business comfortably and evolve with new technology.

- **Stay ahead of the competition**: Users are always looking for the latest stuff and tend to move to new applications that give a better experience. The modernization of your application helps you to stay ahead of the competition by following the latest trends. For example, voice integration is being widely provided in apps, and you can enhance security with face detection. This is only possible when your application is adopting the latest technology.

- **Application reliability and performance**: Every new version of a software API and an operating system tries to address and improve performance issues. Using the latest software and hardware helps you to achieve better performance, scalability, and high availability. Application modernization helps you to reduce operational outages and enhance security.

- **Ability to use cutting-edge technologies**: Legacy systems prevent you from getting insights from data that could help you grow your business. By modernizing your database and creating a data lake, you can use big data and machine learning to get all kinds of insights. This also helps you to retain employees when people get the opportunity to work with new technologies.

- **Cost savings**: Overall, any modernization leads to cost savings by reducing operational maintenance and providing a more natural upgrade. Utilization of open source software reduces licensing costs, hardware flexibility helps to adopt a cloud pay-as-you-go model, and automation reduces the human resources needed for routine jobs and improves overall efficiency.

By migrating legacy core systems, organizations can modernize their core systems to reduce the cost of ownership, automate manual back-office processes, eliminate data silos, improve customer experience, and launch new market-facing applications faster.

However, there are several benefits of legacy system modernization, but they can be very complex and require lots of effort. A careful assessment needs to be conducted to take the right approach. Let's explore the assessment techniques of a legacy application.

Defining a strategy for system modernization

Often, a legacy system gets left out of an enterprise's overall digital strategy, and issues get addressed on an as-needed basis. Taking a reactive approach holds back organizations from executing overall system modernization and benefits.

If your legacy system has serious business challenges, such as security and compliance issues, or cannot address the business need, you can take a **big-bang approach**. In the big-bang method, you build a new system from scratch and shut down the old system. This approach is risky but addresses a business need that can be mitigated from the existing legacy system.

The other approach you can take is a **phased approach**, where you upgrade one module at a time and keep running both the old and the new systems. A phased approach is less risky but takes a long time and may be more expensive as you need to maintain both environments, with the concomitant increased network and infrastructure bandwidth.

Approaching your application portfolio, prioritizing certain applications, and having an overall plan is the first step. As you use the cloud, you design a new operating model, and you end up with a combination of tools. You can choose to use third-party tools to frame your needs and your tool preferences. And finally, you can use a consulting partner for a more successful and faster time to complete migration and modernization projects.

Taking any of these approaches can provide various benefits once the modernization of an application is completed.

Assessment of a legacy application

There may be multiple legacy systems in an organization, with tens of thousands to millions of code lines. In a modernization situation, a legacy system needs to align with the business strategy and the investment cost. Also, it is possible to reutilize some parts of it or completely write it from scratch, but the first step is to conduct the assessment and better understand the overall system. In the Assessment phase, the solution architect needs to make it easy to assess more quickly and make informed decisions. Assessments can be done in days and weeks. The following points are the primary areas that solution architects need to focus on when conducting an assessment:

- **Technology assessment**: As a solution architect, you need to understand the technology stack used by the existing system. If the current technology is entirely outdated and lacks vendor support, you might need to replace it entirely. In the case of a better version of the technology being available, then you can consider upgrading. Often, newer versions are backward-compatible, with minimal changes required.

- **Architecture assessment**: You need to understand the overall architecture to make it future-proof. There may be a case where you need to make a minor upgrade to the technology, but the overall architecture is monolithic and not scalable. You should audit the architecture in the aspects of scalability, availability, performance, and security. You may find significant architecture changes are required to align the application with business needs.

- **Code and dependency assessment**: Legacy systems often have hundreds of thousands of lines of code in a monolithic setting. Various modules tied to each other make the system very complicated. Code that appears not to be used in one module might impact other modules if it is removed without due diligence. These code lines may have been written decades back and may have missed regular refactoring and review. Even if the technology and architecture look fine, you need to determine if the code is upgradable and maintainable. We also need to understand if any UI-related upgrades are required to make the user experience better.

As a solution architect, you want to determine the dependencies across various modules and code files. Modules may be tightly coupled, and you need to define an approach to perform simultaneous upgrades when modernizing the overall architecture. During your assessment, you may find the following patterns:

- First, many customers realize that they have many old apps that do not relate well to the future business model; they can be retired. For example, around 10-20% of the app portfolio can be retired.

- Second, thousands of SaaS vendors didn't exist 5-7 years ago; these SaaS vendors can replace many on-premises apps. For example, most large customers have landed on Salesforce as a CRM platform. This shift to SaaS shrinks down the operational portfolio managed by IT operations — it still presents security and identity work but has lower operations costs.

Then, decisions can be made to lift and shift and, during a move, re-platform the operating system, database, or language to reduce costs, such as customers choosing to re-platform from Windows Server to Linux and from Oracle to Postgres to reduce database licensing costs. If you choose to modernize, there should be a focus on modernizing apps that are true differentiators to your business. Let's look into the modernization approach.

Defining the modernization approach

For stakeholders, there may be no immediate incentive for application modernization. You need to choose the most cost-effective method and deliver results faster. The following diagram shows the modernization approach:

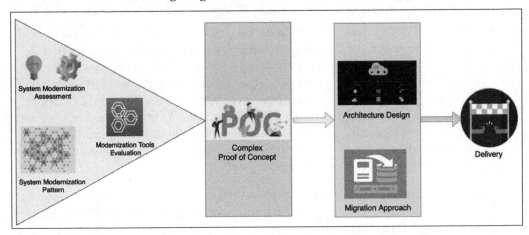

Figure 17.3: The legacy system modernization approach

After your system assessment, you need to understand the existing architecture pattern and its limitations. As per your tech stack, you need to evaluate migration tools. For example, you may choose to use an emulator for mainframe migration or vCenter if you're rehosting your application to VMware. You can select various modernization approaches and create a **proof of concept (POC)** to identify gaps. Some approaches are listed here:

- **Architecture-driven modernization**: The architecture-driven approach is required to achieve the most agility. Often, an architectural approach is language-independent and platform-independent by applying service-oriented patterns, which gives the development team the flexibility to be more innovative. You may want to choose this approach if your assessment shows that you need to make significant architectural changes. Start implementing the most critical feature first and then build a POC to highlight the gaps and the effort required. Take the microservices approach to achieve scalability and ensure better integration with other systems, depending on your legacy application.

- **System re-engineering**: In the re-engineering approach, the solution architect needs to understand the legacy system in depth and perform reverse engineering to build a new modernized application. You need to be sure to make technology choices that help you to create a future-proof system. You may want to take this approach if the legacy system is over-complicated and requires long-term projects. Start with application modernization first and upgrade the database as a final cutover in a phased approach. You need to build a mechanism where the legacy and upgraded modules co-exist, with the ability to communicate in a hybrid manner.

- **Migration and enhancements**: You can use migration and minor enhancement approaches if your existing system technology works relatively well but is restricted due to hardware limitations and cost. For example, you can lift and shift the entire workload to the cloud for better infrastructure availability and cost optimization. In addition to that, a cloud provider extends several out-of-the-box tools, which help you to make changes more frequently and apply better automation. A migration approach enables you to modernize your application with less effort and makes it future-proof, keeping it relevant for the long term. However, lift and shift is limited and may not be suitable for all kinds of workloads.

As you aim to migrate and modernize, make sure to consider specific IT domains that require substantial redesign and modernization. This modernization includes developer operating system environments as it affects patch management. Security, network, and identity are next and offer a great opportunity for scalability, resilience, and cost reduction. After that comes storage, backup, and database tools as more apps move to the cloud. Also, you need to modernize your monitoring and management tools, and all these require training and re-skilling. Let's look into various strategies for modernizing legacy systems.

Looking at legacy system modernization techniques

As per your existing application analysis, you can take various approaches to upgrade your legacy system. The most straightforward approach is migration and rehosting, where you don't need to change the existing system. However, a simple migration may not solve the long-term problem or provide any benefits.

You can take a more complex approach, such as rearchitecting or redesigning the entire application if the system no longer meets business needs. The following diagram illustrates the impact of the various methods:

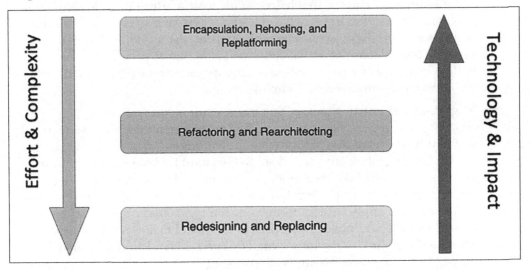

Figure 17.4: Legacy system modernization techniques

Let's look in more detail at the various modernization techniques shown in the preceding diagram.

Encapsulation, rehosting, and replatforming

Encapsulation is the most straightforward approach. If the system is business-critical and needs to communicate with other applications running on the latest technology, you may want to use this approach. With encapsulation, you need to build an API wrapper around your legacy system, which will allow other business applications to communicate with a legacy application. An API wrapper is a common approach whereby you start migrating your applications to the cloud but keep the legacy application in the on-premises data center for modernization in the later phase. You can choose the encapsulation option if your legacy code is well written and maintained but, again, you will not be able to benefit from technology advancements and hardware flexibility.

The **rehosting** approach is also among the most straightforward strategies, whereby you migrate your application into another hardware provider, such as the AWS cloud, without any code changes. Again, as with encapsulation, the rehosting option can reduce costs due to vendor contracts but you may not benefit from technology advancements and hardware flexibility.

An organization often takes this approach when it needs to move out of an existing contract quickly. For example, you can take the first step to the cloud in phase one and apply modernization in phase two.

The **replatforming** approach may get a bit more complex than the rehosting approach but will provide immediate benefits. Organizations often choose this approach if the server reaches **End of Life** (EOL), where no support is available, and an upgrade is necessary to handle security issues. For example, if Windows Server 2008 is reaching EOL, you may want to upgrade the operating system to the Windows Server 2019 or 2022 version. You need to rebuild your binaries with the new operating system and carry out testing to make sure everything works properly, but there are no significant code changes. Again, as with rehosting, with replatforming you may not benefit from technology advancements. However, it will allow you to have continuous support from the vendor.

While the preceding three approaches are the simplest ones, they cannot provide the full benefit of the application upgrade. Let's look at approaches that help you to take full advantage of application modernization.

Refactoring and rearchitecting

In the **refactoring** approach, you can refactor your code to accommodate the new system. In refactoring, the overall architecture will be the same, but you are upgrading your code to suit the latest programming language and operating system version. You can refactor the portion of code to apply automation and perform feature enhancement. If your technology is still relevant and can accommodate business needs with code changes, you may want to take this approach.

In the **rearchitecting** approach, you decide to change the system architecture by reutilizing the existing code as much as possible. For example, you may create a microservices architecture out of your existing monolithic architecture. You can take one module at a time and convert it into a service-oriented architecture by giving each module a RESTful endpoint. The rearchitecting option helps you achieve the desired scalability and reliability; however, overall performance results may be average due to the utilization of existing code.

Redesigning and replacing

The **redesigning** approach is the most complex but provides the maximum benefit. You can choose this approach if the legacy system is completely outdated and cannot accommodate business needs at all. With redesigning, you need to build the entire system from scratch while keeping the overall scope intact.

The following diagram shows the legacy mainframe system migration to the AWS cloud:

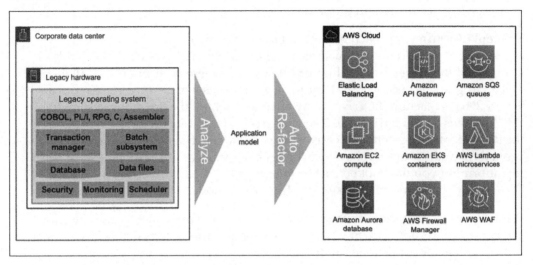

Figure 17.5: Legacy mainframe system modernization to the cloud

Here, a legacy mainframe system is rearchitected and refactored to similar cloud services as a *modernization approach*. Building a cloud-native application helps you utilize and fully benefit from cloud services in aspects of scalability, performance, reliability, and cost. It helps your team to be more agile and innovative by accommodating rapidly changing technology in your system.

Redesigning a legacy system requires a long-term project with lots of effort and increased cost. Before kicking off modernization, as a solution architect, you should do careful analysis if any SaaS product or **commercially available off-the-shelf (COTS)** products can handle your business need with a lower cost. It is essential to do a **Cost Benefit Analysis (CBA)** between *redesign* and *purchase* before proceeding with the redesigning option.

Sometimes, it's more beneficial to replace the existing legacy system with new third-party software. For example, your organization may have a decade-old **Customer Relationship Management (CRM)** system that cannot scale and provide the desired feature. You can look for the option to subscribe to SaaS products such as Salesforce CRM to replace the legacy system. SaaS products are subscription based and offer per-user licenses, so they may be the right choice if you don't have many users. For a vast enterprise with thousands of users, it may be more cost-effective to build its application. You should conduct a CBA to understand the ROI when investing in SaaS products.

Defining a cloud migration strategy for legacy systems

As the cloud becomes ever more popular, more organizations are looking to migrate into the cloud for their legacy application modernization needs. You learned about various cloud migration techniques in *Chapter 5, Cloud Migration and Hybrid Cloud Architecture Design*. The cloud provides you with the flexibility to scale your application while keeping costs low and helps you to achieve desirable performance, high availability, and reliability while maintaining application security.

Cloud providers such as **AWS**, **Microsoft Azure**, and **GCP** provide many options out of the box that can help you to modernize your system. For example, you can take a serverless approach to build a microservice using AWS Lambda and Amazon API Gateway, with Amazon DynamoDB as the backend. We discussed various legacy system modernization techniques and their application in the context of moving to the cloud in the previous section. The flow illustrated in the following diagram will help you decide whether to use cloud migration to modernize your legacy application:

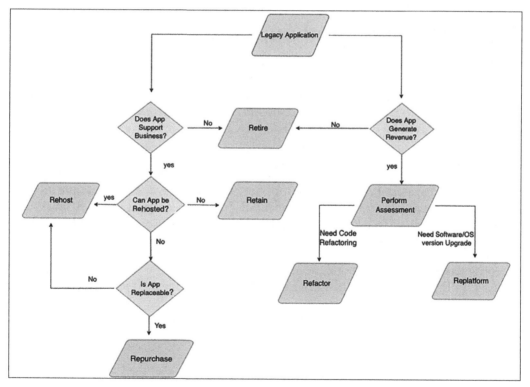

Figure 17.6: Cloud migration path for legacy system modernization

As shown in the preceding diagram, if your application is still heavily used by businesses and generates revenue, you may want to continue with minimal changes. In that situation, you can refactor your application into the cloud or re-platform it into the cloud if the server is reaching EOL.

If you don't want to change existing applications to sustain business and still want to move to the cloud entirely to save and optimize costs, then take the *lift and shift approach* to rehost the legacy application in the cloud. If your legacy application is replaceable, then you can buy a cloud-native SaaS version of the product and retire your legacy application. Sometimes, you may want to retain your legacy system in the on-premises data center if there are too many business dependencies and it cannot move into the cloud due to incompatibility.

You should perform a **total cost of ownership** (TCO) analysis to understand the advantages of moving to the cloud. It is recommended to take the most complex module of the legacy application and build a POC to ensure your entire system will be cloud-compatible before starting the full project. A detailed POC covering the critical business cases will help you identify gaps and reduce the migration risk significantly.

Documentation and support

For the long-term sustainability of a new system and graceful migration to it, make sure to prepare proper documentation and support. Provide documentation for your coding standards that everyone can follow and that helps to keep the new system up to date. Keep your architecture documents as working artifacts and keep them updated as technology trends change. Keeping your system updated will ensure that you don't fall into the legacy system modernization situation again.

Prepare a comprehensive runbook to support new and old systems. You may want to keep the old system for some time until the new system can accommodate all business requirements and run satisfactorily. Update the support runbook and ensure that you don't lose knowledge due to employee attrition and that the overall knowledge base is not processed in a people-dependent manner.

Keeping track of system dependencies helps you to determine the impact of any changes in the future. You will learn more about documentation in the next chapter.

Prepare training content to train staff on the new system and ensure they can support it in case there's an operational outage.

Mainframe migration with the public cloud

Many enterprises are moving their mainframe workloads to the cloud to take advantage of factors such as cost reduction, increased agility, technical debt reduction, digital strategy support, the legacy mainframe skills gap, and data analytics. Mainframe workloads are more challenging to migrate than x86-based workloads because legacy mainframe applications are often developed and deployed in a tightly coupled manner. For example, a mainframe application might include programs that are used by a number of subsystems or are directly called by other applications. In these cases, changes made to the underlying programs also affect the associated subsystems and applications.

For legacy applications, you need to take an incremental approach, where the migration is planned in waves, as a best practice. This approach helps to reduce risks because you select and prioritize closely related applications to be migrated together. However, this approach sometimes isn't as straightforward for mainframe migrations because the mainframe application code can use temporal coupling (invoked synchronously) or deployment coupling (using linked modules). Migrating the coupled application code affects dependent applications and therefore carries some risks. To reduce these risks, you can decouple the mainframe application code without impacting dependent applications. From a code migration perspective, the two main types of legacy mainframe applications are standalone applications and applications with shared code. Let's look into the details of each migration pattern.

Migrating standalone applications

Let's assume that there are two applications, A and B, that are standalone mainframe applications. Each application consists of programs and subprograms that it uses exclusively.

Because the applications are self-contained, you can group the **COBOL** programs and subprograms by application for code refactoring, as shown in the following diagram.

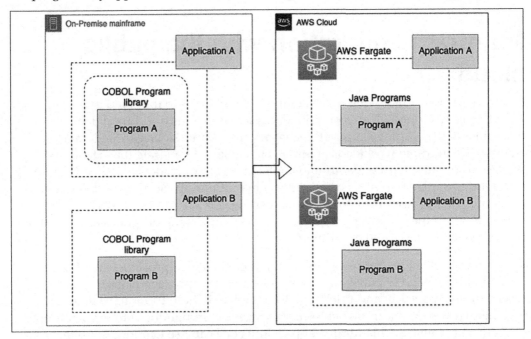

Figure 17.7: Mainframe modernization for a standalone application

In the preceding diagram, The mainframe programs and subprograms are written in COBOL, and the code is migrated to Java on AWS. However, you can use these decoupling patterns with your programming languages of choice. The migration pattern is legacy automated refactoring, where code, data, and dependencies are automatically converted to a modern language, data store, and framework while guaranteeing functional equivalence with the same business functions. Refactoring involves using automated tools to convert the mainframe programming language (such as COBOL) into modern programming languages (such as Java or . NET).

Refactored applications are deployed on containers that are provisioned and managed by **AWS Fargate**. Fargate is a serverless compute engine for containers that work with both Amazon **Elastic Container Service (ECS)** and Amazon **Elastic Kubernetes Service (EKS)**. Here, mainframe database tables and mainframe files are migrated with the application.

After grouping, you can migrate applications A and B in the same wave or in different waves. In either case, for each application, package the refactored modern components and deploy them together into a runtime environment. After migration, retire the on-premises mainframe applications and their components. Now let's look at more complicated scenarios where code is shared by multiple applications.

Migrating applications with shared code

Let's assume mainframe applications A and B run shared code called program AB. You need to perform an impact analysis of the shared program AB to migrate applications A and B and program AB together. Based on the impact analysis, identify the number of dependent applications that use shared programs, such as program AB. You need to complete a business domain analysis to determine whether the shared program can be aggregated into a domain with applications and exposed as an API as one of the domain services. Let's look at some approaches you can take to decouple the applications in preparation for migration.

Application decoupling using a standalone API

Using this approach, you instantiate a standalone API by converting the shared COBOL program AB into a Java program. You can use automated refactoring tools provided to generate network APIs for the program to minimize refactoring efforts. You can take this approach when the shared program can be instantiated as a standalone service. The remaining components of applications A and B are refactored into Java as a whole and migrated to the cloud. You can migrate the applications in the same wave, as shown in the following diagram:

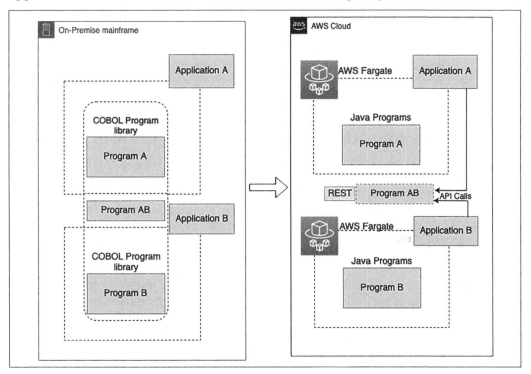

Figure 17.8: Migration of shared program applications using a standalone API

In this approach, you need to refactor both applications with their respective programs and migrate them to the cloud. You need to use the impact analysis report from the analysis phase to help developers and teams identify the refactored applications that call the shared program AB. Replace the inner program call to the shared program AB with network API calls. After the migration, retire the on-premises mainframe applications and their components.

Application decoupling using a shared library

In this approach, the shared program AB is converted into a Java common library and packaged with the migration applications. You should take this approach when the shared program is a supporting library instead of a standalone service. The remaining components of applications A and B are refactored into Java programs and migrated to the cloud.

This approach refactors applications A and B with their associated programs into Java and migrates them to the cloud. You should maintain the source code of the applications in a fully managed source control service such as AWS CodeCommit. The teams that use the shared program can collaborate on code changes by using pull requests, branching, and merging and can control the changes made to the shared program code. After the migration, retire the on-premises mainframe applications and their components.

When applications are too big to be grouped into the same migration wave, you can migrate them in multiple waves and maintain service continuity during the migration. With this approach, you can modernize your applications in phases without bundling them together. Migrating your applications in separate waves decouples them without requiring significant code changes in the mainframe.

Application decoupling using message queues

In this approach, the shared program AB is converted into a Java program and migrated to the cloud as part of application A. A message queue is used as an interface between the refactored application in the cloud and the legacy application on-premises. Using this approach, you can break up tightly coupled mainframe applications into producers and consumers and make them more modular to function independently. The additional advantage is that you can migrate the applications in different waves.

You can take this approach when applications on the mainframe can communicate with the migrated applications in the cloud through a message queue. It would be best to make sure that the queuing architecture pattern meets the business requirements for the applications that reside on the mainframe because it involves re-architecting the existing applications. You should take the message queue approach if applications that aren't part of the first wave require a longer time (six months or more) to be migrated to the cloud.

When applications are too big to be grouped into the same migration wave, you can migrate them in multiple waves, as shown in the following diagram, and maintain service continuity during migration.

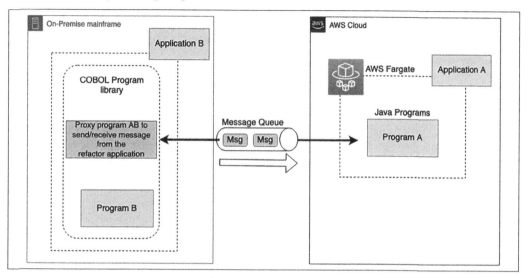

Figure 17.9: Migration of shared program applications using a message queue

As shown in the preceding diagram, you need to follow these steps for migration:

1. Migrate (refactor) application A with its associated programs to the cloud while application B continues to reside on-premises.

2. Refactor application A (in the cloud) to communicate with application B (on-premises) through a message queue.

3. Refactor application B on-premises to replace the shared program with a proxy program that sends messages to, and receives messages from, application A through the message queue.

4. After application A is migrated successfully, retire the on-premises application A and its components (including the shared program). Application B and its components continue to reside on-premises.

5. In the next set of migration waves, migrate application B and its components. The loosely coupled queuing architecture continues to act as an interface between applications A and B in the cloud. This reduces the refactoring effort for application B without impacting application A.

As a best practice, you should perform code analysis to produce a dependency map for the mainframe applications and identify the list of programs that are shared by applications. After that, group applications that share the same programs for the same migration wave to reduce program calls between the on-premises environment and the cloud.

In the planning stage, run an impact analysis to identify applications that share programs with the application you're planning to migrate and select the right decoupling patterns for application migration. When possible, perform mainframe migration incrementally to reduce complexity and risk. By doing incremental migration, migration teams can provide faster feedback regarding the migration progress, and businesses can use the feedback to optimize internal processes to accelerate the pace of migration.

Summary

In this chapter, you learned about various challenges with legacy applications and why it is essential to modernize them. You learned about the different benefits an organization can get by upgrading its application to the latest technology. Application modernization can be a complicated and risky task, but is often worth the effort.

The outcome you get from the upgrade is a trade-off against the amount of investment and energy you put into it. Before defining the modernization approach, it's essential to understand your legacy system thoroughly. You learned various assessment attributes of an application in the aspects of technology, architecture, and code.

After the assessment, the next step is to define the modernization approach. You learned about various modernization approaches, including architecture-driven, system re-engineering, and migration approaches. You also learned about multiple techniques of system modernization, including straightforward approaches (encapsulation and rehosting) and complex approaches (rearchitecting and redesigning). The cloud can provide a significant value proposition, and you learned about the decision-making approach you need to take with modernization in the cloud.

You focused on the various technical aspects of solution architecture; however, documentation is one of the critical elements of architecture design to keep your system maintainable in the long run. The next chapter will discuss the documentation required for a solution architect to prepare, contribute to, and maintain maximum business value.

Join our book's Discord space

Join the book's Discord workspace for a monthly *Ask me Anything* session with the authors: https://packt.link/SAHandbook

18

Solution Architecture Document

In previous chapters, you learned about various aspects of solution architecture design and optimization. As the solution architect works on the design, it is essential to have consistent communication with other stakeholders for successful application delivery. The solution architect needs to communicate a solution design to all technical and non-technical stakeholders.

The **Solution Architecture Document (SAD)** provides an end-to-end view of the application and helps everyone be on the same page. In this chapter, you will learn about various aspects of the SAD, which addresses the needs of all stakeholders associated with the development of the application.

You will learn about the structure of the SAD and other types of documents of which the solution architect needs to be aware, such as the request for proposal, where the solution architect needs to provide input to make strategic decisions. We will cover the following topics to gain a deeper understanding of the documentation involved in solution architecture:

- Purpose of the SAD
- Views of the SAD
- Structure of the SAD
- IT procurement documentation for a solution architecture

By the end of this chapter, you will know about the SAD, its structure, and the various details that need to be accommodated in the documentation.

You will learn about various IT procurement documentation such as the request for proposal, the request for information, and the request for quotation, in which a solution architect participates to provide feedback.

Purpose of the SAD

The need for architecture documentation often gets ignored, and teams start working on implementation without understanding the overall architecture. A SAD provides a broad view of the overall solution design to keep all stakeholders informed.

The SAD helps to achieve the following goals:

- Communicate the end-to-end application solution to all stakeholders
- Provide high-level architecture and different views of the application design to address the application's service-quality requirements such as reliability, security, performance, and scalability
- Provide traceability of the solution back to business requirements and look at how the application will meet all functional and **non-functional requirements (NFRs)**
- Provide all views of the solution required for design, building, testing, and implementation
- Define the impacts of the solution for estimation, planning, and delivery purposes
- Define the business process, continuation, and operations needed for a solution to work uninterrupted after the production launch

SADs define the purpose and goal of the solution and address critical components such as solution constraints, assumptions, and risks that often get overlooked by the implementation team. The solution architect must make sure they create the document in an easy language that business users can understand and relate business context with technical design. Documentation helps to retain knowledge due to resource attrition and makes the overall design process a people-independent one.

For existing applications where modernization effort is needed, a SAD presents an abstract view of current and future architecture, along with a transition plan. The solution architect understands the existing system dependencies and documents them to uncover any potential risk in advance. The migration plan helps businesses understand the tools and technology required to handle the new system and plan resources accordingly.

The solution architect conducts various assessments during solution design by building a **proof of concept** (**POC**) or through market research. A SAD should list all architecture assessments and their impact, along with the choice of technology. A SAD presents a conceptual view of the current and target state of the solution design and maintains a record of change. Let's understand various aspects of a SAD in the next section.

Views of the SAD

The solution architect needs to create a SAD that is understandable by both business users and technical users. A SAD bridges the communication gap between the business user and the development team to understand the function of the overall application. The best way to capture all stakeholders' input is by putting yourself in their situation and looking at problems from the stakeholders' perspectives. The solution architect evaluates both the business and technical aspects of architecture design to take cognizance of all technical and non-technical users' requirements.

As illustrated in the following diagram, the holistic view of the SAD comprises various views derived from business requirements to cover different aspects:

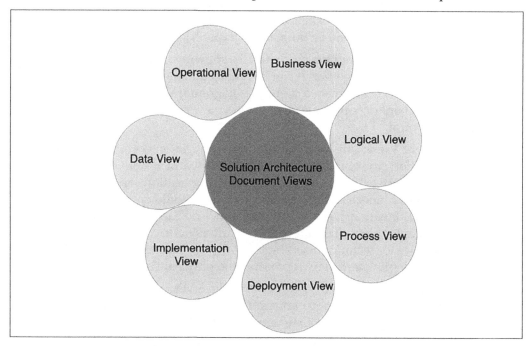

Figure 18.1: SAD views

Solution architects can choose standard diagrams such as a **Unified Modeling Language (UML)** diagram or a block diagram from **Microsoft Visio** to represent various views. Overall, the diagram should be easy to read and understandable by all business and technical stakeholders. A SAD should include the following views, wherever possible, to address everyone's needs:

- **Business View**: Architecture design is all about addressing business concerns and solving business purposes. The business view shows the value proposition of the overall solution and product. To simplify, the solution architect may choose to detect high-level scenarios related to business and present these as a use case diagram. The business view also describes stakeholders and the required resources to execute the project. You can define the business view as a use case view as well.

- **Logical View**: This presents various packages on the system so that business users and designers can understand the various logical components of the system. The logical view offers a chronicled order of the system in which it should build. It shows how the multiple packages of the system are connected and how the user can interact with them. For example, in a banking application, the user first needs to authenticate and authorize using a security package, log in to the account using the account package, apply for a loan using a loan package, and so on. Here, each package represents a different module and can be built as a microservice.

- **Process View**: This presents more details, showing how the key processes of the system work together. It can be reflected using a state diagram. The solution architect can create a sequence diagram if they want to show more details. In a banking application, a process view can present the approval of a loan or account.

- **Deployment View**: This presents how the application is going to work in the production environment. It shows how different system components (such as the network firewall, load balancer, application servers, and database) are connected. The solution architect should create a simple block diagram that business users can understand. You can add more details to the UML deployment diagram to show various node components and their dependencies for technical users, such as the development and DevOps teams. The deployment view represents the physical layout of the system.

- **Implementation View**: This is the core of the SAD and represents architectural and technology choices. The solution architect needs to put the architecture diagram here—for example, if it is 3-tier, *N-tier*, or event-driven architecture—along with the reasoning behind it.

You also need to detail technology choices—for example, using Java versus Node.js, along with the pros and cons of using them. You want to justify the resources and skills required to execute the project in the implementation view. The development team uses an implementation view to create a detailed design such as a class diagram, but that doesn't need to be part of the SAD.

- **Data View**: As most applications are data-driven, this makes the data view important. The data view represents how data will flow between the different components and how it will be stored. It can also be used to explain data security and data integrity. The solution architect can use the entity-relationship diagram to show the relationship between different tables and schemas in the database. You will learn more about the entity-relationship diagram in the *Data architecture* section. The data view also explains the reports and analytics needed.

- **Operational View**: This explains how the system is going to be maintained post-launch. Often, you define **service-level agreements (SLAs)**, alert and monitoring functionality, a disaster recovery plan, and a support plan for the system. The operational view also provides details of how system maintenance will be carried out, such as by deployment of a bug fix, patching, backup and recovery, and handling security incidents.

All the views listed make sure the SAD covers all aspects of the system and stakeholders. You may choose to include additional views—such as a physical architecture view, a network architecture view, or a security (controls) architecture view—as per the stakeholders' requirements. As a solution architect, you need to provide a comprehensive view of system functioning and understanding. Let's explore the structure of the SAD in more detail in the next section.

Structure of the SAD

The structure of the SAD can differ from project to project as per stakeholder requirements and the nature of the project. Your project could be creating a new product from the ground up, modernizing a legacy application, or moving the entire system to the cloud.

For each project, the SAD document may differ, but, overall, it should consider various stakeholders' views and consider the necessary sections, as shown in the following screenshot:

Contents

1. **Solution Overview**

1.1 **Solution Purpose**

1.2 **Solution Scope**
  1.2.1   In Scope
  1.2.2   Out of Scope

1.3 **Solution Assumptions**

1.4 **Solution Constraints**

1.5 **Solution Dependencies**

1.6 **Key Architecture Decisions**

2. **Business Context**

2.1 **Business Capabilities**

2.2 **Key Business Requirements**
  2.2.1   Key Business Processes
  2.2.2   Business Stakeholders

2.3 **Non-Functional Requirements**
  2.3.1   Scalability
  2.3.2   Availability and Reliability
  2.3.3   Performance
  2.3.4   Portability
  2.3.5   Security

3. **Conceptual Solution Overview**

3.1 **Conceptual and Logical Architecture**

4. **Solution Architecture**

4.1 **Information Architecture**
  4.1.1   Information components

4.2 **Application Architecture**
  4.2.1   Application components

4.3 **Data Architecture**
  4.3.1   Data Flow and Context

4.4 **Integration Architecture**
  4.4.1   Interface Component

4.5 **Infrastructure Architecture**
  4.5.1   Infrastructure Component

4.6 **Security Architecture**
  4.6.1   Identity and Access Management
  4.6.2   Application Threat Model

5. **Solution Implementation**

5.1 **Development**

5.2 **Deployment**

5.3 **Data Migration**

5.4 **Application Decommissioning**

6. **Solution Management**

6.1 **Operational Management**
  6.1.1   Monitoring and Alert
  6.1.2   Support and Incident Management
  6.1.3   Disaster Recovery

6.2 **User On-boarding**
  6.2.1   User system requirement

7. **Appendix**

7.1 **Open Items**

7.2 **Proof of Concept findings**

Figure 18.2: Structure of a SAD

In the preceding SAD structure, you can see different sections covering multiple solution architecture and design aspects. The solution architect may choose to add additional subsections or remove some sections as per the project requirements. For example, you can add another introduction section to talk about the document's purpose, with a summary. For a transition project, you may add a subsection to present the existing architecture and compare it with the target architecture, and so on. Let's look into the details of each section.

Solution overview

In the solution overview section, you need to briefly introduce the solution in a couple of paragraphs, describing the functioning of the solution and its different components at a very high level. It's nice to add a high-level block diagram showing various components in one place. The following diagram illustrates the solution overview of an e-commerce platform:

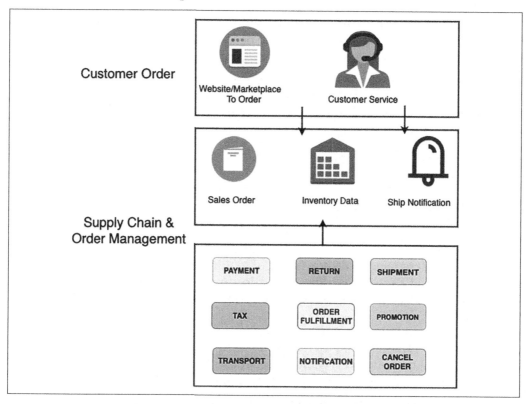

Figure 18.3: Solution overview of an e-commerce platform

You need to provide a brief about each component in simplified language so that the business user can understand the overall working of the solution. Major subsections include:

- **Solution purpose**: This provides a brief about a business concern that the solution is solving and the justification to build a given solution.

- **Solution scope**: This states the business scope that the proposed solution will address. **Clearly** Describes out-of-scope items that the solution will not accommodate.

- **Solution assumptions**: List down all the assumptions based on which solution architect came up with the solution—for example, minimum network bandwidth availability.

- **Solution constraints**: List all technical, business, and resource constraints. Often, constraints come from industry and government compliances, which need to be listed in this section. You can also highlight the risk and mitigation plan.

- **Solution dependencies**: List all upstream and downstream dependencies. For example, an e-commerce website needs to communicate with a shipping system such as UPS or FedEx to ship a package to customers.

- **Key architecture decisions**: List major problem statements and the corresponding proposed solution options. Describe the pros and cons of each option, why a particular decision was made, and the rationale behind it.

After giving a solution overview, you want to relate it to the business context. Let's look at the business context view in more detail in the next section.

Business context

In the business context section, the solution architect needs to provide a high-level overview of the business capabilities and requirements that the solution will address. This section only contains an abstract view of requirements. Detailed requirements need to be a part of a separate requirements document. However, the external link of the requirements document can be provided here. You should include the following primary subsections:

- **Business capabilities**: Provide a brief description of the business capabilities for which the solution is being designed. Make sure to include the benefits of capabilities and how they will address customer needs.

- **Key business requirements**: List all key business concerns that the solution is going to address. Provide a high-level view of key requirements and add a reference to the detailed requirements document.

- **Key business processes**: Solution architects should show key processes with a business process document. The following diagram illustrates a simplified view of an e-commerce application business process model:

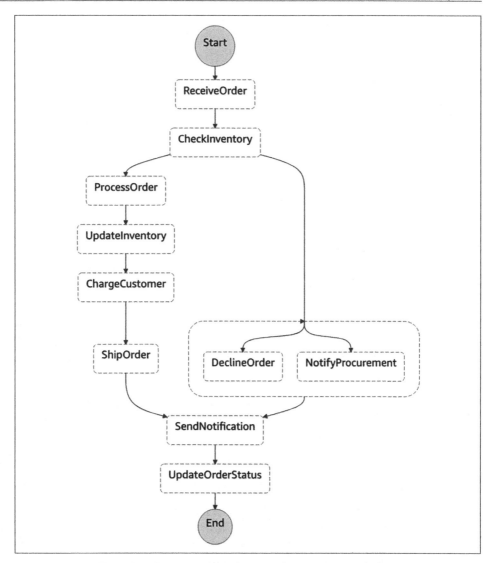

Figure 18.4: Business process diagram of an e-commerce platform

- **Business stakeholders**: List stakeholders who are directly or indirectly impacted by the project. This includes sponsors, developers, end users, vendors, and partners.

- **NFRs (Non-Functional Retirements)**: Solution architects need to focus more on NFRs as these often get missed by the business user and development team. At a high level, an NFR should include:

    - **Scalability**: How can the application scale as workloads fluctuate? (For example, scale from 1,000 transactions per second to 10,000 transactions per second in a given day or month.)

    - **Availability and reliability**: What is the acceptable downtime for system availability? (For example, 99.99% availability or 45 minutes' downtime per month.)

    - **Performance**: What is the performance requirement? Where can the system handle the load increase without impacting the end user experience? (For example, the catalog page needs to load within 3 seconds.)

    - **Portability**: Can the application run on multiple platforms without any additional work? (For example, the mobile app needs to run in the iOS and Android operating systems.)

    - **Capacity**: What is the maximum workload that the application can handle? (For example, the maximum number of users, the number of requests, the expected response time, and the expected application load.)

The conceptual view of architecture is a sweet spot that provides a good system overview for both business and technical stakeholders. Let's learn more about the conceptual view in more detail.

Conceptual solution overview

The conceptual solution overview section provides an abstract-level diagram that captures a big-picture view of the whole solution, including business and technical aspects. It provides a basis for analyses and trade-off studies to help refine and optimize the solution architecture in sufficient detail, to support solution design and implementation. The following diagram illustrates a conceptual architecture diagram of an e-commerce platform:

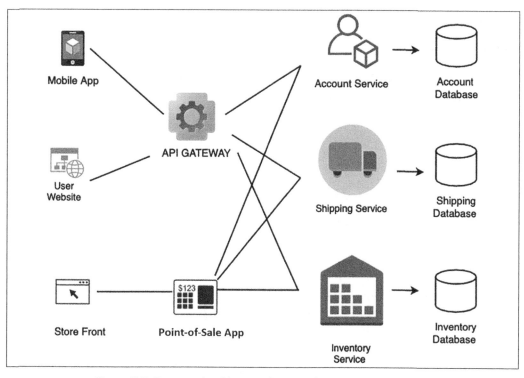

Figure 18.5: Conceptual architecture diagram of an e-commerce platform

The preceding diagram shows an abstract view of significant modules and information flowing between them. The conceptual architecture provides a good understanding of the overall architecture for both business and technical users. However, technical users need further architectural depth. Let's dive deeper into the solution architecture in the next section.

Solution architecture

The solution architecture section dives deep into each part of the architecture. It provides different views that the technical team can use to create a detailed design and work on implementation. These views could target other user groups, such as developers, infrastructure engineers, DevOps engineers, security engineers, and **user experience (UX)** designers.

Let's get into the following major subsections to learn more details.

Information architecture

This section provides a user navigation flow to the application. At a high level, the solution architect needs to put in an application navigation structure. As shown in the following diagram, for an e-commerce website, it is taking three clicks for the user to navigate to the desired page:

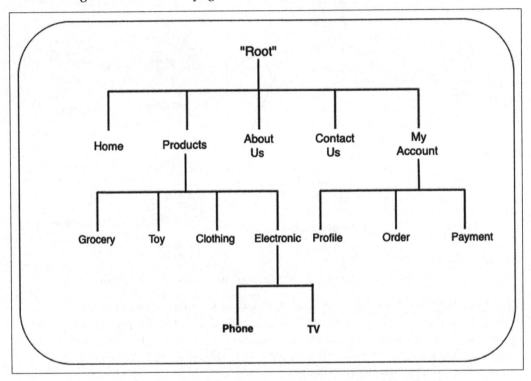

Figure 18.6: Informational architecture diagram of an e-commerce platform

Solution architects can add more details, such as website navigation, taxonomy, or a high-level wireframe that UX designers can use to generate a detailed wireframe.

Application architecture

This section targets the development team. It provides more implementation details upon which a software architect or development team can build a detailed design. The following diagram shows the application architecture for an e-commerce website, with technology building blocks such as caching, networking, content distribution, and data store:

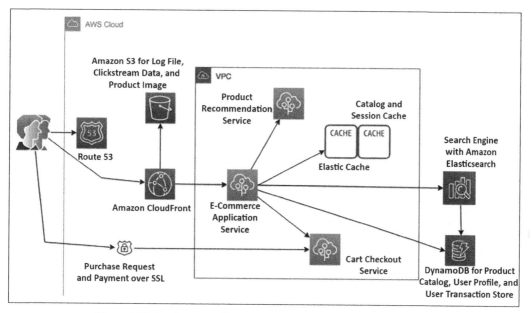

Figure 18.7: Application architecture diagram of an e-commerce platform

This section lists all application modules that need to be retired, retained, replatformed, and transformed for an application modernization architecture.

Data architecture

This section is primarily utilized by the database admin and development team to understand database schemas and how tables are related. This section often includes an **entity-relationship diagram** (**ERD**) showing the relationships of entity sets stored in a database, as shown in the following screenshot:

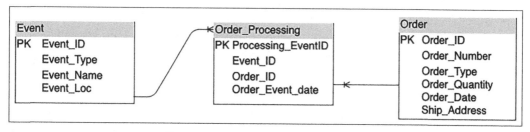

Figure 18.8: ERD of an e-commerce platform

The data architecture section lists all data objects that need to be considered during application development.

Integration architecture

This section mainly targets vendors, partners, and other teams. For example, the following diagram shows all integration points with other systems for an e-commerce application:

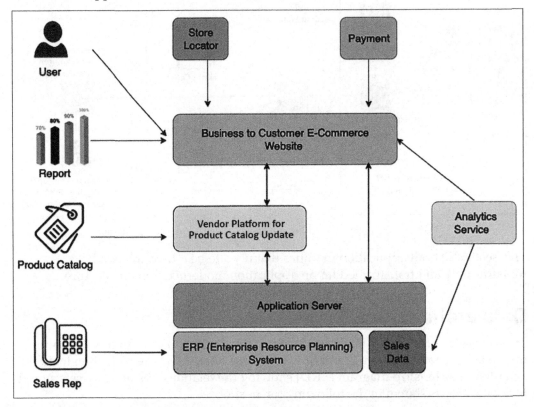

Figure 18.9: Integration architecture diagram of an e-commerce platform

The integration architecture section lists all upstream and downstream systems and their dependencies regarding your application.

Infrastructure architecture

This section is primarily targeted at the infrastructure team and system engineers. The solution architect needs to include the deployment diagram to view the logical server location and its dependencies.

For example, the following diagram illustrates the production deployment diagram for an e-commerce application. You can produce a separate diagram for other environments, such as dev, **quality assurance (QA)**, and **User Acceptance Testing (UAT)** environments:

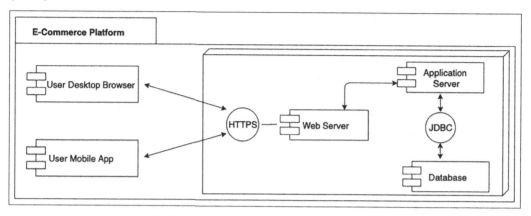

Figure 18.10: Deployment diagram of an e-commerce platform

This section lists all server configurations, databases, networks, and switches to deploy the application.

Security architecture

This section includes all the security and compliance aspects of the application, including:

- **Identity and Access Management (IAM)** such as **Active Directory (AD)**, user authentication, and authorization management

- **Infrastructure security** such as the firewall configuration, **intrusion prevention system (IPS)/intrusion detection system (IDS)** required, and antivirus software

- **Application security** such as WAF and **Distributed Denial of Service (DDoS)** protection

- **Data security** at rest and in transit using **Secure Sockets Layer (SSL)**, encryption algorithms, key management, and so on

Overall, the solution architect can include an application security threat model to identify any potential vulnerabilities, such as **cross-site scripting (XSS)** and **SQL injection (SQLi)**, and plan to protect the application from any security threat.

Solution implementation

The solution delivery section includes essential considerations to develop and deploy a solution. It can consist of the following major subsections:

- **Development**: This section is essential for the development team. It talks about development tools, programming language, code repository, code versioning, and branching, with the rationale behind the choices.

- **Deployment**: This section mainly focuses on DevOps engineers and talks about the deployment approach, deployment tools, various deployment components, and deployment checklist, with the rationale behind the choices.

- **Data migration**: This section helps the team to understand data migration and the ingestion approach, the scope of data migration, various data objects, data ingestion tools used, sources of data and data formats, and so on.

- **Application decommissioning**: This section lists existing systems that need to be decommissioned and an exit strategy for the current system if the **return on investment (ROI)** is not being realized. The solution architect needs to provide an approach and timeline for decommissioning the old system and carry out an overall impact assessment.

The SAD includes a development approach and tools. However, it does not have an application-level detailed design, such as a class diagram or adding pseudocode. Such details need to be handled by the software architect or senior developer under the corresponding software application details design document. As a solution gets deployed, it needs to be managed in production. Let's learn about the details that go into the solution management section.

Solution management

The solution management section is focused on production support and ongoing system maintenance across other non-product environments. The solution management section is primarily targeted at the operations management team. This section addresses the following areas:

- Operational management such as system patching and upgrades of dev, test, staging, and prod environments

- Tools to manage application upgrades and new releases

- Tools to manage system infrastructure

- System monitoring and alerts; operations dashboard

- Production support, SLA, and incident management

- Disaster recovery and **Business Process Continuation (BPC)**

A solution architect needs to do research and collect data to validate the right solution during solution design. Such kinds of additional details can be put in the Appendix section. Let's learn more details of the Appendix section of a SAD.

Appendix

Like every business proposal document, a SAD also has a pretty open Appendix section for containing any data that supports your overall architecture and solution choices. In the Appendix section, the solution architect can include open issues and any research data, such as the outcome of the POC, tools comparison data, and vendors' and partners' data.

In this topic, you got a good overview of the SAD structure with different sections. A SAD should include the major sections mentioned previously; however, the solution architect may exclude some sections or include additional sections as per organization and project requirements. As with other documents, it's essential to continue to iterate upon SADs and look for an opportunity to improve. More robust SADs lead to well-defined implementation guidelines and reduce any risk of failure.

A SAD is a running document created during the initial stages and kept up to date over the years based on various changes throughout the application life cycle. In addition to the SAD, solution architecture often gets involved in a significant procurement proposal with a specific requirement known as a **request for x (RFx)** document. Let's become familiar with RFx documents.

IT procurement documentation for a solution architecture

IT procurement documents are popularly known as **RFx documents**. This is a term that includes different stages of the procurement process. When you refer to RFx, it references the formal requesting process. RFx documents are categorized as **request for proposal (RFP)**, **request for information (RFI)**, and **request for quotation (RFQ)** documents.

Solution architects are often involved in the procurement process to provide their input or lead them. These procurements may be related to outsourcing, contracting, procuring software such as a database or development tools, or buying SaaS solutions.

As these documents could be highly technical and have a broad, long-term impact, the solution architect needs to provide input or respond to any procurement requirement and prepare the invite. Let's understand the difference between different RFx documents, as follows:

- **RFI**: RFI comes early in the procurement process, where buyers invite information from different vendors to make an informed decision regarding their choice of procurement for a later stage. An RFI document collects information about the capabilities of the various suppliers, where the buyer can compare all suppliers in a similar parameter and proceed to the next proposal steps with shortlisted suppliers.

- **RFP**: In this process, shortlisted suppliers from the RFI process have more information about the project's outcome. An RFP document is more open than an RFI one, where suppliers can provide the best way to acquire solutions for the buyer. The supplier can include multiple choices, with the pros and cons of each approach.

- **RFQ**: In this process, buyers narrow down the requirement compared to the RFP and list down the exact requirements of work, equipment, and supplies. Suppliers need to provide a cost for the listed requirements, and the buyer can choose the best quotation among them to award the contract.

RFP is the most popular choice, as often, to speed up the process, the buyer's organization often chooses to ask for the RFP document only from potential vendors. In such a situation, the RFP document needs to have the structure in place so that that buyer can put a clear comparison between preferred vendors in terms of capabilities, solution approach, and cost to make a quick decision.

Due to the technicalities of procurement in IT organizations, solution architects play an essential role in evaluating vendors' capabilities and approaches from the buyer side and responding to RFP documents from the supplier side.

Summary

A SAD aims to keep all stakeholders on the same page and get formal agreement on solution design and requirements. As stakeholders comprise both business and technical users, you learned about various SAD views that the solution architect needs to consider. You need to include views for non-technical users, such as business, process, and logical views. For technical users, include views such as application, development, deployment, and operational views.

In this chapter, you learned about the detailed structure of the SAD, with major sections and subsections.

Various sections of the SAD include details such as an overview of the solution, business, and conceptual architecture. In the architecture diagram, you also learned about various architecture views, such as application, data, infrastructure, integration, and security. You learned about other sections for solution delivery consideration and operations management.

It was a long journey of learning. You are almost at the end of the book, but before closing, you need to learn some tips for becoming a solution architect and continuing to improve your knowledge.

In the next and final chapter, you will learn various soft skills such as communication style, ownership, critical thinking, and continuous learning techniques to become a better solution architect.

Join our book's Discord space

Join the book's Discord workspace for a monthly *Ask me Anything* session with the authors: https://packt.link/SAHandbook

19

Learning Soft Skills to Become a Better Solution Architect

In the previous chapters, you learned how a solution architect needs to accommodate all stakeholders' needs. Even if the solution architect's role is technical, they need to work across the organization, from senior management to the development team. To be a successful solution architect, soft skills are essential and critical factors.

Solution architects should keep themselves up to date with current technology trends, keep evolving their knowledge, and always be curious to learn new things. You can become a better solution architect by applying continuous learning. In this chapter, you will learn about methods to learn new technologies and how to share and contribute back to the technical community.

Solution architects need to define and present an overall technical strategy to address business concerns. They need to work across business and technical teams to negotiate the best solution, which requires excellent communication skills. In this chapter, you will learn the soft skills a solution architect must have, including the following:

- Acquiring pre-sales skills
- Presenting to C-level executives
- Taking ownership and accountability
- Defining strategy execution and objectives and key results

- Thinking big
- Being flexible and adaptable
- Design thinking
- Being a builder by engaging in coding hands-on
- Becoming better with continuous learning
- Being a mentor to others
- Becoming a technology evangelist and thought leader

By the end of this chapter, you will know about the various soft skills required for a solution architect to succeed in the role. You will learn about methods to acquire strategic skills (such as pre-sales and executive communication) and develop design thinking and personal leadership skills (such as thinking big and ownership). You will learn about techniques to establish yourself as a leader and continue improving your skill set.

Acquiring pre-sales skills

Pre-sales is a critical phase for complex technology procurement, whereby the customer collects detailed information to make a buying decision. In the customer organization, a solution architect is involved in the pre-sales cycle to validate technology and infrastructure resources from various vendors. In the vendor organization, the solution architect needs to respond to customers' **requests for proposals (RFPs)** and present a potential solution to acquire new business for an organization. Pre-sales requires a unique skill set that combines strong technical knowledge with soft skills, including the following:

- **Communication and negotiation skills**: Solution architects need to have excellent communication skills to engage the customer with the correct and latest details. Presenting precise details of the solution and industry relevance helps customers understand how your solution can address their business concerns. Solution architects work as a bridge between the sales and technical teams, which makes communication and coordination a critical skill. Solution architects also need to create agreements by collaborating with customers and internal teams, which requires excellent negotiation skills. In particular, strategic-level decisions have a significant impact across multiple groups. Solution architects need to negotiate between the team, work on trade-offs, and develop an optimized solution.
- **Listening and problem-solving skills**: Solution architects need to have strong analytical skills to identify the right solution per customer need.

The first thing is listening to and understanding customer use cases by asking the right questions to create a good solution. You need to understand gaps and develop a solution to result in immediate business impact with long-term **return on investment (ROI)**. For some customers, performance is more important, while others may be more focused on cost based on their application's user base. The solution architect needs to provide the right solution per their customer's primary **key performance indicator (KPI)** goal.

- **Customer-facing skills**: Often, the solution architect needs to work with both the internal team and the external customer's team. They influence stakeholders at all levels, from C-level executives to development engineers. They present solutions and demos to senior management, who look at your proposal more from a business perspective. C-level executive support and commitment to initiatives always result in the success of the adopted solution, which makes customer-facing skills very important. The C-level executive needs details of the solution in a defined time-bound meeting, and the solution architect needs to utilize the allotted time to their best advantage. You will learn more information about the executive conversation in the next section of this chapter—*Presenting to C-level executives*.

- **Working with teams**: The solution architect establishes a relationship with the business team and the product team. To prepare an optimal application, the solution architect needs to work with the business team and technical team at all levels. The solution architect needs to be a good team player and work with multiple teams, share ideas, and find a way of working.

The skills mentioned above are not only required for pre-sales but are also applicable to the solution architect's day-to-day job functions. Solution architects come from a technical background, and, being in such a role, they need to acquire critical skills to communicate at an executive level. Let's learn more about executive conversations in the next section.

Presenting to C-level executives

A solution architect needs to handle various challenges from a technical and business perspective. However, one of the most challenging tasks could be to get executive buy-in. Senior executives such as the **Chief Executive Officer (CEO)**, **Chief Technology Officer (CTO)**, **Chief Financial Officer (CFO)**, and **Chief Information Officer (CIO)** are regarded as C-level as they have a tight schedule and need to make lots of high-impact decisions. As a solution architect, you may have lots of details to present, but your C-level meetings are very time-bound. Here, a solution architect needs to get the maximum value out of their meeting in the allotted time slot.

The primary question is: *How do we get senior executives' attention and support in a limited time?* Often, during any presentation, people tend to put a summary slide at the end, while, in the case of executive meetings, your time may further reduce as per their priority and agenda. The key to an executive presentation is to summarize the primary points upfront in the first 5 minutes. You should prepare in such a way that if your 30-minute slot reduces to 5 minutes, you should still be able to convey your points and get buy-in for the next step.

Explain your agenda and meeting structure even before the summary. Executives ask lots of questions to utilize their time properly, and your agenda should convey that they will get the chance to ask a clarification question. Support your summary with facts and data that align with their industry and organization. Keep the details with you in case they want to dive deep into a particular area; you should be able to pull up and show all the data.

Don't try to present everything in detail by stating information that may seem relevant from your perspective, but maybe doesn't make much sense for an executive audience. For example, as a solution architect, you may focus more on the benefits from the technical implementation. However, senior management focuses more on ROI by reducing operational overhead and increasing productivity. You should be ready to answer the following questions that concern executives more:

- **How will the proposed solution benefit our customers?**: Business revolves around the customer. While executives are looking at their company's growth, that is only possible if their customers are satisfied. Make sure to do your research on their customer base and their needs. Be ready to present benefits backed by reliable data.

- **What assumption did you make to baseline the solution?**: Often, these meetings are at the initial phase when you may not have enough details. Solution architects always need to make some assumptions to baseline the solution. List down your hypothesis in bullet points, and have a mitigation plan associated with it, in case things don't work as per assumption.

- **What will be my ROI?**: Executives are always looking for ROI by determining the **total cost of ownership (TCO)**. Be ready with data to provide an estimated cost of ownership, solution maintenance costs, training costs, overall cost savings, and so on.

- **What happens if we continue as it is today and do nothing?**: Senior management may go into extreme vetting mode to identify ROI. They want to understand if the investment is worth it. You need to be ready with your market research—for example, technology trends, customer trends, and the competitive situation.

- **What will be our competitor's reaction regarding your solution?**: Competition is everywhere, and often, the executive worries more about it. They want to understand if your solution is innovative to beat the competition and give their organization the edge. It's better to do some upfront research and add competitiveness data relating to their industry and customer base.

- **What is your suggestion, and how can I help?**: You should always have a crisp list of action items as the next step while providing your suggestion. You need to get buy-in from executives and make them feel involved by asking for help. For example, you can ask the CIO to connect you with the engineering team or product team to take an overall solution to the next step.

Till now, in this chapter, we have talked about various soft skills, such as communication, presentation, and listening. Let's now look more at the leadership skills a solution architect should have as a technical leader for the organization.

Taking ownership and accountability

Taking ownership and positioning yourself as a leader helps you to win trust with accountability. Ownership doesn't mean that you need to execute things alone; it is more about taking new initiatives and holding on to them as it is your organization. You can have ideas that can benefit your organization in terms of productivity, agility, cost savings, and increasing the customer base. Sometimes, you may not have the time or resources to execute your idea, but you should always try to bring it forward as a new initiative and engage others for execution.

Accountability is about taking responsibility to drive the outcome. Ownership and accountability go hand in hand, where you are creating initiative and working on getting the result. People can trust you to execute any job and drive results. Accountability helps you build trust with your customers and team, which ultimately results in a better work environment and achieving a goal.

As a solution architect, when you take ownership, it helps you see things from the customer's and sponsor's perspectives. You feel motivated and a part of something meaningful that you enjoy doing. Make sure to define and create key successes and the objective key result. The goal/objective should be measurable using specific key results, and they must be time-bound. Let's learn more about **Objectives and Key Results (OKRs)**.

Defining strategy execution with objectives and key results

Strategy execution is complex and challenging. Excelling in strategy execution is essential for realizing the organizational vision, mission, and goals. The idea needs to be converted into actionable elements to keep teams aligned and everyone moving in the same direction. Goal setting and managing goals are some of the best-established ways to get things done.

Objective Key Results (OKRs) are principles and practices (vision and execution) of goal setting. OKR is a strategy management system that focuses on strategy execution. It is a simple framework that lets you define the organization's primary strategy and its priorities. Objectives are the principles, and key results are the practice—it is a *what and how* of organizational vision. OKRs are based on four superpowers, as illustrated in the following diagram:

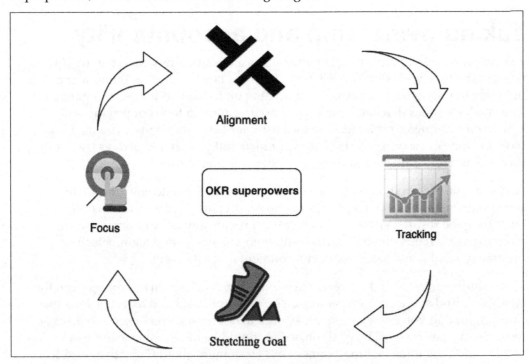

Figure 19.1: Superpowers of OKRs

OKRs' superpowers include the following:

- **Focus**: Start with the question: *What are our main priorities, and where should people concentrate their efforts?* Commit to what truly matters and provide clarity on what is essential.

- **Alignment**: Make goals public and transparent. Connect with the team and get cross-team, bottom-up, and sideways alignment.
- **Tracking**: Visually track the key results of each objective, down to the percentage point.
- **Stretching Goal**: Create ambitious goals to achieve something remarkable. Stretching goals allow people to reimagine and rethink.

OKRs provide visibility and a meaningful outcome to all stakeholders at various levels, from executive sponsors to teams. OKRs make the vision and mission of the organization clear. Team members that are working on day-to-day activities need visibility and clarity to the mission. They need to see how their everyday work has an impact on that organizational mission. The OKR framework allows you to define this link and provide visibility and meaning for everyone on the team.

Thinking big

Solution architects should have the ability to see the big picture and think ahead. A solution architect creates a foundation upon which the team puts building blocks and launches the product. Thinking big is one of the critical skills that solution architects should possess to think about the long-term sustainability of an application. Thinking big doesn't mean you need to make a very unrealistic goal. Your goal should be big enough to challenge you and bring you out of your comfort zone. Thinking big is critical for success at both a personal and an organizational level.

You should never doubt your capability while thinking big. Initially, it may seem challenging to achieve, but you will find the way as you start working toward the goal. Believe in yourself, and you will notice that others start supporting and believing in you. Thinking big helps to inspire people around you to become a part of your success. Set up long-term goals, such as *where you want to see yourself and your organization in the next decade*. Take one step at a time to gear a short-term goal to a long-term goal.

Once you set up the stretching goal by thinking big, it will help you take the initiative and explore new challenges. However, you need support from your peers and team to deliver the result, who can provide you with the right feedback and extend help as needed. Become a person that people want to help; of course, this is a two-way door. To get help, you need to be open to helping others. Adaptability is another critical skill for solution architects to work with others. Let's learn more about it.

Being flexible and adaptable

Adaptability and flexibility go hand in hand, and you need to be flexible to adapt to the new environment, working culture, and technology. Adaptability means you are always open to new ideas and to working with the team. Teams may adopt a process and technology that is best suited for them. As a solution architect, you need to be flexible in accommodating team requirements during solution design.

For example, in a microservices architecture, each service communicates via a standard RESTful API over the HTTP protocol. Different teams may choose to write code in a different language or tool of their choice, such as Python, Java, Node.js, or C#. The only requirement is that teams need to expose their APIs securely so that the entire system can build upon utilizing them.

You need a different mindset and perspective to look into the problem to get a more innovative solution. Encouraging teams to fail fast and innovate helps an organization to be competitive. The personal traits of flexibility are demonstrated by the following:

- Thinking about various solutions to solve a problem with the team and take the best approach

- Helping team members to offload their work

- Volunteering to fill up a place if a team member needs to take time off for weeks due to personal work reasons

- Being able to collaborate effectively with teams across different locations and time zones

You need to be open-minded and adaptable to changes in technology and processes. You may face resistance when bringing change to your team or organization. You need to encourage others to be flexible and convey the importance of change. For example, when an organization wants to move its workload from on-premises to the cloud, they often face resistance, as people have to learn a new platform. You need to explain the value proposition of the cloud and how it will help them be more agile and innovate faster.

As a solution architect, you need to be adaptable to carrying out multiple assignments and setting the right execution priority. You should have the ability to adjust to the situation and work under pressure. A solution architect needs to have critical design thinking to create an innovative solution. Let's learn more about design thinking in the next section.

Design thinking

A solution architect has the primary role of system design, which makes design thinking an essential skill. Design thinking is one of the most successful approaches adopted across industries to solve a challenging and unclear problem. Design thinking helps you to look at problems and solutions from a different perspective, which you might not have considered in the first instance. Design thinking is more focused on delivering results by providing a solution-based approach to solve the problem. It helps to question the problem, solution, and associated risk, to come up with the most optimized strategy.

Design thinking helps you redefine problems in a more human-centric way by putting yourself in the place of end users and customers. The following diagram illustrates the primary principles of design thinking:

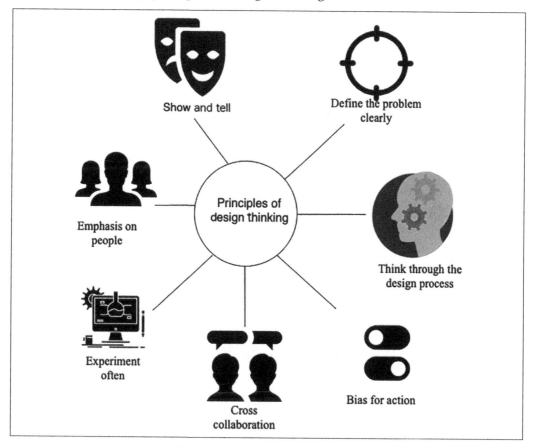

Figure 19.2: Principles of design thinking

The following points are some design-thinking principles:

- **Emphasis on people**: Collect feedback from various users and put yourself in their place to understand the problem from a different perspective.

- **Cross collaboration**: Bring in people from different backgrounds to look for problems in a diversified way, and make sure solutions accommodate everyone's needs.

- **Think through the design process**: Understand the overall design process, with clear goals and methods.

- **Show and tell**: Present your thoughts in visuals to be easy to grasp for everyone in the room.

- **Define the problem clearly**: Create a well-defined and clear vision for a given challenge, which can help others understand clearly and encourage them to contribute more.

- **Experiment often**: Create a prototype to understand the implementation of the idea in real-life situations. Adopt a fail-fast strategy and experiment more often.

- **Bias for action**: The ultimate design to deliver a solution rather than just thinking. Be proactive in pushing forward and coming up with activities that can result in a workable solution.

Design thinking has a solid foundation to apply empathy and create a holistic view of the given problem. To adopt design thinking, there is a five-phase model proposed by **d.school** (https://dschool.stanford.edu/resources/getting-started-with-design-thinking). They are pioneers in teaching and applying design thinking. The following diagram illustrates the five phases of design thinking:

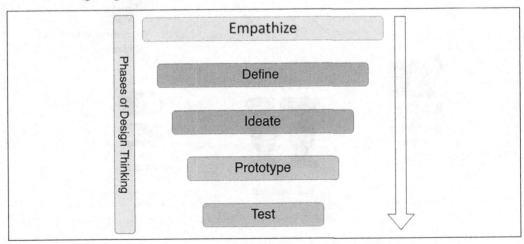

Figure 19.3: Five phases of design thinking

Design thinking is an iterative approach that needs to evolve continuously. The output from one phase can recursively be input to other phases until the solution gets solidified. A brief overview of the phases follows:

- **Empathize**: Empathy is the building block and foundation of design in the human context. To empathize, you should observe your user behaviors and engage with them to understand the actual issue. Try to immerse yourself in — and experience — the problem by putting yourself in the situation.

- **Define**: Empathizing helps define the problem as you experience the user's needs and the problem they face. In the define mode, you apply your insight and define the problem clearly, which can fuel brainstorming to find an innovative yet simple solution.

- **Ideate**: The ideation phase is about moving from problem to solution. You work with the team to find various alternative solutions by challenging assumptions. You need to get an obvious solution out of your head and work collaboratively to find all possible solutions, which allows for innovation.

- **Prototype**: The prototype phase helps to convert ideas into concrete solutions. Prototyping can provide lots of learning and help resolve disagreements by showing a **proof of concept** (POC). It helps you to find gaps and risks. You should build a quick prototype without lots of investment, which allows you to handle failure and increase learning.

- **Test**: The test phase is about getting feedback on your solution and reiterating accordingly. The test phase helps you to redefine the solution and learn more about your users.

Design thinking accommodates all the phases required to come up with a logical and practical solution. When designing application architecture, you can relate the phases and principles of design thinking to your real life. There is special stress on prototyping, as that is the only way to solidify your proposal and existing solutions with data and facts. A solution architect's primary job is to understand the business concern and create a technical solution design with a prototype that the team can implement. To build a prototype, the solution architect needs to get their hands dirty and engage in coding hands-on. Let's learn more about it.

Being a builder by engaging in coding hands-on

A solution architect is a builder who learns by doing. A prototype is worth a thousand pictures. It helps to reduce miscommunication and ideate solutions. Presenting a POC and prototyping is an integral part of the solution architect's role.

Prototyping is the pre-solution phase, which helps to deepen your understanding of the application design and user. It helps you to think and build multiple solution paths. With the testing of the prototype, you can refine your solution and inspire others, such as teams, customers, and investors, by demoing your vision.

A solution architect is a technical leader who works closely with the development team. In the empowered agile team of developers, a solution architect needs to show a piece of code as a POC, in addition to a PowerPoint presentation. A solution architect doesn't need to be part of the development team, but works collaboratively to convey the solution to the dev team in their language. Successful delivery is only possible if the solution architect can understand the deep technical aspect of a solution that comes with continuous coding, hands-on.

A solution architect is often seen as a mentor and player-coach; having some hands-on coding helps them establish credibility. A solution architect needs to decide which programming languages and tools the team should use. A hands-on approach helps identify gaps that may not fit your team or solution requirements—always learning new technology enables the solution architect to make a better decision on behalf of the organization. Let's learn more about the techniques of continuous learning.

Becoming better with continuous learning

Solution architects need to continually absorb new knowledge and enhance their skill set to help the organization make better decisions. Continuous learning keeps your skill set relevant and builds confidence. It opens up your mind and changes prospects. Learning could be challenging with a full-time job and a busy family life. Continuous learning is about developing the habit of always learning something new, whereby you have to be motivated and disciplined. You first need to set up learning goals and apply effective time management to achieve them. This often slips through the net when you get busy with regular daily work.

Everyone has their style of learning. Some people may like formal education; some may read books; others may want to listen to and watch tutorials. You need to find the learning style that is most effective for you and suited to your lifestyle. For example, you can choose to listen to audiobooks and tutorials when commuting to work. You can read books during a business-trip flight or watch video tutorials during exercise hours in the gym. Overall, you need to make some adjustments to put time aside from your busy work life for continuous learning. Here are some of the ways to engage yourself in constant learning:

- **Learning new technologies, frameworks, and languages by trying them out**: Solution architects are the builders and are ready to experiment hands-on. As a successful solution architect, you need to keep learning new technologies by building a small POC. Understanding modern programming languages and frameworks will help you provide the best advice on technology adoption for an organization and team.

- **Learning new skills by reading books and tutorials**: Online learning has brought a revolution and has made it easy to understand and dive deep into any area. You now have massive knowledge bases at your fingertips to learn anything. An online platform such as Udemy or Coursera provides thousands of video tutorial courses in all areas that you can watch online or download to your device for offline learning.

  Similarly, there are millions of books available on Kindle to read anytime and anywhere. Audiobook platforms such as Audible and Google Play's audiobooks can help you listen to the book during your commute. There are so many convenient resources available that there is no excuse not to apply continuous learning.

- **Keeping up with technology news and developments by reading articles on websites and blogs**: The best way to keep yourself updated with technology trends is by subscribing to technical news and blogs. `TechCrunch.com`, `Wired.com`, and `Cnet.com` are some of the popular websites to get the latest technology trends. Major newspapers such as *CNBC* or *The New York Times*, and the BBC News and CNN channels have technology articles that provide a good insight into industry trends. You can subscribe to blogs for new learning in the respective technology area. For example, for cloud platform learning, you can subscribe to **Amazon Web Services** (**AWS**) blogs, which have thousands of articles and use cases in the area of the the AWS cloud, and similar blogs are available from other public clouds such as Azure and **Google Cloud Platform** (**GCP**).

- **Writing a blog, whitepaper, or book**: Sharing knowledge is the best way to learn as you think through use cases when trying to present to others. Publishing blogs and articles in popular blog-publishing platforms such as *Medium*, Blogger, and LinkedIn helps you share your learning and learn from others. Active participation in question-and-answer platforms enables you to find an alternative solution for any given problem. Some popular question/answer platforms are Quora, Reddit, Stack Over flow, and Stack Exchange.

- **Solidify your knowledge by teaching others**: Teaching others helps you collaborate and get a different perspective of your knowledge. Often, use cases proposed by participants give you different ways of finding a solution. Running a full-day workshop with a hands-on lab and concept building helps you solidify your learning and learn with others.

- **Taking online classes**: Sometimes, you want to go for formal learning to be more disciplined, and you want to be flexible. Online courses provide flexibility and help you to adjust to other priorities and save time. Online courses can offer you an organized way to learn new technologies and help to enhance knowledge.

- **Learning from teammates**: Teammates share the same working environment, and you spend most of the day with them. Learning with team members can help to speed up your learning. The team can adopt a divide-and-conquer strategy whereby each team member can share their topics and present deep-dive lunch-and-learn sessions. These sessions are a standard method used by many organizations to conduct regular learning sessions among team members. Each team member shares their new learning in a weekly learning session, and everyone quickly learns new topics.

- **Attending and participating in user groups and conferences**: All large vertical industry and technology organizations conduct conferences to provide insight into new technology trends and hands-on sessions. Participating in industry conferences and user group meetings helps to develop networking and understand technology trends. Some of the large technology conferences from industry leaders include AWS re:Invent, Google Cloud Next, Microsoft Ignite, SAP SAPPHIRE, and Strata Data Conference. You can create a local user group and conduct a meetup in your local area, which will help you to collaborate with professionals across industries and organizations.

A solution architect plays a technical leadership role, and good leadership warrants preparing more leaders like you, which is possible through mentorship. Solution architects should play a player-coach role and mentor others. Let's look at this in more detail.

Being a mentor to others

Mentoring is about helping others and setting them up for success based on your learning and experience. It is an effective way to develop leaders by having one-to-one mentor/mentee relationships. To be a good mentor, you need to establish an informal communication style where the mentee can develop a comfort zone. The mentee can seek advice in multiple areas such as career development, or personal aspects such as work-life balance. You should do an informal needs assessment and set up mutual goals and expectations.

Mentorship is more about listening. Sometimes, people need someone to listen to them and advise as required. You should listen carefully first and understand their point of view.

Help them to make their own decisions as this will make them feel more accomplished. As a good mentor, when advising for a career, you need to be open to advise what the best fit for the mentee is, even if it may not necessarily be the best fit for the company. Always provide honest, constructive feedback to help them identify gaps and overcome them.

The critical trait of a mentor is the ability to inspire people. Often, people may choose you as a mentor if they see a role model in you. Help your mentee realize their full potential without putting your view forward, and help them achieve what they never thought of earlier. There are always mutual benefits to being a mentor; you also learn from mentees about people's behavior and growth. Being a mentor to others will ultimately help you to become a better leader and person.

Becoming a technology evangelist and thought leader

Technology evangelism is about being an expert to advocate technology and your product. Some organizations with an extensive product base roll out a separate technology evangelist role. Still, often, a solution architect needs to assume the role of an evangelist as part of their job. As a technology evangelist, you need to be aware of current technology trends to understand real-world problems and advocate your technology to solve their business concerns.

Technology evangelism involves participating in an industry conference as a public speaker and promoting your respective platform. It allows you to become a thought leader and an influencer, which can help the organization increase its platform and product adoption. Public speaking is one of the critical skills required for a solution architect to interreact on various public platforms and present in front of a large audience.

An evangelist also creates and publishes content such as blog posts, whitepapers, and microblogs to advocate their product. They socialize the content to increase adoption and interact with the user to understand their feedback. An evangelist works backward from the customer and communicates feedback to the internal team to help to make the product better. With time, as an evangelist, you will refine the message that works in the organization's best interests.

Overall, a solution architect is a role with multiple responsibilities, and taking more ownership will help you to better succeed in your career.

Summary

In this chapter, you learned about the various soft skills required for a solution architect to be successful. A solution architect needs to have pre-sales skills such as negotiation, communication, problem solving, and listening, which help them support the organization's pre-sales cycle, such as with the RFP. You learned about the presentation skills required for executive conversations and buy-in.

You learned about the strategic understanding that a solution architect should define key objectives and results for an organization. To execute at various levels, solution architects should have the ability to think big and be flexible and adaptable. You learned details about solution architects taking ownership and being accountable for their actions.

A solution architect's role has the primary responsibility of architecture design. You learned about design thinking, with its principles and phases. You also learned about the importance of continuous learning and different techniques to carry on learning and keep yourself up to date with market trends. You also learned about the additional responsibilities of the solution architect—to work as a mentor and evangelist.

It has been a long journey through this book learning all about solution architects, from their roles and responsibilities to different aspects of solution design and architecture optimization. I hope you have learned a lot and that it will help you develop your career as a solution architect or help you succeed in your current role.

Happy learning!

Join our book's Discord space

Join the book's Discord workspace for a monthly *Ask me Anything* session with the authors: https://packt.link/SAHandbook

packt.com

Subscribe to our online digital library for full access to over 7,000 books and videos, as well as industry leading tools to help you plan your personal development and advance your career. For more information, please visit our website.

Why subscribe?

- Spend less time learning and more time coding with practical eBooks and Videos from over 4,000 industry professionals
- Improve your learning with Skill Plans built especially for you
- Get a free eBook or video every month
- Fully searchable for easy access to vital information
- Copy and paste, print, and bookmark content

At www.packt.com, you can also read a collection of free technical articles, sign up for a range of free newsletters, and receive exclusive discounts and offers on Packt books and eBooks.

Other Books You May Enjoy

If you enjoyed this book, you may be interested in these other books by Packt:

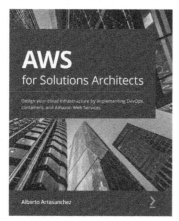

AWS for Solutions Architect

Alberto Artasanchez

ISBN: 978-1-78953-923-3

- Rationalize the selection of AWS as the right cloud provider for your organization
- Choose the most appropriate service from AWS for a particular use case or project
- Implement change and operations management
- Find out the right resource type and size to balance performance and efficiency
- Discover how to mitigate risk and enforce security, authentication, and authorization
- Identify common business scenarios and select the right reference architectures for them

Software Architecture with C# 9 and .NET 5 - Second Edition

Gabriel Baptista

Francesco Abbruzzese

ISBN: 978-1-80056-604-0

- Use different techniques to overcome real-world architectural challenges and solve design consideration issues
- Apply architectural approaches such as layered architecture, service-oriented architecture (SOA), and microservices
- Leverage tools such as containers, Docker, Kubernetes, and Blazor to manage microservices effectively
- Get up to speed with Azure tools and features for delivering global solutions
- Program and maintain Azure Functions using C# 9 and its latest features
- Understand when it is best to use test-driven development (TDD) as an approach for software development
- Write automated functional test cases
- Get the best of DevOps principles to enable CI/CD environments

Packt is searching for authors like you

If you're interested in becoming an author for Packt, please visit `authors.packtpub.com` and apply today. We have worked with thousands of developers and tech professionals, just like you, to help them share their insight with the global tech community. You can make a general application, apply for a specific hot topic that we are recruiting an author for, or submit your own idea.

Share Your Thoughts

Now you've finished *Solutions Architect's Handbook - Second Edition*, we'd love to hear your thoughts! If you purchased the book from Amazon, please `click here to go straight to the Amazon review` page for this book and share your feedback or leave a review on the site that you purchased it from.

Your review is important to us and the tech community and will help us make sure we're delivering excellent quality content.

Index

Q

Quality Assurance (QA) environments 271
quantum algorithms 466
quantum annealing 467
quantum circuits 465
  basic modules 466
  Boolean circuit 465
quantum computers
  building blocks 458
  working mechanism 460, 461
quantum computers, types
  D-Wave-built quantum computers 467
  IonQ 467
  Rigetti 467
  Rydberg Atoms 467
  Superconducting Qubits 467
  Trapped Ions 467
quantum computing (QC) 457
  in AWS cloud 469, 470
  real-time use cases 468
quantum gates 462
  Hadamard gate 464
  Pauli gate 462
  S-Gate 465
  T-Gate 465
  X-Gate 464
  Z-Gate 464
qubits 458
queue-based architecture
  building 167
  job observer pattern 169, 170
  queuing chain pattern 168, 169
  terminology 167
queue-based decoupling 91
queuing chain pattern 168
  architecture 169
  benefits 169

R

R3 Corda 392
Rally 44
random access memory (RAM) 173
random forest 423
reactive scaling
  traffic patterns 82

real-time operating systems (RTOS) 441
real-time use cases, quantum computing (QC)
  cryptography 469
  Internet searches 469
  machine learning 469
  optimization 468
  simulation 469
real-time voting application architecture
  building 165-167
rearchitecting approach 487
Recovery Point Objective
      (RPO) 32, 64, 83, 194, 273
Recovery Time Objective
      (RTO) 32, 64, 83, 195, 273
Recurrent Neural Networks (RNNs) 435
red-black deployment 359
redesigning approach 487
Red Hat Enterprise Linux (RHEL) 298
Redis 96, 175
  versus Memcached 182
redundant array of independent disks
      (RAID) 217
refactoring approach 112, 487
rehosting approach 109, 110, 486
Relational Database Management System
      (RDBMS) databases 381
relocate 111
remaining useful life (RUL) 417
rename distribution pattern 177
replaceable resources
  using 87
replatforming approach 110, 487
Representational State Transfer
      (REST) 6, 261
repurchase 112
request for information (RFI) 5, 513
request for proposal (RFP) 5, 513, 518
request for quotation (RFQ) 513
request for response (RFP) 33
resiliency 60-62
resilient architecture
  building 83-85
resilient distributed datasets (RDDs) 393
resource cost tagging 331, 333
Responsible, Accountable, Consult, Inform
      (RACI) 122
RESTful service model 97

Made in the USA
Middletown, DE
08 June 2022

66833923R00329